Developments

Developments in Russian Politics 5

Edited by

Stephen White
Alex Pravda
Zvi Gitelman

Duke University Press
Durham 2001

First published in 1990 as *Developments in Soviet Politics*.
Second edition (*Developments in Soviet and Post-Soviet Politics*) 1992.
Third edition (*Developments in Russian and Post-Soviet Politics*) 1994.
Fourth edition (*Developments in Russian Politics*) 1997.

Published in the United States in 2001 by
Duke University Press
Durham, NC 27708

First published in Great Britain in 2001 by PALGRAVE
Houndmills, Basingstoke, Hampshire RG21 6XS

Library of Congress Cataloging-in-Publication Data
Developments in Russian politics 5 / edited by Stephen White, Alex Pravda, and Zvi Gitelman – 5th ed.
    p.cm.
    Includes bibliographical references and index.
    ISBN 0-8223-2761-9 (cloth) – ISBN 0-8223-2770-8 (pbk.)
    1. Russia (Federation)–Politics and government–1991– I. Title: Developments in Russian politics five. II. White, Stephen, III. Pravda, Alex, IV. Gitelman, Zvi Y.

DK510.763 .D48 2001
947.08–dc21

                                                                              2001023931

Printed and bound in Great Britain by
Creative Print & Design (Wales) Ebbw Vale

Contents

List of Figures and Tables

Figures

Tables

Preface

The fifth edition of this book finds Russia, once again, at a new stage in its political evolution. We began life as *Developments in Soviet Politics* back in 1990; soon we were *Soviet and Post-Soviet Politics*, then *Russian and Post-Soviet Politics*, and then simply *Russian Politics* for our fourth edition. We keep the same title in the fifth edition, but we deal with a political system that is undergoing further changes under the presidency of Vladimir Putin, towards a greater degree of centralisation and a strong assertion of state authority at what some think is the cost of some of the political freedoms that had been won under Mikhail Gorbachev and Boris Yeltsin.

As before, we have attempted to provide an account of this changing system that covers events and institutions but goes on to explore issues and interpretations. This edition has three new chapters – on crime, the mass media and the tentative search for a 'national idea' – and three other chapters have new authors; in other cases still, the same authors have tackled new subjects. But in every case, these are chapters that have been written specially for this edition, and they draw not just upon a wealth of specialist experience but also upon first-hand research, some of which is reported in these pages.

We hope that all those who found earlier editions of this book of some value will enjoy this new edition for a new century.

Stephen White
Alex Pravda
Zvi Gitelman

Notes on Contributors

Zvi Gitelman is Professor of Political Science and Preston Tisch Professor of Judaic Studies at the University of Michigan, Ann Arbor, where he is director of the Frankel Center for Judaic Studies. Author or editor of eight books, he is editor of *Bitter Legacy: Confronting the Holocaust in the USSR* (1997). He is currently researching the meanings of Jewish identity and communal reconstruction in Russia and Ukraine.

James Hughes is a Senior Lecturer in Comparative Politics at the London School of Economics specialising in Russian and post-Soviet politics. His research interests are in problems of democratisation and federalism in Russia, and nationalism and ethnic conflicts in post-Soviet states. His most recent relevant publications have appeared in Mike Bowker and Cameron Ross (editors) *Russia After The Cold War* (1999) and in the *British Journal of Political Science* (with others, 2001).

Sarah Oates is a Lecturer in the Politics Department at the University of Glasgow, and has served as a monitor at both the 1995 and 1999 Russian Duma elections, and in Kazakhstan. She is co-editor of *Elections and Voters in Post-Communist Russia* (Elgar, 1998), and author or co-author of contributions to *Political Studies*, *Journal of Communist Studies and Transition Politics*, *International Politics*, *Problems of Post-Communism*, and the *Harvard Journal of Press/Politics*.

Alex Pravda is Director of the Russian and East European Centre and Fellow of St Antony's College, Oxford University, where he is also Lecturer in Russian and East European Politics. His books include *The End of the Outer Empire: Soviet-East European Relations in Transition* (edited, 1992) and *Internal Factors in Russian Foreign Policy* (with Neil Malcolm, Roy Allison and Margot Light, 1996).

Thomas F. Remington is Professor of Political Science at Emory University. His research concerns the development of representative institutions in Russia. He is author of *The Russian Parliament: Institutional Evolution in a Transitional Regime, 1989–1999* (2001), *Politics in Russia*, 2nd edn (2001) and, with Steven S. Smith, *The Politics of Institutional Choice: Formation of the Russian State Duma* (2001).

Richard Sakwa is Professor of Russian and European Politics at the University of Kent. He has published widely on Soviet, Russian and postcommunist affairs. Recent books include *Soviet Politics in Perspective* (1998), *The Rise and Fall of the Soviet Union, 1917–1991* (1999) and *Postcommunism* (1999). His current research interests focus on problems of democratic development and the state in Russia, the nature of postcommunism, and the global changes facing the former communist countries.

Judith Shapiro joined the pioneering New Economic School in Moscow in 2000 as a Professor of Health Economics and resident academic coordinator. Most of her academic life has been spent in London, at Goldsmiths College, but before returning to Moscow she served two years at the United Nations Economic Commission for Europe in Geneva. As part of the Economic Programme Group of the European Forum for Solidarity and Democracy she is the co-author of three widely-translated books on economic policy in the transformation of Central and Eastern Europe, the most recent of which is *Hard Budgets, Soft States* (2000).

Louise Shelley is a Professor in the Department of Justice, Law and Society and the School of International Service at American University. She is the founder and the Director of the Center for Transnational Crime and Corruption at American University. She is the author of *Policing Soviet Society* (1996), executive editor of *Demokratizatsiya*, and editor of *Trends in Organized Crime* and *Organized Crime Watch*.

Darrell Slider is Professor of Government and International Affairs at the University of South Floria, Tampa. His publications include *The Politics of Transition: Shaping a Post-Soviet Future* (with Stephen White and Graeme Gill, 1993) and a series of papers in *Europe-Asia Studies*, *Slavic Review*, *Post-Soviet Affairs* and other journals with a particular focus on regional issues, federalism, elections and privatisation.

Gordon B. Smith is a Professor of Government and International Studies at the University of South Carolina. His recent books include *State-Building in Russia: The Yeltsin Legacy and the Challenge of the Future* (1999) and *Reforming the Russian Legal System* (1996). His numerous published articles focus on Russian politics and law, especially the role of the Procuracy.

Vera Tolz is Reader in Russian History and Politics at the University of Salford. She is the author of *The USSR's Emerging Multi-Party System* (1990) and *Russian Academicians and the Revolution* (1997); her study of *Russia: Inventing the Nation* appeared in 2001. She has also edited books and published articles on various aspects of the twentieth century Russian history and politics.

William Tompson is Senior Lecturer in Politics and Head of the School of Politics and Sociology at Birbeck College, University of London. He is the author of *Khrushchev: A Political Life* (1995) and of numerous articles and chapters on Soviet/Russian high politics and the political economy of post-Soviet Russia. He is also currently at work on a history of the USSR from Khrushchev to Gorbachev.

Stephen White is Professor of Politics and a Senior Associate of the Institute of Central and East European Studies at the University of Glasgow. He was President of the British Association for Slavonic and East European Studies in 1994–7, and is chief editor of the *Journal of Communist Studies and Transition Politics*. His recent publications include *How Russia Votes* (with Richard Rose and Ian McAllister, 1997), *Russia's New Politics* (2000) and *The Soviet Elite from Lenin to Gorbachev* (with Evan Mawdsley, 2000).

John P. Willerton Jr is Associate Professor of Political Science at the University of Arizona, Tucson. Author of *Patronage and Politics in the USSR* (1992), his articles have appeared in numerous disciplinary and area studies journals and professional symposia. His current research agenda is focused both on the Russian presidency and Russia's foreign policy interests in northern Europe and the area of the former Soviet Union.

Matthew Wyman is Lecturer in Politics at the University of Keele. His study of *Public Opinion in Post-Communist Russia* appeared in 1997, and he has also authored or co-authored papers in *Europe-Asia Studies*, the *Journal of Communist Studies and Transition Politics, Electoral Studies* and *Party Politics*.

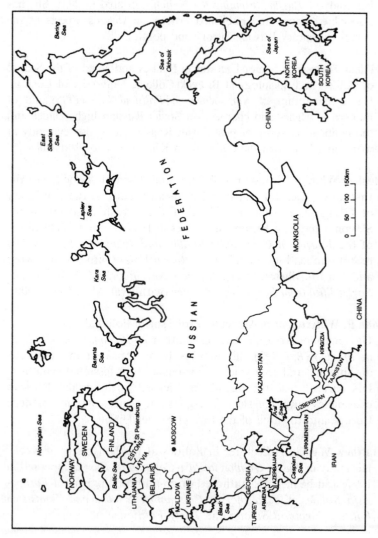

MAP *Russia and the Former Soviet Republics*

List of Abbreviations

ABM	Anti-Ballistic Missile Treaty (1972)
AUCCTU	All-Union Central Council of Trade Unions
CC	Central Committee
CEC	Central Electoral Commission
CIS	Commonwealth of Independent States
CPD	Congress of People's Deputies
CPRF	Communist Party of the Russian Federation
CPSU	Communist Party of the Soviet Union
CSCE	Conference on Security and Cooperation in Europe
FITUR	Federation of Independent Trade Unions of Russia
FSB	Federal Security Service
GDP	Gross Domestic Product
GUUAM	Treaty embracing Georgia, Ukraine, Uzbekistan, Azerbaijan and Moldova
IMF	International Monetary Fund
KFOR	NATO Kosovo Force
KGB	Soviet secret police
LDPR	Liberal Democratic Party of Russia
NATO	North Atlantic Treaty Organisation
NDR	Our Home is Russia party
NMD	National Missile Defence
OMON	Special-purpose police detachment to combat armed criminals, counter terrorist attacks and maintain public order
OMS	Compulsory Medical Insurance
OSCE	Organisation for Security and Cooperation in Europe
OVR	Fatherland-All Russia party
PR	Proportional Representation
RF	Russian Federation
RSFSR	Russian Soviet Federated Socialist Republic
SPS	Union of Right Forces
UNAIDS	United Nations lead agency on AIDS
USSR	Union of Soviet Socialist Republics
VTsIOM	All-Russian Centre for the Study of Public Opinion

Glossary of Terms

Duma	Lower house of Federal Assembly (parliament)
Glasnost	Openness, publicity
Goskomstat	State Statistics Committee
Ispolkom	Executive committee
kompromat	Smear tactics
Komsomol	Young Communist League
Krai	Territory
Matreshka	'Nested-doll' bidding game
Neformalnye	Informal organisations
Nomenklatura	List of party-controlled posts
Obkom	Regional CPSU committee
Oblast	*Region, province*
Perestroika	Restructuring
Politburo	Key decision-making body in the Communist Party
Praktiki	Directors or former directors of major enterprises in regions
Pravovoe gosudarstvo	
	Law-based state
Raion	Rural district
Rossiiskaya	Civic Russian
Rossiyane	Russian Federation population
Sobranie	Regional Assembly
Soglasitelnaya komissiya	
	Reconciliation commission
Soviets	Councils
Ukazy	Presidential decrees
Vekselya	Bills of exchange
Yedinstvo	Unity movement
Zemskii sobor	Assembly of nobility, clergy and merchants

1

From Communism to Democracy?

STEPHEN WHITE

In the event, it has proved much easier to dismantle communist rule than to construct a democratic political system in its place. With all its faults, the Soviet system had lasted more than two generations. By the time of the last Soviet census, in 1989, more than 90 per cent of the population had been born since the October revolution, and 70 per cent since the Second World War, leaving very few who had a conscious recollection of another form of society. More positively, it was a system that had 'won the war', with Communist Party members in the front line; indeed, more than two million party members had lost their own lives (Pospelov *et al.*, 1970, p. 643). It had eliminated illiteracy (or at least it claimed to have done so; the 1989 census found that over four million, mostly elderly, were still unable to read and write). Levels of education had risen remarkably; the proportion with a higher education, in particular, doubled during the 1960s and had doubled again by the end of the 1980s. The circulation of daily newspapers, another indicator of 'modernity', was among the highest in the world. Once a rural society, more than two-thirds were living in cities by the 1970s, and more than a third were working in industry. It was, indeed, one of the explanations for the end of communist rule that it had been outgrown by the complexity of Soviet society as a result of the changes that the party itself had sponsored.

Clearly, the passage of time could be no guarantee of regime survival. But in the Soviet case, it meant that there was no precommunist past to which the new administration could readily return. There was no precommunist constitution, as there had been in each of the Baltic republics. There were no precommunist parties ready to step out of the history books into the centre of public life. And there were no traditions of political organisation and electoral competition, as there had been in most of East Central Europe. Equally, there were very few members of the governing group that had not acquired their political experience in the Soviet system, and usually within the senior ranks of the communist party. There was no equivalent in Russia of a Havel or a Walesa, dissidents propelled to power by a mass movement: Boris Yeltsin, who headed the drive against communist rule, had been a party member for 30 years and a member of its Politburo; Viktor Chernomyrdin, his prime minister and still prominent in public life in the early years of the new century, had been a member of the CPSU Central Committee. About three-quarters of the presidential administration, and the same proportion of the new government, had a career background in the communist *nomenklatura*; at the regional level the continuity was even greater (Kryshtanovskaya and White, 1996). Indeed, in some respects communist rule continued: the Communist Party of the Russian Federation was the largest in the State Duma after the 1995 and again after the 1999 elections, and it controlled a series of local assemblies and governorships.

Much, accordingly, had changed; but much remained the same, not just in terms of the Soviet past but in a much longer time perspective. One of the most obvious of these continuities was the relative powerlessness of the ordinary citizen. There was no longer a communist party with a monopoly on power – indeed the new constitution guaranteed multiparty politics – but political parties were weakly developed, and in any case government seemed to have little influence over what was going on, in Moscow or throughout the country. There was little point in appealing to the courts, or hoping they would provide protection against organised crime and abuse of office; a civil society of groups and associations had scarcely begun to develop; and although there was a wide diversity of opinion in the press, circulations had fallen to low levels, and state television continued to give an interpretation of events that closely reflected the changing priorities of the Kremlin leadership. Indeed there was open speculation that there might be no presidential elections at all in 1996 if Yeltsin had been unable to overtake his communist opponent in the polls, or if in 2000 the Kremlin had not been able to find a credible successor (there were various constitutional pretexts that could have been used to postpone a contest). This was communist rule no longer (and the elections did, in the end, take place); but it fell some distance short of the accountable relationship between rulers and ruled, within a framework of law and human rights, that is central to most definitions of democracy. How far short is the central issue in nearly every chapter of this book.

The Failure of Communist Reform

A very different atmosphere had prevailed in March 1985 when a vigorous, stocky Politburo member from the south of Russia became the leader of what was still a united and ruling party. Gorbachev, according to his wife, had not expected the nomination and spent some time deciding whether to accept it; all that was clear was that (in a phrase that later became famous) 'We just can't go on like this' (Gorbacheva, 1991, p. 14). The advent of a new general secretary had certainly made a significant difference in the past to the direction of public policy, although any change took some time to establish itself as the new leader marginalised his opponents and promoted his supporters to positions within the leadership. Gorbachev, however, told the Politburo meeting that agreed to nominate him there was 'no need to change [their] policies' (Tsentr, 1985), and there was little indication at the outset that he was likely to advance what eventually became a comprehensive reform programme. The new general secretary had not addressed a party congress, and had no published collection of writings to his name; and he had made only a couple of official visits to other countries, to Canada and the United Kingdom, on both occasions as the head of a delegation of Soviet parliamentarians. Only a few important speeches – in particular an address to an ideology conference in December 1984 and an electoral address in February 1985, which mentioned *glasnost*, social justice and participation – gave some indication of his personal priorities.

It was some time, in fact, before a new policy agenda began to take shape. In his acceptance speech Gorbachev paid the customary tribute to his immediate predecessors, Yuri Andropov and Konstantin Chernenko, and pledged himself to continue their policy of 'acceleration of socio-economic development and the perfection of all aspects of social life', which was the political language of the Brezhnev era. At the first Central Committee he addressed as leader, in April 1985, he spoke in a fairly orthodox manner about the need for a 'qualitatively new state of society', including modernisation of the economy and the extension of socialist democracy. The key issue, in these early months, was the acceleration of economic growth. This, Gorbachev thought, was quite feasible if the 'human factor' was called more fully into play, and if the reserves that existed throughout the economy were properly utilised. This in turn required a greater degree of decentralisation, including cost accounting at enterprise level and a closer connection between the work that people did and the payment that they received; but there was still no talk of 'radical reform', let alone a 'market'. The months that followed saw the gradual assembly of a leadership team that could direct these changes and the further extension of what was still a very limited mandate for change (for a more detailed account of the reform programme see Sakwa, 1990; Miller, 1993; White, 1994; Brown, 1996; Hough, 1997).

Of all the policies that were promoted by the Gorbachev leadership, *glasnost* was perhaps the most distinctive and the one that had been pressed furthest by the end of communist rule. *Glasnost*, usually translated as openness or publicity, was not the same as freedom of the press or the right to information; nor was it original to Gorbachev (it figured, for instance, in the constitution that had been adopted in 1977 under Leonid Brezhnev). It did, however, reflect the new general secretary's belief that without a greater awareness of the real state of affairs and of the considerations that had led to particular decisions there would be no willingness on the part of the Soviet people to commit themselves to his programme of *perestroika* or restructuring. Existing policies were in any case ineffectual, counterproductive and resented. The newspaper *Sovetskaya Rossiya* reported the case of Mr Polyakov of Kaluga, a well-read man who followed the central and local press and never missed the evening news. He knew a lot about what was happening in various African countries, Polyakov complained, but had 'only a very rough idea what was happening in his own city'. In late 1985, another reader complained, there had been a major earthquake in Tajikistan in Soviet Central Asia, but no details had been made known other than that 'lives had been lost'. At about the same time there had been an earthquake in Mexico and a volcanic eruption in Colombia, both covered extensively with on-the-spot reports and full details of the casualties. Was Tajikistan really further from Moscow than Latin America?

Influenced by considerations such as these, the Gorbachev leadership made steady and sometimes dramatic progress in removing taboos from the discussion of public affairs and exposing both the Soviet past and present to critical scrutiny. The Brezhnev era was one of the earliest targets. It had been a time, Gorbachev told the 27th Party Congress in 1986, when a 'curious psychology – how to change things without really changing anything' – had been dominant. A number of its leading representatives had been openly corrupt, and some (such as Brezhnev's son-in-law, Yuri Churbanov) were brought to trial and imprisoned for serious state crimes. More generally, it had been a period of 'stagnation', of wasted opportunities, when party and government leaders had lagged behind the needs of the times. The Stalin question was a still more fundamental one, as for all Soviet reformers. Gorbachev, to begin with, was reluctant even to concede there was a question. Stalinism, he told the French press in 1986, was a 'notion made up by enemies of communism'; the 20th Party Congress in 1956 had condemned Stalin's 'cult of personality' and drawn the necessary conclusions. By early 1987, however, Gorbachev was insisting that there must be 'no forgotten names, no blank spots' in Soviet literature and history, and by November of that year, when he came to give his address on the 70th anniversary of the revolution, he was ready to condemn the 'wanton repressive measures' of the 1930s, 'real crimes' in which 'many thousands of people inside and outside the party' had suffered.

In the course of his speech Gorbachev announced that a Politburo commission had been set up to investigate the repression of the Stalinist years, and this led to the rehabilitation of many prominent figures from the party's past (and thousands of others) from 1988 onwards. The most important figure to be restored to full respectability in this way was the former *Pravda* editor Nikolai Bukharin, whose sentence was posthumously quashed in February 1988 (his expulsions from the party and the Academy of Sciences were also rescinded). Trotsky had not been sentenced by a Soviet court and there was therefore no judgement to be reconsidered; but his personal qualities began to receive some recognition in the Soviet press, and from 1989 onwards his writings began to appear in mass-circulation as well as scholarly journals. An extended discussion took place about the numbers that Stalin had condemned to death: for some it was about a million by the end of the 1930s, but for others (such as the historian and commentator Roy Medvedev) it was at least 12 million, with a further 38 million repressed in other ways (for a discussion see Getty and Manning, 1993). Some of the mass graves of the Stalin period began to be uncovered at the same time, the most extensive of which were in the Kuropaty forest near Minsk. The victims, as many as 40 000, had been shot between 1937 and 1941; this, and the other graves that were still being discovered in the early 1990s, was an indictment of Stalinism more powerful than anything the historians could hope to muster.

Glasnost led to further changes in the quality of Soviet public life, from literature and the arts to statistics and a wide-ranging discussion on the future of Soviet socialism. Public information began to improve, with the publication of new figures on abortions, suicides and infant mortality. Subjects that had been taboo during the Brezhnev years, such as violent crime, drugs and prostitution, began to receive extensive treatment. Many events of the past, such as the devastating earthquake in Ashkhabad in 1948 and the nuclear accident in the Urals in 1957, were belatedly acknowledged. Figures for defence spending and foreign debt were revealed to the newly elected Congress of People's Deputies when it met in 1989; figures for capital punishment followed in 1991. The Congress itself was televised in full and followed avidly throughout the USSR; so too were Central Committee plenums and Supreme Soviet committee hearings. Still more remarkably, the Soviet media were opened up to foreign journalists and politicians, and even – in a few cases – to open opponents of Soviet socialism; and the first 'spacebridges' were instituted, linking together studio audiences in the USSR and Western nations (we take these themes further in Chapter 13). Opinion polls suggested that *glasnost*, for all its limitations, was the change in Soviet life that was most apparent to ordinary people and the one they most valued.

The 'democratisation' of Soviet political life was an associated change, and was similarly intended to release the human energies that, for Gorbachev, had been choked off by the bureaucratic centralism of the Stalin and Brezhnev years. The Soviet Union, he told the 19th Party Conference in the summer of 1988, had pioneered the idea of a workers' state and of workers' control, the right to work and equality of rights for women and all national groups. The political system established by the October revolution, however, had undergone 'serious deformations', leading to the development of a 'command-administrative system' that had extinguished the democratic potential of the elected soviets. The role of party and state officialdom had increased out of all proportion, and this 'bloated administrative apparatus' had begun to dictate its will in political and economic matters. Nearly a third of the adult population were regularly elected to the soviets, but most of them had little influence over the conduct of government. Social life as a whole had become unduly politicised, and ordinary working people had become 'alienated' from the system that was supposed to represent their interests. It was this 'ossified system of government, with its command-and-pressure mechanism', that was now the main obstacle to *perestroika*.

The Conference agreed to undertake a 'radical reform' of the political system, and this led to a series of constitutional and other changes from 1988 onwards that – for the reformers – had as their ultimate objective the development of a model of socialism that would recover what they believed to be its democratic potential. An entirely new electoral law, approved in December 1988, broke new ground in providing for (though not specifically requiring) a choice of candidate at elections to local and national-level authorities. A new state structure was established, incorporating a smaller working parliament for the first time in modern Soviet history and (from 1990) a powerful executive presidency. A constitutional review committee, similar to a constitutional court, was set up as part of a move to what Gorbachev called a 'socialist system of checks and balances'. Judges were to be elected for longer periods of time, and given greater independence in their work. And the CPSU itself was to be 'democratised', although the changes were less far-reaching than in other parts of the political system and in the end were not sufficient to preserve the party's authority or the confidence of its individual members. Leading officials, it was agreed, should be elected by competitive ballot for a maximum of two consecutive terms; members of the Central Committee should be involved much more directly in the work of the leadership; and there should be much more information about all aspects of the party's work, from its finances to the operation of its decision-making bodies.

Together with these changes, for Gorbachev, there would have to be a 'radical reform' of the Soviet economy. Levels of growth had been declining since at least the 1950s. In the late 1970s they reached the lowest levels in Soviet peacetime history, and there was no growth at all once the increase in population had been taken into account. Indeed, as Gorbachev explained in early 1988, if the sale of alcoholic drink and of Soviet oil on foreign markets were excluded, there had been no increase in national wealth for at least the previous 15 years. Growth, for many reformers, could not be an end in itself: what was important was the satisfaction of real social needs, not 'the plan for the sake of the plan'. But it was equally apparent that without some improvement in living standards there would be no popular commitment to *perestroika*, and no prospect that socialism would recover its appeal to other nations as a means by which ordinary working people could live their lives in dignity and sufficiency. There was indeed a real danger, in the view of economists like Nikolai Shmelev (1988, p. 179), that without radical reform the USSR would enter the twenty-first century a 'backward, stagnating state and an example to the rest of the world how not to conduct its economic affairs'.

Radical reform, as Gorbachev explained to the 27th Party Congress and to a Central Committee meeting in the summer of 1987, involved a set of related measures. One of the most important was a greater degree of decentralisation of economic decision-making, leaving broad guidance of the economy in the hands of the State Planning Committee (Gosplan) but allowing factories and farms throughout the USSR more freedom to determine their own priorities. They should be guided in making such decisions by a wide range of 'market' indicators, including the orders they received from other enterprises and the profits they made on their production. Retail and wholesale prices would have to reflect costs of production much more closely so that enterprises could be guided by 'economic' rather than 'administrative' regulators, and so that the massive subsidies that held down the cost of basic foodstuffs could be reduced and if possible eliminated. Under the Law on the State Enterprise, adopted in 1987, factories that persistently failed to pay their way could be liquidated; some economists were willing to argue that a modest degree of unemployment was not simply a logical but even a desirable feature of changes of this kind. The state sector, more generally, should be reduced in size, and cooperative or even private economic activity should be expanded in its place. Gorbachev described these changes, which were gradually brought into effect from 1987 onwards, as the most radical to have taken place in Soviet economic life since the adoption of the New Economic Policy – which had allowed some private trading and a wider range of political freedoms – in the early 1920s.

There was a still larger objective, discussed by academics and commentators as well as the political leadership: the elaboration of a 'humane and democratic socialism' that would build on Soviet achievements but combine them with the experience of other nations and schools of thought, including environmentalism and feminism. Khrushchev had promised that the USSR would construct a communist society 'in the main' by 1980 in the Party Programme that was adopted under his leadership in 1961. His successors dropped that commitment and began to describe the USSR, from the early 1970s, as a 'developed socialist society', whose evolution into a fully communist society was a matter for the distant future. Brezhnev's successors in turn made it clear that the USSR was at the very beginning of developed socialism, and that its further development would require a 'whole historical epoch'. Gorbachev, for his part, avoided the term 'developed socialism' and opted instead for 'developing socialism', in effect a postponement into the still more distant future of the attainment of a fully communist society. Later still, in 1990, the objective became 'humane, democratic socialism'; in 1991, the revised version of the Party Programme was entitled 'Socialism, Democracy, Progress', with communism mentioned only in passing.

It remained unclear, these generalities apart, how a socialist society of this kind was to be constructed. Gorbachev resisted calls to set out the way ahead in any detail: did they really want a new *Short Course*, he asked the Party Congress in 1990, referring to the discredited Marxist primer that had been produced under Stalin's auspices in 1938? And what was the point of programmes like railway timetables, with objectives to be achieved by particular dates: wasn't an authentic socialism the achievement of people themselves, not something they were directed towards by others? Gorbachev's objectives emerged as a set of fairly general propositions: a humane and democratic socialism would accommodate a variety of forms of ownership and would not necessarily exclude small-scale capitalism; it would be ruled by a broad coalition of 'progressive' forces, not just by communists; it would guarantee freedom of conscience and other liberties; and it would cooperate with other states in an 'interconnected, in many ways interdependent' world. However adequate as an expression of general principle, this could scarcely offer practical guidance to party members and the broader public in their daily life; nor did it carry conviction at a time of economic difficulty, nationalist discontent and the acknowledgement of mistakes in public policy for which a party that had monopolised political power for 70 years could hardly avoid responsibility.

In the end, the search for a 'third way' that would combine Western-style democracy with a Soviet commitment to equality and social justice turned out to be a delusion. More open elections led, not to the return of committed reformers, but to the success of nationalist movements in the non-Russian republics and to the election of anti-communist mayors in Moscow and Leningrad (which once again became St Petersburg). The opportunity to organise outside the CPSU led to 'informal' movements and then to political parties that were openly hostile to communist rule. There were demonstrations, not in support of a humane and democratic socialism but (in early 1990) for the removal of the party's political monopoly from the constitution. Writers, protected by *glasnost*, moved towards an

explicit critique of Lenin as the founder of what they described as a
'totalitarian' system, and to a more general attack upon revolutions
as progenitors of violence and repression. The USSR as such was still
very popular: 76 per cent voted in favour of its retention as a
'reformed federation' when the matter was put to a referendum in
March 1991, and surveys in the late 1990s showed that the principle of
a larger union of some kind had lost none of its appeal. But belief in
communist rule had fallen to a very low ebb by the end of 1991, after
the failure of an attempted coup by hardliners which accelerated the
disintegration of a state they had sought to preserve; and there was
little support for a return to a system that had clearly failed, although
there was even less consensus about the form of government that
should take its place.

Negotiations continued even after the failure of the attempted coup
to construct a new union state, and it was agreed in November 1991
that there should be a new 'Union of Sovereign States', with its own
president and parliament. There was no doubt, Boris Yeltsin told
journalists, that there would be a new union; the only question was
how many of the former Soviet republics would be members. On 1
December, however, a referendum took place in Ukraine that produced an overwhelming majority in favour of full independence (these
were the same voters that had supported a 'renewed federation' the
previous March). Yeltsin, as Russian President, decided there was no
point in further discussions about a new form of union, and on 8
December he, the Ukrainian president and the speaker of the
Belarusian parliament gathered at a hunting lodge outside Minsk
and agreed to establish a Commonwealth of Independent States. The
new Commonwealth – which the other post-Soviet republics, apart
from the three Baltic republics, joined later – was not a state, and it
did not have a capital. It was rather an intergovernmental framework
for dealing with the common affairs of what had become fifteen
independent states. On 25 December Gorbachev resigned as the first
and last Soviet president, the Russian flag replaced the Soviet flag on
top of the Kremlin, and the Russian Federation became the successor
state of the USSR.

Constructing Postcommunism

A decade later, had Russia become a democracy or was it still in a
vaguely-defined 'transition'? Formally at least, there was no doubt

about the commitment to key liberal principles. Under the 1993 Constitution there was to be 'ideological diversity', and there could be no official belief system of any kind. There was also to be 'political diversity' and multiparty politics (Art. 13). The state was a secular one, but there was freedom of conscience, including the right to practise and to 'disseminate religious and other views and act according to them' (Art. 28). The rights and freedoms of citizens were inalienable, and based on internationally recognised norms and principles (Art. 17). And they extended to all spheres of life: there was equality before the law (Art. 19), private life and the home were inviolable (Arts. 23 and 25), and there was freedom of movement (Art. 27), speech (Art. 29), association (Art. 30) and peaceful assembly (Art. 31). Most of these had already been included in a Declaration of the Rights of Man and the Citizen that had been adopted by the Soviet and then, in a broader formulation, by the Russian parliament in late 1991; the new constitution incorporated these basic liberties into the legal foundations of the state.

There were several further rights that related to ownership and economic activity, which had particular significance in a formerly communist system. The right of private property, for instance, was protected by law, including the right to hold and to dispose of property and to pass it on by inheritance (Art. 35). There was also recognition for private property in land, on a basis to be established by subsequent legislation (Art. 36). And there was protection for the right to engage in entrepreneurial activity (Art. 34). Many of these rights – including the right to practise a religion, or to engage in entrepreneurial activity – were 'entrenched', in that they could not be limited even by the declaration of a state of emergency (Art. 56). The entire chapter on rights and freedoms (Chapter 2), moreover, could not be modified by the Federal Assembly, but only by a constitutional conference or a referendum (Art. 135). Many of the provisions of the new constitution were modelled on those of its Western counterparts (it even began 'We, the multinational people'). Indeed, the new constitution took the rights of citizens further than in many other countries, as in the requirement that official bodies allow access to the information they held on citizens that were relevant to their rights and freedoms (this was close to the 'freedom of information' legislation that existed in the USA, but not in most of Western Europe).

At the same time there were serious doubts about the constitution as a political and legal basis for a new and consolidating Russian democracy. For a start, although it was meant to be the 'basic law', there had been some doubt about the legality of its own adoption. Under the much-amended Russian constitution of 1978 that obtained at the time of its adoption, the new constitution should have been submitted to a referendum, not (as it was described) a 'national vote'. It was submitted to a national vote, in turn, because the president had no power to call a referendum on his own authority: that power belonged to the Russian parliament, originally elected in 1990 and dominated by his political opponents. The rules that applied to the national vote were different as well: a referendum was carried if a majority of the electorate voted in favour of the proposition, but Yeltsin decreed that his national vote would be carried if it secured the support of a majority of those who had actually voted. There was a further requirement, that at least half of the electorate take part in the exercise: and there was continuing controversy about whether this requirement had actually been satisfied, although 54.8 per cent of the electorate were officially reported to have taken part (see White, Rose and McAllister, 1997, pp. 98–101).

The real concerns about the new constitution had less to do with the circumstances of its adoption, and more to do with its central provisions. Above all, it imposed a strongly presidential system for which there was no national consensus, and which raised political and constitutional difficulties of its own. There was strong and widespread support for the constitution's provisions on right and freedoms, many of which codified existing legislation. But there was no corresponding agreement on the adoption of what *Izvestiya* described as a 'super-presidential republic' (12 October 1994, p. 4). It clearly reflected the president's own preferences – what else could you expect, Yeltsin explained to the press, 'in a country that is used to tsars and strong leaders?' (*Izvestiya*, 15 November 1993, p. 4). But much of the political opposition were committed to a parliamentary system with a ceremonial president, or even (as the communists proposed) no president at all. The new constitution appeared likely to withstand legal challenge (under the new system, in any case, the president appointed the constitutional court), and neither Yeltsin nor his successor Vladimir Putin showed any interest in considering an entirely new document. If anything, it was likely that Putin would strengthen, rather than weaken, its strongly centralist character. But it remained a set of rules of the game that had been imposed by one side upon the other, rather than the consensual document that might have emerged from a 'pacted' transition of the kind discussed in Chapter 15. This obviously prejudiced its ability to provide a framework within which the contending parties in a divided society could attempt to resolve their differences by the peaceful process of politics.

There were further difficulties arising from the strongly presidential character of the new constitution. As Chapter 2 makes clear, the formal powers of the Russian president are extremely far-reaching. He has important powers of his own, including the right to issue decrees that have the force of law, to initiate and reject legislation, and to dissolve parliament. He makes appointments to almost all positions of importance, including the powerful Security Council and government itself (he appoints the prime minister 'with the agreement of the State Duma', and on his proposal appoints and dismisses other ministers). In addition, he forms his own administration, in effect a super-government that for many is reminiscent of the apparatus of the Central Committee of the CPSU. The president, certainly, must be elected; but he is not accountable to the Federal Assembly, and can only be removed from office for 'high treason or other grave state crime' after a very complicated procedure has been invoked. Yeltsin had been impeached by the old parliament in 1993 after he had suspended its meetings by a decree that was an admitted violation of the constitution that prevailed at the time. The present constitution, adopted after he had suppressed the 'parliamentary insurrection' that followed, made it extremely difficult to impeach any future president, and none of the attempts that were made to do so, including the presentation of five indictments in the spring of 1999, got past their first reading in the lower house of parliament.

A strongly presidential system is one that depends upon the health, and not simply the formal powers of the president. And upon the president alone: the Soviet constitution after 1990 made provision for a vice-president, and so did the Russian presidency that was established in 1991. Yeltsin, however, found himself at odds with the vice-president who had been elected with him in 1991, Alexander Rutskoi, and the position disappeared entirely under the constitution that was approved two years later. In the event of resignation, incapacity or impeachment, under Article 92, the president's duties are taken over by the prime minister until new elections can be called. But there is no indication who is to decide if the president is suffering from a 'stable inability because of health reasons to exercise the functions vested in him'. The president himself could scarcely be expected to offer a medically qualified opinion, and might be in no position to offer an opinion of any kind. Indeed, he might be reluctant to leave office at all even if medical advice was very clear. But if not the president, who else could take a decision of such constitutional significance? These were far from abstract questions as Boris Yeltsin underwent a quintuple bypass operation in November 1996 that removed him from official duties for several months. And they had not seemed abstract on other occasions, as the president conducted himself erratically in a manner that appeared to suggest a familiar Russian weakness. There was particular embarrassment when the president failed to emerge from his plane at Shannon airport in 1994 to greet the Irish prime minister, leading to later accusations that he was in a 'permanent state of visiting Ireland'. Vladimir Putin was certainly a younger and a fitter man, a judo black belt who worked out every morning. But it was the job of the constitution to provide for all eventualities, particularly in a system in which a single figure was invested with so much authority.

Presidents, in other systems, are limited not simply by their formal powers but also by countervailing institutions, such as political parties and the courts, and by an informed and assertive public. There were weaknesses in both of these in early postcommunist Russia. Political parties, in particular, had few members and very little public support (see Chapter 5). The only party in a Western sense was the Communist Party of the Russian Federation, which had a national membership and a functioning organisation. But all the parties were mistrusted, more so – according to the survey evidence – than almost all other public institutions. When these questions were put to a representative sample of Russians in early 2000, only 9 per cent were prepared to express some degree of confidence in political parties; 74 per cent took the opposite view. Parties were trusted more than foreign advisers to the Russian government, but less than parliament, the trade unions, the police, courts and private entrepreneurs, and much less than the army, the church and ordinary people themselves.[1] Fewer were interested in politics than they had been in the Gorbachev years, and fewer subscribed to a newspaper – particularly a national newspaper (the annual circulation of all newspapers fell from 37.8 billion in 1990 to just 7.5 billion in 1998: *Rossiya*, 2000, p. 133). Russians were still likely to be members of a trade union, and often of a cooperative; but there was little sign of a flourishing civil society that might sustain a newly democratic system of government.

What about control over government, the central element in definitions of democracy? Everyone, certainly, had a better chance to say what they thought; they were free to join any organisation they liked, and to take an interest in politics or (just as important) not to take an interest. There was more freedom of travel (though there were relatively few that could afford to take advantage of it), and there was much more freedom to practise a religion than in the Brezhnev years. But there had been fewer changes in the relationship between citizens and the government that ruled in their name (see Figure 1.1). Indeed, in early 2000, a majority thought their elected government was actually less likely to treat them 'fairly and impartially' than the government they had experienced in the Brezhnev years. And in a question that is asked internationally about the ability of 'people like me' to influence government, only 19 per cent thought their influence had increased as a result of fully competitive elections and the other changes of the postcommunist period; a third thought they had less influence, and almost half thought there had been no change of any significance. Nor was there much belief, according to the surveys, that

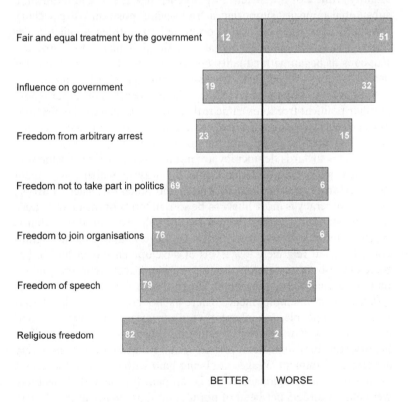

FIGURE 1.1 *A balance sheet of postcommunist rule*

ordinary people were less at risk of arbitrary arrest than had been the case in the communist period. In most respects, clearly, personal liberties were thought to be much better protected than in the years of Soviet rule (the comparison was with the Brezhnev years, before *perestroika*, and the present). But the relationship between citizens and government had shown no real improvement, in the view of ordinary Russians, and in some respects a worsening.

What about the way forward? Russians, on the survey evidence, were certainly committed to their own path of development, rather than a simple repetition of the experience of other countries. Just 16 per cent, in early 2000, wanted to develop along the lines of a West European country; a massive 83 per cent preferred to develop 'in their own traditions'. It was less clear what that tradition might be. What kind of ideas, for instance, did ordinary Russians most readily identify with? For a quarter (24 per cent), it was still communism; a substantial minority supported a 'right-wing' position (18 per cent), but still larger numbers were committed to nothing at all (35 per cent). And what was a 'democracy' in the first place? For ordinary Russians, it began with equality before the law (87 per cent); but for nearly as many (83 per cent) it was economic prosperity, and not far behind was a 'guaranteed income' (73 per cent). The other, more familiar political freedoms came rather later: multicandidate elections (63 per cent), freedom to disregard the advice of politicians (58 per cent), and freedom to criticise the government (51 per cent).

Attitudes towards democracy are not a 'given': they reflect the way in which democracy is defined, and the way in which government itself performs – particularly in Russia and much of Eastern Europe, where democracy is more likely to be seen in terms of the maintenance of living standards rather than in the formal, procedural way that is more common in Western countries. Countries have sustained democratic forms at relatively low levels of development (as in India), but there are also more developed nations – like Germany in the 1930s – that have seen democracy break down in the face of high levels of inflation and unemployment. There is no reason to believe that Russians, as people, are inherently authoritarian. But they have had little opportunity to experience self-government in the course of their history, and they are attempting to acquire that experience in a very adverse environment. Wages are being paid with considerable delays or not at all, and organised crime is rampant (in the mid-1990s there were more murders per head of population than in any other country in the world apart from South Africa). The environment is increasingly unhealthy, unemployment is mounting, and the education and health care systems are in grave difficulty with the withdrawal of the kind of state support they had enjoyed until the recent past.

The future of a Russian democracy, accordingly, will be shaped by the nature of its political system, and the formal liberties that it provides; but it will also be shaped by the performance of government – in the economy, in health, and in family matters – in ways that are considered in the subsequent chapters of this book. All that could safely be said at the start of a new century was Russians were sick of experiments, bitter about the failures of their political class, and desperate for the first time in their lives to 'live normally' – whatever the regime might choose to call itself.

Notes

1. These and the figures that follow are taken from a nationally representative survey conducted by the All-Russian Centre for the Study of Public Opinion (VTsIOM) in January-February 2000 for the present author and associates; a full presentation of results is available in Rose, 2000.

PART ONE

The Framework of Government

2

The Presidency: From Yeltsin to Putin

JOHN P. WILLERTON JR

A decade after the collapse of the USSR, the Russian Federation finds itself at a political crossroads as it struggles to consolidate the fledgling democratic institutional arrangements now in place. Central to such democratic consolidation is the definition of the role and responsibilities of the federal presidency and the federal executive. Established in the waning days of Soviet power and forged during Boris Yeltsin's first term as Russia's chief executive (1991–6), the presidency has evolved into a powerful institution affecting all aspects of Russian political life. Even a dispassionate observer might be inclined to characterise the post-Soviet political system as a presidential democracy.

Ten years of institution building and governance under Yeltsin yielded a 'hegemonic presidency': that is, a federal presidency, composed of dozens of agencies and literally thousands of political functionaries, which assumes primacy in both decision-making and policy supervision. Led by a popularly elected president, this hegemonic presidency – with overwhelming resources at its command – dominates the country's political landscape. The 1993 Constitution defines and legitimates this institutional presidency, with its considerable powers derived not only from these formal constitutional arrangements, but also from a decade-long pattern of assertive use of those powers by the two men who have held the office, Boris Yeltsin and Vladimir Putin.

Yet the 'logic' of a hegemonic Russian presidency also lies with past Tsarist and Soviet preferences for a strong executive, with power concentrated with the executive as supported by a massive underlying bureaucracy. While the Russian public was politically deferential, state coercion reinforced the decision-making prerogatives of the supreme leader, whether Tsar or Communist Party General Secretary. Post-Soviet Russian society continues to wrestle with this historical past of executive domination and public submission, yet in the midst of ongoing turbulent transformational politics, many Russians continue to desire – as consistently revealed in opinion surveys – a strong, stabilising hand at the state's helm.

How is the interested observer to explore the fundamental realities of the new – but still evolving – Russian democracy? We concentrate here on the presidency, examining its institutional makeup, its functions and role in Russian politics, and the two men who to date have held the office. We consider not only the actions of the federal presidency, but the forces operating upon it. To better understand the realities of contemporary Russian politics and, in particular, to appreciate the nature of post-Soviet decision-making and governance, we must draw a number of distinctions among forces affecting the current political process. Firstly, we need to differentiate between the institution of the Russian presidency and the officeholder standing at its helm. The 1993 Constitution invests the presidency with considerable formal powers, but these are separate from the abilities, intentions, and authority of the individual assuming the country's highest office. Both Yeltsin and Putin struggled to consolidate their power bases and promote their agendas; their power was distinguishable from their authority. Secondly, we must distinguish between the formal duties and prerogatives of the presidency and the informal powers that permit it to so dominate the Russian political landscape. In doing so, we consider the informal and extralegal arrangements that can bring together the often-conflicting policy interests of government officials, legislators, and private sector interests.

As we illuminate the Russian presidency and federal executive, we necessarily give attention to the two men who assumed Russia's highest political office since the Soviet collapse: Boris Yeltsin (1991–9) and Vladimir Putin (2000 to date). As we shall see, Yeltsin and his supporters shaped the post-Soviet system and created an all-powerful presidency, with Yeltsin's own constitutionally legitimated transfer of power to Vladimir Putin at the end of 1999 setting yet another precedent in the consolidation of this new system. Now more than a year into his tenure, Putin began to put his own mark on the institution. He and his allies further concentrated presidential power, actively pursing an anti-corruption campaign while advancing a programme to investigate the country's still troubled economy. The longer-term significance of Putin's early initiatives is yet to be determined but, as we shall see, they are constructed on a past tradition of executive assertiveness and dominance that many see as at the heart of Russian political order.

Tradition of Strong Executives

The desire and ability of Yeltsin, Putin, and their allies to craft a powerful post-Soviet federal presidency must be considered against the backdrop of the Russian public's traditional desire for strong and decisive leaders. Moreover, the size and diversity of Russia have been viewed by many as requiring some level of power concentration and bottom-up public deference to the elite to ensure political stability and economic wellbeing.

Past Russian political systems have been characterised by a strong executive, as political power was concentrated with a small ruling elite. During Tsarist times, the centralised autocracy was organised on the basis of a steep power hierarchy. It was the Tsar who had ultimate decision-making authority, as he stood atop a massive state bureaucracy and was legitimated by his position as the formal head of the Russian Orthodox Church. From the nineteenth century on, the Tsar was assisted by an impressive array of government ministries and advisory councils. These bodies assumed critical information-gathering, consultative and policy coordinating roles. Meanwhile, representative bodies such as the *Zemskii sobor* (first selected in the mid-sixteenth century) and the State Duma (created in 1905) emerged at points in Russian history, but they never constrained the actions of the Tsar. Such bodies were ignored and even dissolved when judged necessary.

The tradition of a strong chief executive standing atop a massive state bureaucracy continued in the Soviet period (1917–91). The core feature of the Soviet political system was its centralised, hierarchical structure, with a massive set of interlocked bureaucracies linking all institutions and interests into an apparatus ruled by a small and relatively homogeneous Slavic and Russian elite. Chief executives such as Joseph Stalin, Nikita Khrushchev, and Leonid Brezhnev, serving as the Communist Party General or First Secretary, devoted considerable attention to consolidating and maintaining power within the party-state apparatus. Their ability to promote their policy agendas was dependent upon their organisational prowess. It was the Communist Party that was responsible for setting policies, with the party supervising the Soviet government's implementation and administration of those policies. Thus, the head of the party was the USSR's chief executive, his position of executive dominance assured.

Mikhail Gorbachev's ill-fated efforts (1985–91) to salvage the Soviet system through political institutional reform only served to fracture this centralised, hierarchical system. Root and branch reforms shifted decision-making power away from the party and governmental bureaucracy to new federal-level executive and legislative bodies, including a federal presidency. An expanding array of complex policy problems required power-sharing among a growing set of established and new institutions, but with the president at the helm. It was intended in this emergent system that a broad political consensus would arise through a viable legislature, guided by a president with an independent basis of authority. History would demonstrate that Gorbachev erred in choosing to assume the presidency through legislative approval rather than through a contested popular election: he was left without a public mandate, leaving his authority to govern open to question. Gorbachev's questionable leadership legitimacy would only be further underscored by the electoral successes of his public rival, Boris Yeltsin, who successfully competed for the Russian Republic presidency a year later.

Gorbachev's federal-level changes set precedents that were followed at lower levels, including in Russia. Yeltsin and other politicians made use of similar institutional arrangements to advance their own agendas even as they challenged Soviet federal authorities. Nuanced executive-legislative struggles in late Soviet period Russia reflected the logic of more open federal-level struggles between President Gorbachev and the new Soviet parliament. Russian institutional and procedural changes in 1990–1 laid a framework for the political conflicts that arose after the Soviet collapse.

Yeltsin and the Forging of the Post-Soviet Presidency

It is hardly surprising, in the wake of Gorbachev's failed reform efforts and the Soviet collapse, that Boris Yeltsin would play the key role in defining the country's highest political office. Indeed, the first occupant of a country's highest executive post will be critical in the shaping of that office, as evinced by the experiences of George Washington and Charles de Gaulle in the American and French cases. We must consider Boris Yeltsin's legacy, grounded not only in his personality and leadership style, but also in the exigencies of the era in which he governed. Definitive judgments about Yeltsin's ultimate contribution to the forging of the Russian presidency – and to the creation of the post-Soviet Russian system – however, will require decades of post-Yeltsin experience.

Boris Yeltsin (b. 1931), a product of the Soviet system, hailed from a poor peasant family, his relatives having suffered during the Stalinist repressions (Yeltsin, 1990). His worldview was highly influenced by this background as he became a champion of the rights and economic interests of common citizens. A regional party functionary from the Sverdlovsk region, he rapidly ascended to the top regional party posts before being pulled in the early Gorbachev period to troubleshoot reform of the corrupt Moscow city party machine. As he fought corruption and inefficiency in the country's capital, he rose to national political prominence. His free-wheeling style and iconoclastic and anti-establishment behaviour quickly earned him high public regard, though it cost him his standing within the Gorbachev-led Communist hierarchy. He successfully manoeuvred around Gorbachev's political reforms to secure election to a newly constituted Soviet parliament (1989) and ultimately to the newly established Russian presidency (June 1991).

The hallmarks of Yeltsin's leadership style, influential in the crafting of the post-Soviet presidency, were evident in his early years as Russia's chief executive. Instinctively a political opportunist, Yeltsin held pragmatic political beliefs which – depending upon the circumstances – permitted him to promote both decisive reform and compromise. Throughout his career, both during and after the Soviet period, Yeltsin demonstrated a strong willingness to navigate around formal rules and procedures to advance his personal and policy agenda. He had risen to power as a Communist Party leader through manipulating the authoritarian system, and he could be quite authoritarian in pursuing his own interests. Yet while willing to use power as needed, he also came to rely on the public for support at critical junctures. Thus, while late Soviet period statutes made the Russian president subordinate to the elected legislature, Yeltsin moved forward after the failed August 1991 coup effort to secure extraordinary powers to introduce a radical reform programme. His bargaining position with the more conservative parliament was bolstered by the extraordinary political and economic crisis in which Russia found itself. It was also bolstered by his previous victories in contested elections, most notably the June 1991 Russian presidential election. By force of personality, assertiveness in taking on the massive dilemmas overwhelming Russia, and directness in garnering palpable public support, Yeltsin consolidated his power position while introducing controversial economic reform measures. We find here a powerful combination of leadership characteristics and political conditions that would be evident during much of Yeltsin's tenure as president as he led Russia through the first phase of its post-Soviet transformation.

Throughout most of his second term, after his second-round victory in the 1996 elections, Yeltsin was tired, withdrawn, some have argued depressed, and certainly inactive. Shadow economic structures, bridging government institutions and the private sector, were critical to the ongoing massive sell-off of state property and to the further marketisation of the Russian economy. As will be discussed later, powerful business interests (the so-called 'oligarchs') assumed important, even highly public, positions within the formal political arena. Meanwhile, Yeltsin's strong predilection to rotate government ministers and presidential functionaries only accelerated as policy problems persisted. With five different prime ministers heading the government during Yeltsin's last two years in office, there was considerable personnel instability and policy inertia. The public perception of incompetence, combined with the image of a mismanaged state, overwhelmed Yeltsin's public standing and his ratings fell to record lows, in striking contrast to the high public approval of his last prime minister, Vladimir Putin (Figure 2.1; and for a discussion, Mishler and Willerton, 2000). Some might argue that Yeltsin's last act as president, his surprise resignation on 31 December 1999, was the final impulsive act of a very volatile career. However, his resignation and passing of power to a hand-picked successor could also be interpreted as a final crafty step both to protect his own personal well-being and to salvage the prospects for continuation of his policy line.

In sponsoring Putin, Yeltsin brought to the country's highest office a former intelligence officer who had been virtually unknown but a year earlier. Putin has been described as 'an entirely random person who basically did nothing to contribute to his own rise' (Radzikhovsky, 2000). Yet in Yeltsin's final year in office, power seemed to accumulate itself around Putin, as Kremlin authorities searched for a politician who would safeguard their interests. Putin technically assumed office as acting president on 31 December 1999, waiting

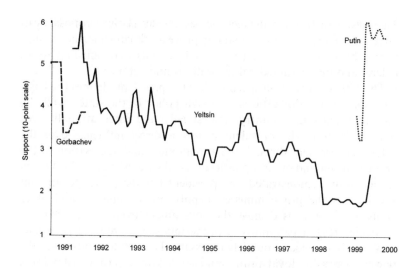

FIGURE 2.1   *Trends in popular support for leaders in Russia and the USSR*

until his first-round election on 26 March 2000 (with 52 per cent of the vote in a multi-candidate election) to claim his own mandate for governance. Elected by the Russian people, he had *de facto* come to power through appointment. Given the circumstances of his rapid ascent, it would be especially incumbent upon Putin to decisively consolidate power over the institutions comprising the federal presidency. His prospects for successfully addressing Russia's pressing policy problems would be fundamentally grounded in these power consolidation efforts.

Institutional Arrangements

The federal president was given extensive decision-making powers under the 1993 Constitution. The full range of presidential prerogatives was used by Boris Yeltsin, while Vladimir Putin, in his first year in office, has moved to expand on them. The federal presidency contoured during the Yeltsin years represents a large pyramid of power that dwarfs those of all other political institutions. What makes the presidency hegemonic is not only the fact that its position is legally superior to that of other bodies, but the institutional independence and freedom of manoeuvre the president possesses.

The president, through decrees, vetoes and legislative proposals can direct the federal decision-making process. Meanwhile, he is supported by a large set of agencies and officials that link him to all federal and major subfederal institutions and actors.

The 1993 Constitution specifies that the president 'defines the basic directions of the domestic and foreign policy of the state', while he also represents the country domestically and internationally (see Articles 80–93). The president possesses direct influence over the federal government through the appointment and supervision of the prime minister and other top officials. As the experience of the Yeltsin regime aptly demonstrated, the president has the power to appoint and dismiss the prime minister, deputy prime ministers and other ministers, as well as dismiss the government overall. He needs no particular reason to remove a prime minister or remove personnel beyond what he deems publicly necessary. Thus, Yeltsin possessed the power to fire his loyal prime minister Viktor Chernomyrdin for a 'lack of energy' in pursuing his reform agenda, and then – less than six months later – attempt to reappoint him to the same post because he was 'the right man for the job'. The president enjoys comparable nominating powers for other top federal officials, including the State Bank chairman, members of the Constitutional and Supreme Court, and members of the Security Council.

The president, operating through his vast apparatus of supporting agencies and officials, initiates legislation, reporting annually to a joint session of parliament on his government's domestic and foreign policy. The bases for the president's and parliament's power are constitutionally defined and separate. In particular, there are conditions under which the president can dissolve the lower house of the parliament, the State Duma. He can call referendums and, as Commander in Chief, he can declare a state of emergency.

Central to the president's hegemonic position are presidential decrees (*ukazy*), which have the force of law. The Constitution (Art. 90) grants him extensive leeway in issuing decrees that are binding throughout the country so long as they do not contradict the Constitution or federal laws. Given the massive size of the Russian state bureaucracy, with its numerous and often-conflicting ministries and agencies, there has been a need for powerful top-down mechanisms – such as presidential decrees – to spur it to action and coordinate its direction. Policy-setting decrees, which have a binding effect on all citizens, may be overridden by parliament, but only upon a two-thirds vote of both legislative chambers – an action unlikely to occur given the weakness of Russia's party system and the highly fragmented, factional structure of parliament.

Both in number and substance, presidential decrees have had a significant effect upon post-Soviet politics. Yeltsin issued over 1500 policy-relevant decrees (excluding appointments and honorific awards) during his nearly nine year tenure, with all major areas affected. The formal impetus for many major governmental institutional changes came from such decrees, including the expansion of judges' powers, the increased professionalisation of the civil service, and the creation of a new passport system. Indeed, many controversial political decisions, such as the September 1993 dissolution of parliament and the December 1994 intervention into Chechnya, were taken by decree. It should be added, however, that the more parochial political interests of the president were advanced through decrees, as nearly 25 per cent of all decrees entailed the dispensing of what could be called 'political pork': that is, the handing out of particularised benefits for regional, sectoral, or other special interests. It is not surprising that during the 1996 presidential campaign, Yeltsin used decrees to grant exemptions to companies in paying their tax arrears, to raise the government assistance levels for certain dependent elements, and to commit federal assistance to certain regions (Mishler, Willerton, and Smith, 2000).

Meanwhile, the ability of the rival legislative branch to remove the president for malfeasance is extremely limited. Procedures for impeaching the head of state are cumbersome and involve numerous federal bodies. The State Duma must formally vote an indictment on the basis of serious violations of the Constitution, with the Supreme Court and the Constitutional Court confirming the appropriateness of such an extreme action and verifying that correct procedures have been followed. Only after these steps have been taken, and the necessary hearings held, can the State Duma and Federation Council subsequently vote for impeachment, with two-thirds majorities in both chambers needed to remove him from office. The closest the parliament came to impeaching the president was in spring 1999, yet even with considerable pent-up frustration with the president's actions (ranging from the state of the economy to the Chechen debacle and the recent firing of a popular prime minister) and doubts about his leadership competence, all five opposition-sponsored counts failed.

Presidential Apparatus

Much of the president's dominant power position stems from the large apparatus of agencies and officials that comprise the federal executive. The vast array of responsibilities falling on the presidency requires a plethora of agencies in both crafting policy and supervising its implementation. Although this presidential administration has been subject to constant organisational modification and highly publicised efforts to downsize, it still encompasses over three dozen separate agencies with perhaps 3000 full-time functionaries. The presidential administration was built on the foundation of the old Communist Party Central Committee apparatus, continuing a centuries-old tradition of massive bureaucratic support for Russia's chief executive. Literally located in many of the same old Central Committee buildings and employing many of the late Soviet party functionaries, the presidential administration's power intrigues and marked tendency to protect the vested interests of the government-bureaucratic elites also harkens back to Soviet era executive norms.

The structure and functioning 'logic' of the presidential administration are subject to the president's – and his top associates' – preferences. The 1993 Constitution is silent on this important set of bodies beyond brief reference to one body, the Security Council. Four organisational components of the presidential administration merit brief discussion as we highlight the impact of this complex set of executive institutions on Russian politics: (1) the Administration of Affairs office; (2) the Chancellery; (3) the Executive Office; and (4) the security apparatus, including the Security Council. While reorganisations of this set of institutions have occurred with the changing political needs of the president and the rise and fall of different heads of the presidential administration, we can offer some general comments tying institutions to broad political tasks (Huskey, 1999).

A number of bodies deal with the technical operations of the federal executive, but their control of information flows and dispensing of resources can be very important to the functioning of the presidency. The Administration of Affairs oversees the significant material resources at the command of the presidency. Through its control over facilities, allocation of offices, handling of business expenses, paying of officials' salaries, provision of goods and services to those officials, the Administration of Affairs has tremendous leverage to advantage individuals and influence their actions. Meanwhile, the Chancellery is responsible for the more mundane processing of documents for the president's consideration, but these can total in the thousands per workday, necessitating a staff of several dozen.

The Executive Office, at the heart of the new Russian presidency, is the umbrella entity composed of nearly 40 agencies responsible for all facets of executive activity: crafting policies, gathering information and generating analyses, coordinating activities with other political institutions, and reviewing actions of governmental bodies in policy implementation. One of its major subunits, the State Legal Affairs Administration, develops presidential decrees and draft laws which are forwarded to the parliament. Since presidential decrees have been major decision-making devices of the Yeltsin and Putin regimes, the ability to influence their content has been a fundamental concern for anyone trying to influence the policy process. As a result, the head of the presidential administration, overseeing the State Legal Affairs and other agencies, is the critical conduit through which such influences must pass. Meanwhile, a related executive body, the Monitoring Administration, examines the actions of officials and state institutions to be sure they are implementing policies and acting in accordance with the law. Related bodies serve in providing information and technical advice. Yeltsin relied upon the Counsellors' Service which, with its approximately one dozen top advisers and their support staffs, provided position papers on the full range of substantive issues before the executive. Essentially disbanded in Yeltsin's second term, the role of providing technical advice was parcelled out among a number of more topically-focused departments. Putin, in formulating his own support structures, created a Presidential Expert Department that potentially assumes a more high profile advisory function.

Finally, a number of agencies dealing with security issues reinforce the executive's pre-eminence in this all-important domain. For example, the Federal Agency for the Protection of Government Communications has responsibilities ranging from control over the government's phone system to control over the nuclear black box. The former may be especially germane to the power politics of competing elites as communications surveillance could advantage those in charge *vis-à-vis* both executive branch rivals and those in the parliament and elsewhere. Another agency, the Main Security Administration, is responsible for protecting officials and government buildings. More importantly, the Security Council, directed by the president, can be a high-level consultative body to assist the chief executive in addressing national security and high stakes domestic issues. Its composition and decision-making role are determined by the president, and it is supported by a good-sized staff of approximately 150. Yeltsin ultimately took the decision to invade Chechnya through a session of the Security Council. With its current membership including the president, prime minister, the heads of the two parliamentary chambers, its executive secretary, and selected top government ministers, the Security Council bridges various institutional and sectoral interests. While its executive secretaries have proven influential to Yeltsin–Putin era national security calculations, its policy significance is entirely dependent upon the president's prerogatives.

Prime Minister and Government

While the Russian president sets the broad direction of government policies, it is the prime minister, standing atop the formal governmental administrative structure, who is responsible for the day-to-day administration of the country. Nominated by the president and subsequently approved by the parliament, the prime minister assumes an important role in linking the executive and legislative branches while marshalling support – both within the parliament and in the large state bureaucracy – for government initiatives. The prime minister helps in selecting ministers, who must be approved by the president and account to the legislature. Together with other government ministers, the prime minister assists the president and his advisers in policy formulation. In the event of the incapacitation, death, or resignation of the president, the prime minister assumes the post of acting president (with an election to select a full-time replacement held within three months of the transfer of power).

The first post-Soviet decade has revealed real limits in the prime minister's power prerogatives *vis-à-vis* the president. It is true that the prime minister stands at the head of a governmental apparatus with approximately two dozen departments and over 1000 full-time functionaries. But unlike the French system of possible 'cohabitation', where a prime minister heading the government has a power base at least partially independent of the president, the Russian prime minister must maintain the president's confidence to remain in office. Viktor Chernomyrdin, Russia's longest-serving prime minister to date (1992–8), demonstrated that there was room for an assertive prime minister to troubleshoot on important policy matters, to influence public opinion, and to affect the smooth operation of executive-legislative relations. However, when circumstances warranted, Yeltsin removed him, and the string of subsequent prime ministers rotated in and out of the top government post in less than two years revealed the president's ability to move top officials and reorganise governments as he saw fit.

The men who have served as prime minister in the post-communist era have been varied in career background and ideological orientation (see Table 2.1). As the president's political needs have shifted, occupants of the highest government office have been moved in and out of office, often with the 'deposed' official drawing a 'golden parachute' into another position and maintaining a good relationship with the president. Reformist economists such as Yegor Gaidar and Sergei Kirienko promoted controversial privatisation and more austere government spending programmes, while long-serving Soviet era bureaucrats such as Chernomyrdin and Yevgenii Primakov were tapped to build bridges to centrist and conservative forces and to forge a more modest reform programme. When the need arose for more assertive, loyal, but organisationally weak functionaries to advance the president's agenda, former security apparatus officials such as Sergei Stepashin and Vladimir Putin were elevated from near obscurity to the prime ministership. All of these former prime ministers continue to assume influential positions in the country's politics, with several members of the parliament. Meanwhile, Mikhail Kasyanov, Putin's prime minister, is an economist with significant governmental and business connections who appeared able to navigate around reformist and centrist elements. Yet with concerns about budgetary struggles with the legislature and mounting doubts about the condition of Russia's anaemic economic recovery, rumours were already spreading during his first year in office that Kasyanov, like his predecessors, might also succumb to Kremlin intrigues and be removed.

TABLE 2.1 *Post-Soviet prime ministers, 1992–2000*

Yegor Gaidar (b. 1956)	January–December 1992
Viktor Chernomyrdin (b. 1938)	December 1992–March 1998
Sergei Kirienko (b. 1962)	March–August 1998
Yevgenii Primakov (b. 1929)	September 1998–May 1999
Sergei Stepashin (b. 1952)	May–August 1999
Vladimir Putin (b. 1952)	August 1999–May 2000
Mikhail Kasyanov (b. 1957)	Since May 2000

Informal Prerogatives and Power Realities

While the 1993 Constitution and related rules and procedures structure the operation of the policy process, the reality of Russian
decisionmaking is that much occurs behind the scenes and involves
informal bargaining relationships among both governmental and
private actors. The interactions among public and business interests
are nearly impossible to observe and evaluate conclusively, but we
know they affect governmental actions and policy outcomes. It is
ironic that while the Russian polity and society are open to a degree
unmatched in the past, complex unmonitored manoeuvrings of
powerful sectoral and bureaucratic interests play an elusive role in
the crafting of decisions (Schroder, 1999).

We have seen that the presidential administration arose in the void
left with the collapse of the Communist Party Central Committee
apparatus. The high-level political intrigues and hidden manipulation
of resources and ideas that surrounded that system have found
resonance in the Yeltsin–Putin era. Within the institutional labyrinth
of the presidency and the government, changing coalitions and
evolving policy calculations are directly tied to these fundamental
power struggles. There is a powerful need for executive discipline, as
the continuing competition among executive and government bodies
structures policy outcomes. Much of post-Soviet federal politics has
involved institutional turf wars. Meanwhile, the ability of executive
and legislative bodies to craft policies often occurs through informal,
'off the record' dealings (see Remington, 2000). And throughout this
system, institutional bargaining and decisionmaking are significantly
influenced by resource-rich 'private' businesses and their top
executives.

Within the executive branch, the changing 'team' of presidential
advisers and functionaries has not only reflected the careful balancing
of diverse ideological and sectoral interests, but the rotation of top
representatives of often competing private sector interests. Personnel
rotation was a hallmark of the Yeltsin period, as officials were
constantly moved from one post to another. Yeltsin himself was
uninterested in the everyday politics of governance and left considerable power and responsibility with trusted subordinates. Top lieute-
nants, in particular the head of the presidential administration,
became gatekeepers in overseeing the recruitment (and removal) of
officials and in the crafting of policies. The preferences of these
gatekeepers varied, as did the 'teams' they helped oversee: where

Yeltsin's first chief of staff, Gennadii Burbulis (1991–2) helped to fashion a group of young, smart economists to drive the early Yeltsin reform programme, his last (and Putin's first), Alexander Voloshin (1998 to date), has cultivated a diverse group of centrist officials who seem quite protective of the powerful business interests with which they have close connections.

Critical to the functioning of both the Yeltsin and early Putin presidencies is what Russians refer to as 'the Family': a varied collection of Yeltsin's close relatives (in particular, his daughter Tatyana Dyachenko), old friends (bodyguard Alexander Korzhakov and tennis coach Shamil Tarpishchev), government allies (such as one-time head of the presidential administration Valentin Yuma-shev), and corporate-business leaders (such as oligarchs Boris Bere-zovsky and Roman Abramovich) who seem quite protective of the power and resources gained by the contemporary government-busi-ness establishment. Yeltsin might personally have stood down, but the influence of 'the Family' lives on through individuals such as Alexander Voloshin, who continues as Putin's head of the presidential administration. This should not be surprising. A frequent observation raised when Putin succeeded to the presidency was that he was little more than a creature of 'the Family', having been cultivated by Voloshin and others during the year preceding his elevation to president with the intention that he safeguard 'the Family's' interests.

Judging the political significance of 'the Family' is difficult, with concrete evidence of its impact on policy not easy to come by. The Russian press is full of anecdotes, claims, and exposés of the actions of members of the so-called 'presidential court', but it is hard to determine the veracity of claims, let alone judge their long-term significance. However, it is reasonable to conclude that 'the Family', operating through powerful senior presidential functionaries, has influenced the content of proposed legislation and presidential de-crees, has affected the dispensing of the considerable resources at the president's command, and has been influential in both the crafting and application of governmental regulations affecting the emerging – and still chaotic – Russian private sector. The impact on the priva-tisation of the Russian economy and its subsequent functioning cannot be overemphasised. The influence of 'the Family' and its friends could be felt in the government's regulation of the so-called 'sale of the century', when Russia's oil and gas industry was bought up by favoured private interests under suspicious circumstances at amazingly low prices. For instance, the government's share of

Russia's richest company, Gazprom, which the International Monetary Fund estimated to be worth $119 billion, was sold off for only $20 million (that is, for one-sixtieth of one per cent of its value). Indeed, the 17 major Russian energy companies, which the IMF estimated as having a market value of $17 billion, were privatised for less than $1.4 billion (see Pirani and Farrell, 1999). And the 'loans for shares' programme whereby these valuable resources were sold was developed and supervised by such 'Family' associates as Anatolii Chubais (one-time presidential administration head) and Vladimir Potanin (one-time first deputy prime minister). Meanwhile, the long-time presidential administration property department head, Pavel Borodin, dispensed considerable resources to public and private sector interests, whether in the provision of offices, goods and services to state functionaries, in the awarding of lucrative construction contracts, or in the selling the valuable Kremlin real estate assets. Careers were advanced and fortunes made as the long-term structure of the privatised post-Soviet economy was set.

Among those most richly rewarded by political favours of 'the Family' and the government establishment were the so-called 'oligarchs': ambitious, risk-taking entrepreneurs who used their political connections and business acumen in the new market environment to build corporate conglomerates and fabulous personal fortunes. In the new regulated market environment, these oligarchs, with their high-placed political friends, took advantage of the very low level of competition to amass considerable property and capital. Their bases of power lay in the extractive industries – in particular energy – and also in banks. Their resources have given them an ability to secure media outlets, signifying that these powerful business conglomerates have a genuine public presence. It may be fair to say that the oligarchs do not care about ideology, but they are concerned about policies affecting the economy and their business interests: in particular, they want to safeguard the new market arrangements and protect their corporate positions. To do so, they involve themselves in government personnel and policy matters. The recruitment of top government and presidential administration officials often has been tied to the interventions and pressures of powerful 'oligarchs'. During the 1996 presidential election, the oligarchs offered high profile public support for Yeltsin's re-election (notably in their published 'Appeal of the 13', in *Nezavisimaya gazeta*, 27 April 1996), but more significantly they committed vast financial resources and media exposure to help maintain Yeltsin in power. Four years later, oligarchs tied with 'the

Family' used their media outlets (particularly Boris Berezovsky's
ORT television channel) to effectively destroy the reputations of
two 'Family' rivals, Moscow Mayor Yuri Luzhkov and former Prime
Minister Yevgenii Primakov, who were positioning to run for the
presidency in 2000. These oligarch-supported media efforts proved
important to the outcome of the December 1999 parliamentary
elections and were probably central to both Luzhkov's and Primakov's withdrawals from the 2000 presidential campaign.

A brief examination of the careers and political influence of two
leading personalities, one an oligarch with a strong political agenda,
the second a politician turned oligarch, illuminates the concrete
political significance of unelected figures who have so influenced
post-Soviet Russia's transformation. Boris Berezovsky, at one time
arguably the most powerful and publicly visible of the oligarchs,
began his rise to economic and then political prominence through a
car dealership, taking advantage of a dismantled supply network in
the late Gorbachev period to make what were then unprecedented
profits. By early 1995 his wealth had enabled him to gain effective
control over a state television station (ORT), and he subsequently
gained control over the Sibneft oil company in the 'loans for shares'
auction. While his ties with the Yeltsin family allowed him to secure
control of the state air company, Aeroflot, it was his outspoken
support for the President in 1996 that helped him to formally move
into the political arena with appointments as the Security Council's
vice secretary (1996) and subsequently as the executive secretary of
the Commonwealth of Independent States (1998). While such formal
positions may have enabled Berezovsky to become involved in a
variety of affairs of states (such as Russian–Chechen negotiations to
resolve the conflict), it was his ability to sponsor individuals either
into presidential and governmental posts (including Alexander Voloshin), or to connect friends with high-level state officials (for
instance, the oligarch Roman Abramovich with 'the Family' and
Putin), that gave Berezovsky almost unmatched political clout.

Meanwhile, Anatolii Chubais, an economist from St Petersburg
who rose to oversee Russia's privatisation programme, is the con-
summate political insider who has operated at the highest decision-
making levels since the early days of the Yeltsin regime. Originally
brought to Moscow in November 1991 as the Minister for State
Property Management, he became the point man for developing and
implementing the privatisation programme. Between 1992 and 1998
Chubais rotated through various senior posts, including service as

first deputy prime minister, presidential administration head, and Russian envoy to international financial institutions. Along the way, he worked as one of the architects of Yeltsin's successful 1996 re-election campaign, though arguably his greatest strategic value to the Yeltsin team centred around his ability to forge strong ties with both domestic Russian businesses and foreign international financial institutions. Indeed, he helped leverage Western support and oversaw hundreds of millions of dollars in subsidised loans and rescheduled debt. A highly controversial figure who was a lightning rod for anti-Yeltsin elements, he found a 'golden parachute' from the presidency through his April 1998 appointment to head the powerful Russian natural electricity monopoly, Unified Energy Systems. His continuing importance to contemporary high power politics is revealed in his monopoly's manipulation of energy subsidies to Russia's regions, no small matter as President Putin uses a range of federal powers to rein in the country's restive provinces.

President Putin's State of the Nation address in July 2000 indicated that Russia would no longer tolerate 'shadowy groups', and his government's early moves against several prominent oligarchs (such as media mogul Vladimir Gusinsky and banker Vladimir Potanin) may signify the imminent ending of 'the good times' for this privileged economic elite. Indeed, the August 1998 financial crisis had already weakened the resource base of many of these corporate executives. However, many government officials continue to have strong associations with oligarchs such as Roman Abramovich and Boris Berezovsky, while corporate executives such as Chubais, Vagit Alekperov (LUKoil president), and Rem Vyakhirev (Gazprom chairman) continue to influence Russian economic policy. There are serious questions as to whether Putin has either the will or the political capital to lessen the oligarchs' centrality to contemporary Russia's political and economic life.

Putin and the Russian Federation's Second Decade

Considerable uncertainty surrounds both the prospects for Russia's socioeconomic revival and the intentions and abilities of the country's new chief executive as the Russian Federation moves into its second decade. There is a universal desire for stability and order, seen as essential to political governance and economic recovery, while public frustrations with corruption and policy inertia abound. Moreover,

Russian power impotence, whether evinced in the continuing Chechen tragedy or in unequal relations with the West, flames the fires of nationalism and encourages at least the appearance of assertiveness on officials' part. Vladimir Putin appears aware of these changes in the public mood, his decisiveness both as prime minister and then as president enabling him to build a high level of popular support (see Figure 2.1). Yet more than a year into his administration, there is still considerable mystery surrounding the man and his intentions.

Who is Vladimir Putin? Born in 1952 into a family of Leningrad (now St Petersburg) workers, he became fascinated with espionage and foreign intelligence, ultimately going on to earn university degrees in law and economics. Recruited into the KGB, he served for 17 years both in Leningrad and East Germany (where his German became fluent, his English certainly being proficient). His movement into the political arena began in Leningrad, where – soon after leaving the KGB – he linked up with the reformist mayor (and his former law professor) Anatolii Sobchak, serving as an international affairs adviser. Putin ultimately became a first deputy mayor to Sobchak, promoting privatisation and economic reforms while being especially involved in the oversight of foreign investments. When a corruption scandal led to Sobchak's electoral defeat in 1996, Putin found himself assisted by another Leningrader, Anatolii Chubais, then head of Yeltsin's presidential administration. He was brought to Moscow to work under Pavel Borodin as the Kremlin's deputy property manager, quickly moving up the hierarchy to become the director of the Federal Security Service (July 1998), the successor to the KGB. For the next year Putin would be a top figure in the coordination of Russia's security and intelligence services before being selected as Yeltsin's (final) prime minister in August 1999.

Putin's reputation as a tough leader who would move decisively began during his brief tenure as prime minister as his government reinitiated hostilities in war-torn Chechnya. A series of bomb blasts in Moscow and other cities had been linked by Russian authorities with Chechen rebels. The major offensive launched in the late summer of 1999 resulted in the capture of the Chechen capital, Grozny, and the short-term consolidation of the Russian position in the republic, and it earned Putin high marks with the Russian public. Putin's stated commitment to consolidate the country's economic reform, in part by cracking down on corruption and refilling the country's coffers with tax revenues, also suggested a serious politician at the country's helm. These themes, combined with Putin's insistence that federal institutions (such as the presidency) be strengthened to bring political discipline to the country, underpinned his successful presidential campaign in early 2000.

Putin has moved at the same time to consolidate his own power while lessening that of a number of potential or real political rivals. Various influential elite elements surround him, including what might be termed liberal reformers (such as Chubais), 'go slow' reformers (such as Abramovich), and representatives of the power ministries (including the police, internal security and military bureaucracies), with Putin's actions suggesting a balancing of these various interests. His creation by decree of seven federal regions, encompassing all of the federation's 89 provinces and major cities (see Chapter 7), was designed to reconsolidate the federal executive's power over the restive periphery. The seven presidential representatives overseeing these federal regions were invested with real power, an ability to oversee the actions of regional officials, and the responsibility to bring those officials' actions and regional laws into conformity with federal laws and intentions. By late 2000 there was already solid evidence they were making inroads in fighting regional separatism. Meanwhile, his initiatives to reorganise and essentially downgrade the influence of the federal parliament's upper chamber, the Federation Council, and to create a new State Council as a consultative body drawing in regional leaders' inputs, were further weakening the autonomy of subfederal authorities.

Other early policy moves such as tax reform with 'tax relief' for Russian citizens reinforced Putin's standing with the electorate. During his first year in office Putin revealed himself as a politician who could adjust to the dynamic realities of a chaotic democracy. He initially mishandled the August 2000 Kursk submarine tragedy by appearing remote and indifferent, but quickly rebounded with his public statements and meeting with deceased crew members' relatives. Indeed, his standing in opinion surveys was little affected by his early miscues. Just weeks earlier, he had favourably impressed Western officials and reporters with his appearance at the Okinawa G-8 meeting.

Yet after a year of governance, there is continuing uncertainty how to read Putin's actions and intentions. Selective crackdowns on media outlets that have been critical of government policies, pressures against certain reformist oligarchs, and the development of a new 'information security doctrine' giving authorities additional levers *vis-à-vis* domestic and foreign journalist, raise disturbing questions.

When summed up, do Putin's initiatives and the actions of his government reflect a new authoritarianism and safeguarding of the elite establishment, or do they constitute a power consolidation necessary to create what Putin calls 'a single economic and legal space' in Russia? Serious observers are divided: very diverse political figures such as the reformist Grigorii Yavlinsky and the communist Gennadii Zyuganov express grave reservations, while the nationalist literary giant Alexander Solzhenitsyn and former Soviet leader Gorbachev offer support. Some even see Putin as a political centrist.

It has been remarked that there are no clean politicians in Russia, and severe measures may be necessary to create what Putin identifies as 'a dictatorship of the law'. Whether a hegemonic presidency can be conducive to the long-term rule of law, and whether Vladimir Putin is committed to such, remain open questions. As the Russian Federation begins its second decade, the actions of the federal executive will prove decisive in the forging of a new polity and society. As in the past, much rests with the country's chief executive, leaving the observer to ponder the meaning of Russia's top-down political development – and whether it can be truly democratic.

3

Parliamentary Politics in Russia

THOMAS F. REMINGTON

The political system of the USSR rested upon the legal fiction that state power resided in the system of *soviets* (councils). Soviets were popularly elected bodies in which, according to Soviet doctrine, legislative and executive power were fused. At the same time, it was understood that actual political power lay with the Communist Party of the Soviet Union, which exercised its power through the soviets and through the executive bodies that were nominally accountable to the soviets.

This system changed significantly when Mikhail Gorbachev launched his political reforms in the late 1980s. Gorbachev used new expanded parliamentary structures and open elections as instruments for awakening and channeling popular political energies. His goal was to bring the country's newly active political life into a new set of legislative structures where he would be able to guide decision-making. Gorbachev created a complicated four-tiered parliament for the USSR, consisting of a huge, 2250-member Congress of People's Deputies, which elected a smaller, full-time parliament called the Supreme Soviet. In turn, the Supreme Soviet was guided by its Presidium, which was overseen by a Chairman. Elections of deputies to this new parliamentary structure were held in 1989; in 1990, elections were held for the equivalent bodies at the level of the union republics and in regions and towns throughout the Soviet Union.

Gorbachev's strategy was to give *glasnost*, his policy of open political communication, an institutional home. He sought to incorporate many diverse groups into the new parliamentary arena while ensuring that he would have the ultimate power of decision over policy. But liberalisation of politics under Gorbachev had unanticipated consequences. Not only did it mobilise radical democrats against defenders of the old order, but it also encouraged coalitions of democrats and nationalists in the republics, including Russia, to rally around demands for national independence. As a result, the new USSR parliament and its counterparts at lower levels *represented* reasonably well the political divisions existing in the country between defenders and challengers of the old order. But they were woefully unsuited to *deciding* the grave policy questions that the country faced. They lacked even the most rudimentary institutional means to generate and deliberate on coherent alternative policy options. They depended heavily on the executive to set their agendas and guide their decision-making. Sessions of the new USSR parliament, and the parliaments in the union republics and lower level territories, were frequently the sites of passionate but inconclusive debate, dramatic walk-outs by embattled minorities, and deep frustration as the deputies found themselves unable to reach majority decisions on difficult issues. Little wonder that they were never able to resolve the most serious crises that the Soviet Union faced.

On the other hand, these transition-era parliaments did achieve some notable results, both in the legislation they passed, and in some of the new institutional innovations they devised. For example, the USSR Supreme Soviet, which existed only from spring 1989 to summer 1991, passed some path-breaking laws on the media, local government, freedom of religion, collective bargaining, and reform of the judicial system and the criminal code. But faced with the fundamental conflict between radical reformers and hardliners over market-oriented reform, the parliament simply ducked: it created a state presidency for the USSR, a curiosity that was logically incompatible with the principle of CPSU rule. Then it delegated extraordinary powers to President Gorbachev, who fell into a trap of own making by constantly expanding the nominal powers of the president. What he failed to recognize at the time was that by doing so, he only encouraged the presidents of the union republics to follow suit at their own level of jurisdiction, thus deepening the disintegration of the Soviet state. The more power Gorbachev claimed for himself as president of the USSR, the less power he had in actuality, and the more he undercut the possibility that *any* central level institution– president, parliament or Communist Party – could have held the union together.

The RSFSR Transition-Era Parliament

A round of elections was held in 1990 for the parliamentary bodies in the union republics and to the soviets at regional and local levels. Russia (formally the Russian Soviet Federative Socialist Republic), the largest of the republics making up the Soviet Union, created a four-tiered legislative structure consisting of Congress, Supreme Soviet, Presidium, and Chairman which was very similar to the structure that Gorbachev devised at the USSR level. In Russia, the 1990 election brought about a new surge of democratic mobilisation among voters. A large group of reform-oriented deputies was elected to the Russian parliament, but a nearly equal number of pro-communist conservatives won mandates as well. This Russian parliament then underwent a history rather similar to the USSR parliament. Unable to cope with the mounting crises of political and economic order, the Russian Congress created a presidency, delegated emergency powers to it, then almost immediately regretted its own decision and tried to win back its prerogatives. Confrontation between parliament and president then intensified to a final, violent peak in the shoot-out of October 1993.

Like the USSR parliament, the RSFSR parliament of 1990–3 was ill-adapted institutionally to form a collective will, especially on contentious issues; its structural problems were exacerbated by the deep and intense gulf separating communist and nationalist forces from radical democrats. The old communist-era soviets never had any difficulty in forming majorities, because everyone understood that the actual decision-making went on elsewhere and that the soviets were there simply to offer their ceremonial and unanimous consent. In fact, for much of the Soviet era, very few laws were ever needed; for most of the post-war period, no more than 10 or 15 laws per year were passed by the USSR Supreme Soviet. But once Russia was faced with the need to choose policies to deal with the most fundamental questions of its constitutional and economic order, these partly-inherited, partly improvised legislative institutions were unable to cope. Although the parliament was formally endowed with vast constitutional authority, it was unable in fact to wield it.

Still, the RSFSR Congress and Supreme Soviet in the 1990–3 period succeeded in passing some important legislation on matters where its communist and reformist camps could find common ground. Among these were laws on taxation and budget formation, privatisation and property relations, banking, bankruptcy, and land relations. Other legislation reformed regional government and the state's territorial-administrative structure. Perhaps of still greater importance were the laws reforming the justice system, including the law creating the Constitutional Court. The Supreme Soviet also passed legislation on social welfare, creating a mandatory medical insurance system, as well as on civil liberties, including a law guaranteeing freedom of religion. Often the legislation was broad and vague, leaving loopholes that executive agencies could fill (as had long been the practice in Russia) with administrative instructions and regulations. These often had the effect of distorting and weakening the intent of the law. The scope of the legislative record of the Supreme Soviet suggests, nonetheless, that many deputies took their law-making responsibilities seriously, and used the institutional resources at hand to fulfill them. The laws passed by the USSR and RSFSR parliaments then were inherited by the new Russian Federation when it became independent following the USSR's dissolution.

Boris Yeltsin and the Crisis of 1993

The 1990–3 period was marked by the rise of Boris Yeltsin, who made Russia's parliament his initial base of power. Yeltsin led a coalition of radical democrats and Russian nationalists in a struggle for greater autonomy for Russia within the union. Yeltsin's own position was strengthened, rather than weakened, by Gorbachev's clumsy attempts to undermine him. In spring 1991, Yeltsin rallied a majority of deputies and won their endorsement of his proposal for a powerful, directly elected Russian president. In June 1991, he was elected president of Russia in a nationwide election.

Once the presidency was established, however, it led to a contest between the legislative and executive branches. The leadership of the RSFSR Congress and Supreme Soviet began to challenge Yeltsin for supremacy, claiming that the legislative branch was the supreme seat of state power. Yeltsin claimed that as popularly elected president, he embodied the Russian people's desire for a decisive break with the communist past. The August 1991 coup attempt further solidified Yeltsin's political position. The surge of popular resistance to the coup in Moscow, Leningrad, and other Russian cities, and his own uncompromising opposition, gave Yeltsin a substantial political bonus. Many of his communist opponents in the Russian Congress lost their political bases through a series of decrees Yeltsin issued which suspended, and later outlawed, the activity of the CPSU and confiscated its considerable property. In October 1991, at the Fifth Congress, Yeltsin sought and received special powers to enact economic reform measures by decree; he won the congress's consent to put off elections of local heads of government until 1 December 1992; he won approval of constitutional amendments giving him the right to suspend the acts of lower authorities in Russia if he found they violated the constitution and to suspend legal acts of the union if they violated Russian sovereignty; and the congress approved his programme for radical economic transformation. A few days later Yeltsin assumed the position of prime minister himself, named a new cabinet dominated by young economists committed to rapid liberalisation, and issued a package of decrees launching the radical 'shock therapy' that is discussed in Chapter 9.

Making full use of his expanded powers, Yeltsin pursued his programme of reform throughout 1992. Although the impetus of 'shock therapy' diminished out as the year proceeded, opposition to Yeltsin grew, and the majority in the parliament shifted further and further away from him. Yeltsin was also unable to win legislative approval of a new constitution that would formalise his powers *vis-à-vis* the government and the legislative branch. Under the old constitution, however, only the Congress had the power to amend the constitution or adopt a new one. Confrontation between Yeltsin and the Congress-Supreme Soviet intensified. In March 1993 the Congress attempted to remove Yeltsin from power through impeachment but fell slightly short of the required two-thirds majority. Yeltsin responded by holding a popular referendum on support for his policies, which gave him a surprisingly strong vote of confidence. However, the constitutional crisis continued to deepen.

Finally, on September 21, Yeltsin issued decrees that lacked constitutional foundation but offered a political solution to the impasse. He shut down parliament, declared the deputies' powers null and void, and called elections for a new parliament to be held on December 12. He decreed that there was to be a national vote on adopting the draft constitution that had been developed under his direction.

Under Yeltsin's constitutional plan, the upper chamber of the Federal Assembly, the Federation Council, was weaker than the lower house, and gave equal representation to each of Russia's 89 constituent territories (called 'subjects of the federation'). The lower house, the State Duma, was to introduce a fundamentally new principle into Russian legislative institutions: proportional representation. Half of the Duma's 450 seats were to be filled by the candidates listed on parties' electoral lists according to the share of votes that party received in the election in a single federal-wide district. To receive any seats, however, a party or electoral association had to win at least 5 per cent of the PR votes. The other half of the seats were to be filled by plurality voting in 225 single-member districts. In the election of 1993, each voter thus had, in effect, four votes for the parliament: two for the two deputies from his or her region to the upper house, and two for the lower house, one to fill the local district seat, and one for a party list.

Not surprisingly, Yeltsin's draft constitution also provided for a very strong presidency. Yet it is an exaggeration to say that the 1993 constitution reflected only Yeltsin's conception of how state power should be organised. Yeltsin and his advisors were shrewd enough to recognise that they needed to provide just enough political concessions to other powerful political interests in the country to keep them in the game. Moreover, Yeltsin's constitution incorporated some ideas that had become generally accepted in political circles. Most political groups agreed, for instance, that the parliament should comprise two chambers: a lower, popular chamber and an upper house giving equal representation to each region making up the federation. In the past, bicameralism had been part of USSR parliaments but had been purely nominal. Both Gorbachev and Yeltsin had experimented with advisory councils made up of the leaders of the regions. The plan that Yeltsin initially intended to put to the voters in the 1993 referendum called for a Federation Council made up of two representatives from each territorial unit of the federation. But at the last moment, Yeltsin also decided that the two representatives should come from the executive and legislative branches – a casual constitutional improvisation that has led to endless difficulty since then. However, most of the 1993 constitution's elements were not the arbitrary interventions of a capricious president; they were the products of struggle and deliberation. Some reflected Yeltsin's calculations about how much power he could give himself without provoking an open revolt by the groups he wanted to participate in the system. Some issues were left unresolved.

After the new parliament convened in 1994, its organisational arrangements reflected other points of consensus among the political elite about what institutional forms were appropriate. One widely accepted notion was that political parties should have a significant place both in the elections and in the lower chamber. Many politicians agreed that something other than a Presidium should be the steering committee for the new parliament. Most agreed that the post of chairman should be substantially weakened in comparison to the previous system, with the power to manage the chamber residing in a collective council of parliamentary leaders. The system of standing legislative committees with specialised jurisdictions that had been used in the previous parliaments aroused no controversy. Thus, to design the new parliament, the deputies drew upon experience with earlier forms as well as international experience, adapting models according to their political aims and ambitions (Remington, 2001).

The Federal Assembly

The 1993 elections gave no one political party or coalition a majority of seats in the Duma. Reform-oriented deputies occupied about a third of the seats; centrist forces about a quarter; and opposition deputies about 40 per cent (these and later Duma election results are set out in Table 4.1). Winning voting coalitions in the 1994–5 Duma often were 'left-centrist' – that is, they included the votes of the Communists, Agrarians, the centrist 'Women of Russia' group and, nearly as often, Zhirinovsky's Liberal Democrats and the Democratic Party of Russia. It was a coalition of centrists and the left, for instance, that succeeded in winning a narrow victory for Ivan Rybkin as chairman of the Duma at the very outset. Formerly a leader of the Communist faction in the old Congress/ Supreme Soviet, Rybkin had run on the Agrarian Party list. His reputation was that of a straight-forward, pragmatic figure, and he was therefore acceptable to many centrist and some democratic deputies. After his election as Chairman, he steered the Duma toward a constructive relationship with the president. He helped avert destabilising confrontation between president and parliament and make parliament into an effective legislature by shaping legislative compromises among parties that could gain majorities on the floor and that the president could accept. He thus helped to make the parliament a counter-weight to the presidency.

Over the 1994–5 period, over a quarter of the members of the Duma changed factional affiliations; moreover, some factions disappeared while others were formed. But the major party factions remained intact and prepared for the December 1995 elections. Altogether 400 (90 per cent) of the deputies ran for re-election to the Duma and 158 (40 per cent) were successful.

Yeltsin had decreed that the Duma elected in 1993 would serve for only two years. Elections were to be held again two years later, in December 1995, for a new Duma with a four-year term. Accordingly, elections were held on 17 December 1995, under a new election law that was passed by both chambers of parliament and signed into law by the president. The new election law was similar in most respects to the law under which the 1993 elections had been held. Once again, voters cast two ballots: one to fill a single-member district seat, the other for a party list. This time, however, a huge number of political groups, 43 in all, registered and ran party lists – far more than could be accommodated in view of the 5 per cent threshold rule for receiving seats.

In the event, four parties crossed the 5 per cent threshold and divided the 225 seats among themselves: the Communists, Zhirinovsky's LDPR, the 'Our Home is Russia' bloc formed around Prime Minister Chernomyrdin, and the Yabloko bloc led by Grigorii Yavlinsky. Of these, the Communists were by far the most successful, with 22.7 per cent of the party list votes. Zhirinovsky's party won 11.4 per cent; Our Home is Russia (NDR, in its Russian initials) took 10.3 per cent, and Yabloko 7.0 per cent. Russia's Democratic Choice, which had been the major reform faction in the previous Duma, failed to receive even 4 per cent. Another 11.5 per cent went to centrist groups that had also failed to clear the threshold. Altogether, nearly half of the votes were cast for parties that failed to win any seats on the party list ballot. These votes were redistributed to the parties that did clear the threshold. As a result, each of the four winners gained about twice as many seats as they would have been entitled to had there been no wasted votes. Moreover, the Communists were quite successful in winning district seats, taking more than 50. Combined with the seats they won through the party list vote, they commanded one-third of the seats in parliament – the highest share that they or any party had held in the previous Duma.

The Communists and the factions allied with them came close to commanding a majority of seats in the new Duma. The Communists therefore became an indispensable member of many majority coalitions. However, their position was not secure. To win majorities, they generally needed to offer concessions to other factions or to moderate their policy stance. They did succeed in electing a leading member of their faction, Gennadii Seleznev, as chairman of the Duma. His relations with the Kremlin were not as close as Rybkin's had been, but he developed a generally smooth working relationship with the president. The Communists refrained from seeking full control over the chamber, although whether it was in their power to gain a clear and lasting majority or not is uncertain. In any case, they generally abided by the previous working arrangements in such matters as the distribution of committee chairmanships among factions, and the practice of forming task forces and legislative commissions by recruiting members from all factions. Most important, they retained the rule under which the Duma's steering committee, the Council of the Duma, comprised the leader of every faction, one leader per faction.

Likewise, President Yeltsin devoted considerable effort to bargaining with the Duma over legislation. Both the president and the government maintained permanent representative offices in the Duma, working closely with deputies to ensure the passage of key legislation. Altogether, around one hundred executive branch officials were detailed to liaison duty with the Duma. Over the four-year term of the second Duma, the president signed nearly three-quarters of the bills passed by the Duma, about the same proportion of bills that he signed that the first Duma had passed. Moreover, the Duma passed a much higher share of legislation submitted by the executive branch than it did of bills its own members submitted, as Table 3.1 indicates.

Much of the bargaining within the Duma and between Duma and the executive went on out of public view; public attention instead tended to focus on the histrionic displays of temper on the floor and high-stakes brinkmanship between president and Duma. One of the most memorable confrontations between the branches came as the Duma tried to remove the president through impeachment. The deputies were well aware that removal of the president by means of impeachment was a long and complicated process of which a two-thirds parliamentary vote was only the first step, and that even if they succeeded in passing a motion to impeach, the odds of actually removing Yeltsin were remote indeed. The action thus served largely symbolic purposes for the parliamentary opposition.

The Communists in the Duma had long tried to put impeachment on the agenda. They finally succeeded in June 1998, when the chamber agreed to form a commission to examine five accusations against Yeltsin: that he had committed treason by signing the agreement in December 1991 to dissolve the Soviet Union; that he had illegally initiated the war in Chechnya in 1994; that he had illegally dissolved the Russian Congress and Supreme Soviet in 1993; that he had destroyed Russia's defence capacity; and that he had committed genocide against the Russian people through the effects of the

TABLE 3.1 *Legislative action by the State Duma, 1996–9*

Sponsor	Accepted for Consideration	Considered*	as % of all bills accepted for consideration	Passed in 3rd reading	as % of all bills considered	No. signed by president	as % of bills passed by Duma
All bills	3303	1693	51	1036	61	771	74
President	165	126	76	106	84	100	94
Federation Council	297	117	39	27	23	16	59
Duma deputies	1629	784	48	488	62	292	60
Government	661	532	80	367	69	332	90
Regional assemblies	528	116	22	33	28	20	61
High courts**	23	18	78	15	83	11	73

Note: * 'Considered' means that the bill reached at least a first reading in the Duma.
** Refers to the Supreme Court, Supreme Arbitration Court, and Constitutional Court.

Source: Federal'noe Sobranie – parlament Rossiiskoi Federatsii (2000) 'Gosudarstvennaya Duma. Analiticheskoe upravlenie, Analiticheskii vestnik', *Statisticheskie kharakeristiki zakonodatel'noi deyatel'nosti Gosudarstvennoi Dumy vtorogo sozyva (1996–1999)*, vyp. 3, pp. 6–8.

economic policies of his government since 1992. In March 1999 the commission approved all five charges and submitted them to the full chamber for its consideration. On May 15 the deputies voted on the five charges. None gained the required 300 votes, although the charge that Yeltsin had illegally initiated and conducted military operations in Chechnya came close. Yeltsin used the full range of carrots and sticks at his disposal to avert impeachment, promising material rewards to some deputies in return for their support, and reminding the Duma that he still had other 'trump cards' in his hand.

In his final address to the second Duma as it recessed in December 1999, Chairman Seleznev praised its accomplishments and glossed over the impeachment episode. Among other things, he noted that the Duma had passed constitutional laws reforming the judicial system and defining the status and powers of the government; it had passed seven codes of law, including a new criminal code and criminal-corrections code; it had passed several laws regulating market relations, including laws on the securities market, on investors' rights, on privatisation, and on production-sharing agreements; it had also passed some important legislation concerning federal relations, including a long-contested law limiting the governors of the regions to two terms of office and another much-fought-over law delineating the jurisdictions of the federal government and the governments of the constituent territories of the country, as well as laws on local self-government, and a law defining the rights of voters throughout the country. Seleznev also acknowledged that the Duma had been dead-locked on the issue of how to regulate the sale and purchase of land, a bitterly disputed issue. Nor had the Duma been able to pass a law regulating the status of political parties (some factions would like to raise the threshold to registration very high and then restrict partici-pation in elections to those few parties that qualify, while smaller groups understandably want a less restrictive bill). Given the decen-tralised, non-majoritarian nature of decision-making in the Duma, on deeply contentious matters such as these, the Duma simply deadlocks. Nonetheless, Seleznev was right to call attention to the sizable record of legislative accomplishment (Gosudarstvennaya Duma, 1999, pp. 1–4).

The Duma in 2000

The December 1999 elections produced a significant shift in the alignment of parliamentary camps. As Prime Minister Vladimir

Putin's popularity rose through the later months of 1999, the two parties that he supported benefited from his favour. First was the 'Unity' coalition, which emerged from the obscurity of its origins in the backrooms of the Kremlin to become one of the two strongest vote-winners in the party-list ballot. The other was a coalition of democratic politicians called the Union of Rightist Forces (SPS). For their part, the Communists ran slightly ahead of their 1995 result, but both their single-member seat results and the results of their allies were far less impressive than in 1995. Consequently, they were somewhat marginalised in the new Duma. Table 3.2 indicates the balance of party factions in the Duma immediately subsequent to the elections, in January 2000.

The third Duma began with a vivid demonstration of Unity's clout. In the two previous Dumas, the faction leaders had devised among themselves a power-sharing arrangement under which they divided up committee chairmanships in rough proportion to their strength on the floor. But in the 2000 Duma, the Unity faction (probably under orders from the Kremlin) formed a shotgun alliance with the communists and a group of pro-president single-member district deputies called 'People's Deputy' and took control of the chamber. Together the three of them commanded a slender majority of votes in the Duma, which they used to reelect the Communist Seleznev as chairman of the Duma, and to allocate nearly all the committee chairmanships among themselves. Other factions were outraged at being left out of the deal. It turned out, however, that the Communists had obtained less than it appeared: they did gain ten committee chairmanships and the position of chairman of the Duma, yet they failed to be assigned any of the powerful committees they had sought – such as the budget, legislation, defence, security, property or banking committees – and they lost some crucial jurisdiction battles. The real winner was Unity, which in this and many subsequent votes proved that it was the pivotal faction in the new Duma. Almost no majority could be assembled that did not include it. On vote after vote, it delivered majorities on legislation vital to Putin, including ratification of the START–II treaty, passage of the new tax code, and passage of a series of major reforms of the federal system, including a complete change in the manner in which the upper house is to be formed in the future. Thus the new balance of forces in the Duma gave Putin nearly a free hand in controlling the legislature, using his leverage over Unity to form either centre-right or centre-left coalitions according to the issue at hand.

TABLE 3.2 The State Duma: faction membership, February 2000

Party	Vote share in PR ballot (%)	PR seats won	District seats won	Total seats won in election	No. Duma faction members (February)	Duma seat share (%)
Reform factions:						
Union of Right Forces (SPS)	8.52	24	5	29	32	7.3
Yabloko	5.93	17	5	22	21	4.8
Centrist factions:						
Unity	23.32	64	9	73	81	18.4
People's Deputy	–	–	–	–	58	13.2
Russia's Regions	–	–	–	–	38	8.6
Fatherland–All Russia (OVR)	13.33	36	32	68	45	10.2
LDPR	5.98	17	2	19	17	3.9
Opposition factions:						
Agro-Industrial Group	–	–	2	2	41	9.3
CPRF	24.29	67	55	124	89	20.2
Totals	81.37	225	110	337	422	95.9

Note: The Agro-Industrial Group, People's Deputy, and Russia's Regions were deputy groups formed after the new Duma convened in order to represent deputies elected from single-member districts, many of whom had been nominated by parties which failed to receive seats in the PR ballot.

The Legislative Process in the Federal Assembly

Basic Legislative Procedure

The State Duma originates all legislation except for certain categories of policy which are under the jurisdiction of the upper house, the Federation Council. Upon final passage in the State Duma, a bill goes to the Federation Council. If the upper house rejects it, the bill goes back to the Duma, where a commission comprising members of both houses may seek to iron out differences. If the Duma rejects the upper house's changes, it may override the Federation Council by a two-thirds vote. Otherwise it votes on the version of the bill proposed by the commission (see Figures 3.1–3.3). When the bill has cleared both chambers of the Federal Assembly, it goes to the president for signature. If the president refuses to sign the bill, it returns to the Duma. The Duma may pass it with the president's proposed amendments by a simple absolute majority, or override the president's veto, for which a two-thirds vote is required. The Federation Council must then also approve the bill, by a simple majority if the president's amendments are accepted, or a two-thirds vote if it chooses to override him.

State Duma

The steering committee of the Duma is the Council of the Duma. The Council of the Duma makes the principal decisions in the Duma concerning the agenda, and acts on occasion to overcome deadlocks among the political groups represented in the Duma. It is made up of the leaders of each party faction or registered deputy group regardless of size. Every party that has won at least 5 per cent of the party-list voting in the proportional representation half of the ballot is entitled to form a faction in the Duma made up of its elected deputies, together with any of the deputies elected in single-member districts who wish to join. Moreover, any group of deputies that can assemble 35 members has the right to register as a recognised deputy group in order to obtain exactly the same rights and benefits as the party factions obtain. These benefits are valuable to deputies: they include funds for staff, office space, and procedural rights. Moreover, the factions and groups divide up all the leadership positions in the chamber, including the committee chairmanships, among themselves. The factions and groups see the Duma as a means for showcasing

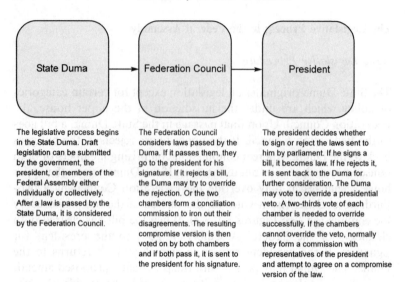

| State Duma | → | Federation Council | → | President |

The legislative process begins in the State Duma. Draft legislation can be submitted by the government, the president, or members of the Federal Assembly either individually or collectively. After a law is passed by the State Duma, it is considered by the Federation Council.

The Federation Council considers laws passed by the Duma. If it passes them, they go to the president for his signature. If it rejects a bill, the Duma may try to override the rejection. Or the two chambers form a conciliation commission to iron out their disagreements. The resulting compromise version is then voted on by both chambers and if both pass it, it is sent to the president for his signature.

The president decides whether to sign or reject the laws sent to him by parliament. If he signs a bill, it becomes law. If he rejects it, it is sent back to the Duma for further consideration. The Duma may vote to override a presidential veto. A two-thirds vote of each chamber is needed to override successfully. If the chambers cannot override the veto, normally they form a commission with representatives of the president and attempt to agree on a compromise version of the law.

FIGURE 3.1   *The legislative process: overview*

their pet legislative projects, giving their leaders a national forum, obtaining crucial organisational support for their party work, and providing service to their constituents. Not surprisingly, nearly all deputies join one of the factions or groups.

The Duma also has a system of standing legislative committees – 28 in the 2000 Duma – whose leadership and membership positions are distributed to factions in accordance with an inter-factional agreement. Each deputy is a member of one committee. The work of drafting and developing legislation goes on in the committees. However, only a few committees do much active legislative work: in the second Duma, which sat from 1996 to 1999, 70 per cent of the bills that came to the floor were handled by just seven committees (*Federalnoe Sobranie*, 2000, pp. 28–9). The most important of these are the committee on legislation, which handles matters concerning the judicial system, federal relations, and other constitutional questions; the budget committee; and the committee on labour and social policy.

Bills are considered in three readings (see Figure 3.3). In the first reading, the Duma simply decides whether or not to approve the basic conception of a piece of legislation. If so, then the bill goes back to the committee, which then sifts through the amendments which are offered to the bill by deputies (sometimes thousands of amendments are offered to a single bill). When the committee has agreed on its recommended version of the bill, it reports it out again to the floor for a second reading, and the whole chamber decides on which amendments to approve and which to reject. At that point the floor votes on the bill in its entirety, and sends it back to the committee for a final editing and polishing. The third reading then gives the Duma's final approval to the bill and it goes to the Federation Council.

The use of working commissions to negotiate solutions to contentious disagreements over legislation is common. Disagreements between the two chambers often go to an 'reconciliation commission' (*soglasitelnaya komissiya*). In instances of disagreement between the branches, three-way commissions can be created, consisting of Duma deputies, Federation Council members, and representatives of the president and government. The work of these bodies is one reason so many legislative compromises are eventually found. Over the 1996–9 period, almost 300 such inter-cameral or inter-branch commissions were created. Two thirds of all bills that were rejected either by the

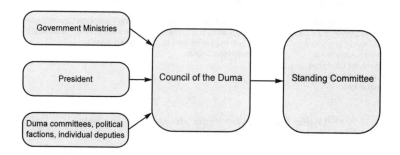

Draft legislation can be submitted by the government, the president, or Duma deputies either individually or collectively. Bills may also be submitted by regional legislatures as well as by members of the Federation Council. The three high courts may also propose legislation on judicial matters. Most draft legislation is introduced by members of the Duma, by the government, and the president.

When a bill is introduced, the Council of the Duma reviews it to ensure it meets the standards for draft legislation, and assigns it to one or more standing committees. The Council of the Duma is made up of the leaders of each party faction or registered deputy group.

The committee to which the bill has been assigned prepares the bill for first reading. When a bill is ready for first reading, the Council of the Duma puts it on the agenda of the floor.

FIGURE 3.2 *The legislative process: bill introduction*

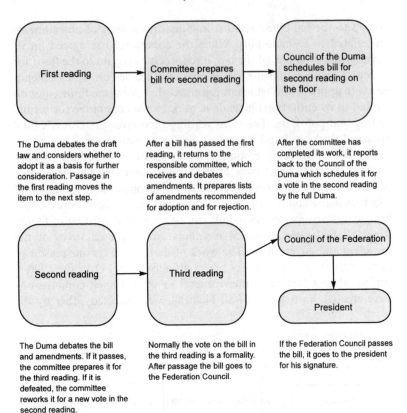

The Duma debates the draft law and considers whether to adopt it as a basis for further consideration. Passage in the first reading moves the item to the next step.

After a bill has passed the first reading, it returns to the responsible committee, which receives and debates amendments. It prepares lists of amendments recommended for adoption and for rejection.

After the committee has completed its work, it reports back to the Council of the Duma which schedules it for a vote in the second reading by the full Duma.

The Duma debates the bill and amendments. If it passes, the committee prepares it for the third reading. If it is defeated, the committee reworks it for a new vote in the second reading.

Normally the vote on the bill in the third reading is a formality. After passage the bill goes to the Federation Council.

If the Federation Council passes the bill, it goes to the president for his signature.

FIGURE 3.3   *The legislative process: three readings*

Federation Council or the president on the first round were eventually passed and signed after such commissions worked out mutually acceptable language.

Federation Council

The Russian upper house is designed as an instrument of federalism in that every constituent unit of the federation is represented in it by two deputies. Thus the populations of small ethnic-national territories are greatly over-represented compared with more populous regions. Members of the Federation Council were elected by direct popular vote in December 1993 but since the constitution was silent on how they were to be chosen in the future, requiring only that one representative from the executive branch and one from the legislative branch from each region be members of the chamber, a law was passed in 1995 governing the formation of the chamber. Under that law, the heads of the executive and legislative branches of each constituent unit of the federation were automatically given seats in the Federation Council.

In 2000 President Putin chose to change this procedure as part of a package of reforms intended to strengthen the power of the federal government *vis-à-vis* the regions. Under the law which he proposed, each region's chief executive would name a full-time representative to serve as a member of the Federation Council, and each regional legislature would name another. This bill passed by a large majority in the Duma (whose deputies had often complained that members of the upper house were not full-time law-makers) and was rejected by comparable majority in the Federation Council. After intense three-way bargaining among the Duma, Federation Council and president, a compromise version was worked out and passed by both chambers. The compromise phases in the new system over an 18-month period, and gives regional executives the right to recall their delegates to the Federation Council (so long as the regional legislature did not block the recall by a two-thirds vote). The right of recall meant that governors would be able to keep their representatives in Moscow on a short leash.

The Federation Council has important rights of its own beyond its role as counterweight to the lower house. It approves presidential nominees for high courts such as the Supreme Court and the Constitutional Court. It approves presidential decrees declaring martial law or a state of emergency, and any actions altering the boundaries of territorial units in Russia. It must consider any legislation dealing with taxes, budget, financial policy, treaties, customs and declarations of war. The Federation Council has defied the president's will on a number of issues, rejecting some of his nominees for the Constitutional Court as well as his candidates for Procurator-General. On matters of ordinary legislation, however, where the Federation Council does not have exclusive jurisdiction, the State Duma can override a veto by the Federation Council with a two-thirds vote. The president can then choose whether to support the Duma's position and sign the law, or to uphold the Federation Council and veto it.

The Federal Assembly in Perspective

The ability of a legislature to exercise its constitutional prerogatives depends not only on its own internal rules and structures, but also on features of its institutional environment. One such factor is the party system. Where political parties are cohesive, stable, and strongly rooted in the electorate, their representatives in parliament can call upon parties to provide them with accurate information about the policy and electoral consequences of particular policy positions. Parties may constrain and discipline their members in parliament, but, because they aggregate the voices of many individual voters, they also provide parliamentary deputies with resources allowing them to act collectively. The weakness of Russia's party system reduces parliament's capacity to form majorities and thus to check the vast powers of the executive.

A second factor influencing the ability of a legislature to work effectively is the degree to which channels of communication and interest articulation are well developed. If parliamentarians only attend to a few powerful interests, citizens grow cynical about representative government – as polls show Russians to be. If the mass media and interest groups do not monitor parliamentary activity and provide regular information to citizens, citizens feel disengaged from political life. In Russia, members of parliament regularly remark that their voters do not understand what they do and have little respect for law-makers; surveys show that the Duma is one of the least-trusted institutions in Russia (only political parties and invest-ment funds are trusted less!) (Rose, 1998). By the same token, poorly functioning media and interest group systems cannot check abuses of office by members of parliament. Both ordinary citizens and political officials alike come to assume that 'all politicians are crooks'. Politicians then reason that if everyone else is crooked, only a fool will stay honest. There is considerable evidence to suggest that this problem is serious in Russia as well.

Third, in a political system where actors are unsure of the stability of constitutional arrangements (for example, if law-makers cannot be sure how committed the president is to abiding by the constitutional rules, and the president suspects that the parliamentary opposition is plotting against him), courts can play a crucial stabilising role by serving as a politically neutral mediator in disputes between the branches. In Russia, the Constitutional Court has played this role on a number of occasions. In several crucial cases, the court has provided guidance to political actors about their obligations under the constitution and, significantly, they have complied with the court's decisions. The court has tended to proceed cautiously, particularly with respect to the president; it has been very reluctant to issue a decision that the president would be likely to ignore. Yet it has adjudicated some sensitive and contentious disputes between the branches, and has laid down some important principles. One of the most dramatic was the 'trophy art' law case in 1998, when the court rejected the president's right to withhold his signature from a law passed by both chambers of parliament by the two-thirds majority that was required to override a presidential veto (the law prohibited the return of works of art and cultural artifacts seized by Soviet armed forces during the Second World War, and it attracted the support of a wide spectrum of deputies).

Thus, in the environment in which Russia's Federal Assembly operates, the party system, the mass media, and the system of interest groups are all very weak mechanisms for aggregating citizens' demands and linking members of parliament with constituencies in society; the Constitutional Court, however, has been relatively effective. Within the parliament, the institutions of party factions and of legislative committees have given Duma deputies means to generate and deliberate on policy alternatives, to build majorities in favour of particular decisions, and thus to form a collective will. Although considerable uncertainty still hangs over the ultimate stability of the system created by the 1993 constitution, Russia's parliament has proven to be a more effective source of political influence in the country than anyone had expected.

4

Elections and Voters

MATTHEW WYMAN

It is now more than a decade since the first competitive national elections of the recent period took place in Russia. In that time, Russians have been to the polls for three presidential and four parliamentary elections and three national referendums. They have also elected regional chief executives and assemblies, in almost every republic or region more than once. Russians choose their leaders via the ballot box, as opposed to the political practices of both Tsarist and Soviet periods, where appointment rather than election was the norm. In the words of one important analyst of postcommunist elections, Russians are no longer subjects but citizens of their own country.

The most recent set of national elections, for the State Duma in December 1999, and the presidency in March 2000, marked a watershed in postcommunist Russian politics. They heralded the end of Boris Yeltsin's eight years in office and the handing over of the Kremlin to his designated successor, Vladimir Putin. They raise a number of important questions for analysts of the Russian scene. To what extent were they genuinely free and fair elections? Had repeated experience of carrying out democratic elections improved their conduct, or had matters deteriorated in some areas? How much was the elective principle, that leaders are elected rather than chosen in some other way, genuinely consolidated in Russian politics? What best explained Russia's presidential choice? To what extent did the generalisations about the political behaviour of Russian society that had been developed during the Yeltsin period still seem to hold true once Russia's first president had left the stage? Did social groups continue to divide their support in largely familiar ways, or did the new political circumstances cause significant realignment?

The Electoral Process

The verdict of the international observers sent by the Organisation for Security and Co-operation in Europe was that 'The 2000 presidential election represented a benchmark in the ongoing evolution of the Russian Federation's emergence as a representative democracy' (OSCE, 2000). Despite this glowing reference, both the Duma and presidential elections raised a number of questions about how free and fair postcommunist elections in Russia actually are. These included issues of the application of electoral law by the central and local electoral commissions, the role of the mass media, and the influence of state authorities on electoral outcomes, as well as evidence of outright falsification in some parts of the country (IFES, 2000).

With the introduction of a new electoral law parties and candidates wishing to stand for election had to undergo an elaborate process to get on to the ballot at all. This involved various rules about financial and property disclosures, and the collection either of a certain number of signatures, or paying a deposit. The application of these procedures twice led to problems for the right-wing maverick Vladimir Zhirinovsky. In the elections to the State Duma, the Central Electoral Commission (CEC) disqualified from the ballot Zhirinovsky's Liberal Democratic Party of Russia, which had come first in the party list voting in 1993 and second in 1995. Ostensibly this arose out of inaccuracies in property declarations for two of the top three candidates on its national party list. However the suspicion lingered that the decision was intended to boost the chances of Prime Minister Putin's favoured party of that time, Unity, which was competing for a similar statist and nationalist vote. Zhirinovsky was eventually allowed to compete, as head of an electoral bloc rather than a party. His share of the vote was halved. At local level there were a number of instances of candidates unwelcome to the local authorities being denied registration on technicalities (in Omsk and Bashkortostan, Duma candidates were not allowed to stand even after local decisions denying them registration had been overruled by the CEC). And in the presidential election, Zhirinovsky also had problems registering as a candidate, although he was once again permitted to compete.

In the years leading up to the 1999 and 2000 votes the mass media in Russia had undergone much change. Ownership had become more concentrated, and financial difficulties had made media outlets more vulnerable to pressures from national and regional political authorities. Accordingly, as we explore in Chapter 13, while the electoral law insisted upon equal access to political advertising opportunities, media coverage of the campaigns tended to be unbalanced. During the Duma elections, programmes on two of the most important national television channels, RTR and ORT, attempted to damage the prospects of Fatherland-All Russia. The two leaders of that bloc, former Prime Minister Yevgenii Primakov and Moscow mayor Yuri Luzhkov, were seen as the Kremlin's most important threats. Consequently, viewers were treated to tirades about Primakov's age and communist past, and Luzhkov's possible links with organised crime. The party came a poor third, ending both men's presidential ambitions for 2000. Meanwhile the 'party of power', the electoral movement Unity, received over a quarter of all the coverage, the majority of it favourable, in a race between 26 different parties (European Institute for the Media, 2000a).

The presidential election too saw national television coverage overwhelmingly favourable towards then acting President Putin. According to the European Institute for the Media, around half of all television coverage was for Putin, and it was largely uncritical. He was portrayed as the ruthless destroyer of Chechen terrorists, the enemy of corruption and the friend of the needy. Particular efforts were made to talk up his human side, as with for example coverage of his grief at the funeral of his former mentor Anatolii Sobchak, the ex-mayor of Leningrad. The worst of the coverage was outright sycophancy in the worst Soviet tradition. For example during his visit to the Federation of Independent Trade Unions, one official was shown on television commenting: 'All the Vladimirs that Russia has ever had have been great, from Saint Vladimir to Vladimir Lenin. But being Vladimir Vladimirovich, you are twice that great' (reported via BBC Monitoring, 14 March 2000).

In the presidential vote, so-called *kompromat*, or 'smear tactics', were not employed against Gennadii Zyuganov, Putin's main opponent. The President's campaign team clearly saw no danger of a Communist victory. Rather the main liberal candidate, Grigorii Yavlinsky, was the subject of the strongest attacks. Examples include the accusation, without evidence, that Yavlinsky had illegally taken money from foreign backers. A few reports even went as far as saying that – in a Russia that has become much more anti-Western in the most recent period – if he became president he would be forced to repay this support by making Russia dependent on the West. Groups of Jews and homosexuals were shown on national news backing him, a clear attempt to exploit anti-Semitic and homophobic prejudice among sections of the electorate. He was also criticised for failing to take part in some of the televised debates and for illegally campaigning at a military base, in spite of the fact that Putin had also declined to debate with his opponents, and visited military bases on several occasions. There were many other equally mendacious reports. So while there was a regulatory structure in place designed to ensure unbiased coverage of the campaign, it, like many other laws in Russia, was simply not consistently enforced. Putin himself conceded after the vote that his rivals had been shut out of the media.

After the 1995 Duma elections, Prime Minister Viktor Chernomyrdin was so disgusted with the performance of his party, Our Home is Russia, in some parts of the country that he publicly threatened to have the leaders of the regions where he did worst removed. This revealing outburst illustrated that, while Russian electoral law forbids state officials from attempting to use their positions to exert influence on voters, the informal expectation among Russia's political elites that votes are delivered to their favoured candidates is much more important. An investigation by the *Moscow Times*, published in September 2000, provided detailed and well-documented evidence for manipulation of the electoral process in the presidential election (Borisova, 2000). In the republic of Dagestan, the territorial electoral commission simply misreported the actual vote numbers from polling stations in Putin's favour, and officials allegedly destroyed ballots cast for his opponents. In several other republics and regions, it is claimed that stuffing of ballot boxes took place on a significant scale. Sometimes officials simply made up extra voters, no doubt part of the reason why, in a country with a declining population, the size of the electorate rose by 1.3 million between December 1999 and March 2000.

As well as direct falsification, the *Moscow Times* investigation cites numerous examples of pressuring of voters by local government officials. The mechanism is straightforward: threats of dire consequences such as dismissal or loss of pension. In a society with high unemployment and widespread poverty, people prefer not to take the risk of defying those who have power over them. That said, not even the most strident critic of the Russian government claims that the result, even without these distortions, would have been anything other than a victory for Putin. However the new president might well have received less than half the votes in the first round, forcing a run-off with Zyuganov. Responding to the *Moscow Times* evidence, however, the head of the Central Electoral Commission had nothing more convincing to say than that it 'relies on assumptions'.

While competitive and reasonably free elections do take place in today's Russia, then, it is certainly clear that the playing field is by no means level. What the evidence shows is that while there is an acceptance that elections must be held to choose office holders, political elites have by no means lost their old habits of seeking to control outcomes. This may in part be a symptom of continuing political insecurity. Given the scale of political disagreements over fundamentals in Russia, people in authority are deeply concerned about the possible consequences of losing power. Not just material well-being, but even their physical freedom might sometimes be under threat. Even the elective principle thus remains unconsolidated. Elections happen, but some outcomes appear to remain excluded.

Trends in Parliamentary Elections

Notwithstanding the above, there is little question that electoral outcomes remain broadly in line with popular preferences. Survey data, for example, reveal essentially the same distributions of reported voting behaviour as is the case in actual election outcomes. Any experienced analyst of poll data will acknowledge that the scale of distortion needed to achieve this outcome in a plausible manner by deception is inconceivable. So what do the elections of 1999 and 2000 tell us about the development of electoral politics in postcommunist Russia?

The main issue at stake in the State Duma elections was the struggle for pre-eminence between competing sections of the Russian elite in the run-up to the presidential vote. A few months before the elections, opinion polls had suggested that the main victors were likely to be the Fatherland-All Russia (OVR) alliance, bringing together Primakov, Luzhkov and a number of important regional leaders such as President Shaimiev of Tatarstan. The Kremlin was less than happy with the prospect, since these were by no means 'insiders' guaranteed to preserve the power and prosperity of the existing Kremlin team. The strategy to deal with the challenge was twofold: the appointment of a new prime minister in the then unknown Putin, and the launch for a second time of military operations in the breakaway republic of Chechnya. The resort to military force was ostensibly in response to a series of serious terrorist incidents, first the incursion by Chechen separatists into the republic of Dagestan, and then the blowing up of three apartment blocks with horrific consequences. These incidents were blamed on Chechen separatists, although hard evidence for responsibility for the bombings was never produced.

Unlike in the first Chechen War, the authorities were anxious to avoid unfavourable media coverage, and exercised strict controls on the information flowing out of the region. This in combination with early military successes made the campaign very popular. Prime Minister Putin quickly gained a reputation as a man of action, someone who could apparently deal decisively with Russia's problems. His background as a former KGB officer contributed to the image. The appeal was nakedly one to Russian national pride: the might of Russian military strength would be the foundation of the modernisation of the country and political system. Putin portrayed people who opposed the attempt to resolve the problem of Chechen separatism by force as traitors.

Electorally, the main vehicle for Putin was the movement *Yedinstvo* (Unity), appropriately, given its associations with Russian military strength, also known by the name of its symbol *Medved*, or Bear. This movement, led by the capable Minister for Federal Emergencies, Sergei Shoigu, had no history, no programme, and no membership. The names on its party list were virtually unknown. However Putin made it clear that this was his favoured group. As described above, the campaign between it and OVR was extremely negative, a fight to destruction between groups of people with largely similar views and backgrounds, played out in the media.

What then of the electoral outcomes? Table 4.1 shows the results of the 1999 ballot, together with information about the two previous State Duma votes. First place, both in the party list section of the vote and in terms of numbers of single member constituencies won, went to the Communist Party of the Russian Federation (CPRF). However, since the experience of the 1996 presidential election had been that the Communist presidential candidate was incapable of generating the support of a majority of voters against almost any moderate non-Communist opponent, this was of no particular concern to the ruling authorities. So the most significant outcome was that Unity, from literally nowhere three months previously, had succeeded in gaining fully 23 per cent of the party-list vote, compared to just 13 per cent for OVR. This was a major personal triumph for Putin, and one that instantly turned him into the front runner for the forthcoming presidential vote.

TABLE 4.1 Trends in Russian State Duma elections, 1993–9

	% vote on party lists			Party List seats		SMD seats	
	1993	1995	1999	1995	1999	1995	1999
Communist Party of the Russian Federation	12.4	22.7	24.3	99	67	58	56
Unity			23.3		64		8
Fatherland-All Russia			13.3		37		30
Union of Right Forces			8.5		24		5
Zhirinovsky bloc*	22.9	11.4	6.0	50	17	1	1
Yabloko	7.9	7.0	5.9	31	16	14	4
Communists – Workers' Russia		4.6	2.2	0	0	1	0
Women of Russia	8.1	4.7	2.0	0	0	3	0
Our Home is Russia		10.3	1.2	45	0	10	9
Russia's Democratic Choice**	15.5	3.9				9	
Agrarian Party	8.0	3.8		0		20	
Others	20.9	28.8	10.0	0	0	31	10
Independents						78	101
Against all	4.3	2.8	3.3				
Turnout (per cent)	54.8	62.5	61.9				

Note: * 1993 and 1995, Liberal Democratic Party of Russia
** 1993, known as Russia's Choice, in 1999 a constituent part of the Union of Right Forces

Source: For 1993, Wyman *et al.* (1998) p. 275; for 1995, Wyman *et al.* (1998), pp. 276–7; for 1999, *Central Election Commission*, available from <http://www.fci.ru> and Radio Free Europe/Radio Liberty *Russian Federation Report* 2:1, 5 Jan 2000

A number of other important points emerge from these data. First of all, as we shall see in more detail in the next chapter, they show how weakly developed programmatic parties remained in Russia. Other than the Communists, only the liberal Yabloko, led by Yavlinsky, and Zhirinovsky's right-wing populists succeeded in passing the 5 per cent threshold for representation in each of the three parliamentary votes. At each election, previously unknown groupings, with no organisational or membership roots in society, successfully emerged, often simply to fade away four years later. Many parties remained vehicles for the personal ambition of their leaders, rather than organisations representing distinct and well-defined sections of society that knew their own interests. Parties, accordingly, come and go with the individuals with whom they are primarily associated. As recent analysis has shown, it is not that voters lack well-defined and consistent views. It is rather that there is no stability in the institutional means of expressing them (Colton, 2000; Rose, Munro and White, 2001).

The electoral system for State Duma elections continues to produce idiosyncratic outcomes. Parties in Russia need to secure 5 per cent of the national vote to obtain seats via the party list. In 1995 just four, representing only a fraction over half of the votes cast, cleared this hurdle. These parties therefore received relatively large proportions of the party list seats. However in 1999, six parties, with 80 per cent of the vote among them, were successful. There were now two competing 'parties of power' in OVR and Unity, and the more pro-government liberal parties had suppressed their policy and personality differences to campaign together as the Union of Right Forces. The fact that more parties cleared the five per cent barrier meant that the incumbent parties received substantially smaller numbers of seats in the Duma on the basis of similar proportions of the votes. Yabloko's representation, for example, fell from 31 to 16 on the basis of a 1 per cent lower share of party list votes.

The use of the first past the post, winner takes all, electoral system for the other half of the State Duma constituencies continued to be a lottery. The overwhelming majority of candidates were elected with substantially less than half of the votes cast. The average share of the vote for the winner in those constituencies where valid results occurred was 32.7 per cent. This was at least an improvement on the average of 27.5 per cent in the 1993 election. Eighteen deputies were elected with less than 20 per cent of the vote. The smallest proportion of the vote gained by a winning candidate was 16.5 per cent in a district of

Archangel region. This situation is an inevitable consequence of using first past the post procedures, without provision for a second ballot, in a situation where there is no established party system. It is at least, though, a system that favours those parties that do have some organisational presence on the ground. In the seats where the CPRF had a candidate, they won an average vote share of 42 per cent, and OVR 28 per cent in districts in which they competed (Turovskii, 2000). Turnout remained at virtually the same level as in 1995, at just over 60 per cent. The majority of Russians evidently valued their right to choose, whatever the flaws in electoral procedures.

The composition of the new Duma was one with which Russia's rulers could happily coexist. At the time commentators made much of the fact that this was the first parliament in which there was not a majority of 'opposition' deputies, whether communist or nationalist, firmly opposed to the direction in which the government was taking the country. However the true balance of power was shown in the first meeting of the Duma, where between them the CPRF and Unity divided up parliamentary posts including committee chairs, excluding the prominent liberal parties. Putin's government would find it easy to work with the Communists because they shared similar goals: a strengthening of the power of the state, restoring Russian pride and enforcing order. The two groups had a great deal in common: similar social backgrounds and political instincts and even styles of dressing, inherited from a shared Soviet past.

The 2000 Presidential Election

Unity's success in the Duma elections was enough to convince Boris Yeltsin that he had at last found, in Putin, a successor who could win a presidential election. With characteristic flair and instinct for the dramatic, Yeltsin surprised the world by announcing his resignation early, on New Year's Eve 1999, exactly eight years after he had become the leader of an independent Russia at the end of 1991. The more generous-minded accepted the explanation that this was due to ill health, while the more cynical saw it as an act of protection for himself and his (personal and political) families. Under the 1993 Russian Constitution, when the president resigns, since there is no vice-President, the prime minister becomes acting president, and there must be a new election within three months. The vote was therefore brought forward from June to March 2000.

Yeltsin's resignation, elevating Putin to the presidency before the election, gave the latter a huge advantage. Whether it is something more deeply rooted in Russian political culture or a much more general truth about political systems, being in a leadership position gives candidates a considerable boost. Wielding the full might of Russian state power itself is legitimation enough for some Russian voters. Holding the presidential election early was a major advantage for Putin in a number of other respects. The 1999 vote had put an end to the presidential challenge of Yevgenii Primakov, and no other truly credible candidate had emerged. Putin's exceptionally high popularity in opinion polls at the time had put off many potential candidates. Indeed most of Russia's political classes were hurrying to endorse the acting president, anxious about their futures after his seemingly inevitable win. The main challengers, Communist Gennadii Zyuganov and liberal Grigorii Yavlinsky, were failed candidates from 1996, and most of the other eleven candidates were unknown. An early vote would also help to guard against serious reverses in Chechnya of the kind that had been so worrying for Boris Yeltsin in 1996.

The campaign itself was an unimpressive affair. Putin did not publish a campaign programme on the grounds that, as he put it, everyone would fall on it and tear it to pieces. The closest to this was a series of interviews with three Russian journalists, published as a booklet entitled *First Person* just weeks before the decisive vote (Putin, 2000). He refused to take part in debates with his opponents, and refused to use political advertising, because, as his staff crudely explained, 'you don't need to know in the middle of an election campaign whether Tampax or Snickers are better'. In an effort to look statesmanlike Putin pretended not to campaign at all, merely relying on reports of his carrying out his presidential duties. Underlying all this though, was the basic message that the Russian state was under threat, and that only he could save it. In words that rapidly became notorious, he threatened to 'destroy the [Chechen] terrorists in their outhouses'. Yeltsin in 1996 had used the threat of a return to communist rule to hold on to power. In 2000 the refrain was the fear of terrorism and of state collapse. Thus the campaign did not involve the systematic comparison of alternative directions of development for the country. There was still, as there had been in Russia for most of its history, a relative absence of public politics. There was, however, just as in 1996, an outbreak of generosity by the ruling elites in the run-up to polling day. As much as 140 billion roubles ($4.9 billion) was made available to pay pension arrears and provide for some increases, and a special bonus for the Second World War veterans was announced. All back wages were to be repaid by April. It also became clear that as President, Putin intended to rein back the powers of unruly regional leaderships.

In the meantime, opposition candidates had great difficulties in articulating distinctive messages. Zyuganov, unlike Yavlinsky, had less difficulty in being heard in the media. However he faced the problem that Putin had moved onto his electoral territory. The Communist Party in the 1990s had espoused very much the same mixture of statist and nationalist ideas that Putin was now campaigning on. Yavlinsky's popularity was undoubtedly damaged among some sections of the electorate by his opposition to the continuation of the Chechen War, at least in its existing form. He was also disliked by sections of the pro-reform electorate because of his stance of permanent opposition to everything the Kremlin had done, rather than ever taking responsibility for the immensely complex task of attempting to create a free market economy. He in turn loathed many other leaders of Russia's so-called democrats for supporting the Yeltsin regime despite the odour of corruption and nepotism surrounding it. Furthermore, liberalism as espoused by Yavlinsky had become associated in the minds of many of the Russian electorate with economic chaos and state collapse.

Sociological researchers took the opportunity of the elections to use focus groups to explore the way that the various candidates were perceived by voters during the campaign (*Imidzh*, 2000). They first asked about the kinds of qualities voters wanted to see in a president. The most important ones were honesty, health and energy, patriotism, competence, professionalism, intelligence and a high level of education. How did the actual candidates measure up? Putin was most often described as intelligent, competent, having a sense of humour, physically and psychologically healthy, not old, a man who kept himself to himself, whose actions spoke louder than his words, honest, and having authority abroad. Asked what words or images he evoked, his supporters mentioned his toughness, describing him as a 'real *muzhik*, strong-willed and a strong hand'. Other traits frequently mentioned were cunning, farsightedness and purposefulness. Animals he reminded people of were the fox, and the wolf who 'holds on to his own territory, and can also snarl'. However all voters, both supporters and opponents, mentioned his enigmatic side. Some described him as a 'black box', 'an unidentified object', or even 'a Malevich black square'. Voters praised his appearance, manner of speaking, restrained behaviour (the comparison with the previous president was no doubt on respondents' minds here), decisiveness and manliness, but also mentioned cruelty, the ability to keep downwind of opponents, cunning and unpredictability. Some women who were intending to vote for him mentioned his 'manly smile'. One said 'we are used to amoeba-like men, but he is something different.' The five most important reasons for voting for Putin mentioned by his supporters were as follows:

- Putin would bring about order in the country, control incomes and prices, strengthen national defence
- Raise the prestige of the country in the world
- Struggle with crime, oligarchy and corruption
- Increase production and lower taxes
- Resolve the crisis in the Caucasus

Those who were not intending to support him, on the other hand, stressed the following:

- The possibility of the establishment of a dictatorship, relating to worry about strengthening the military and police structures
- Putin's connections with the Yeltsin entourage, and the nepotism that had been shown in his appointment as acting president
- Yavlinsky supporters believed that the economy would remain in the same parlous state

Gennadii Zyuganov's public image had fewer positives. The most frequent descriptors of him were 'energetic', confident in himself', 'stable and calm', but also 'aggressive', 'mendacious', 'contradictory', 'demagogical and a windbag'. The most common views about his policies were that he would improve matters in the social sphere (free education and health care), and raise wages and pensions and increase social equality. Opponents were concerned, in this order, about the possibility of returning to a socialist past, the absence of real plans for Russia's development, and the possibility of civil war or dictatorship. As regards personal qualities, supporters liked his understanding of the needs of the poor, his energy, professionalism, organisational abilities and his lack of associations with Yeltsin and the oligarchs. Opponents saw him as 'aggressive', 'thick-headed' and criticised his 'disagreeable appearance'.

In the event, the overall outcome of the election, shown in Table 4.2, was predictable. Turnout remained consistent at 68 per cent, and Putin secured a narrow first round victory by gaining 53 per cent of

TABLE 4.2   Trends in Russian presidential elections, 1991–2000 (as percentage of votes cast)

1991		1996 (round 1)		1996 (round 2)		2000	
Boris Yeltsin	59.7	Boris Yeltsin	35.3	Boris Yeltsin	53.8	Vladimir Putin	52.9
Nikolai Ryzhkov	17.6	Gennadii Zyuganov	32.0	Gennadii Zyuganov	40.3	Gennadii Zyuganov	29.2
Vladimir Zhirinovsky	8.1	Alexander Lebed	14.5	Against all	4.8	Grigorii Yavlinsky	5.8
Aman-Geldy Tuleev	7.1	Grigorii Yavlinsky	7.3			Aman-Geldy Tuleev	3.0
Others	7.5	Vladimir Zhirinovsky	5.7			Vladimir Zhirinovsky	2.7
		Others	2.2			Others	3.5
		Against all	1.5			Against all	1.9
Turnout	74.7		69.7		68.8		68.0

Source: For 1991, White *et al.* (1997), p. 39; for 1996, Wyman *et al.* (1998), pp. 278–9; for 2000, *Central Election Commission*, available from <http://www.fci.ru>

the votes cast. Zyuganov obtained 3 per cent and Yavlinsky 1.5 per cent smaller shares of the vote than they had in the first round in 1996, and none of the other candidates performed above expectations. In the case of two, Aman-Geldy Tuleev and Alexei Podberezkin, this was hardly surprising since they had already publicly expressed their support for Putin. Summing up the results, one commentator mordantly observed that 'To the fact that we don't have parliamentary parties, we must also note the absence of politicians as such, with the exception of the leaders of these same "ghostlike" parties' (Petrov, 2000).

Social Characteristics of Voters

Theories of voting behaviour in established democracies do allow for policy preferences and short-term factors such as attitudes to individual politicians, but the basic explanatory factor in most is social background. Voters act politically as they are socially. Candidates and parties are understood in large part as the political expression of particular social groups. These ideas have proved broadly robust in postcommunist Russia (Colton, 2000; White, Wyman and Oates, 1997; Wyman, 1996; Wyman *et al.*, 1998), although the lack of a consolidated party system tends to raise the importance of short term factors. So to what extent did established patterns of voting behaviour continue to hold in the 1999–2000 electoral round? Table 4.3 illustrates the nature of party support in the State Duma election.

The distribution of voting by age remained broadly similar to the patterns that had been seen in previous elections. Voters for the Communist Party tended to be significantly older than those for other parties. Many Communist voters have memories of a time when the communist system did not appear to be failing, or are nostalgic for a period of order and superpower status. The two competing parties of power, Unity and OVR, also tended to have somewhat older electorates. The style of governing they both represented, with its ingrained habits of paternalism and even the legacy of the command-administrative habits of office holders under communism, is a practice with which older people seem to be more comfortable. The other ideological parties, by contrast, appealed more strongly to younger Russians. Zhirinovsky's aggressively populist nationalism and the Union of Right Forces' pro-market idealism both found more fertile ground among younger, less resigned voters. In this respect, one notable

TABLE 4.3 *The social characteristics of party voters, December 1999*

	CPRF	Unity	Fatherland-All Russia (OVR)	Yabloko	Union of Right Forces	Zhirinovsky bloc
Age						
18–24	5	10	10	12	25	18
25–39	17	38	29	40	37	42
40–54	26	24	25	29	23	23
55 plus	53	28	36	19	15	18
Sex						
Men	48	50	44	47	42	62
Women	52	51	56	54	58	38
Education						
Elementary or less	15	8	8	5	3	10
Incomplete secondary	36	24	26	16	17	26
Secondary	20	27	22	24	26	30
Vocational	18	25	21	28	29	29
Higher	11	16	23	27	25	5
Living standard						
Hardly make ends meet	45	33	28	24	17	32
Have enough to buy food	40	41	46	41	44	37
Have enough to buy food and clothes	13	23	21	30	31	28
Can afford consumer durables easily	2	3	5	6	8	3

Source: VTsIOM pre-election polls, conducted in December 1999, N = 6400, accessed via Russia Votes, available from <http://www.RussiaVotes.org >

change from past Duma elections is that Yabloko's electorate had a slightly older age profile than its rival in the 'democratic' camp. Previously, pro- and anti-Kremlin democrats tended to have rather similar social profiles. Perhaps the effect of greater political experience had been to increase voter cynicism about the gap between promise and reality in postcommunist Russian governments, to Yabloko's advantage?

Gender and education differences continued to be noticeable. Men were in 1999 much more likely than women to vote for what have to be described as the more aggressive parties, those in favour, for example, of a military 'solution' in Chechnya, such as Zhirinovsky's bloc, Unity and the CPRF. Women voters were more likely to prefer the more pacific, and indeed more anti-Kremlin political forces. The trend continued of more educated voters preferring pro-reform and pro-market parties, while less educated (who also tended to be older) preferred communists, nationalists, or the parties of power. And as education in Russia as in most societies, tends to be related to income, the poorer tended to prefer the communists. The parties of the 'democrats', Yabloko and the Union of Right Forces, had larger portions of their electorates made up of the relatively wealthy than did the parties of power. This is unsurprising, since these are the people who have done best out of the attempt to introduce a free market economy in Russia.

Table 4.4 illustrates voting trends among various social groups in the 2000 presidential elections. It provides a more detailed account of where the main candidates' appeal was stronger or weaker. As can be seen, Putin's electorate was, unsurprisingly, similar in nature to Unity's. He did relatively better among older voters, those with at least secondary education, people occupying more senior positions, and the better off. The gender effect seen in the Duma elections disappeared. Since neither of the top two candidates could by any stretch of the imagination be described as pacific, there was perhaps little way of expressing opposition to excessively forceful or violent forms of politics. Unlike Yeltsin, Putin was able to gain votes from rural areas just as easily as big cities, and this was the main difference between the social base of the two presidents. In addition, Putin was able to gain votes from supporters of all the major parliamentary parties. A third of Yavlinsky voters, and even one in eight CPRF voters, were willing to transfer their support to him.

The patterns of support for Zyuganov remained absolutely consistent with CPRF voting and with patterns of support in his previous

TABLE 4.4 *Presidential voting behaviour among social and political groups (in percent), March 2000*

	Proportion of sample	Putin	Zyuganov	Yavlinsky	Non voters
All Russians		36	20	4	31
Age					
18–23	12	29	4	5	55
24–29	13	29	13	6	35
30–39	20	39	10	3	37
40–49	17	39	22	6	26
50–59	14	39	26	2	25
60–90	25	37	33	3	19
Sex					
Men	46	34	20	4	31
Women	55	38	20	4	30
Education					
Less than secondary	37	32	25	2	34
Secondary	48	39	18	4	29
Higher	15	38	12	11	26
Rurality					
Rural	26	36	26	2	28
Town / small city	36	33	20	3	32
Large city	38	38	15	7	31

Employment					
Manager	5	40	9	7	29
Specialist	11	44	14	8	22
White collar worker	8	36	17	6	30
Worker	25	37	20	3	31
Student	5	31	1	10	48
Pensioner	30	36	32	3	23
Housewife	7	40	5	4	39
Unemployed	10	22	16	2	49
Consumption status					
Hard-pressed for food	34	29	28	3	32
Can't afford clothes	44	39	18	4	29
Can't afford consumer durables	18	39	12	5	32
Can afford consumer durables	4	48	4	8	26
Recalled parliamentary election vote					
Yabloko	32	32	3	47	14
Union of Right Forces	54	54	4	2	19
Unity	77	77	6	1	9
CPRF	12	12	75	0	5

Source: adapted from VTsIOM post election poll, n = 1580. Accessed at <http://www.wciom.ru/EDITION/elprdem.asp>. (Note that voters for other candidates have been omitted, which is why rows do not add to 100 per cent.)

presidential bid, in that his strengths were among the old, poorest, and least educated sections of Russian society, especially in rural areas. Yavlinsky, too, had a stable social base, polling best among those with higher education and students, among people with relatively higher social status and in the biggest cities, especially Moscow and St Petersburg. He was the candidate of choice of a section of Russia's intelligentsia. However the weakness of his performance was illustrated by his failure to retain the support of even half of 1999 Yabloko voters, according to these data.

Patterns of non-participation also remained consistent with previous national votes. The young, who tend to be much more physically and psychologically mobile, voted in significantly lower numbers than older people. Around half the unemployed, with very little stake in the status quo, did not take part in the presidential election. The existence of a party claiming to represent the poor and excluded meant that participation rates among this section of society remained high in comparative perspective. Communist party structures were able to mobilise their potential support effectively. Although women and men voted in similar numbers, women who were not currently in employment were less likely to take part in the elections.

Regional Voting Trends

In earlier elections supporters of economic and political reform had normally polled more strongly in northern and eastern Russia, while Communists had achieved higher votes in southern and southwestern areas. A notion which is commonly used to explain Russian regional voting patterns is that of the 55th parallel: reformers did better above this latitude, Communists and their allies better below it. More sophisticated analyses have sought to explain this observation, as well as the other patterns of regional voting that have been discussed (Clem and Craumer, 1995a and 1995b; Medvedkov *et al.*, 1996, Slider *et al.*, 1994). Out of these studies some clear propositions have emerged. For example, anti-reformers do better in the south of European Russia because this is the agricultural heartland, and Russia's agriculture remains dependent on the continuation of a system of state subsidies that is supported by the Communist and associated parties. Additionally, in many of these areas, the old communist *nomenklatura* retains a firm grip. By contrast, reformers

TABLE 4.5 Results of the 1999 and 2000 elections by region

% of total population		CPRF	Unity	Fatherland-All Russia	Union of Right Forces	Yabloko	Zhirinovsky bloc	Putin	Zyuganov	Yavlinsky	Zhirinovsky
		1999 State Duma election						2000 presidential election			
4	North	15	31	7	10	8	9	64	19	6	3
6	Northwest	16	24	12	13	9	5	64	19	8	2
22	Central	21	17	23	9	7	5	50	28	10	2
6	Volga-Vyatka	28	22	12	11	4	6	54	34	3	2
6	Central Black Earth	32	29	7	5	4	5	50	39	3	3
11	Trans-Volga	27	24	16	10	4	5	56	30	3	2
11	North Caucasian	34	14	6	2	2	2	58	32	4	2
14	Urals	21	22	15	10	6	6	57	27	6	3
9	West Siberia	28	25	6	9	8	7	42	32	6	3
6	East Siberia	25	32	5	7	5	8	49	34	4	4
5	Far East	23	29	6	7	6	10	47	32	7	5
	Russia	24	23	13	9	6	6	53	29	6	3

Source: author's calculations from data of the Central Electoral Commission, available from <http://www.fci.ru>.

have done better in more urban regions where the population is better educated, and also in the natural resource-rich areas of the far north and Far East. The oil and gas industries are concentrated in the latter area, are one of the few parts of the Russian economy to have performed relatively well in recent years, and of course require a continuation of a policy of Russia's ongoing integration with the world economy. Votes in a number of 'deviant' areas, such as the republic of Tyva, which has been consistently pro-government despite being southern and predominantly agricultural, may be explained by the strong influence exerted by local leaderships over voters and outcomes – 'the gubernatorial ten per cent' as it has become known (Wyman *et al.*, 2001).

The most recent round of elections shows patterns of regional support shifting in significant ways. Most notable, Unity and Putin were able to make significant inroads into the 'red belt' of communist strength in Southern and Western Russia. This may be explained by the combination of two factors. The first is the increasing convergence between the policies and styles of Putin and his Communist opponents. Second, as discussed above, regional leaderships in the period between the 1999 and 2000 votes became extremely keen to demonstrate their loyalty to the man everyone expected to be the winner of the presidential election. If it is the case that local leaderships in parts of southern Russia are able to exert more control over local outcomes, then this helps to explain the move. It is also noticeable that Putin did much less well in Russia east of the Urals. It may well have been the case that his centralising and controlling instincts looked rather less desirable to both voters and local political elites at such a distance from Moscow.

Conclusions

So to what extent is the practice of electoral democracy consolidated in postcommunist Russia? We can certainly say that the structures for holding free and fair elections exist. There are clear and well established rules governing the conduct of elections and their administration. As with any country, there is room for improvement in these structures (IFES, 2000). However what the Russian case demonstrates is that while clearly structures are an important part of democracy, the surrounding culture is still more crucial. For example the laws governing the role of the media, or the conduct of ballots at individual polling stations, are adequate to the purpose. The problem is that officials, journalists and the courts simply don't always follow the laws and regulations that exist. In the Soviet period, laws were only arbitrarily applied, and the legacy continues into the postcommunist period, although in a much less extreme fashion.

After three rounds of national elections, what generalisations seem to hold about the Russian electorate? Clearly, this remains an electorate largely without partisan loyalties. The proportions of the vote gathered by ideologically definable political parties that have maintained their presence through the three rounds of elections is very small. This does not mean that voters are without consistent views, just that the means to express them change from election to election. In other words the party system is mostly unconsolidated, and politics remains highly personalised. This matters a great deal. Democracy, if it is to be an effective form of government, offers a means of changing the direction of development of a country peacefully, without revolution. But up to the year 2000, there had not really been a national election in Russia where there was any serious prospect of forces coming to power who would seek dramatically to shift the directions of development. While allowing opposition to exist, so long as it does not get too powerful, the existing leadership has managed to control the elections sufficiently to ensure no real threat to their hegemony. As one commentator succinctly put it, '26 March 2000 completed the eleven year process of the transformation of Soviet decorative democracy into a Russian managed democracy' (Petrov, 2000). However optimists will note that, in a situation where the leadership is much more unpopular than was the case in 1999–2000, it may be that the structures do exist for a genuine democratic transfer of power to take place. This will be the real test of how consolidated democratic practices have become in the Russian Federation.

5

Parties and Organised Interests

RICHARD SAKWA

Political parties and organised interests such as trade unions play a fundamental role in modern representative democracy. They connect civil and political society, advance the perceived interests of individuals, groups and social strata while aiming consciously to develop these constituencies, and provide a link between civil society and the state, espousing the claims of the one and enforcing the rules of the other (Sartori, 1976; 1987). In postcommunist Russia, parties and organised interests only marginally fulfilled these functions. The relative independence of government from both parliamentary oversight and party control, and the emergence of a powerful presidential system based on the apparatus of the state, marginalised the political role of organised social interests. Trapped between an ill-formed state system and a rudimentary civil society, the nascent representative system was unable to assert itself against other political actors like the military and security apparatus, oligarchical financial and commercial interests, regional governors, and the government itself. Indeed, rather than parties forming the government, the pattern in most parliamentary democracies, in Russia it was the executive branch that tended to take the initiative in party formation. Nevertheless, despite all the odds, parties became an essential element in the Russian political scene.

The Emergence of Pluralism

Four stages can be identified in the political life cycle of organised interests in the emerging democratic order of postcommunist Russia.

The first was the insurgency stage of movements and *neformal'nye* (informal) organisations accompanying the dissolution of the power of the Communist Party of the Soviet Union (CPSU) during *perestroika* (1985–91). The second stage was the period of constitutional crisis between August 1991 and October 1993, when the presidency and parliament struggled for supremacy. In the absence of elections and the bare-knuckle fight for political power between rival elite factions, this period can be characterised as a peculiar sort of 'phoney democracy'. The third stage was inaugurated by the dissolution of the old Russian Congress of People's Deputies (CPD) and its Supreme Soviet led by Ruslan Khasbulatov on 21 September 1993 and the events of 3–4 October, when the White House was stormed and President Boris Yeltsin's opponents crushed. This adaptation stage was marked by the adoption of a new constitution and the first genuine national multiparty elections of 12 December 1993. The elections began to clarify the pattern of party affiliation but failed to consolidate the party system.

This period, lasting up to the end of Yeltsin's period in power in December 1999, was characterised by a contradictory dual adaptation. Political leaders and organised interests adapted themselves to constitutional and democratic mass politics, largely renouncing the street politics of the insurgency and 'phoney democracy' phases. Democratic forms and constitutional norms, however, were adapted to the needs of the political leadership, thus undermining the real impact that organised political interests could have on the conduct of government and the shaping of policy. In the fourth phase, accompanying Putin's presidency from March 2000, the role of political parties was formalised and the policy process broadened to allow the voice of organised interests to be heard more effectively. We will examine all four phases – insurgency, 'phoney democracy', adaptation and formalisation – in more detail below.

The Insurgency Phase

One of the cardinal principles of communist rule had been the incorporation of organised interests into the political regime itself. The CPSU, as the only legal political party, took on itself the burden of political management, while organised interests existed as little more than emanations of the party itself. The trade union movement, for example, organised in the form of the All-Union Central Council of Trade Unions (AUCCTU) was a vast bureaucratic organisation whose leadership was appointed by the party and whose role was reduced to little more than provider of rest homes, holiday vouchers, pensions and welfare entitlements. The AUCCTU administered a large part of the social security budget, but this only served to underline the administrative nature of the organisation: functions that in most countries are undertaken by special ministries in the USSR was fulfilled by a body nominally representing workers' interests. In 1920 Lenin had talked of trade unions and other mass organisations acting as 'transmission belts', relaying party policy to the people, and under Stalin this was achieved with a vengeance for all social organisations, including the youth movement (Komsomol) and women's organisations. Although under the post-Stalin leadership mass organisations became a little more responsive to the needs of their members, they remained heavily bureaucratised organisations with a relatively low status in the Soviet pecking border.

The party jealously guarded its constitutionally entrenched rights, as asserted in Article 6 of the 1977 (Brezhnev) Constitution:

The Communist Party of the Soviet Union is the leading and guiding force of Soviet society and the nucleus of its political system, of all state organisations and public organisations. The CPSU exists for the people and serves the people. The Communist Party, armed with Marxism-Leninism, determines the general perspectives of the development of society and the course of the home and foreign policy of the USSR, directs the great constructive work of the Soviet people, and imparts a planned, systematic, and theoretically substantiated character to their struggle for the victory of communism.

Only with the onset of Gorbachev's *perestroika* was there an attempt to revive mass social organisations, and ultimately even the party formally became no more than one among many competing social organisations. In March 1990, Article 6 was modified to remove the party's 'leading role', and formally the era of pluralistic multi-party politics was inaugurated as *the* party became *a* party. Already since 1987 the relaxation of the prohibition against independent political and social organisations had seen an upsurge of citizen activity. The establishment of the Democratic Union on 9 May 1988 represented the symbolic moment when the new era of multiparty politics in Russia began. Movements covering social, environmental, gender and other issues, as well as popular fronts and proto-parties, were established (Sedaitis and Butterfield, 1991). By late 1990 some 500 political or politicised organisations had been established as the informal movements began to take on more structured forms.

The tumultuous proliferation of informal organisations and an independent press revealed the strong currents of civic endeavour flowing beneath the stagnant surface of Soviet life. While Russian political culture is often described as passive and individualistic, this upsurge of social activity suggested that, given the right circumstances, Russians were as ready to enter into associational life as any other people (White, 1999). The problem, however, was that much of this activity was united by little other than its anti-systemic character, devoted to overcoming the dominance of the CPSU. When it came to a positive programme, Russian society proved deeply fragmented (Fish, 1991), quite apart from its inability to impose accountability on the authorities and even on its own leaders. Although the informal movement was only one route of party formation in this period, with others including groups emerging from within the CPSU itself, openly anti-communist alliances and the 'revolutionary movement' represented by the creation of the umbrella body called 'Democratic Russia' in mid-1990 (Urban and Gel'man, 1997), all reflected a rather simplistic bipolarity. There remained a gulf between insurgent political elites and the political system. This gulf was reproduced once a section of the insurgent elite, headed by Boris Yeltsin, came to power after August 1991 in what became an independent Russia.

Elections shape party systems, and the one held in March 1990 to the Russian CPD was dominated by the anti-politics of opposition to the communist regime. Democratic Russia won about a quarter of the seats in the new parliament. However, unlike much of Central Europe, the social movements associated with the insurgency phase were largely unable to make the transition from mobilisational to representational politics (Waller, 1993). Unity in the insurgency phase of party formation was forged by the negative programme of opposition to the communist regime, in favour of greater civic freedom and a looser form of federation. A survey of middle level Democratic Russia activists revealed the extent to which the negative programme of removing the CPSU from power was ingrained in the movement (Gordon and Klopov, 1993). The informal movement origins of most parties left its stamp on the nascent party system. Civil society type 'anti-politics' was typical of the insurgency phase, marginalising political parties as instruments of mobilisation and political communication (Lewis, 1993).

'Phoney Democracy' (August 1991–October 1993)

Duverger (1954) stresses the electoral and parliamentary origins of modern political parties, and in the absence of either in the phoney democracy phase party formation inevitably stagnated. The unity promoted by the common struggle against communism, now shattered in response to the disintegration of the USSR in December 1991, and the launching of radical economic reform in early 1992. The period was characterised by a distinctive type of dual power in which a presidential apparatus was superimposed on the nascent parliamentary system, with little coordination between the two. Parties were left hanging in the air with little constructive purpose. The official trade union movement was reformed and de-étatised, while the new trade unions were subject to the factionalism and splits typical of the pseudo-parties (*Kto est chto*, 1993). Although a number of independent new unions were formed, the vast majority remained under the umbrella of what was now called the Federation of Independent Trade Unions of Russia (FITUR, in Russian FNPR). The Komsomol movement lost almost all of its membership now that it was no longer compulsory, leaving only a rump of radical socialists to continue the tradition of Leninist youth activity. The old Soviet women's organisation also dissolved and a number of independent women's organisations were created. Notable among them was the political party Women of Russia that, drawing on the organisational resources of the earlier period, successfully entered parliament in the December 1993 elections.

After December 1991 'national' politics were no longer Soviet but Russian. The disappearance of the CPSU removed the incentive for the 'opposition' to unite, while much of the old CPSU elite made a smooth transition and became part of the new establishment. The second phase was marked by a strong ebb tide of social activism. Environmental movements were marginalised under the impact of severe economic recession, and housing and other movements failed to respond to the new challenges. The so-called 'democratic' anti-communist movement ceded ground to numerous patriotic and nationalist organisations. The ideological homogeneity of the insurgency phase now gave way to programmatic divergence over such issues as the powers of the presidency, relations with the 'near abroad' and, above all, economic reform (Golovin, 1994). Most of the parties spawned by the struggle against communism were not proto-parties, destined to become fully-fledged parties, but pseudo-parties sustained by a variety of extraneous circumstances that reflected neither their popular appeal nor organisational resources. Very few social movements were able to convert themselves into effective parties. This was the case with Democratic Russia and also the Civic Union later, and is one of the distinctive features of the transition in Russia.

The proto-parties of the first stage of party formation gave way to a period marked not by their evolution into fully-fledged parties but by a system marked by numerous pseudo-parties, all seeking a niche in the ideological spectrum and organisational life of the postcommunist polity. The Communist Party of the Russian Federation (CPRF), revived at a congress in February 1993 and claiming to be the successor to the old Communist Party, was one of the few political forces that transcended the politics of insurgency and could draw on organisational experience and reserves of political experience matched by few other parties. Yet it, too, like all other parties in this period, was disconnected from the political system. Parties neither nominated the president nor formed the government, and parliament and the parties in it were marginalised. The absence of disciplined party blocs endowed parliamentary politics with a fractious fluidity. Parties were often divided internally, usually dominated by a single strong personality, and were unable to play an effective role in the new order. Parties emerged but not a party system. Parties and social movements failed to fulfil the communicative and link functions between the political elite and the people. The failure to integrate parties into the operation of the political system undermined the stability of the new democratic institutions and forced ever-greater reliance on a technocratic ideology of democratic and marketising reforms from above. The executive formulated its policies largely independent of any party, movement or bloc.

The Dual Adaptation Stage (December 1993–December 1999)

In December 1993 the pseudo-parties of the earlier periods were now faced with the hard school of an election. Their inflated claims of support were finally put to the test. Few withstood the challenge, and most faded into the obscurity whence they had come. The elections, however, did contribute to the development of parties by forcing the development of organisations and alliances, while the adoption of the constitution finally provided a stable institutional framework in which parties could operate. A new generation of parties emerged, most of whom drew their provenance from earlier stages but which had been able to respond to the dramatically changed political climate following the October events.

The electoral system was designed to encourage the development of a multiparty system. In the new mixed system half the seats to the new 450-member State Duma were elected by the traditional 'first-past-the-post' single-member constituencies, but the other half were elected from party lists according to a weighted system of proportional representation. In order to be eligible to stand a party or bloc required at least 100 000 nominations with no more than 15 000 signatures drawn from any one of Russia's 89 regions and republics; the bloc or party had to have demonstrable support in at least seven regions or republics. This provision was designed to stimulate the creation of a national party system, to overcome the proliferation of small parties, and to avoid the dominance of Moscow. To enter parliament on the 'list' system a party had to take at least five per cent of the national vote, with the whole country considered one giant constituency.

Although the details changed, this was the system in operation for the rest of the 1990s (see Chapter 4). Its results, however, were hardly those anticipated by the institutional engineers. The adoption of this hybrid system only revealed more starkly the fault lines in Russian society. Thirteen parties and electoral blocs negotiated the hurdles to stand in the 1993 election, and of these only eight cleared the five per cent threshold. Once again party representation in parliament was fragmented, with nearly a dozen relatively small factions preventing the establishment of a stable majority, inhibiting the development of parliamentary government and helping to perpetuate the supraparty system of presidential politics. Political fragmentation was strongly evident in the December 1995 election, with 43 electoral blocs standing but only four crossing the five per threshold to enter parliament. By the time of the December 1999 election the situation had somewhat stabilised with 26 blocs standing and six entering parliament, including the newly-formed Unity (Yedinstvo) organisation supporting Putin's presidential ambitions.

Although Yeltsin on several occasions floated the idea of establishing a presidential party, every time he fought shy of undertaking the organisational work required for such a venture. Instead he claimed to be president of all Russians. Attempts to unite the 'democratic' forces behind a single presidential candidate came to nothing, and instead in the 1996 presidential elections the organisational and financial resources of the presidency itself, allied with powerful 'oligarchs' to which the presidency then became indebted, were the key resource that ensured Yeltsin's re-election.

The frantic regrouping of parties in the adaptation phase could not disguise the weakness of the party system and the marginalisation of all forms of social representation. Politics were focused on private, top-level intrigues and lost transparency, while political organisations only slowly sank roots into society itself. No overall legislation had been adopted to regulate the sphere of social organisations, and the absence of direct instructions in the new constitution concerning the adoption of a law on political parties was seen by the opposition as part of the broader chaos in political relations, inhibiting effective work in the Duma and one of the reasons for the disorganisation of local elections. The lack of rules concerning the financing of political organisations meant that commercial organisations were given a free hand, and sought to ensure the maximum benefit from their 'investment'. In the absence of structured party politics lobbies formed their own parties, as with the Agrarian Party. At the same time, the presidency relied on quasi-political 'parties of power', combining the organisational and financial resources of the executive branch with access to the media.

The retrogression can partly be explained by the type of resources available for party formation. In the insurgency phase mobilisation took place largely on ideological grounds, whereas later this shifted to a variety of forms but was marked by the weakness of organised social groups in civil society coming together to seek political representation. Instead, parties drew on the organisational resources of the state itself, with various ministries providing the organisational resources for a number of parties. Above all, those groups fortunate enough to enter the Duma were able to draw on the administrative and technical resources allowed deputies (up to five advisers paid by the state, plus secretarial and other help) to promote the development of the associations to which they belonged. In party formation as elsewhere a process of territorialisation of politics was apparent, with insiders carving out areas of concern and resources to further their own political ends. The role of prominent personalities, often with access to sources of financial support, is striking. The career of Konstantin Borovoi, the founder of Russia's first post-Soviet commodity exchange and of the Party of Economic Freedom, is a case in point. Although most parties had adapted to the conventions of parliamentary politics, they had also succumbed to the intrigue-ridden regime-dominated politics of the Yeltsin years (Sakwa, 1997).

The Formalisation Stage (January 2000–)

Although Putin's rise had been sponsored by Yeltsin, his policies and political style in many respects represented a repudiation of Yeltsinism. This was nowhere more true than in the sphere of party development. Putin came to power proclaiming the need for his government to have proper social support reflected in political organisation. On several occasions Putin argued that 'Russia needs a real multiparty system', not parties 'that represent only themselves, but rather . . . reflect the interests of large groups of society', which could 'shape the policies of the state' (*Washington Post*, 8 September 2000). It appeared that this would take the form of a two or three-party system. The centre-right would be represented by Unity (a party that did not hide its aspiration to become the 'ruling party'), the left niche would be occupied by the CPRF, while the liberals would be represented by a unified grouping comprising Grigorii Yavlinsky's Yabloko and the Union of Right Forces (SPS), a bloc bringing together the many small parties forged to fight the 1999 elections.

It was in this period that there was much talk about revising the legislative framework for the activities of political parties. In the wake of the December 1999 elections Alexander Veshnyakov, the chair of the Central Electoral Commission, argued that a law on political parties was required to make their financing and organisation more transparent. In return only genuine political parties would be allowed to participate in parliamentary elections. Such a reform would at a stroke eliminate the pseudo-party electoral associations. Already in the 1998 Ukrainian election only parties were allowed to stand on the party list. Consolidation would also be achieved by Unity's proposal to raise from 5 to 7 per cent the share of votes necessary enter the Duma in the party-list system. Not surprisingly Yabloko, which barely crossed the five per cent threshold in the 1999 elections, sought to retain the existing level (*Izvestiya*, 18 August 2000). Other ideas in the draft legislation was to require that in order to be registered parties had to have a membership of at least 10 000 nationwide, with no fewer than 200 members in each region (*Segodnya*, 10 October 2000).

Civil Society Today

In their study of postcommunist party systems Kitschelt *et al.* (1999, p. 1) argue that 'In the final analysis, whether democracy becomes the "only game in town" depends on the *quality of democratic interactions and policy processes* the consequences of which affect the legitimacy of democracy in the eyes of citizens and political elites alike'. Democratic consolidation in their view was very much a matter of the quality of democratic procedures and not only a question of the durability of the system. This is particularly pertinent for Russia, where the formal institutions of democracy often masked quite undemocratic practices. Robert Michels (1962) had long ago argued that political parties, whatever their programmatic aspirations, tend to succumb to the oligarchical tendencies inherent in modern social organisation. Russia appears to have fallen victim to this 'iron law of oligarchy' even before party life had become routinised. Similarly, most of the larger social organisations, above all the trade unions, tended to be top-heavy bureaucratic organisations with weak links with the mass of their membership.

Nevertheless, despite repeated setbacks the Yeltsin years had provided conditions for the development of associational life and representative institutions. A number of questions emerged as Putin reorganised Russian governance: would his support for a more structured party system recognise and incorporate the pluralism that had emerged since the late 1980s, or would he try to reduce parties to little more than departments of state responsible for organising public politics; to what extent would a genuine system of governmental accountability to society emerge; and would the environment (above all, a free media, free and fair elections, an independent judiciary and a transparent funding regime) allow parties and other social organisations effectively to participate in Russian public life? Above all, as Putin used the presidency as an instrument of political change would the presidency itself become responsible to public and parliamentary accountability? From Putin's public utterances in his first period in power, it was clear that he himself did not know the answer to these questions. The contours of the post-Yeltsin Russian polity would emerge not simply out of decisions, but would reflect the balance of political and social forces and institutional arrangements.

Party geography mutated from one election to the next, with only four parties fighting all three Duma elections in the 1990s. Russia's 'floating party system' inhibited stable party identification as electors were forced to become floating voters as parties came and went (Rose *et al.*, 2001). In mid-2000 some 180 parties were registered in Russia, but the vast majority were of little significance. Of the six parties that crossed the five per cent representation threshold in 1999, three were new: Unity as the reconstituted 'party of power' gained 23 per cent of the party-list vote; the centre-left grouping Fatherland-All Russia (OVR) led by the former prime minister Yevgenii Primakov and the mayor of Moscow, Yuri Luzhkov, gained 13.3 per cent; and the liberal Union of Right Forces (SPS) won 8.5 per cent. Despite the lack of continuity, however, a number of parties survived the turmoil of the 1990s to play an important part in the politics of the new century. The organisation that most properly deserved the title of 'party' was the CPRF. With a network of regional organisations covering the entire country, some 20 000 primary cells and a membership of about half a million, and a large deputy fraction in all three postcommunist State Dumas, the CPRF was potentially an important political force. The CPRF became one of the cornerstones of Russian parliamentarianism and although somewhat eclipsed in December 1999 by Unity, the CPRF remained the largest group in parliament. However, the party was unable to realise its potential and its leader, Gennadii Zyuganov, appeared forever to be the runner-up and never the victor, as in the 1996 and 2000 presidential elections. The CPRF's ideology was a potent and largely incompatible mix of nationalist, imperialistic (in the Soviet sense) and communist principles; its policies were incoherent in that elements of the market were accepted as long as market *forces* were to be constrained; and its politics appeared to place its own institutional comfort (above all in the Duma) above principle. The party was the main oppositional force in the Duma, yet its policy stances too often appeared opportunistic and contradictory.

The CPRF was also riven by problems of political identity. Was it a revolutionary party intending to overthrow Russia's nascent capitalist institutions, or was it more of a social democratic party seeking to humanise the workings of the capitalist market? What would be the balance between nationalism and socialism? These questions, faced by the whole social democratic movement in the early part of the century and by the West European communist parties in the postwar era, was one that confronted postcommunist communist parties in a particularly stark form. These ideological questions were far from abstract since on them hinged questions oforganisation and strategy. To what degree would the party support strikes and street demonstrations; would the emphasis be on the working class or the intelligentsia; what would be the party's economic policy; how would the party relate to the other former Soviet republics? On all these questions the CPRF equivocated. The absence of a clear-cut ideology and the aged profile of its membership inhibited the mobilisation of the party's resources. Above all, its nationalist ambitions, socialist aspirations and its democratic commitments were far from integrated. Following the December 1999 election some of the tension in the CPRF came out into the open. A new political movement of the moderate left, headed by the Speaker of the State Duma, Gennadii Seleznev, was formally established in September 2000. Called 'Rossiya' (Russia), the new movement remained allied to the CPRF but the relationship was strained.

Yavlinsky's Yabloko party had since its foundation in 1993 represented the anti-Yeltsin wing of the 'democratic' movement. It too, like the CPRF, lacked a clear ideological orientation: it was clearly a liberal party, but opposed some of the neo-liberal policies pursued by the reformers; but it was also a social democratic party, although one with few links to the working class. The party seemed locked in a trajectory of gentle decline, hence following the 1999 election it accepted some form of alliance with the Union of Right Forces. Of the other groups, only a limited number could be considered parties as such. One of these was the Liberal Democratic Party of Russia (LDPR), headed by the flamboyant Vladimir Zhirinovsky. In the early 1990s the party was rampantly nationalist and imperialist, in the sense that it sought to recreate the USSR, but by the end of the decade it had lost some of its fire and, indeed, had become a steady supporter of the government in the Duma.

The most significant of the new parties that emerged out of the 1999 parliamentary elections was Unity. Party forms of representation have traditionally been over-shadowed in Russia by the predominance of conglomerate pseudo-parties like Our Home is Russia (NDR), Fatherland-All Russia (OVR) and now Unity. Unity was neither a modern political party nor a mass movement but was instead a political association made to order by power elites to advance their interests. There was the danger that Unity would become the core of a new type of hegemonic party system in which patronage and preference would be disbursed by a neo-*nomenklatura* class of state officials loyal to Putin. Unity could become the core of a patronage system of the type that in July 2000 was voted out of office in Mexico after 71 years.

We have noted above that after every election there were plans to change electoral legislation. Following the December 1999 election attention focused on campaign financing, the role of the media in elections and the structure of political parties. The question of party financing remained a crucial one. The financing of the CPRF in particular aroused considerable speculation. In the 1995 election the party received considerable infusions of cash as the banks and corporations hedged their bets on the outcome, but by 1999 the CPRF was perceived as less of a threat, and its income fell commensurately. The party was forced to find alternative sources of support. It might be noted that of intake of 450 deputies in December 1999, 60 were businessmen, of whom eight represented the CPRF, a party that was allegedly hostile to capitalism. Changes in legislation in 2000 proposed that parties would have to present an annual financial account reporting the amount received from donors and be open to auditors to examine their financial activities. Federal assistance would no longer come before elections but be paid afterwards in proportion to the number of votes won. Changes to the role of the media sought to draw a clearer line between information and commentary in an election campaign. As for the nature of parties, the key point here was to try to reduce the number of parties by several orders of magnitude.

The law on political parties became part of the larger package of changes to the electoral system. Moser (1998) notes the effects of Russia's dual electoral system, favouring parties that can combine both high name recognition with local organisation. The main party that fitted this bill, as we have seen was the CPRF, allowing it to maintain strong representation in the Duma while consolidating its position in a number of so-called 'red belt' regions. In a situation of party and candidate proliferation (in December 1995 an average of 12 candidates fought for every single-mandate seat) the more disciplined and organised CPRF was able to win in single-mandate seats with a small proportion of the total vote. Governors themselves favoured a revision of Russia's electoral law to increase the number of deputies elected directly from local constituencies, something that would allow them greater leverage than the party-list system.

If parties struggled to define their identities in postcommunist Russia, other social organisations found the task no easier. The USSR had been an 'over-industrialised' economy, and now in the 1990s the proportion of GDP coming from the production of goods fell from 60 to 40 per cent, while the service sector, including trade and transport, rose sharply. Total employment in the same period fell from 72 million to 63 million, with the fall sharpest in the industrial sector, falling a third from 21 to 14 million (*Goskomstat,* 1999, p. 81). In these conditions it was not surprising that trade union membership declined, especially since it was no longer compulsory. In 1992 FITUR boasted that it represented 60 million Russian workers, but even then that claim was doubted and now no more than 40 million are union members. At the same time, their role changed. In free market conditions strikes are one of the main weapons of the labour movement, yet the number of workers involved in a strike in any one year remained remarkably low, hovering at the half million mark except for a peak of nearly a million in 1997 (ibid., p. 93). Remarkably, in May 2000 no strikes at all were recorded. In conditions of dramatic economic decline, huge wage inequality and mass impoverishment the persistence of social peace is surprising (Greskovits, 1998).

Old Soviet practices, when trade unions were part of the troika of management and party bosses to ensure the fulfilment of the five-year plan (Cook, 1997), lingered on. The defence of workers' interests played little part, but in return workers could not be sacked, however poorly they worked. This neo-Stalinist bargain, where 'the workers pretend to work and the state pretends to pay them', is today reflected in relatively low official unemployment rates. Underemployment rather than unemployment became chronic as workers and management often presented a common front against outsiders, and workers became ever more dependent on management. New independent trade unions found it difficult to break in, although they attracted members in sectors that had demonstrated solidarity and militancy in the past, like the coal miners. Reflecting the under-development of Russian parties, in the 1995 and 1999 parliamentary elections trade unions sought directly (albeit in loose electoral alliances) to achieve representation in the Duma.

Problems of Social Representation in Contemporary Russia

Democratic theory usually thinks in terms of representative democracy but it is party democracy that is most commonly meant, focusing above all on competition between parties to win votes and form government. While the age of mass parties may everywhere be in decline, the political party as a representative institution remains central to any model of democratic institutionalisation. The classical cleavage structure of modernising West European states, according to Stein Rokkan (1997), cut along lines of class/capital, religion/secularism and centre/periphery conflicts, giving rise to certain categories of parties (socialist, Christian, conservative, liberal and so on). In postcommunist Russia the lines of such a cleavage structure are blurred to the point of illegibility. Instead, identity, ideological and interest conflicts interact in unpredictable ways and mostly do not line up to reinforce each other. In fact, the very opposite appears to be the case, with political affiliations torn by cross-cutting concerns. Identity conflicts, for example, are particularly pronounced in the ethnic republics, but they are reinforced neither by economic interests nor by ideological concerns and hence remain relatively marginal. In addition, mechanisms of patronage and political clientelism are divorced from the party system (Afanas'ev, 1997), and thus one of the main factors that promotes party development elsewhere is largely absent in Russia. This may change, of course, if Putin's plans to reinforce the party dimension to Russian politics bear fruit.

How can we explain the amorphousness of Russian party development? Is there something specifically Russian inhibiting the development of an effective party system, or is the problem broader, reflecting a general crisis of party systems in mature industrial democracies? We can identify at least eight groups of factors that have inhibited the development of an effective party and representative system in Russia: the provenance of parties as part of the insurgency against the decaying communist regime; presidential patterns of politics and governance; the electoral system; parliamentary politics; Russian political culture; the regionalisation of politics; the post-totalitarian legacy of a fragmented society; and the general crisis of parties and organised interests in modern societies. Having said this, we should immediately add the caveat that the role of parties and organised interests in postcommunist Russia has been far from negligible.

The Politics of Insurgency

The formative phase of a social formation is crucial, and never more so than in the case of Russia's transition from communism. As Golosov (2000) notes, the roots of the fragmented and undeveloped party system lie in its genesis (see also Panebianco, 1998, p. 50). During *perestroika* the negative connotations of the concept of 'party' led many groups to call themselves 'unions', 'movements' or 'associations'. The fluid politics associated with the insurgency phase continued into later years, with few associations imposing rigorous membership criteria, or even maintaining membership registers. Another feature of insurgency politics was the weakness of the link between parties and political representation in legislative bodies. A great mass of deputies had been swept into the soviets as part of the democratic tide of 1990, yet once elected they lacked a structured political identity and as a mass reflected the amorphousness of the party system in its entirety. Above all, the politics of insurgency were marked by the ability of small groups and leaders to achieve victories and fame with relatively small organisational, membership and, indeed, financial, resources. Parties until well into the postcommunist era remained stamped by the formative stage and largely remained elitist organisation with a fairly small mass base and fluid organisational structures. The major legacy of the politics of insurgency, indeed, is the gulf between the elite (above all those elected to legislative bodies) and the mass membership.

Presidential Politics

The emergence of presidential government inhibited the emergence of a party system. The development of a dominant presidency is discussed elsewhere in this book (Chapter 2); here we shall only identify some of the implications for party development. The key point is that the representative system, epitomised by parties, is largely divorced from the process of forming governments. The very structure of government was inimical to the development of a party system, with the premier and cabinet chosen on a non-party basis and forced to resign their seats as deputies on appointment. The idea was to maintain the separation of powers, but this rather crude principle, typical of presidential systems, only divorced the power and representative systems from each other, and weakened the accountability and responsibility of both.

Apart from systemic factors, Yeltsin's own personal preferences played their part. Although Yeltsin on coming to power had promised to support parties, the financial and material support was relatively insignificant. Yeltsin declared himself to be above party politics, and on resigning from the CPSU in July 1990 declared that he would join no party. He missed perhaps the best opportunity to establish a presidential party in late 1991 when, following the attempted coup, his prestige and support were at their height. At his press conference on 21 August 1992 Yeltsin observed that he was often asked to create a presidential party, but he refused because 'My support is the Russian people' (*Nezavisimaya gazeta*, 22 August 1992, p. 1). In the December 1993 elections Yeltsin refused to endorse Yegor Gaidar's Russia's Choice, the successor to the Democratic Russia movement that had so loyally supported him in the past. Yeltsin's understand-able desire to be president of all Russians, however, only strengthened the tendency towards charismatic above-party leadership that freed him of all constraints. Yeltsin later toyed with the idea of creating a presidential party, but never gave any firm indication of how this was to be achieved. Instead, as we have seen, various quasi-political 'parties of power' emerged to provide the presidency with parliamen-tary and structured popular support. In the event they were unable to provide the executive with cohesion, and political power remained fragmented.

Only with the emergence of Unity did the 'party of power' strategy really work, but by then Yeltsin had given way to Putin, and it was the latter who enjoyed the support of a loyal majority in the Duma. Unity was registered formally as a political party in June 2000 and at that time claimed a membership of 186 000, making it second only to the CPRF in size. Putin's ideological syncretism meant that he appealed to voters across the political spectrum, and once elected allowed the CPRF to be brought in effectively as part of the governing coalition. The presidency's sponsorship of attempts to create a two- or three-party system from above, however, was in danger of reducing all parties to little more than shades of a single 'party of power'.

The Electoral System

The institutional design of an electoral system lies at the heart of a new democratic system (Gel'man, 2000). The mixed plurality and proportional electoral system used in Russia has certain political consequences, some of which have been noted above. The key point is that competitive elections played a significant role in adapting the nascent party system to the conventions of party politics. This may appear obvious, but with the country on the verge of civil war in 1993 the role of elections in stabilising the political situation should not be underestimated. However, while elections may be necessary, they are not a sufficient condition for democracy, and the very weakness of

Russia's party system allowed executives partially to co-opt the electoral process for their own ends. Elections make parties, but party affiliation made little difference to the vote in majoritarian districts. Parties did not fight the majority of seats in the constituencies. In all three Duma elections in the 1990s a large proportion of all constituency deputies were elected as independent deputies rather than by party affiliation, and this was then reflected in the relative fluidity of factions in the Duma. This fluidity was exacerbated by the lack of continuity in the choice of parties offering themselves up for votes from one election to the next. Instead of parties in search of an electorate, we appeared to have an electorate in search of parties.

Parliamentary Politics

Just as the engineers of democracy sought to mould the electoral system to promote party development, so, too, there were attempts to shape the working arrangements of the State Duma in 1993 to create cohesive party groups. The weakness of party groups in the 1990–3 Congress of People's Deputies was widely considered to be one reason for it having been captured by radical rejectionists. In the Duma there are strict rules about the minimum number of deputies required to form a group (35), and only those parties crossing the five per cent threshold have the right to call themselves party factions. The formation of parliamentary committees on the party principle was yet another attempt to kick-start the party system. According to Mikhail Mityukov, the chair of the presidential commission on legislative proposals and the main author of the regulations governing the work of the new assembly, the rules prevented the emergence of a new Khasbulatov, and by focusing on party factions promoted the development of a party system (*Izvestiya*, 24 December 1993, pp. 1–2). The chair of the Duma and the vice-chairs were to belong to different factions, and instead of a Presidium there was a Conference made up the chair and vice-chairs and delegates from factions and groups with voting power in proportion to the size of the faction, and the Conference's role was to be purely organisational. The rules, moreover, allowed a faction or bloc to recall a deputy and replace him or her with one further down the party list.

The rules governing Duma organisation are designed to support party politics, but these attempts were undermined by the nature of Russia's political system. The upper house of the Federal Assembly, the Federation Council, in the form in which it existed up to 2000, was based not on party but on regional representation. Extensive individual cooptation, personalised ties and a relatively fluid party system meant that the distinction between parties in government and those in opposition was unclear. A syncretic political process predominated. The CPRF had tacitly supported Chernomyrdin's government on several occasions, and during Primakov's premiership from September 1998 to May 1999 the CPRF in effect became part of the governing coalition. Voters, understandably were often confused by the 'choice' offered to them, and even more so since the relationship between parties and the government, let alone the government and the presidency, was not always clear. Various extraconstitutional 'accords' and 'fora' were established as part of Yeltsin's attempts to incorporate active political forces into a dynamic and mobile form of consensus politics run firmly from the top. It appeared that Yeltsin, quite simply, did not understand the principles on which a multiparty system operates.

Russian Political Culture

It is often asserted that Russian political culture is hostile to the emergence of political parties because of a popular commitment to collective values and a predilection for a single authoritative source of political authority (Biryukov and Sergeev, 1993). As Stephen Welch (1993) has pointed out, however, political culture is far more malleable than sometimes suggested, and in place of the traditional static approach instead suggests a dynamic model stressing the evolutionary dynamics of political culture. This is illustrated by the case of America where, as Richard Hofstadter (1970) argued, the political culture was originally hostile to parties but gradually a party system became accepted. In Russia, too, traditional appeals to collectivism, both of the traditional Russian sort (*sobornost'*) or of the Soviet communist variety, do not necessarily undermine ideological cleavages and policy preferences taking the form of partisan alignment. The experience of over a decade of free multiparty elections suggests that the Russian voter is as sensitive to party affiliations as electors in any other country even though, as we have suggested above, this may not take the form of voting for the same party from one election to the next. The extraordinary stability of electoral preferences, with roughly a third of the vote from one election to the next supporting the left nationalist opposition, and a fifth the liberal democrats, suggests the presence of the political base for a two-party system.

Regionalism and Politics

The Russian party system is highly fragmented and its reach is partial. Historically, parties have emerged as the coalition of local or sectional interests that have only later been aggregated at the national level. In postcommunist Russia regionally-based parties are weak and have minimal impact on national politics, while parties based on ethnic politics are wholly delegitimated. Most party formation in Russia has been top down, only reinforcing the tendency for much of politics to be conducted outside the framework of party politics, whether national or local. One of the reasons for this is the fragmentation of political space itself. Under Yeltsin a rich variety of regional political systems and regimes emerged, ranging from the democratic to the outright authoritarian, and national parties had to accommodate themselves to local circumstances. Local name recognition and political capital derived from non-partisan sources are often as important as organisation in regional elections.

Gubernatorial elections repeatedly demonstrate the lack of correlation between national elections and those held on the regional level. Although the CPRF enjoys the advantages of a national organisation, it is unable to dominate the political life of even 'red belt' regions. The CPRF is not the source of patronage or advancement, even where its governors identify with it. The communist governor of Voronezh, Ivan Shabanov, for example, insisted that no party would enjoy any privileges in his administration, much to the distress of local communists who had hoped to enjoy the spoils of victory. A similar pattern was repeated elsewhere. In Volgograd region under communist governor Nikolai Maksyuta, for example, communists complained that there were too few comrades in his administration. Political parties there and elsewhere remain underdeveloped and out of the loop of power and patronage.

In addition, regional parties appeared unconnected with ideologies. Although proclaiming an anti-market ideology, the CPRF in the regions accepted that the triumph of capitalism was irrevocable. As one analyst noted:

Ideologies are merely a kind of political label – tools in the struggle for a place in the capitalist sun. Group identification arises not from a common system of values but from a pragmatic assessment of the advantages or disadvantages of occupying this or that niche in the political market (*Prism*, vol. 6, no. 9, part 4, 2000).

There were greater incentives for regional elites to exploit personal connections and to cultivate local sponsors than to devote their energies to the long-term strategy of building up party organisations. In polarised national elections, moreover, like that for the presidency in 1996, regional leaderships were able to counteract any organisational advantages that the CPRF's candidate, Zyuganov, may have enjoyed. In the first round Zyuganov won in 45 regions, but by the second round this had declined to 31 (with a decisive victory in only 19 of these). This was even more accentuated in the 2000 presidential elections, where Zyuganov won in only three regions. Putin's attempts to homogenise Russia's political and legal space will in all probability create a more auspicious environment for the development of a national party system. The emergence of Unity as the putative presidential party has the potential to transform the Russian party scene by bringing together power and electoral maximisation strategies of governing elites while provoking the counter-mobilisation of oppositional parties on a national scale. A classic two-party system may emerge.

The Post-Totalitarian Society

Whereas in most postcommunist Central European and Baltic countries functioning national party systems based on the classic left-right division have consolidated themselves, in Russia, where communism lasted much longer and with greater intensity, only a glimmer of such a consolidation is evident. The legacy of the unprecedented concentration of political power and claims to ideological predominance by the CPSU provided an inauspicious terrain for parties to claim a share in power. We have noted the popular 'anti-party' mood, but the problem was deeper. The deceptive ease with which the Soviet regime fell masked the resilience of the former structures, both formal (for example, the *nomenklatura* elite) and informal (mafia-type structures). In postcommunist countries political and social structuration takes distinctive forms. Traditional social institutions, groups and practices are deeply embedded despite the formal change of political regime, and new social forces and democratic social institutions (above all political parties) remain superficial. Classic theories of party development connected particular interests with party alignment, but Russia's post-totalitarian social structure blurred the link between party choice and socio-economic structure. However, the correlation existed, as evidenced for example by the consistent support of the

agrarian sector for the CPRF and of young upwardly mobile urba-
nites for Yabloko and other liberal parties.

The weakness of the state and Yeltsin's personalised style of rule,
moreover, encouraged the development of a type of mimetic pluralism where political bargaining took informal forms and subverted
institutionalised patterns of interest aggregation. Political integration
tended to bypass political parties, and mechanisms whereby parties
can be integrated into the governmental process remain undeveloped.
The mass mobilisation that does take place is derived not from social
cleavages but by the organisational capacity of 'political machines'
(Gel'man and Golosov, 1998). In short, the postcommunist psychological atmosphere, social structure and political processes inhibited
party development. Socio-economic and other social interests acted
directly on the state without the mediation of traditional 'gatekeeper'
organisations like parties. In these circumstances the running of
'party' elections in an atomised and essentially 'non-party' country
could not but have perverse consequences. Few parties represented
the interests of specific social groups, although gradually programmatic crystallisation has taken place and the outlines of a traditional
political spectrum along which party align themselves is beginning
to emerge.

The General Crisis of Parties and Partisan Representation

Party development in Russia reflects only in more extreme form what
some have identified as the 'unfreezing', if not general crisis, of parties
in European politics (Inglehart, 1984). The shift from materialist to
post-materialist preferences in the value system of voters and the
apparent decline in the role of parties as such, eclipsed by new forms
of participation such as social movements and alternative forms of
political communication (such as television), have given rise to a new
volatility in established party systems (Katz and Mair, 1994).
Although there is much evidence to suggest overall stability in party
systems (Ware, 1996, Chapter 7), the end of the Cold War has
promoted increased fluidity in some party systems. The 'end of
ideology', the thesis advanced by Daniel Bell (1960) and taken up
by Francis Fukuyama (1989, 1992) in the form of the 'end of history',
promoted a more managerial approach to social development, while
ideology itself, as reflected in party programmes and manifestos,
became more symbolic rather than a guide to action. Everywhere
the old cleavage between left and right was blurred, the left itself took

on new forms, and the era of mass parties appeared over. The fusion of information and communications technology has accelerated the creation of 'virtual' communities in which politics has become even more spectral, reduced to the level of images and attractions that have little relation to the realities of public life. Jacques Derrida (1994) argues that the media has rendered the professional politician 'structurally incompetent' by generating a set of demands associated with performance on air and image projection that displaces parties and parliaments. Parties in general, from this perspective, appear obsolete as vehicles of popular mobilisation, regional and national identity, individual development, and, in the Russian context, even as instruments of power. As Schmitter (1992, p. 160) has argued, substantial changes have taken place in the role and nature of parties in established Western democracies, and it would be anachronistic to assume 'that parties in today's neodemocracies will have to go through all the stages and perform all the functions of their predecessors.

Conclusion

Parties are an expression of the attempt to institutionalise the diverse interests of civil society, but in Russia's fragmented society parties only fitfully achieve this function. The formation of a structured party system is inhibited both by the intrinsic weakness of Russian civil society, by the institutional framework of government, and by the general failure to represent social interests. The Russian party system was atomised, with every category contended by numerous groups in a constant process of formation and separation. The death of the Soviet system put an end to some of the cruder forms of the antagonism between the state and society, but the gulf between power and the individual remained, and the failure of Russian political parties to fulfil the traditional role of channelling political communication between the elite and the people was the subjective aspect of a structural problem. Parties only fitfully acted as intermediaries between state and society.

We usually understand 'democratisation' as the extension of mass democracy through active citizenship. However, if we look at the stunted development of popular representation in Russia and the limited reach of parties we are forced to conclude that, though formally a democracy, the quality of democratic life in Russia remains impoverished. Political parties appear to be more a way of communicating within the elite and of mobilising ideological and political resources in intra-elite struggle rather than a way of representing social interests. The communicative functions between state and society are fulfilled more by the mass media than by parties. Nevertheless, although the strains of postcommunist transition have tested the very notion of a political party, the case remains that a structured party system is an essential element in pluralist democracy. Having missed the golden age of party politics in the late nineteenth and early twentieth centuries and having endured the trauma of one-party rule for seven decades, the crystallisation of a party system in contemporary Russia will inevitably be long drawn-out; but it is taking place.

6

Russia and the Rule of Law

GORDON B. SMITH

Since the time of Stalin, one of the consuming interests of the intelligentsia and, to some extent, the entire Soviet/Russian population has been the development of a law-based state (*pravovoe gosudarstvo*). As we have witnessed in many transitional countries, the process of developing norms of rule of law is complex. It entails overcoming the legacy of the communist past that devalued law and the norms of equal treatment and due process. It also necessitates the drafting of new legislation, including whole new codes of law. Finally, it requires the creation of new judicial and other law enforcement institutions, or the fundamental reorientation of pre-existing institutions. This chapter assesses progress toward the development of rule of law in Russia, examining each of these requisite tasks. We conclude by assessing the status of norms of rule of law in several critical areas.

Communist Legacy

Until the mid-1950s, law was seen by the leaders – whether tsars or Communist Party first secretaries – as a weapon of the state. Given the general absence of private property and the belated and short-lived development of a capitalist class in Russia prior to the revolution, law did not evolve as the natural means for protecting property nor rights and interests *vis-à-vis* the state. Rather, under Marx's formulation, law was an instrument of the state used to insure the power and privilege of the ruling class. After the revolution Lenin continued this notion, declaring, 'All law is politics'.

Lawyers were on the forefront of reforms in the 1950s, following Khrushchev's denunciation of Stalin at the 20th Party Congress. Implicit in Khrushchev's scathing attack was the intention of developing legal means for protecting citizens' rights. In December 1958 the Supreme Soviet enacted new Fundamental Principles of Criminal Law and Criminal Procedure that substantially reduced the level of repressiveness of the Soviet criminal justice system, shortened the maximum prison sentence from 25 to 15 years, and raised the age limit for juvenile offenders from 12 to 14. Although the new procedures did not go so far as to recognise a formal presumption of innocence, they did clearly establish that the burden of proof rested on the state. They also obliged state prosecutors investigating criminal acts to collect and verify all pertinent information, including evidence that might exonerate the accused.

Only modest progress was realised in elevating citizens' rights in relation to the state, however. Soviet citizens had very restricted ability to initiate civil actions against state agencies; instead they had to rely on state prosecutors to investigate their grievances under their powers of general supervision. The new Fundamental Principles of Civil Procedure enacted in 1961 permitted judicial review in a few areas of interest to average citizens: imposition of administrative fines, disputes arising from the assignment of state-owned housing, and work-related grievances. Other important areas were excluded from judicial review, such as grievances arising from health care, pensions, and education.

Before any further progress could be made in expanding citizens' ability to utilise the courts to protect their interests, the conservative Brezhnev leadership ousted Khrushchev and shifted the focus of legal reform to actions that would enhance the powers of the state, especially in combating economic crimes such as fraud, theft of socialist property, and the padding of accounts and plan-fulfilment records. The Constitution of 1977 reaffirmed the central role of the party and reinforced the interests of the state, but did little to expand the rights of citizens. For example, the constitutional provision granting freedom of speech, press, association, assembly, and public meetings was preceded by the caveat, 'In accordance with the people's interests and for the purpose of strengthening and developing the socialist system'. Under Brezhnev the crackdown on dissidents resumed after the relatively relaxed Khrushchev years. Among the thousands of intellectuals arrested or banished on trumped-up charges were Andrei Sinyavsky, Yuli Daniel, Alexander Solzhenitsyn and Andrei Sakharov.

Gorbachev was the first General Secretary of the CPSU since Lenin to have a university education and, like Lenin, he was trained as a lawyer. His agenda for legal reform did not begin to emerge until mid-1988, however. Speaking to the 19th Party Conference, Gorbachev called for the development of a legal system in which 'the supremacy of law is ensured in fact' and proclaimed his intention of creating a socialist *Rechtsstaat*. According to Soviet jurists, in order for the rule of law to exist the following principles had to be observed:

- The rights of individuals must be paramount. The 19th Party Conference's resolution 'On Legal Reform' called for 'the legal protection of the individual and secure guarantees of the Soviet people's political, economic and social rights and freedoms'
- The role of law in Soviet society must be enhanced. All activities must take place within the strict framework of the law. The powers of the CPSU and legislative, executive and judicial bodies should be made explicit
- State and party officials and bodies must be made subordinate to the law. Judicial officials and law enforcement agencies must enjoy independence from the party and state agencies
- A meaningful system of constitutional law must be developed. A constitutional court must be established with full enforcement powers, including the power to annul legislation and administrative acts that are deemed unconstitutional
- Laws must be fairly and uniformly enforced

Following the 19th Party Conference commissions began drafting an impressive array of laws designed to achieve the goals that Gorbachev had articulated. Among them were new codes of criminal law and property, land and leasing, the judicial and tax system, the enterprise and pensions, constitutional review and the status of judges, the press, the police, and freedom of conscience. Much of this legislation was enacted by the USSR Supreme Soviet over the course of the next three years. However, as in the 1950s, progress was slowed by the bureaucratic might of the Procuracy, the KGB, the Ministry of Internal Affairs and the party itself. The progress of legal reform was also retarded by the destabilizing effects of the Gorbachev reforms. As the country fell deeper and deeper into crisis, the scope of reformist discourse broadened from expanding citizens' rights within the context of the Soviet legal system to a fundamental break with communism. The August 1991 attempted coup greatly accelerated the political disintegration of the USSR. In the process, the aspirations of legal reformers for a democratic society governed by Western norms of rule of law gained widespread support.

The legacy of communism in the legal sphere was largely one of unfulfilled expectations. Incremental reforms had been undertaken to reduce state repression, arbitrariness, and extra-judicial procedure. Progress toward a more fundamental and sweeping reform was resisted by powerful conservative vested interests. However, other legacies of communism – the extensive provision of secondary and post-secondary education, universal literacy and the rise of a stable, urban middle class – created the prerequisites and fostered expectations for a society governed by rule of law.

Drafting the Rules

Emerging from the ashes of the USSR, the Russian Federation under Boris Yeltsin began the laborious task of building a new legal infrastructure. The first item of business was the drafting of a new constitution to replace the 1978 constitution of the now-defunct RSFSR. Throughout 1992 and most of 1993 several draft constitutions were circulated and widely discussed and debated. A version drafted by Yeltsin's advisors called for a strong presidential republic, while the parliament sponsored a draft vesting most power in the legislative branch with a figurehead president. A third draft, developed by a commission led by the constitutional scholar and deputy Oleg Rumyantsev, called for a federal republic with a president and a new bicameral parliament. The debate between Yeltsin and the parliament over various constitutional drafts culminated with Yeltsin's decree disbanding the Supreme Soviet and the use of the armed forces to drive his opponents from the White House in October 1993. By overcoming his opponents, Yeltsin cleared the way for passage of a new constitution in December 1993. That constitution, not surprisingly, incorporated most of the provisions of the earlier 'presidential' draft.

The Duma, which was also elected in December 1993, worked closely with President Yeltsin over the course of the next two years to enact more than 185 major pieces of legislation. During this period, new or greatly revised laws or codes were passed relating to criminal law and procedure, commercial law, tax law, family law, maritime law, administrative law, environmental protection law, and laws on the judiciary, the Procuracy, the police, and political parties. The years 1994–5 represent the most active period of legislative reform in the history of Russia. Nevertheless, there were some notable gaps in the legislative drafting. For example, the rapid privatisation of state industrial, commercial, and agricultural assets was widely perceived by Russian citizens as benefiting only a relative few. Before a law on privatisation of land could be enacted, Russian nationalistic pressures rose to block land sales. Negotiations between the parliament and president over the new land code collapsed in 1998 and were resumed in 2000; however, major differences remain. In the meantime, several regions and republics have taken the initiative to recognise private ownership of all types of land.

In other instances, it was not the absence of law, rather the fluidity of laws that stymied fundamental reforms. For example, the laws on taxes have changed radically over the years since 1992, making it virtually impossible for businesses (whether domestic or foreign) to assess risks and opportunities. The absence of a stable and predictable tax system is a primary cause of the loss of billions of dollars in foreign investment in 1998, but this trend has now been reversed.

'If You Build It, They Will Come'

The transition from communism experienced in Russia, rather than expanding the state's capacity to make and implement policy, has resulted in the creation of political vacuums, institutional malaise, chaos, and lawlessness. As the state has withdrawn from vast areas of social, economic, and political life, we have witnessed an erosion of the power of the state and a lack of consensus about what the proper boundaries of state activity should be in the new Russia. The principal problem confronting the Russian government since 1992 has been how to go about creating new powerful, effective political institutions to fill these vacuums.

In the previous section we noted the extensive efforts to rewrite Russian codes and laws to reflect the new realities of the postcommunist Russian Federation. However, laws and codes alone are not sufficient for the rule of law to exist. Equally necessary for a functioning legal system in a civil society is the creation of institutions, such as courts, bailiffs, police, and other agencies to implement and enforce legislation. These institutions must have sufficient authority and independence to ensure fair and uniform enforcement of laws without political intrusion. They also require sufficient funds, equipment, personnel, and other resources to function effectively. Below we summarise progress toward strengthening various judicial and law enforcement agencies in Russia.

Constitutional Court

The Constitutional Court was first established in July 1991, prior to the break-up of the USSR. The Court was to be comprised of 15 judges elected by the parliament for a limited life term (until age 65). Initially, the parliament could agree on only 13 of the nominees; the other two seats remained vacant. Modelled on the constitutional courts of Western Europe, especially the German Federal Constitutional Court, the Court is the only body empowered to review constitutional questions. Decisions of the court are final and not subject to appeal. Initially, the Constitution Court, under the leadership of Chief Justice Valerii Zorkin, carefully screened the cases it heard to avoid sharp clashes with either the parliament or the presidency. However, by 1993, Zorkin and several other justices had clearly aligned themselves with the parliament against President Yeltsin. On 17 October 1993, two weeks after the shoot-out at the White House, President Yeltsin issued a decree suspending the Constitutional Court pending the adoption of a new constitution.

The Constitution of 1993 and a new 'Law on the Constitutional Court', enacted on 21 July 1994, enlarged the court to 19 members. In order to handle the rapidly increasing caseload, the new law permitted the court to handle multiple cases simultaneously. Under the provisions of the new law, judges no longer serve for life; rather they have 12-year terms and may serve until age 70.

In contrast to the previous court, the present Constitutional Court of the Russian Federation has tended to focus on cases involving the rights of the individual. In the period 1995–6, more than 70 per cent of the cases considered dealt with individual rights, while only 12 per cent dealt with separation of powers and 17.6 per cent dealt with questions of federalism. By contrast, in 1992 and 1993, cases involving questions of separation of powers and federalism each accounted for 31 per cent of the cases heard and individual rights cases represented only 38 per cent. It is evident that the court is carefully directing its attention to the types of cases that are likely to build its legitimacy and solidify its place in the judicial system, while avoiding conflicts with other branches of government and with the powerful regional governors. One of the justices, Boris Ebzeev, candidly observes: 'The Court must avoid getting involved in current political affairs, such as partisan struggles. ... We must revive our prestige and status. We must find a stable niche in the state machinery.'

Under President Putin, the Constitutional Court appears to be adopting a more assertive role again, especially in cases that relate to Russia's federal system. Consistent with Putin's desire to rein in the republics and regions, in July 2000 the Constitutional Court ruled that the constitutions of several republics violated the Basic Law of the Russian Federation. It is a good sign for the future of federal relations in Russia that these regions have acknowledged the Court's decision and have begun revising their constitutions accordingly.

The 1996 Law on the Judicial System of the Russian Federation enabled the constituent republics and regions of the federation to establish charter courts. These courts, which have been created in eight regions, have exclusive jurisdiction to determine whether the laws and regulations promulgated by their respective executive and legislative authorities and local governmental bodies are consistent with the regions' constitutions or charters. The courts may rescind any such laws or nullify actions.

The Judiciary

At the lowest level of the judicial hierarchy are the city and district courts. These courts function as the courts of first instance for the vast majority of civil and criminal cases. Directly above the district courts are the courts of the republics, regions, and territories, and the cities of Moscow and St Petersburg. These courts hear cases on appeal from lower courts and also routinely serve as the courts of first instance in major cases. The provincial courts have separate chambers for civil and criminal cases.

At the pinnacle of the judicial hierarchy is the Supreme Court of the Russian Federation. The Supreme Court is charged with supervising subordinate courts and resolving disputes between them. The court regularly issues instructions to inferior courts directing them in the handling of various types of cases or pointing out mistakes and shortcomings in their practice. The Supreme Court hears cases on appeal from inferior courts and in a limited number of cases of 'exceptional importance', the court has original jurisdiction. The court includes 20 justices and 45 lay assessors and is divided into three chambers or collegia – for civil, criminal, and military cases respectively. In all three chambers cases are heard by a panel of three judges, and in cases of original jurisdiction, one judge and two lay assessors.

The Ministry of Justice administers the judicial system and is responsible for drafting relevant legislation on courts, judges, and substantive law codes. In addition, the ministry undertakes the training of judicial personnel and gathers and analyses court statistics. Recently President Putin has sought to expand the responsibilities of the Ministry of Justice. Speaking to top-level ministerial personnel in January 2000, he declared his intention of establishing a 'dictatorship of law' in Russia with the Ministry of Justice in the forefront of this effort. Specifically, he noted the necessity of expanding the Ministry's involvement in drafting legislation. He also recognised the need to enlarge the Ministry beyond its current 380 000 employees. Putin's decision to divide the Russian Federation into seven 'super-regions' further centralises judicial, procuratorial and police functions. Putin specifically challenged the Ministry of Justice to form 'a single legal space' in Russia, by bringing the regions into strict compliance with federal law.

On 1 July 1995 a new system of commercial courts was introduced, governed by a new Commercial Procedure Code. These courts replaced the former system of arbitration tribunals. The commercial courts resolve commercial disputes, including disputes involving foreign companies and foreign entrepreneurs. The jurisdiction of the commercial courts extends to a wide array of issues, including privatisation, taxes, bankruptcy, reorganisation, and administrative proceedings related to commercial activities. At the lowest level, there are 82 regional, republic and territorial commercial courts. Above these courts are ten federal commercial courts which function as courts of cassation. The Higher Commercial Court of the Russian Federation oversees the commercial courts and hears cases on appeal.

The 1993 Constitution, in Article 46, provides that 'decisions and actions (or inaction) by bodies of state authority or bodies of local self-government, public associations or officials may be appealed in court.' Article 118 refers to constitutional, civil, administrative, and criminal judicial proceedings, implying that a separate system of administrative courts was envisaged. In fact, Putin's government, together with the Supreme Court of the Russian Federation, has moved to establish a new administrative court system. Under the plan revealed by Supreme Court Chairman Vyacheslav Lebedev, 21 administrative judicial districts will be created as early as 2001 with each court staffed with 200 judges. The primary purposes of the new courts are to rein in high-handed regional officials and alleviate the large backlog of cases pending in regular district courts. The administrative courts will hear complaints about public officials, including cases questioning the constitutionality of laws and regulations passed by local and regional authorities, and cases of voters' rights. Appeals against the decisions of district administrative courts can be made to the administrative collegia of regional or republic courts and then to the Supreme Court.

At all levels, the performance of the courts today is severely hampered by shortages of personnel, antiquated facilities and equipment, and inadequate operating funds. Many local courts meet in old buildings without elevators and in which the heating and plumbing do not work properly. According to the former Minister of Justice, more than 1000 courts are located in buildings that should be condemned. Most courts do not have working photocopy machines, and even typewriters are difficult to obtain. Trials often encounter long delays due to shortages of police guards and vehicles to shuttle defendants from jail to court. Budgets are also inadequate to pay jurors for their time, to ensure their anonymity and safety, and to compensate judges adequately. Salaries of judges have not kept pace with inflation, prompting many judges to take positions in private practice or as legal consultants to private enterprises, which offer much higher salaries.

Caseloads are so heavy that long delays ranging from seven to 18 months occur. In an effort to alleviate overcrowding of the courts' dockets, President Yeltsin signed a law 'On Justices of the Peace in the Russian Federation' in December 1998. Justices of the peace, who share the same status and protections as judges in courts of general jurisdiction, may either be elected for a five-year term by the public or appointed by their respective legislative body. They consider cases that do not require lengthy proceedings: divorces not involving custody disputes or large property settlements; labour disputes resulting from late wages or severance benefit disputes; and property disputes up to 500 times the minimum monthly wage. The justices can also hear criminal cases in which the possible punishment is no more than two years incarceration.

The Procuracy

During Soviet times, the Procuracy was the most powerful legal institution, eclipsing the courts. Dating back to 1702, the Procuracy was established by Peter the Great to be 'the eyes of the tsar', to ensure that the tsar's edits were implemented throughout the empire. Although the Procuracy's powers were severely reduced during the legal reforms of 1864, the institution was resurrected by Lenin in 1922 and charged with supervising the legality of administrative officials, agencies, and citizens.

The Procuracy has long been viewed by liberal jurists and legal reformers as a bastion of conservatism. Some argue that as long as the Procuracy retains such sweeping powers, the courts will never develop the independence and status to function properly. Despite the controversy surrounding the role of the Procuracy and its powers, the 1993 Constitution made only minor changes in the institution. The constitution established the Procuracy as a single, centralised, hierarchical system of prosecutors. Some controversy arose during the drafting phase, whether procurators at the regional and local levels should report hierarchically to the Procurator-General or to the governments at their respective levels. A new 'Law on the Procuracy of the Russian Federation', enacted in 1995, settled the dispute in favour of the Procurator-General.

At the time of the drafting of the 1993 Constitution there was considerable discussion and debate over restricting the Procuracy to prosecuting criminal cases and coordinating the fight against crime. Proponents of this position wanted to strip the Procuracy of its traditionally board-ranging power of supervision (*nadzor*). Others felt that they needed to weaken the Procuracy in order to permit the courts and the Ministry of Justice to assume dominance in the evolving legal system. Rather than tackle these contentious issues, it was decided to leave out of the Constitution any listing of the Procuracy's powers and functions. These were addressed in detail in the 1995 law.

The functions of the Procuracy prescribed in the 1995 law include: supervision over implementation of laws by ministries, departments and their officials; supervision of the protection of rights and freedoms of citizens by all organisations, including private commercial establishments; supervision over the conduct of criminal investigations; supervision over places of detention and correctional facilities; prosecution of criminal cases and appealing decisions on behalf of the state; initiating civil actions, appealing court decisions arising from civil actions, and seeking arbitration decisions on behalf of the state's interests; coordinating the fight against crime; and investigating citizens' complaints. Thus, the Procuracy retained most of its traditional powers and functions. The only major responsibility lost was the supervision of the courts, which was vested in the Ministry of Justice and the Supreme Court. Supervision over the acts of private business establishments was restricted to actions that violate citizens' or human rights. The retention of the 'general supervision' powers of the Procuracy means that citizens who encounter acts of government officials that impinge on their interests or rights now have two alternative courses of relief: to the courts or lodging complaints with the Procuracy. Every year the Procuracy looks into more than one million such complaints.

The 1995 'Law on the Procuracy' also retains the Procuracy's right to supervise criminal investigations, whether they are conducted by the police, the security police or the Procuracy itself. With a staff of approximately 28 000, including some 7000 investigators, the Procuracy issues more than 400 000 arrest warrants and takes 1.2 million cases to court each year. The continued central role of the Procuracy in the Russian legal system remains a point of contention with legal reforms and liberal jurists. However, President Putin's recent centralisation of law enforcement agencies and his vigorous anti-crime campaign both indicate that the Procuracy's place in legal system will not be challenged in the near future.

The Police

Police in the Russian Federation, unlike in federal states elsewhere, report through a unified, hierarchical chain of command to the Ministry of Internal Affairs. The basic structure of the Ministry did not change radically even with the collapse of the USSR. The Ministry and its subordinate police departments in every city and region are charged with a wide array of duties: investigating crimes, apprehending criminals, supervising the internal registration system, maintaining public order, combating public intoxication, supervising parolees, and controlling traffic. Perhaps the most notorious division of the police is the OMON, a special-purpose police detachment established in 1987 to combat especially dangerous armed criminals, maintain order at public events, and counter terrorist activities. There are 117 OMON special detachments, ranging in size from fewer than 70 to more than 2000 in Moscow.

President Putin's creation of seven federal districts in mid-2000 resulted in a reorganisation of police services. Police departments no longer report to regional or local authorities and are now funded from the central treasury, giving them more autonomy to pursue cases of corruption by local or regional officials. Like other law enforcement agencies, the police suffer from inadequate resources. Police officers routinely complain about shortages of ammunition, equipment for forensic laboratories, and fuel for police vehicles. Since 1992 more than 600 000 police officers have left their jobs. Svyatoslav Golitsyn, Director of Russian Internal Affairs Ministry's Internal Security Administration, recently reported that the mass exodus of experienced officers, especially those assigned to regular operational units, has forced the Ministry to recruit young employees with insufficient professional training. According to Internal Affairs Ministry data, the Moscow police department is understaffed by approximately 5000 officers. The problem of insufficient numbers of police has been exacerbated in recent years by the proliferation of private security firms in Russia. Today there are an estimated 8000 such firms employing more than 65 000 personnel, many of whom are former police officers. Given the shortage of experienced personnel, law enforcement agencies have been forced to employ poorly trained recruits. In 1998 approximately half of Russia's 1.6 million police officers were younger than 30. The lack of training of police officers, their youth and inexperience are seen as principal causes of an alarming increase in police casualties. In 1996 approximately 300 police officers were killed and almost 600 were wounded.

The average salary for patrol officers is less than $170 per month and even at that level policemen go months with no pay or only partial pay because of the government's budgetary crisis. Wage arrears and on-the-job stress are cited as principal causes for 400 policemen who commit suicide every year.

Given these problems, it should not be surprising that some law enforcement officers succumb to accepting bribes or engaging in other forms of corruption. In 1996, 21 347 police officers were dismissed and disciplinary or criminal proceedings were instituted against 12 000. The deputy Chief of the Moscow Procuracy estimates that 60 to 80 per cent of all criminal investigators are 'on the take'. In high-profile cases against suspected mafia figures evidence is lost, witnesses change their testimony, and even judges and jurors have been threatened.

The picture that emerges from this survey of the institutional infrastructure for rule of law in Russia today is decidedly mixed. New institutions, such as the commercial courts, have been created and have proven to be very popular mechanisms for resolving citizens' disputes. The extraordinarily heavy caseloads of the regular courts and the large number of citizens' complaints investigated by the Procuracy each year testify to citizens' willingness to utilize state-sanctioned institutions for protecting their interests and rights. On the other hand, all legal institutions suffer from inadequate resources, insufficient and poorly trained personnel, minimal operating budgets, antiquated equipment, and crumbling infrastructure. These problems are having a direct negative impact on the ability of these institutions to function, which in turn erodes their public support and legitimacy. However, it is worth noting that these problems are not unique to Russia, neither are they insurmountable. Recent improvements in Russia's economy, including balancing the government budget, positive trade balances, and a recovery in economic growth all indicate that Putin's government should be able to direct increasing resources to the fight against crime and the establishment of rule of law.

We now turn to examine some of the most problematic areas in which the development of rule of law in Russia is being tested.

Criminal Procedure

The enactment of a new Code of Criminal Procedure of the Russian Federation has bogged down in partisan wrangling between the president and parliament since 1998. As a result, Russia continues to operate under the 1960 code of the RSFSR, which was substantially amended in 1992. Under the terms of that code and the Constitution, persons accused of committing criminal offences are entitled to having their cases heard by courts with the participation of jurors. They are also guaranteed the right to receive qualified legal assistance. Citizens accused of committing crimes have the right to be informed of their rights and the right to see all evidence gathered during the course of the investigation. There is now an officially-stated presumption of innocence and citizens are not obliged to testify against themselves, their spouses, or close relatives. Double jeopardy is prohibited, as is the use of evidence gathered in violation of the law. Finally, persons convicted of crimes have the right to appeal those convictions.

While these procedural rights represent important steps forward in Russian criminal procedure, their full implementation leaves much to be desired. A recent study of the Human Rights Watch group reported that in Astrakhan, Nizhnii Novgorod, Yekaterinburg, St Petersburg and Moscow during the period 1994–9 interviews with accused persons and their relatives, judges, defence attorneys and police officers revealed that police beat or torture approximately one-half of all detainees. Unfortunately, the Stalinist notion that the confession is the 'queen of evidence' continues to hold among many police officers and prosecutors in Russia today.

Under Russian criminal procedure, when a person is charged with a serious felony the investigator, procurator, or judge may chose to impose a 'measure of restraint' to prevent the accused from fleeing. Rates of pretrial detention in Russia are quite high – approximately 35 to 40 per cent of all persons charged with crimes, or 150 000 to 200 000 detainees per year. Moreover, the process of deciding whether to detain someone is highly individualised and unpredictable. A 1995 joint ruling of the Russian Procurator-General and the Minister of Internal Affairs recommend maximal application of Article 96 of the Russian criminal procedure code that makes detention automatic for a long list of offences, including some non-violent crimes. Since 1992, a person who has been detained has the right to contest, in front of a judge, the legality and reasonableness of the detention. Such hearings result in the release of the accused in only approximately 20 per cent of the cases.

Another problematic area of criminal procedure today concerns illegal searches and seizures. Both the Constitution and the Code of Criminal Procedure guarantee citizens privacy and protection against unwarranted searches. However, these guarantees are being eroded by subsequent laws and decrees. In 1998 the Constitutional Court ruled that a new 'Law on Detective and Undercover Investigatory Work' is legal. According to the court ruling, undercover investigative activity including surveillance, phone taps, videotaping and other invasions of privacy can be authorised by a judge and that those records can be kept as state secrets. The case arose when Irina Chernova, an editor of a newspaper in Volgograd, brought a suit claiming that she had been blackmailed and harassed by police who had violated her privacy. To prove her claims, she was requesting access to taped telephone conversations and videotapes that were in the possession of the local police. The Court ruled that the police were not required to release such evidence because they fell under a broad protected category of 'state secrets'.

Shortly before his resignation as president, Yeltsin signed an amendment to the 'Law on Detective and Undercover Investigative Work' extending its application to the Federal Tax Police. Previously, only the Ministry of Internal Affairs and the Federal Security Service (FSB) could conduct surveillance. Authorisations to tap telephone lines or read mail may be obtained from local and regional procurators or a court. In practice, law enforcement agencies generally prefer to obtain warrants from the procurator.

Violations of citizens' privacy have tended to increase with the rise of crime and terrorism. Crime rose in the Russian Federation in 1999 by 16 per cent over the previous year. More than three million crimes were committed, and the majority were 'especially grave in nature', including murder, armed robbery, acts of terrorism, large-scale fraud and larceny. When confronted with an alarming increase in violent crimes, it should not be surprising that local police sometimes disregard procedural protections.

Similarly, an 'Anti-Terrorism Action Plan', developed in mid-1999 by then-Prime Minister Putin in response to the apartment building bombings in Moscow, grants to the president the power to declare martial law or a state of emergency in the country. Under the terms of this plan, the president can impose curfews, suspend normal criminal procedure for searches, and detain suspects without the right to defence counsel. The most intensive application of these powers to date has been in Dagestan and Chechnya where security forces are conducting searches of individuals and their property, dwellings, vehicles; seizing documents; detaining suspects, imposing temporary bans on the free movement of vehicles and individuals, and quarantining borders.

Jury Trials

After a hiatus of 76 years, jury trials have been reintroduced in Russia on an experimental basis. The jury trial programme began in 1993 in five regions and was extended to four more districts the following year. Jury trials are available only in the most serious cases – cases involving punishment exceeding ten years incarceration or the death penalty. Defendants are given the option of having their cases heard by a jury or by a regular court, consisting of one professional judge and two lay assessors. The jury trial is overwhelmingly preferred and has significantly higher acquittal rates than do the regular courts, approximately 20 per cent compared to less than one per cent in regular trials.

In Russia the jury is composed of 12 citizens between the ages of 25 and 70. Jurors decide questions of guilt or innocence, while judges rule on questions of law and procedure. The jury deliberates in private and reaches its decision based on a majority vote, with a vote of at least seven to five necessary for conviction. It is up to the judge, guided by the Criminal Code, to set punishment; however, the jury may recommend leniency in a case.

While jury trials have enjoyed popularity with defence attorneys and persons accused of crimes, the experiment has been resisted by the Procuracy, the Ministry of Internal Affairs, and other law enforcement agencies. Conservative resistance was sufficient to stop any further extension of the 'experiment' to more regions and today there is active discussion of discontinuing jury trials altogether, despite the constitutional provision guaranteeing them to all Russian citizens. In 1998 in Ryazan region, officials petitioned the Ministry of Justice to be dropped from the jury trial experiment on the grounds that jury trials were too costly. Local authorities claimed that jury trials were costing 80 000 rubles per year, mostly in payments to jurors for missed wages.

Death Penalty

Capital punishment was widely practised in the USSR, even for some non-violent, white-collar crimes, such as embezzlement on a massive scale. During the 1980s criticism of the death penalty and its application began to be heard from human rights groups both inside and outside the Soviet Union. Foremost among its critics was the Council of Europe. As a condition for admission to the Council of Europe in 1996, President Yeltsin pledged to eliminate the death penalty within three years. However, due to the explosion of violent crime and the proliferation of mafia groups in Russia, capital punishment remains popular with many Russian citizens and with deputies in the Duma. The Duma repeatedly rejected Yeltsin's attempts to abolish the death penalty. Consequently, in 1998 Yeltsin ordered a moratorium on executions and began clemency reviews for all persons awaiting execution. Anatolii Pristavkin, Chairman of the President's Commission on Clemency, estimated that 30 per cent of death row inmates were mentally ill and that as many as 15 per cent of all death sentences were imposed on innocent persons. In 1999 more than 1000 death sentences were reviewed and commuted to life or 25 years in prison. Nevertheless, the Criminal Code of the Russian Federation still permits capital punishment for a limited number of offences. Continued observance of the moratorium on executions will depend on continued Western pressure and Putin's resolve in standing up to the Duma.

Pretrial Detention and Corrections

Other human rights concerns arise from Russia's overcrowded and under-funded penal institutions. Unquestionably the worst correctional facilities in Russia are its pretrial detention centres, which are currently holding 130 000 more inmates than they were designed to accommodate. Individual cells sometimes house more than 100 people, necessitating detainees sleeping in shifts. Rates of infection with tuberculosis, HIV, and other sexually transmitted diseases are very high. The Ministry of Internal Affairs reports that 1800 inmates are HIV positive. Unfortunately, no special facilities exist for these inmates, and most are kept in pretrial detention centres rather than being sent to correctional labour camps.

It is not uncommon for accused persons being held in detention centres for periods up to four years to confess to crimes they did not commit, so that they will be transferred to labour camps or other correctional facilities where conditions are better. In 1999 pretrial detention centres were still housing some 800 people condemned to death but who had not yet been granted clemency by the President. Some of them had been awaiting commutation of their sentences for five to eight years.

The maximum term of incarceration is 25 years although prisoners condemned to death are now having their sentences commuted to 'life in prison' by a presidential decree signed by Yeltsin in 1999. An estimated 800 prisoners are currently serving time in Russia's two prison camps specifically designed for long-term or 'life' inmates. Living and working conditions in these 'special colonies' is so hard that after ten years most of the inmates are permanently disabled and surviving 15 years is considered virtually impossible.

Given the chronic overcrowding in Russia's prisons and pretrial detention centres, the Duma voted in June 1999 to declare an amnesty for an estimated 94 000 offenders convicted of minor crimes. Other convicts serving sentences of up to five years had their remaining time cut in half. Most of those released had less than one year to serve and many were suffering from tuberculosis. Released inmates had so little money that they had difficulty returning to their homes. An estimated 8000 released prisoners were stranded in Kemerevo alone. Those sentenced prior to 1995 have lost their residency permits. Others, whose relatives have died, are now homeless.

Freedom of the Press

Article 29 of the Constitution guarantees freedom of the mass media. Since the introduction of *glasnost* by Mikhail Gorbachev in the mid-1980s, censorship has been abolished and some 13 000 new, independent newspapers and magazines have sprung up, representing every conceivable political, ethnic, or social faction. However, the federal government maintains a dominant ownership share in the major nationwide television networks.

Privatisation of the media during the Yeltsin years resulted in most television and radio stations, newspapers, and magazines being owned by large energy companies, banks, and tycoons, such as Boris Berezovsky and Vladimir Gusinsky (see Chapter 13). Berezovsky reportedly owns 49 per cent of the stock of ORT, Russia's largest television network. In addition, he owns controlling interests in TV-6, the newspaper *Nezavisimaya gazeta*, and the leading news magazine, *Ogonek*. Gusinsky's media holdings – before most of them were taken over by state interests in 2001– included 51 per cent of NTV, the only non-government television network; a radio network, *Ekho Moskvy*; the newspaper *Segodnya*; and the news magazine, *Itogi*. The concentration of so many media outlets in the hands of a few tycoons has raised concerns about the maintenance of press freedoms and potential government interference.

Gusinsky's NTV was an ardent critic of President Putin's conduct of the Chechen war and his behaviour during the Kursk submarine tragedy. NTV's popular, hard-hitting satiric programme 'Kukly' (Puppets) regularly lampoons the President. Yevgenii Kiselev, the general director of NTV, claims that he was contacted by a high Kremlin official and told to drop the puppet of Putin from the show.

In May 2000 tax police raided Gusinsky's Media-Most offices and a few days later he was briefly jailed on charges of embezzlement. Responding to an international outcry, the charges were dropped, Gusinsky was released, and fled to Spain. In exchange for not being prosecuted for tax fraud, the heavily indebted Gusinsky agreed to transfer $300 million in Media-Most property to Gazprom, a government-dominated energy company. Berezovsky has also come under pressure from the government to relinquish his stake in ORT, but so far has successfully resisted.

The fire at the Ostankino transmission tower in Moscow in August 2000 knocked out all television and radio broadcasting in the city for several days. In the wake of the fire, the government has sought to impose tougher rules on registration, licensing, license revocation, and suspension of broadcasting activities.

Another trend that has had a chilling effect on freedom of the press in Russia has been the broadening of 'state secrets', as defined in the Law on State Secrets. The law encompasses information on emergency situations, catastrophes, disasters; ecological health and demographic problems, crime, privileges, compensations and benefits granted by the state, violations of human rights, gold and hard currency reserves, the state of health of top politicians, and violations by government agencies and officials. While in practice many of these topics are reported on in the Russian media, the arrests of Alexander Nikitin, Grigorii Pasko, and Andrei Babitsky served as a reminder to journalists that the state can and will enforce protection of 'state secrets' whenever it wishes. Nikitin and Pasko were charged with divulging state secrets about environmental contamination by the Russian military. Babitsky was detained as he tried to report on the renewed fighting in Chechnya and was later charged with using a false passport.

In recent years there has been an alarming increase in violence against journalists. In the first eight months of 1998, at least nine journalists were murdered, six of whom were investigating criminal structures and corruption among government officials. During the same period, there were 66 attacks on journalists, editors, and newspaper offices.

Freedom of Religion

The Law on Freedom of Conscience and Religion, passed in September 1997, requires the registration of all religious groups in the Russian Federation. Non-orthodox groups, such as the Pentecostal Church and Jehovah's Witnesses, have experienced difficulties obtaining registration permits because local authorities consider them 'sects'. In some jurisdictions, the failure to be registered has resulted in evictions from church property.

The 1997 law also recognised conscientious objection to military service based on religious beliefs. However, in practice conscientious objectors have been prosecuted. In 1999 three members of a Jehovah's Witness church in the Kursk region were arrested and convicted to prison terms for refusing military service. The Kursk regional court ruled 'groundless' their claims that their objection to military service was based on religious belief. The court described them as members of a 'sect'.

Conclusion

This assessment of the extent to which there is rule of law in Russia today produces a decidedly mixed picture. On the one hand, Russia has largely overcome a centuries-long tradition of arbitrary and despotic rule and disregard for legal protections for the individual, especially protection from the coercive power of the state. Moreover, many of the badly needed laws giving meaning to democracy and rule of law have been passed. Finally, judicial and other institutions have been created to implement those laws. Some of these institutions, such as the commercial and magistrate courts, are proving to be popular and effective.

On the other hand, the courts and law enforcement agencies have been severely hampered by inadequate resources, decaying infrastructure, personnel shortages, and insufficient public and governmental support. The rapid rise of violent crime, increasing instances of terrorism and widespread official corruption inevitably push public policy toward stringent 'law and order' measures that may reverse some of the gains Russia has achieved over the past decade. When President Putin speaks of a 'dictatorship of law', Russians speculate which element will be the more dominant – dictatorship or law?

The challenge for Western observers is to temper our assessment with a broader historical perspective. Norms of rule of law evolved gradually over centuries in European and North American democracies. Although these societies set a world standard for human rights and rule of law, problems remain with the death penalty, overcrowded prisons, insuring equal justice, and preserving civil liberties. We should remind ourselves that 'rule of law' is not an absolute, rather it is a relative concept in any society. The question is not whether there is rule of law in Russia, but how well are the norms of rule of law being realised. From this perspective, Russia's progress in dramatically improving rule of law in the past decade is quite impressive.

The immediate challenge facing Putin's government is to reassert the state's rightful role in maintaining law and order, curbing crime and corruption, protecting normal legal commerce, enforcing contracts, guaranteeing public safety, and the humane treatment of detainees and incarcerated people, but to do so without succumbing to the temptation to undermine individual liberties essential in a society of laws. Perhaps the most positive factor working to insure that Russia succeeds in this complex endeavour is the fact that all of the critical actors – President Putin, the Russian people, the press, and even the tycoons – have a vested interest in building a society governed by rule of law.

7

From Federalisation to Recentralisation

JAMES HUGHES

The existence of the Russian Federation is, in a sense, an anachronism. It is the exception to the rule since the other communist federal states in Europe disintegrated as a result of the fall of communism in 1989–91. The three federal states – the USSR, Czechoslovakia and Yugoslavia – fragmented into numerous entities, 22 of which so far have achieved international recognition as independent states. This pattern suggests to some that the combination *democratising state/ multinational society/federal institutions* is 'subversive' (Bunce, 1999), and certainly not one that is 'usable' (Linz and Stepan, 1996) for democratic state-building in a transitional regime. How and why, then, did Russia manage to reconfigure its federal system?

Defining Federalism

We should clarify, at the outset, whether the terms 'federation' and 'federalism' are applicable in the Russian context. For much as with the term 'democracy', a state may be a nominal federation without operationalising federalism as an organising principle for government. The key distinguishing features of a federal state from a decentralised unitary system are the jurisdictional autonomy of different constituent units and a constitutionally defined separation of powers adjudicated by a higher court. These are the core elements, though there is immense variation in what political scientists term 'intergovernmental relations' – the fiscal arrangements for revenue sharing, conditional and unconditional grants, equalisation arrangements, and the political bargaining which may involve all units collectively, separately, or as blocs.

In federal states government is spatially multi-level and operates according to a principle of 'shared sovereignty' or, at its most basic form, 'self-rule and shared-rule' (Elazar, 1997). Key powers (defence, foreign relations, commerce, finance) will be pooled to centralised federal institutions, usually including a bicameral parliament, while other powers will be reserved to the jurisdiction of the territorial governments. As a system that institutionalises power-sharing, federalism has been frequently chosen as a conflict-regulation mechanism in deeply divided societies in order to protect territorialised minorities. Stepan distinguishes between 'coming together federalism' (as in the USA), 'holding together federalism' (India, Belgium and Spain), and 'putting together federalism' (the USSR). Depending on their institutional features he sees federal states as falling along a spectrum between poles that are 'demosconstraining' or 'demos enabling' (Stepan, 1999, pp. 20–4).

There is general agreement that the Soviet Union lay at the far end of the 'demosconstraining' side of the spectrum and was only a 'nominal' or 'quasi' federation in terms of the operation of its institutional architecture. The Soviet 'federal' constitutions of 1924, 1936 and 1977 created and developed an elaborate institutional veneer, with Russia as a sub-federation within the USSR. Real power, however, resided in the Communist Party of the Soviet Union, which was not organised on a federal basis but rather on the Leninist principle of 'democratic centralism'. The Soviet federal state structure, consequently, was essentially a 'rubber stamp' for decisions taken by the Communist Party. Thus the USSR and RSFSR had all the attributes of federalism but none of the substance. This is not to say that there was not lower-level input into decision-making or lower-level autonomy in practice. In fact, there was a growing trend in the post-Stalin era for increased autonomy of decision-making by republican and regional elites (Bahry, 1987). In the absence of meaningful federal institutions and courts, however, lower-level decisional autonomy is something quite distinct from federalism.

There is a strong argument that the ethnified federal institutional structure of the Soviet Union, termed 'institutionalised multinationality', contributed to the breakdown of Soviet authoritarianism (Brubaker, 1996). Stalin's USSR Constitution of 1936 defined the Soviet ethnic hierarchy and reformulated its territorialisation for fifty years. When democratising pressures were unleashed by Gorbachev in the second half of the 1980s, and accompanied by his undermining of the Communist Party's will for coercion, the largely symbolic ethnified federal Soviet structure was activated as a natural platform for elite mobilisation of a hitherto deeply moribund ethnic nationalism. There was also, undoubtedly, a secession 'contagion' effect on the Soviet Union from the revolutions in Eastern Europe. A kind of *matreshka* or nested-doll bidding game resulted in a 'war of sovereignties' between the various federal units and Gorbachev's USSR government in 1989–91. Gorbachev's final bid to reconfigure the USSR into a more confederal arrangement by the Novo-Ogarevo Agreement of May 1991 (the so-called '9 + 1 agreement') was undermined by the failed August 1991 putsch. Why did the USSR's collapse not trigger a parallel disintegration of Russia? Russia, after all, was as multiculturally diverse (with some 140 ethno-linguistic groups) and had the same ethnified federal structure as the USSR. It was equally subject to contagion effects and sovereignty demands from its own federal units, in particular its own 'ethnic' republics.

Perhaps, the state that emerged in post-Soviet Russia was not a 'real' federation at all, despite its label. The Soviet nomenclature of Russian Soviet Federated Socialist Republic (RSFSR) was changed formally to Russian Federation on 25 December 1991, with effect from 1 January 1992. Whether and when nominal Soviet federal institutions were empowered in a 'federal' way in Russia is much less easy to define. Nevertheless, the fact that Russia's territorial integrity has been preserved and has been challenged by only one major ethnic secessionist conflict, that of Chechnya, sets it apart from other communist-era federations. The federal structure as it now stands under the Russian constitution is set out in Table 7.1.

There are four main explanations as to why the disintegration of Russia did not occur in the 1990s. Firstly, there were structural *limiting conditions* against the emergence of ethnic separatism. Secondly, there was a process of experimentation with the whole federal *institutional design* in 1991–3 in an attempt to manage the demands for greater autonomy while the thornier issues of separatism that were most serious in just two republics, Tatarstan and Chechnya, were continually postponed. Thirdly, from late 1993 the experimentation changed as the Yeltsin administration focused on a more selective federal institutional design to manage the demands from the most powerful recalcitrant republics and regions. A hierarchical framework of *bilateral power-sharing treaties* between the federal government and republics and regions was developed. The treaties were natural off-shoots of the institutional changes that had occurred at the federal centre after the violent events of October 1993 and Yeltsin's imposition of strong presidential rule in the December 1993 constitution. Fourthly, Yeltsin's management of federal relations was inextricably linked with the nature of his presidential 'system', which rested more on his charismatic authority than constitutional provision. Yeltsin's presidentialism reflected his preference for the soft institutional constraints of informal patrimonial networks, and this was fully evident in the new executive *patrimonial federalism* that developed from early 1994 based on the bilateral treaties. Patrimonial federalism was the key to the mutually agreed accommodations with President Mintimer Shaimiev of Tatarstan, President Murtaza Rakhimov of Bashkortostan and President Mikhail Nikolaev of Sakha. Equally, however, it proved to be the main stumbling block to an accommodation with the other significant challenge to an integral Russian Federation – President Dzhokar Dudaev's secessionist Chechnya.

Limiting Conditions for Ethnic Separatism

Demography

One of the most potent elements making for separatism is the presence of a territorially concentrated and dissatisfied minority group. Although Russia's titular ethnic republics account for 29 per cent of the territory of the federation, this spatial significance is not matched by demographic presence. An important force for territorial cohesion in Russia, therefore, is the high level and spatial spread of Russian ethnic homogeneity. At the time of the 1989 census Russians constituted a bare majority (50.8 per cent) of the USSR's 286.7 million population. In contrast, in the Russia Federation ethnic Russians were an overwhelming majority (81.5 per cent) of the 147 million population. Of the 88 constituent units of the Russian Federation in late 1991, 31 had a titular ethnic designation, of which 20 were republics and the rest autonomous districts. Of these only four (Ossetia, Tuva, Chechnya, Chuvashia) had an absolute majority of the titular ethnic group. In three republics (Tatarstan, Kabardino-Balkaria and Kalmykia) the titular ethnic group constituted a simple majority. For example, the largest ethnic minority in the Russian Federation, the Tatars (6.6 million), are a minority within their own

TABLE 7.1 *Russia's republics and regions (according to the 1993 Constitution)*

REPUBLICS (21)

Republic of Adygeya	Ingush Republic	Republic of Marii El
Altai Republic	Karbardino-Balkar Republic	Republic of Mordovia
Republic of Bashkortostan	Republic of Kalmykia-Khalmg-Tangch	Republic of North Ossetia
Republic of Buryatia	Karachai-Cherkess Republic	Republic of Sakha (Yakutia)
Chechen Republic	Republic of Karelia	Republic of Tatarstan
Republic of Dagestan	Khakass Republic	Republic of Tuva
Chuvash Republic	Republic of Komi	Udmurt Republic

KRAIS OR TERRITORIES (5)

Altai Krai	Krasnodar Krai	Primorskii Krai
Khabarovsk Krai	Krasnoyarsk Krai	

OBLASTS OR REGIONS (46)

Amur Oblast	Kursk Oblast	Samara Oblast
Arkhangel Oblast	Leningrad Oblast	Saratov Oblast
Astrakhan Oblast	Lipetsk Oblast	Smolensk Oblast
Belgorod Oblast	Magadan Oblast	Sverdlovsk Oblast
Bryansk Oblast	Moscow Oblast	Tambov Oblast
Chelyabinsk Oblast	Murmansk Oblast	Tomsk Oblast
Chita Oblast	Nizhnii Oblast	Tula Oblast
Irkutsk Oblast	Omsk Oblast	Tver Oblast
Ivanovo Oblast	Orel Oblast	Tyumen Oblast

Kaliningrad Oblast
Kaluga Oblast
Kamchatka Oblast
Kemerovo Oblast
Kirov Oblast
Kostroma Oblast
Kurgan Oblast

Orenburg Oblast
Penza Oblast
Perm Oblast
Pskov Oblast
Rostov Oblast
Ryazan Oblast
Sakhalin Oblast

Ulyanovsk Oblast
Vladimir Oblast
Volgograd Oblast
Vologda Oblast
Yaroslavl Oblast

FEDERAL CITIES ENJOYING STATUS EQUIVALENT TO A REGION (2)

Moscow
St Petersburg

AUTONOMOUS REGION (1)

Jewish Autonomous Oblast

AUTONOMOUS DISTRICTS (10)

Komi-Permyak
Koryak

Taimyr
Ust-Orda Buryat

Agin Buryat
Chukchi
Evenk
Khanty-Mansi
Nenets
Yamal-Nenets

titular ethnic homeland, the Republic of Tatarstan (Tatars are 48 per cent of the population, Russians 43 per cent). In 12 republics ethnic Russians are an absolute majority or the majority group. It is not, therefore, simply numerical superiority at the state level that makes ethnic Russian homogeneity such an important factor in limiting ethnic separatism, but also the spatial dispersion of Russians in strength throughout the bulk of the territory of the federation. Moreover, the spatial spread of Russians is not a recent phenomenon of 'settler colonialism' but occurred as a historically gradual development linked to Russian imperial expansion from the mid-sixteenth century, and the Tsarist and Soviet modernisation policies from the late nineteenth century onward.

This is not to underestimate the accumulating evidence for 'ethnification' or nationalising policies in these republics ('Tatarisation' or 'Bashkirisation'), which may in time accentuate the ethno-national cleavage. It would be an oversimplification, however, to assume that the ethnic cleavage is always drawn against Russians. The Bashkirs are more concerned by the presence of the large Tatar minority (about one-third of the total population) in Bashkortostan than by ethnic rivalry with Russians. Baskortostan's language law of 1999 illustrates this point. The population of Bashkortostan is only 20 per cent Bashkir, ethnic Russians account for 40 per cent and Tatars almost 30 per cent; indeed Ufa, the capital, is only 10 per cent Bashkir. The language law recognises only Bashkir and Russian as official languages and excludes Tatar. Apart from Chechnya, there is little evidence of an 'ethnic' mobilisation *against* Russians within the republics. There are even signs, for example, of an emergent 'Tatarstani' civic identity (Hanauer, 1996). Also with the exception of Chechnya, there has been a high level of elite continuity with the Soviet period and, consequently, these elites are highly sovietised culturally and operate through *nomenklatura* networks inherited from the Soviet period (McAuley, 1997). Only in Chechnya has there been something akin to an 'ethnic' war in post-Soviet Russia, but the factors involved make it a deviant case.

Regional Political Economy

The single most important common factor among the four most 'secessionist' or autonomy-seeking republics (Chechnya, Tatarstan, Bashkortostan and Sakha) is that they all have significant economic resource endowments. Tatarstan accounts for around one quarter of

Russia's oil output and is a key industrial region, Sakha produces 99 per cent of Russia's diamonds, and Bashkortostan and Chechnya are also key energy producing or transit regions. The question of 'ethnic' separatism, consequently, is blurred by distributive politics and the issue of local control of economic assets. Distributive issues have equally fostered regionalism in the ethnic Russian regions, where there is much resentment at the lack of revenue sharing and weakness of local control over local resources, and antagonism at the 'ethnic privileging' of republics. In the early 1990s so-called 'inter-regional associations' were created, broadly on the basis of the horizontal inter-regional ties of the Soviet-era economic planning regions. There was much discussion at this time about whether the associations could be the basis for a regionalist disintegration of Russia. The most politically significant were those of the Urals, Siberia and the Far East, whose territories contain the bulk of the natural resources from which most of Russia's export revenues are derived. In fact, even the more regionalist 'inter-regional associations' such as Siberian Agreement proved to be fragile coalitions that were easily fractured by competing inter-regional interests and a policy of divide and rule by the centre (Hughes, 1994). Regional elite mobilisations against the federal government were, in any event, weakly institutionalised and rarely took the form of a specific regional political party. In fact, federal electoral law from 1993 created legal barriers to regionalist parties by requiring cross-regional registration, and even at local elections regionalist parties are rare (Gel'man and Golosov, 1998).

Finally, we should note that *geographical location* significantly affects capacity for secession. An ideal position for the assertion of secession would be a location on or close to an international frontier. Tatarstan is situated in the centre of European Russia far from the international frontier, and is surrounded by predominantly ethnic Russian regions. Its political economy is, consequently, wholly dependent on its good relations with Russia. Chechnya, in contrast, is located on Russia's post-Soviet international frontier in the Caucasus, which gives it a much wider flexibility in its dealings with Russia.

Presidentialism and Patrimonial Federalism

Russia's asymmetric federal institutional architecture, under the constitution of 1993, would have been less viable had it not been for the establishment of a strong presidency. Juan Linz has observed that presidentialism tends toward a dangerous personalisation of power, polarising zero-sum politics in a way that has a corroding effect on institutional norms. There is much evidence of Yeltsin's reluctance to compromise and preference for unilateral action when dealing with central political actors and institutions (Colton, 1995b). When dealing with federal actors, however, Yeltsin used a combination of institutional measures and great charismatic authority to project some systemic order into the federal system. His preference for informal patrimonial relations with the leaders of the republics and regions tended to subvert institutional mechanisms of control.

Presidential patrimonialism was most evident in his relations with the presidents of the ethnic republics, whereas his relations with most of the regions was characterised by administrative controls. In late 1991, one of the extraordinary decree powers given to Yeltsin by the Russian Congress of People's Deputies was the right to appoint governors (a power retained until autumn 1995) and to place his own 'representative' in each region and republic as a kind of monitor. In principle, the representatives should have provided the president with a controlling and coordinating instrument in the regions, in practice they often went native or proved weak in standing up to assertive governors.

Yeltsin's forcible dissolution of parliament in late September 1993 averted a parliamentary republic where any autonomy of republics would most likely have been erased by ethnic Russian domination. Such an outcome might well have led to other ethnic conflicts besides that with Chechnya. Having erased the segmental autonomy of republics in the 1993 Constitution Yeltsin employed his extensive decree powers under the same Constitution to bypass the new parliament and implement a new federal design based on the selective bilateral power-sharing treaties. Yeltsin's role was instrumental to the implementation and success of this process in the face of strong opposition from the Duma, regional governors and even many of his key advisors on federal questions. There is little doubt that Yeltsin approached the issue of federal relations with a great deal of pragmatism, perhaps best illustrated when he attempted to entice leaders of key republics and regions into sacking the Prosecutor General (then investigating Yeltsin's role in Kremlin corruption) by promising: 'we will give you more independence than set down in the bilateral agreements we have signed. Let us gradually revise these agreements' (Russian Public TV, 20 April 1999).

The presidential personalisation of power, so widely viewed as destabilising in transition, was central to the establishment of a rapport with the executives in the republics and regions. In this way Yeltsin's presidential patrimonialism eased the negotiating process on the treaties. To a great extent it replicated the traditional patrimonialism of the Soviet *nomenklatura* system with which almost all of these leaders felt most comfortable.

Chechnya and the Failure of Refederalisation

Chechnya was excluded from the bilateral power-sharing treaty process, according to the official Russian account, as a punishment for its strenuous assertion of sovereignty in late 1991. This is clearly disingenuous since Tatarstan had pursued its sovereignty claim even earlier. Similarly, it is argued that the secessionist conflict in Chechnya was largely driven by Russia's strategic political and economic interests in the Caucasus, notably Caspian Sea oil, the major pipeline for which traversed the republic. Yet, economic distributive issues were a characteristic feature of conflicts between the federal government and other republics, and were stabilised by treaties. When the treaty with Tatarstan was signed Shakhrai believed that a similar agreement would most likely be the basis of a solution for the Chechnya crisis. It has also been suggested that conflict with Chechnya was a tactic used by the federal government to strengthen its credibility in the negotiations with other republics over power-sharing. In fact, the key negotiations and treaties were completed by the end of 1994, well before the Russian invasion of Chechnya. A power-sharing treaty offered the best prospect for a peaceful resolution to the conflict and might well have prevented the war of 1994–6. Why, then, did such a treaty prove elusive?

Chechen nationalism, unlike that of Tatarstan and other republics, was mobilised around a much more vivid historical memory of resistance to Russian imperialism, which had been ingrained and embittered by the genocidal deportation of 1944 – a catastrophe that was within living memory for many Chechens (Dunlop, 1998, p. 187). This factor was a considerable political constraint on the Chechen leader Dudaev's ability to compromise with Russia. Such poor background conditions for stable Russian–Chechen relations were further aggravated by the personality clash between Yeltsin and

Dudaev. A close adviser to Yeltsin on his policy towards Chechnya suggests that a treaty-based solution could not be reached in 1991–4 because the conflict became a 'highly personalised' battle of egos between Yeltsin and Dudaev (Tishkov, 1997). An influential Western account attributes the descent into war to some kind of mutual primordial 'ethnic' hatred (Lieven, 1998, p. 76).

A major stumbling bloc to a political accommodation lay in the fact that Dudaev, unlike Shaimiev and the executives in the other republics, was not a former member of the party *nomenklatura*, and consequently lacked the personal skills for operating within the informal networks that controlled Russian politics. Dudaev, like Chechen nationalism, was a dissonant phenomenon in the new Russia and was incapable of adjusting to an executive federalism constructed around Yeltsin's new presidential patrimonialism. That Yeltsin himself was personally central to the conflict is indicated by the fact that the war was pursued even after the removal from office of the key ministers who formed the so-called 'party of war' by summer 1996. The war was only ended after the death of Dudaev in April 1996. A key mediating role was played by Tatarstan president Shaimiev who also mobilised pressure from a core group of republics, the 'Cheboksary Seven', named after their first meeting in the capital of Chuvashia in January 1995 to denounce the invasion. The war became a military disaster for Russia and forced Yeltsin to make peace with Chechnya a key platform in his re-election campaign in spring 1996. He delegated the negotiations for peace to his subordinates, at first Viktor Chernomyrdin who struck a deal for electoral convenience in May 1996, and then General Alexander Lebed who delivered a more durable peace through the Khasavyurt Agreement of August 1996 in exchange for a withdrawal of Russian forces from Chechnya and the postponement of a decision on Chechnya's final status for 'up to' five years. A formal treaty was signed in May 1997 confirming the end of hostilities and a special status of 'association' and 'common economic space' between the Russian Federation and Chechnya. As if to confirm Yeltsin's personal antipathy to Chechnya, he could neither bring himself to negotiate personally with the newly elected Chechen president, Ruslan Maskhadov (he could barely shake his hand in public), nor even sign the treaty (that task was left to prime minister Chernomyrdin).

The Khasavyurt Agreement ended effective Russian sovereignty over Chechnya. Nevertheless, the Russian government ruled out *de jure* independence and ensured that Chechnya's claim to independence was not recognised by the international community. In practice, from late 1996 Maskhadov attempted to rule Chechnya *de facto* as an independent state, and this was most obviously demonstrated by the introduction of *Shariat* law in a clear departure from the Russian Constitution. Chechnya, devastated by the war, and with its traditional clan-based social fabric even further fragmented, soon descended into a militarised anarchy, with rampant crime, kidnappings and smuggling organized by competing warlords. Consequently, Chechnya became a disastrous model for separatism in the Russian Federation. Putin's options as president remained very similar to those of Yeltsin in 1996: an increasingly unpopular war of attrition, an all-out military onslaught, or a negotiated settlement on Chechnya's status. Having bolstered his authority with a vigorous military campaign in Chechnya and a first round win in the election of March 2000, Putin set about using his decree powers to refashion the federal structure created by Yeltsin.

Putin's Federal Recentralisation

Since much of the federal structure and practice that developed under Yeltsin was a product of his presidential patrimonialism, it is no surprise that a radical shake up would follow his resignation. The bilateral power-sharing treaties were based on narrow institutional supports, being the outcome of executive agreements and excluding the parliament. Their imprecise status in parallel to the constitution makes them vulnerable to unravelling once the interests of the centre might change through a presidential alternation. This is precisely what occurred as Putin preferred a federal recentralisation. On becoming acting president on 31 December 1999 Putin issued a credo, 'Russia at the Turn of the Millennium', which declared that one of his key policy aims was the reversal of the 'weakening of state power' that had occurred under Yeltsin and the remaking of a strong centralised state in Russia. During the presidential election campaign in February–March 2000 Putin toured the republics and regions condemning the state of legal chaos in the country whereby many thousands of legal acts passed at these levels contradicted the federal constitution and federal law. Putin made the 'dictatorship of law' – the construction of a new less corrupt model of governance and administrative coherence – one of his first tasks.

New Federal Districts

By a decree of 13 May 2000 Putin added a new commanding tier of administration to the federal structure by dividing the country into seven new federal districts, broadly based on the existing military districts, each headed by a presidential appointee named the plenipotentiary representative, or more commonly 'governor-general' after the Tsarist military governors of the provinces. The districts are: Central, North West, North Caucasus, Volga, Urals, Siberia, and Far East. There was a strong military-security bias in the appointments; two of the new presidential representatives had been commanders in the 1994–96 Chechen war, and two others had been drawn from the internal security apparatus.

The governor–generals will have ultimate control of the republic and regional economies in their districts. Taken together with the reform of the Federation Council (see later), Putin's aim appears to be to marginalise the governors and introduce more stringent central control of budget transfers to the regions and tax returns to the centre. There is a suspicion that the governor–generals will turn into a new bureaucratic–oligarchic superstructure that will apply sanctions against governors and mayors who do not conform to policies and decisions set by the centre. Just what kind of role will be played by the governor–generals remains to be seen and much will depend on their personal authority and the overall administrative capacity of their staffs. Their main power is patronage: they control appointments in the local departments of federal agencies such as the prosecutor's office and the tax police. Not surprisingly, the appointments have given rise to fears that Putin has opted for a simplistic military-bureaucratic solution to the complex problems of centre-regional and federal relations in Russia. As President Nikolai Fedorov of Chuvashia stated, it was the 'easiest and most primitive, Russian road ... [another] structure at one fell swoop' (BBC Summary of World Broadcasts, 16 May 2000).

Reform of the Federation Council

On 17 May 2000 Putin used the occasion of his first post-inaugural address to the country to map out his plans for federal reform. His target was the powerful regional governors whom he wanted the power to sack, and end their automatic right to a seat in the

Federation Council. Only by strengthening the 'executive vertical', Putin claimed, could he 'cement Russian statehood'. Such radical changes to the composition of the Federation Council required a new federal law, which was duly passed by both houses of parliament in early August 2000. It removed the governors and replaced them with representatives appointed by the governors and approved by a republic's or region's legislative assembly for a four-year term (if the assembly does not approve of the appointment, a two-thirds vote in the regional assembly can remove the appointee). The law also gave the president the power to remove and replace governors for repeated violations of federal law.

The reform deprived the governors of their most important forum for organising collective action. Admittedly, given their part-time attendance it was rare for Federation Council members to meet in committee to discuss legislation. Nevertheless, the upper house was their main institutional channel for the exercise of collective pressure if and when it could be mustered. In principle, the reform could lead to a significant redistribution of power in favour of the upper house. The new members will be more active representatives, since they will be full-time and not burdened by the immense administrative responsibilities involved in regional governance. Once they begin working in 2001 not a single law will be passed by the upper house without being discussed at length in committee, a factor that will sharply increase legislative gridlock. Consequently, this reform may yet backfire badly on Putin.

Unpicking the Bilateral Treaties

A federal law on centre-periphery relations passed in June 1999 stipulated that all of the existing treaties must be revised to comply with the Russian Constitution by 2002. Putin astutely began his assault on the bilateral power-sharing treaties in the most powerful republics, Tatarstan and Bashkortostan, during visits in March 2000. Concessions here would make his task much easier in the rest of the country. Moreover, President Shaimiev of Tatarstan had weakened his political credibility by joining Fatherland-All Russia against Putin's Unity Bloc in the Duma elections of 1999. Putin forced Shaimiev to yield back to the federal government some of the fiscal privileges that had been allocated by the 1994 treaty. From now on, Tatarstan was to direct the same amount of tax revenue to the federal budget as other regions, though Putin accepted a symbolic face-saving formula for Shaimiev whereby the revenues would stay in Kazan at the regional branch of the federal treasury and would be spent on federal projects in Tatarstan. Afterwards, Putin visited Bashkortostan and agreed similar forfeits of fiscal exceptions with President Rakhimov. In 1999, for example, Bashkortostan was the only republic or region to not transfer income tax revenues to the centre. The treaty revisions, therefore, strengthen the federal treasury and give the federal government greater control over tax collection in these wealthy resource-rich republics.

In addition to face-to-face negotiations, Putin relied on the judicial activism of the Constitutional Court. In an important test case on the treaties in June 2000, the Constitutional Court struck down a Bashkortostan law that required candidates for the Bashkortostan presidency to be bilingual (effectively disqualifying four out of five Baskortostani citizens). Bashkortostan argued that its constitution was protected by exceptions contained in its treaty. The case established the important precedent that the constitutions of republics must comply with the federal constitution. On 7 August Sakha amended its constitution to comply with the court's ruling. It remains uncertain how this process of judicial review of the treaties will be given effect as on 3 November 2000 the Bashkortostan parliament approved a new law to bring the republic's constitution into conformity with the federal constitution, but concurrently included the full text of the 1994 power-sharing treaty in its new constitution.

Fiscal squeeze

Putin has intensified the fiscal squeeze on the regions that began in spring 1998 under the Kirienko government. Russia's federal budgets are wholly non-transparent, unrealistic, and normally in deficit (the first balanced budget of the post-Soviet era was only approved for 2001). Consequently, many of the projects with official budget lines are not allocated funds and the Ministry of Finance has considerable discretion in determining which projects proceed and which regions receive their federal subsidies. The federal government also has extensive powers to grant or curtail lucrative export-import privileges, tax waivers to specific enterprises in a region, or state debt roll-overs for enterprises or regional administrations that can dramatically boost local economies. The federal government may use its influence over the key public utilities and natural monopolies (the Unified Energy System, Gazprom, the Railroads, Transneft), which set prices for vital services. Many regions are massively in debt to these monopolies and are easily subjected to pressures and threats of cuts in supplies. The most thorough study so far of the balance of federal fiscal flows (including non-budgetary funds) revealed that by 1998 only 26 of the 89 regions and republics were net 'donors' to the federal budget and the rest were dependent on federal transfers (Lavrov and Matushkin, 2000). Putin's fiscal squeeze in 2000 has delivered another blow to the power of the governors as the balanced budget for 2001 significantly redistributed tax revenues in favour of the federal authorities.

The State Council

A new consultative forum for regional leaders, the State Council, was created by Putin on 1 September 2000, and held its opening session on 29 September. The State Council is composed of the heads of all 89 Russian regions and republics, but its presidium has only seven members who are appointed by Putin. Presidium meetings are chaired by Putin and its membership will rotate six-monthly to include a regional leader from each of the new federal districts. The current seven include many of Russia's most powerful regional leaders: the Tyumen Governor Leonid Roketsky, Tomsk Governor Viktor Kress, Moscow Mayor Yuri Luzhkov, Khabarovsk Governor Viktor Ishaev, Dagestan State Council Chairman Magomedali Magomedov, Tatarstan President Mintimer Shaimiev, and St Petersburg Governor Vladimir Yakovlev. Whereas the State Council will meet in plenary session only four times a year to discuss two issues at a time and reach a 'consensus' on them, the presidium will meet monthly. The State Council and presidium are clearly much weaker bodies than the Federation Council. The State Council has no permanent staff or apparatus, whereas the Federation Council played a crucial role in making or stopping legislation. The formation of the State Council has raised questions over what its functions and role in Russian government will be, particularly in light of Putin's attempts to eviscerate the power of the regional leaders.

Putin has engaged in a careful act of cooption to the presidium by appointing Luzhkov, Yakovlev and Shaimiev, the OVR leaders. In contrast, prominent regional leaders left out include Sverdlovsk

Governor Eduard Rossel and Primorskii Governor Yevgenii Naz-dratenko both of whom are out of favour with Putin (Nazdratenko, indeed, was persuaded to resign in early 2001). Currently, the State Council exists outside the constitution. Putin claims that its role will be to tackle the most important issues and that it will not supplant parliament. Nevertheless, the State Council may consider draft laws and decrees, and discuss the federal budget and its implementation. The fact that the State Council itself will meet only four times a year suggests that this body will be more of a talking shop for regional leaders. The presidium's membership demonstrates that it will have a much more influential role in policy making and in improving coordination between the federal and regional governments.

In a Kremlin ceremony to mark Russian Constitution Day on 12 December 2000 Putin declared that he had acted 'strictly within the limits of the constitution' in order to 'pull the state together'. There can be little doubt that Putin has engaged in an unprecedented transformation of the role of the regions in Russian government, the aim of which is to strengthen the federal centre. The institutional building blocks are now in place with the creation of the seven federal districts and Putin-appointed governor-generals, a weakened Federal Council (certainly in the short term), a purely consultative State Council, and a much smaller and easily managed Putin-appointed presidium. The next step in the process of subordinating the regions is to change the governors. A federal law of October 1999 ended the era when governors held their regions as personal fiefs by limiting them to two five-year terms in office. We can expect Putin to use gubernatorial electoral cycles to challenge incumbents who oppose his reforms.

Conclusion

The development of post-Soviet Russian federalism has proceeded through several stages and along a spectrum of change from feder-alisation under Yeltsin to a trend for recentralisation under Putin. The kernel of the problem of federalisation in Russia has been how to reconcile the multicultural nature of its society, and the territorialisa-tion of ethnicity in a few key areas, with the demands of ethnic Russian elites for a constitutional equalisation of status and power among the federal sub-units. On the whole, Russian and Western scholars have viewed asymmetric federalism as destabilising. The tension between recognising and institutionalising the asymmetric features of the society in Russia's federal state structure came to the fore in 1992–3. Political pressure from the ethnic Russian regions forced the abandonment of the asymmetrical Federal Treaty of 1992 and the institutionalisation of equal status in the 1993 Constitution. Yeltsin, however, used his enhanced presidential patrimonial powers from late 1993 to build an alternative, more selective asymmetrical federal regime through the bilateral power-sharing treaties. In this sense Russia is a case where a strong presidency imposed a stabilising institutional design that would have been avoided had there been a parliamentary ethnocracy.

As with the Federal Treaty, the new treaties were a form of 'ethnic privileging' that antagonised Russian regional elites, though generally the discontent at the symbolic and economic distributive effects of the treaties was cloaked under the guise that they threatened the territorial integrity of the state by encouraging secessionism (as in Chechnya) and fragmenting sovereignty. In fact, separatism was an exceptional political phenomenon in post-Soviet Russia as only Chechnya asserted and fought for its independence, and this case had very particular causes. A more relevant argument against asymmetric federalism is that it may have entrenched authoritarianism in certain republics and regions by conceding power-sharing. The problems of embedding democratic practice, enforcing rule compliance, order, and state administrative coherence exist in Russia, however, irrespective of whether a constituent unit is a republic or region, or has a power-sharing treaty or not.

Asymmetric federalism has had many stabilising effects. Firstly, by decentralising power over a wide range of policy domains the treaties have acted as a counterweight to the strongly centralist state tradition in Russia. Secondly, the treaties engineered a new institutional structure for the accommodation of Russia's plural society. The key treaties involved lengthy and complex negotiations (three years in the case of Tatarstan) that have by their very nature helped to regularise federalism as a political, if not constitutional, process of institutionalised bargaining, even though it is as yet non-transparent. The Russian experience of federal transition has even had a beneficial contagion effect on other ethnic conflicts in the former Soviet Union. For example, asymmetric federal arrangements have been applied to the Crimean Autonomy in Ukraine, and are being discussed for the Abkhazia–Georgia and Nagorno–Karabakh conflicts.

On balance, the development of an asymmetric federalism has contributed to the promotion of political stability and the institutionalization of elite bargaining in Russia. These are factors that have been so problematic for democratic consolidation by their very absence in central politics. It is doubtful whether the process of recentralisation under Putin will be as stabilizing in the absence of coercion, since comparative experience suggests that there is as yet no alternative institutional arrangement that would work as well in an ethnically and territorially divided society.

8

Politics in the Regions

DARRELL SLIDER

The system of federal relations discussed in the preceding chapter sets the framework within which regional politics develop, but political life in the provinces follows its own dynamic. The 89 regions that make up the Russian Federation are characterised by widely varying economic and political conditions. Regions differ in the extent to which they depend on agriculture or a particular industrial sector (for example, textiles in Ivanovo, oil processing in Bashkortostan, coal mining in Kemerovo, the defence industry in Udmurtia). Politically, as demonstrated in national and regional elections, the provinces differ markedly in their relative support for communists, reformers, or nationalists. Other politically significant variation is caused by the presence of non-Russian ethnic groups, particularly in the 21 ethnically based 'republics'.

This diversity greatly complicates the analysis of the state of affairs in Russian regions. There is no such thing as a 'typical' region that could be used to show common patterns or tendencies. Nevertheless, all regions shared the formative impact of the communist political-economic system and responded to a set of incentives that was implicit in Yeltsin's policies toward the regions in the 1990s. Important changes in regional political institutions had their origins in the political crisis of October 1993 and the new Russian constitution that followed.

Overall, the regions have seen a consolidation of power in the hands of regional executives, most often called governors in the *oblasts* (regions) and *krais* (territories), and presidents in the republics. This tightening hold on power has been, in part, an unanticipated result of policies adopted by Moscow that were intended to expand the role of market forces and democracy. By 2000, governors and republic presidents were increasingly referred to in the popular press in Russia as 'feudal lords' who ran their territories as fiefdoms. As we have seen in the previous chapter, this brings into question the very nature of federalism in Russia. This chapter seeks to examine the nature and impact of political and economic developments within the regions – developments that have potentially devastating implications for Russia's future progress as an emerging free market democracy.

Institutional Development in the Regions

In the Soviet period, regional politics were defined by a uniform, hierarchical pattern, at least on the surface: the Communist Party designated regional party first secretaries who were the principal decision-makers at that level. As Jerry Hough (1969) demonstrated in his classic work on Soviet regional politics, the provincial party bosses acted much like 'prefects' in the French administrative system: they were agents of the 'centre' that carried out its policies. At the same time, they were accountable for the region's performance and had considerable discretionary power in performing their duties. Promotions to the Central Committee and Politburo often came from the ranks of regional party leaders. Both Mikhail Gorbachev and Boris Yeltsin first achieved national prominence while serving lengthy stints as regional party first secretaries in the Brezhnev era – in Stavropol *krai* and Sverdlovsk region, respectively. Separate from the party structure was a hierarchy of legislative-executive bodies, called soviets (the Russian word for 'council'). Until the 1990 elections, regional soviets were large bodies that met infrequently and that provided little more than formalised participation in decision-making. The soviets also served as the institutional home for provincial administrators – the *ispolkom* or executive committee that constituted the core of regional government. The *ispolkom* included departments that provided or supervised education, health care, services, local industry and infrastructure, housing, police, and other local agencies.

Regional legislatures elected in Russia in 1990, while still called soviets, took advantage of the changes in Soviet politics under Gorbachev and Yeltsin to push for a more assertive role over policy and local government. They continued, however, to be large, unwieldy bodies with few permanent members and staff. A presidium, headed by a chairman, often dominated the setting of their agenda.

After the failed August coup in 1991, Yeltsin disbanded the communist party hierarchy that controlled the regions and confiscated party property, which included the chief administrative buildings in every region and city. Yeltsin initially considered holding elections of chief executives in the provinces, but when it became evident that communists might win many of these posts, elections were postponed 'for the period of radical economic reform'. Earlier, exceptions had been granted for the two largest cities that were full-fledged 'subjects of the federation' – Moscow and Leningrad (soon to be renamed St Petersburg). In both cases, as was expected, leading reformers (the economist Gavriil Popov and the legal scholar Anatolii Sobchak) won the elections that were held in 1991. In other regions, Yeltsin used direct appointments to fill the vacuum left by the removal of the *obkom* first secretaries. In a number of cases, Yeltsin's appointments encountered serious local opposition, and he often compromised to allow local favourites to remain in power – including many from the old communist *nomenklatura*. New chiefs of admin-istration (known informally as 'governors') took over the party offices and buildings; in virtually every provincial capital this repre-sented the best office space – especially in telecommunications, given that they were equipped with direct phone lines to the Kremlin separate from the normal phone system. Though Yeltsin was creating a new administrative structure separate from the soviets, he left in place the regional soviets that had been elected in 1990. A number of local communist leaders had enough foresight to run for seats in the soviets, and many became chairmen of the soviets or took top administrative posts in their regions prior to the end of the Soviet Union.

From the beginning, there was a marked difference between the republics within the federation (not to be confused with the 14 union republics that gained independence along with Russia when the USSR collapsed) and other entities. The leaders of Russia's 21 republics followed Yeltsin's own example and were able to legitimise their standing through popular election as early as 1991, usually to the newly created post of president. Republic leaders tended to come from the old regional communist party *nomenklatura*. Among com-munist-era republic first secretaries who became republic leaders were Mintimer Shaimiev of Tatarstan, Aslan Jarimov of Adygeya, Leonid Potapov of Buryatia, Yuri Spiridonov of Komi, Valerii Kokov of Kabardino-Balkaria, Vladimir Khubiev of Karachai-Cherkessia, and Akhsarbek Galazov of North Ossetia. Others, while not serving in the top party post, had party or government responsibilities near the top of the hierarchy; these include Dagestan's Magomedal Magomedov, Valerii Chaptynov of Altai Republic, Viktor Stepanov of Kareliya,

Vladimir Shtygashev of Khakasia, Vladislav Zotin of Mari El, Sherig-ool Oorzhak of Tuva, Alexander Volkov of Udmurtia, and Mikhail Nikolaev of Sakha (Yakutia). Murtaz Rakhimov of Bashkortostan (Bashkiria) had been director of one of the largest oil refineries in the region, the top post in the region's economic *nomenklatura*.

In a few republics, the first set of elections brought to power new, post-communist elites. The most controversial was Kirsan Ilyumzhi-nov, a millionaire with money of unknown provenance, who set up an autocratic regime that has been described as a new 'khanate'. Another outsider was Yeltsin's former justice minister, Nikolai Fedorov, who was elected president in his home region of Chuvashia. Ruslan Aushev, an ethnic Ingush with a military background, was elected president of Ingushetia after Yeltsin appointed him to serve as acting chief of the republic in the wake of ethnic clashes in the region. In Chechnya, an important factor in the drive for independence was the election of Dzhokar Dudaev, a former Soviet air force general, as president. These elections were not recognised by Moscow and took place after Dudaev had made substantial progress toward achieving *de facto* independence. (The Russian army later intervened, at the end of 1994, and Dudaev was killed by a Russian rocket attack.)

As of 2000, the majority of the first elected republic leaders remained in power after easily winning re-election. In several cases, including Tatarstan, Mordovia, and Kabardino-Balkaria, republic presidents won over 90 per cent of the vote because they ran either unopposed or with only token opposition. There were exceptions, however. Several republic leaders were defeated by prominent local political figures. In Karelia, Stepanov was defeated by the mayor of Petrozavodsk, Sergei Katanandov. The former communist leader of North Ossetia, Galazov, was replaced by another former *obkom* first secretary, Alexander Dzasokhov. The president of the Mari El republic was easily defeated by Vyacheslav Kislitsyn, a former collective farm chairman and district administration head. In Altai Republic, a former government finance auditor and 'democrat' Sergei Zubakin narrowly won a plurality of votes (23.5 per cent) in a seven-candidate race. Candidates with military backgrounds won election in several republics. In Khakassia, General Alexander Lebed's brother, Aleksei, also a paratroop commander, won election to the post of head of state. At the conclusion of the first Chechen war, Aslan Maskhadov, commander of the rebel forces, was elected president of Chechnya with Moscow's tacit support. In Karachai-Cherkessia, General Vladimir Semenov, a Karachai former ground troop commander who was dismissed following embezzlement charges, won a hotly disputed contest. Mari El had a succession of one-term presidents. The first president of the Mari El republic, Zotin, was easily defeated in 1996 by Vyacheslav Kislitsyn, a former collective farm chairman and district administration head. Kislitsyn, in turn, was defeated in 2000 by Leonid Markelov, deputy head of the state insurance company.

The first direct popular elections in other administrative units – *oblasts* and *krais* – took place in seven regions in April 1993 without Yeltsin's approval. Most of those elected governor were communist-era regional leaders who were opposed to Yeltsin and his policies. In one case, in Chelyabinsk, Yeltsin refused to recognise the outcome of the election and appointed his own candidate, but the others were allowed to keep their posts. Two years later, Yeltsin began to allow elections for governor on a case-by-case basis. In December 1995, 12 governors were elected. Finally, in late 1996, elections were held for governor or president in 52 of the remaining regions.

Political organisations at the national level began for the first time to get involved in regional politics during the 1996 gubernatorial elections. Candidates favored by Yeltsin received support from the 'party of power', Prime Minister Viktor Chernomyrdin's party Our Home is Russia (NDR). The party provided financing and expert assistance in campaigns for over 20 incumbent governors. Yeltsin's office, including then chief of staff Anatolii Chubais, served as a national headquarters for coordinating these campaigns. The Communist Party of the Russian Federation (CPRF), which in previous national elections had dominated voting in the southern provinces known as the 'red belt', put forward candidates in most regions or supported sympathetic incumbents. They were successful in many regions where the party had done well in presidential voting. Among the candidates who won with communist support was Yeltsin's nemesis from the 1993 events, former vice president Alexander Rutskoi (in Kursk region). Vladimir Zhirinovsky's ultranationalist Liberal Democratic Party of Russia (LDPR) succeeded in November 1996 in getting its candidate, Yevgenii Mikhailov, elected governor in Pskov region.

In most cases, however, political parties or other national affiliations played little role in the outcome of the elections. Even where they did, parties had few instruments of influence over candidates they had supported. Many of those elected governor were so-called *praktiki* – directors or former directors of major enterprises in the region who were not closely identified with any political movement, but who were well known locally and long-time members of the economic *nomenklatura*. The fact that governors lacked substantial party ties hindered the further development of Russia's party system and made governors less accountable for their actions.

The establishment of new, provincial legislatures was marked by difficulties. Despite the fact that Yeltsin's early appointees as governors had been approved by the soviets and often included chairmen or chairwomen of soviets, conflicts soon arose between regional executives and soviets in the period 1992–3. These conflicts between governors and the heads of regional soviets mirrored the struggle for power between the Russian President and the Chairman of the Russian Supreme Soviet, Ruslan Khasbulatov. Governors largely supported Yeltsin, while Khasbulatov found support among chairmen of the regional soviets. When Yeltsin used the Russian army to resolve the constitutional crisis of September–October 1993 by disbanding the Russian parliament, he took advantage of the situation to also dissolve soviets in almost all regions of Russia. The result was a major shift in local power to the benefit of the regional executive, paralleling the changes that took place at the national level.

Starting in December 1993 and extending into 1995, elections were held in most regions of the country for regional assemblies. New names were chosen for these bodies – most often 'assembly' (*sobranie*) or 'duma'. These assemblies differed in both size and function from the soviets they replaced. The major advance made in the creation of new institutions was that the new assemblies were smaller than in the past and were to include a subset of members who would be designated to act as permanent legislators. These positive features, however, were outweighed by other developments. Officials from the regional administration and local economic elites dominated the new assemblies to a much greater extent that was true in the old soviets. In over 65 of the 89 assemblies, executive branch officials and enterprise directors or farm managers made up over half the members. Almost all continued to hold their posts, since this was the source of their real power, rather than devote themselves to full-time legislative activity. This virtually guaranteed substantial conflicts of interest; it also meant that assemblies would meet infrequently. Political parties were weakly represented in most of the new regional assemblies; according to data from the Central Electoral Commission, fewer than 14 per cent of deputies were affiliated with a political party at the time of their election. About half of these deputies were from the Communist

Party (CPRF), but the party had a majority of deputies in just six regions. The only majority by a reformist party was held by Russia's Choice in the Moscow city duma.

Most regional legislatures were subject to re-election in either two or four years. A second series of elections began in late 1996 and were concluded in most regions by 1999. These elections produced a slightly different mix of deputies, though the political significance of these changes appeared to be minimal. Enterprise managers, farm directors, and executive officials continued to be the largest category of deputies. The second elections to regional assemblies produced a larger number of deputies who had been nominated by political parties: national parties had deputies in 56 of 78 regions for which data were available. As before, however, this presence was sufficient to produce a working majority in only a few regions. The CPRF again won a majority in the assemblies in Krasnodar *krai* and Volgograd region. At the same time, the second elections deprived the communists of majorities they had won before in regional assemblies in Chuvashia, Kamchatka, Vladimir and Orel.

The sharp conflicts between regional assemblies and chiefs of administration that were common in the early 1990s diminished as a result of the institutional changes just described. Once governors were elected (rather than appointed by Yeltsin), there were fewer cases of political/ideological mismatches between legislative and executive branches. Also, the changes in composition of the assemblies meant that a majority was beholden to the governor or republic president, either for their careers or for the economic wellbeing of their enterprises. There were few truly independent deputies, and often assemblies had no organised political opposition. As a result, most assemblies could be accurately described as 'in the governor's pocket' (in Russian, *karmannye*).

Through most of the 1990s, regional political institutions developed in a legal vacuum. General principles were set out in the 1993 constitution on executive and legislative institutions, with further elaboration expected in a future federal law on legislative and executive organs in the regions. No such law was adopted, however, until October 1999. The delay was mostly due to opposition by regional leaders through the Federation Council, which vetoed the draft law four times before the Duma was finally able to override their veto. In the meantime, constitutions in the republics and charters (*ustavy*) in the oblasts moved into the void, setting out the basic relationships between the organs of power. These began to be adopted in most regions in 1994, though most were approved only in 1995–6, after the formation of new legislative bodies. Given the political balance of forces in the regions and regional assemblies at that time, the institutional arrangements favoured the executive.

The October 1999 law 'on general principles on organising legislative and executive organs of state power of subjects of the Russian Federation' did little to impose uniformity on the regional political institutions that had developed in the interim period, nor did it seek to further democratisation at the regional level. Instead it left most decisions to the regions and codified some of the framework that Yeltsin had established earlier by decree. These provisions also worked to reinforce the dominance of the executive over the legislative branch. One measure, for example, permitted a legislature to override an executive veto only it if had the support of two-thirds of the total number of deputies who were supposed to be elected to the assembly. Many legislatures had empty seats due to insufficient turnout in some – usually urban – districts, and deputies who were not full-time legislatures were frequently absent. Thus, it was very difficult for a legislature to assert itself against a governor or president.

One controversial aspect of the 1999 law, and a major reason for Federation Council opposition, was the introduction of term limits for the top executive post in the region. Henceforth, regional leaders were limited to two consecutive terms of no more than five years each. The law did not clearly specify, however, how the term limits would be applied to sitting governors. The ambiguity was tested only in late 2000 when many governors were coming to the end of their first terms and many republic presidents were approaching the end of their second terms. If applied to terms already served, the law would have prevented most republic presidents from running again, and most governors would be limited to one more term in office. Sitting governors and presidents lobbied to 'clarify' the law so that only elections occurring after October 1999 were to be covered by the limit, thus allowing them to run for a third or even a fourth term in office. In January 2001 the Duma bowed to the governors' wishes and amended the law, thus giving the 70 regional executives who had been in office in October 1999 a new lease of life.

Local Government

Thus far, we have discussed political institutions at the provincial level. There were also dramatic developments at lower levels – in cities and rural districts (*raiony*). Again, the events of October 1993 and the new constitution played a major role. Yeltsin's October 1993 degree disbanding regional soviets was accompanied by an order to dissolve local soviets. Virtually all functions of local government were placed in the hands of chiefs of administration, most of whom were appointed by governors or republic presidents. This was true even for most city mayors, though exceptions were made for mayors who had won elections held in several cities in 1994 or earlier. Republic or oblast executive control over local government was meant to be a temporary measure, and the new constitution established a framework for the democratisation and empowerment of local government.

In August 1995 the Duma passed a new law on local self-government, again over the objections of the Federation Council, to implement the provisions of the 1993 constitution. It mandated the popular election of local assemblies organs that would have wide-ranging powers, including independent tax and budgetary authority, control over municipal property, and the right to make decisions that were binding on all organisations or factories (including those that were privatised or federally owned) that were located within its territory. Representative bodies at the local level had to be directly elected, while local executives (mayors or *raion* chiefs of administration) could be either popularly elected or chosen by a representative assembly from among its elected members. It was up to the regions to adopt laws implementing this federal law in their regions. Federal law explicitly prohibited regions from directly appointing local officials or creating assemblies without elections.

There was considerable opposition to the law on local government, particularly by the group that had the most to lose – oblast governors and republic presidents. In September 1995, eleven chief administrators sent requests that their territories be exempt from the law. Even Anatolii Sobchak, a leading reformer and at the time mayor of St Petersburg, predicted that the law would 'bring nothing but chaos to the country'. One way opposition to the law was manifested was through delays in implementation. The law set a time frame of six months from the adoption of the law to the holding of local elections, in other words, by the end of February 1996. By that time at least 40 regions still had not even drafted laws on local government. The delays left local government at the mercy of governors and presidents, who continued to appoint (and dismiss) local administrators. Republics were the most resistant to introducing lower-level elections, especially republics that had signed agreements with the centre giving them the right to form their own governmental institutions. In the republic of Udmurtia, for example, the legislature adopted a law in September 1996 making all local governmental posts appointed. The Russian Constitutional Court nullified the republic's law and similar measures in other republics, but often was unable to enforce its rulings. Other regional leaders were more subtle. In Sverdlovsk region, local officials were elected by late 1996. However, Eduard Rossel, the governor, created six new 'administrative districts' all headed by officials he appointed, who would take on many of the functions of local government.

Elections to local government bodies were finally completed in 82 of 89 regions by September 1997. The effect on the power of regional executives was mixed. In most rural districts, it appears that chiefs of administration who had been appointed by the governor were successful in winning election to their posts. In other districts, the winners were most often chairmen of collective farms. In any event, because rural districts tended to be dependent on the province for budgetary allocations (taxes collected in the cities were redistributed to the rural districts), financial levers preserved the dominance of governors and republic presidents. The story was much different in the larger cities, however, particularly the provincial capitals. Elected mayors often came in conflict with governors or republic presidents. Since the relationship between holders of the two posts was poorly defined, disputes quickly emerged over privatisation, control over state and city property, tax receipts and budgets, and other issues. Frequently the mayor of the largest city in a region became the only serious political opponent to a sitting governor or republic president and as such attracted the support of economic interests 'on the outs' with the region's leader. When sitting governors ran for re-election, it was frequently the case that their most dangerous opponent was the mayor of the region's capital.

The Fate of Reform in Russian Regions

To what extent have the political institutions created in the regions affected Russia's progress toward a deepening of democracy and economic reform? The caveats and criticisms expressed elsewhere in this volume about the results of attempts at reform take on an even more negative colouring when the level of analysis is shifted to Russia's regions. One fundamental reason has already been discussed:

the background of most governors or republic leaders in the 1990s. Most often they came from the senior levels of the regional communist party *nomenklatura*. While it is true that an official's background in the communist party apparatus or other top administrative posts is not a foolproof predictor of attitudes or behaviour in post-Soviet Russia, the training, habits, and mindsets of communist-era provincial elites have little in common with what is needed to facilitate progress in such areas as marketisation and democratisation.

Countering this argument is the view is that the logic of devolution to the regions will encourage or even force regional elites to change their behaviour in ways that will advance political and economic reform. Elections, privatisation, liberalisation of trade, financial reforms, and other institutional changes taking place at the national level could cause local elites to seek to respond with complementary policies that are simultaneously in their own interest and that are necessary for their regions to cope in an evolving free market democracy. Decentralisation to the regions, in this view, should be encouraged, and it ultimately will result in an effective federal system that allows its component parts to respond flexibly to local conditions.

What would regional politics and economics look like, if a province were on the path of democratic reform and marketisation? In politics, one would expect to see an expansion in the role of political parties, especially those active nationally, in regional and local politics. There would be free and fair elections with incumbents subject to challenges from serious opponents nominated and supported by political party organisations in the region. Political parties would help structure the work of elected assemblies, introducing greater political accountability. Regional legislatures would play a key, independent role in adopting budgets and laws and would develop the expertise and organisational foundations necessary for this. One would expect democratising regions to show signs of the development of civil society in the form of new types of non-government organisations, including the growth of genuine trade unions that would do more than administer employee benefits. Local government would begin to play an independent role in determining policies and setting priorities that corresponded to the needs of citizens and groups at the lowest level. Governmental and legal institutions would exhibit less arbitrariness in their operations and show increasing respect for human rights. Law enforcement, local prosecutors and the courts would be less subject to political influence. A democratising region would also exhibit an increasing diversification of the media marked by the growth of independent regional sources of information.

In the economic sphere, progress toward the development of a free market would be marked by a diminished role of government in economic management and regulation. There would be a decreasing role for government subsidies and price controls. Antimonopoly policies would facilitate competition in all areas, and barriers to entry from outside the region would be minimalised. Small private businesses would begin to flourish in many sectors of the economy.. Previously privatised state enterprises would come under the control of new owners who would improve corporate governance. Managers would seek to find a niche for their enterprises in the emerging market economy rather than engage in asset stripping. Enterprises that failed to adapt would be subject to bankruptcy proceedings that would either find new owners or shut them down. A new financial infrastructure would emerge at the regional level that would provide local sources of investment. At the same time, regional governments would actively seek to attract outside investment to their regions.

Do any Russian regions fit the above description? The short answer to this question is no. While clearly a few regions score better in some categories than others, all exhibit major deficiencies that can be attributed to the actions (or inaction) of regional officials. Furthermore, there is little evidence that leaders in the regions see these deficiencies as problems that need to be addressed. Comprehensive studies of policies in the regions provide little cause for optimism; there are no 'ideal' regions. In October 2000 the Moscow Helsinki Group, an independent, non-governmental human rights advocacy group, issued the first comprehensive report on civil and human rights in Russian regions. The report found that not a single Russian region of the 60 that were investigated (and they observed the most 'open' regions) met internationally accepted standards for observing human rights. Press freedoms in Russian regions are monitored by several groups led by the Glasnost Defence Foundation. In their reports for 1999 and 2000, press monitors rated 87 regions on the basis of the journalists' access to information and the availability to the public of independent media. The reports concluded that none of the regions studied had created a favourable climate for free expression. Relative progress on economic factors can be gauged through ratings of the investment climate in regions. The Moscow-based Expert Institute annually evaluates factors that influence the attractiveness of regions for investment or entrepreneurial activity. Their findings show serious problems of local origin even in regions that would otherwise present attract opportunities for business.

The north-west region of Novgorod is often cited as a progressive, 'reform-friendly' region. The governor is Mikhail Prusak, who was appointed in 1991 to head the region by Yeltsin at age 31 after drawing attention as a 'democrat' in the Soviet Congress of Peoples' Deputies. Novgorod has distinguished itself as a region that aggressively seeks foreign investment and offers numerous tax advantages. A number of Western corporations, including Cadbury, have selected Novgorod for building new production facilities. In this, the region is helped by its location on the main transportation link between St Petersburg and Moscow. Novgorod is also one of the few regions where an understanding has been reached on the division of responsibilities and budgetary funds between provincial and local government. Praise for the region is also based on evidence of the beginnings of civil society in Novgorod – a rapid expansion in the number of civic associations.

On the other hand, Prusak has not made a serious effort to increase the importance of political parties in Novgorod, even though he has himself been a prominent member, successively, of three 'parties of power' in post-Soviet Russia: Yeltsin aide Sergei Shakhrai's Party of Unity and Accord, Prime Minister Viktor Chernomyrdin's Our Home is Russia, and the main party supporting President Putin, Unity. The Novgorod regional assembly is one of the few in Russia that has no deputies nominated by a national political party or movement. In other areas of civil and human rights, Novgorod fares little better than other regions. The Moscow Helsinki Group found little progress in implementing the rule of law in Novgorod and pointed to widespread abuses by the police and courts. Approximately 95 per cent of the region's newspapers are financially dependent on the authorities, a figure rivalled only by the most authoritarian regions in Russia. Prusak arranged for early elections for his second term in September 1999 (rather than concurrent with parliamentary elections in December). This ploy allowed him to avoid the two-term limit passed in October 1999, and it definitely helped him to vanquish the opposition – Prusak won 92 per cent of the vote.

Another region, Nizhnii Novgorod (formerly called Gorky), which is located on the Volga east of Moscow, has also been identified as one of the most progressive. Under Boris Nemtsov, governor from 1991 to 1997, the region was literally turned into a laboratory for policy experiments including auctioning off collective farm property, new approaches to industrial and small-business privatisation, conversion of military industry, and the issuing of government and corporate bonds to finance special projects. Nemtsov subsequently left Nizhnii to take a post in Yeltsin's government, and in the Duma elected in 1999 he became the most prominent leader of the reformist party, the Union of Right Forces. The former mayor of the capital of Nizhnii Novgorod, Ivan Sklyarov, became governor after Nemtsov's departure. Under Sklyarov, the region became notably less hospitable to reforms, and many of Nemtsov's initiatives languished. In the area of press freedom, Nizhnii Novgorod has a mediocre to poor record in journalists' access to information and in the availability of independent media.

By far the most popular destination for Western investment has been the Russian capital, Moscow. Even though Moscow is a city that has consistently voted for reformers in national elections, it has elected a mayor, Yuri Luzhkov, who is far from being a reform advocate. The Moscow city government constantly sought and won the right not to implement a number of Yeltsin-era policies in privatisation and tax policy. The city government maintains tight control over the Moscow economy, which is heavily regulated and taxed, and it is assumed that the construction projects for which Luzhkov is famous are rife with corruption. Human rights violations in the city are widespread, particularly for 'persons of Caucasian nationality' who are routinely harassed by police. Although Moscow is perhaps the freest city in Russia in terms of independent media availability, there is very little critical reporting or commentary on the mayor and his administration. Luzhkov has been particularly adept at filing lawsuits in local courts against newspapers that allege corruption, and he always wins.

If relatively progressive regions such as Novgorod, Nizhnii Novgorod, and Moscow have serious flaws that undermine their reformist credentials, what is the status of political and economic development in other regions? On almost any of the reform criteria listed above, other regions are as bad or significantly worse. Some of the systemic causes for this are outlined in what follows.

Economic Aspects

In the economic sphere, governors and republic presidents have become extraordinarily powerful players. In Soviet times, control of the regional economy was dispersed, with major enterprises most often under the direct supervision of Moscow-based ministries. This had the effect of limiting the power of regional party first secretaries. Economic and administrative changes that took place in the 1990s made it possible for governors to consolidate local control over much of the regional economy and its institutions.

The method by which initial privatisation of industrial enterprises was carried out in Russia had the effect of turning over control to local economic and political elites. The inside track to gaining effective control over enterprises was given to enterprise managers, in other words the regional economic *nomenklatura*. Local officials frequently altered the procedures for privatisation to provide additional advantages to the local economic elite – such as closing share auctions to outside bidders, and creating regional share funds. Further consolidation of local control began in 1996 as the national government began turning over their shares in privatised federal-level enterprises to local government as a substitute for budgetary financing. The result of this transfer was, if not a controlling share, then a substantial voice in enterprise affairs through a place on the board of directors.

In the aftermath of the August 1998 financial crisis, regional elites tightened their grip over the local economy through strategies that relied on cooperative local courts to take control over key enterprises. A new bankruptcy law adopted in 1998 allowed even small debts to used as a basis for 'restructuring' enterprises; with the help of the regional courts, the governor could arrange for the enterprise to be declared bankrupt and, with the help of the local police, install his choice as manager – by force, if necessary. One of the most profitable plants in Russia, Novokuznetsk Aluminum, was taken over in this way at the instigation of Aman Tuleev, governor of Kemerovo region, where the plant is located. The net impact of such actions was to make enterprises that were formally in the private sector dependent on regional government. Governors and republic presidents took advantage of this dependence in various ways. They frequently resorted to Soviet-era practices in their relations with leading enterprises: Enterprises were pressured to provide financial or in-kind assistance to the region, for everything from construction projects to supporting local schools. Often this took the form of 'voluntary' contributions to off-budget (*vnebyudzhetnye*) funds controlled exclusively by the governor. In the new conditions of an emerging market economy, of course, these contributions represented a burden on the economic wellbeing of an enterprise; they were the equivalent of a regional tax, but one that often would not officially appear on the financial balance sheet. In return, favoured enterprises were given preferential treatment in other areas, such as the awarding of government contracts or the writing off of enterprise debts. A major instrument used to allocate benefits was the valuation of in-kind contributions by enterprises to the province. The potential for abuse of these practices was great, and it created an environment that distorted market forces and fed corruption in the regions. It also had the effect of reducing the amount of money collected by the centre in the form of taxes on enterprises.

The suppliers of electrical power in the regions were still part of a national entity – Unified Energy Systems headed by Anatolii Chubais. Regional leaders, however, controlled the regional energy commissions that set rates, and political factors often determined who got subsidies. Before elections, it was common practice for governors to lower rates for individual consumers (voters) at the expense of major enterprises. Enterprises thus accumulated huge debts to energy suppliers, which exacerbated their already precarious financial position and provided new levers of influence to governors.

Banking reforms in post-Soviet Russia led to the creation of numerous regional commercial (private) banks which could have formed the basis for the development of a financial infrastructure in the regions. As Juliet Johnson (2000) has shown, most of these failed to survive the financial shakeout of the mid-1990s, when Moscow-based banks were given major advantages. An aggravating factor was the actions of regional officials, who often set up their own government-owned banks to control budgetary funds. As a result, regional private banks were squeezed out of existence or taken over by these privileged state banks. Ties to regional officials led to financial abuses and ill-advised loans, which along with other factors weakened the regional banking system. This, in turn, forced regions to accept the expansion into the regions of branches of Moscow-based banks, though many of these were later forced to close by the August 1998 financial crisis. After the crisis, state-controlled banks with close ties to regional leaders again moved into the void, setting the stage for a further entrenchment of Russia's regional variant of 'crony capitalism'.

Political Aspects

Rampant corruption by regional elites is an obvious manifestation the overall lack of reform in the regions. It also is an important explanation for the lack of interest in democratisation and market reforms among regional leaders. These are leaders who, in part because of their past behaviour, have an interest in remaining in power for as long as possible. The introduction of elections of governors, while seemingly a step toward the democratisation of Russian politics, in fact made possible a number of abuses that were decidedly undemocratic.

The advantages of incumbency are present in any political system, but in Russia governors and republic leaders possessed extraordinary 'administrative resources' that could be used to manipulate the electoral process to their advantage. Russian election laws forbid incumbent governors from using the advantages of office to conduct their campaigns, but the practice was widespread and usually went unchallenged. One exception was the October 2000 gubernatorial election in Kursk oblast, where Alexander Rutskoi sought a second term. Literally on the eve of the elections, Rutskoi was removed from the ballot by the regional court based in part on the charge that he had used his official status to conduct the campaign. Rutskoi's case was unusual, however, in that by the time of the election he had lost control not only of the local courts, but also of the police (who surrounded the local television facilities to prevent the governor from addressing the voters) and the provincial electoral commissions (who prevented Rutskoi's representatives from observing the voting, since their candidate was now disqualified). It was also apparent that the Putin administration was happy to see Rutskoi go, even though his successor turned out to be Alexander Mikhailov, a Communist.

In a typical Russian region, resources at the disposal of the governor provided almost unassailable advantages. Since regional legislators were, as a rule, subservient to the governor, they could be pressed to adopt changes in the electoral system that would give additional advantages to the incumbent. In most regions, a second round of voting if no candidate won over 50 per cent in the first round was standard procedure. This followed the example of Russia's presidential elections and gave a divided majority the chance to unite around a single candidate. Several regional assemblies eliminated the second round by introducing a rule that declared the candidate with the most votes – if they exceeded 25 per cent of the total votes cast – the winner. In Pskov, for example, this allowed Yevgenii Mikhailov, the sitting governor originally from the LDPR and now in the Unity Party, to win re-election with only 28 per cent of the vote in November 2000. Another common ploy was to request moving up the date for elections – even if this would greatly add to the cost of the election. Calling early elections could catch the opposition off-balance and preempt the rise of a well-funded, consensus candidate. (This was the thinking behind Yeltsin's early resignation at the end of 1999.) We have already seen that this strategy was used by Novgorod's Prusak; it was also employed by Konstantin Titov of Samara, another reputedly 'democratic' regional leader, and Yuri Luzhkov of Moscow, among others. In republics, election laws and constitutions were drafted to eliminate possible candidates who might present the strongest challenge to the incumbent president. In both Yakutia and Mari El, for example, Russians make up the majority of the population. Yet in Yakutia, candidates for president had to be between the ages of 40 and 60, speak fluent Yakut, and must have lived in the republic at least 15 years. In Mari El, candidates were required to speak both mountain and valley dialects of Mari.

Once the election campaign was under way, the governor's team typically mobilised the entire regional apparatus in support of his re-election. Local police could be used to disqualify opposition candidates through house-by-house verification of signatures on petitions required to register candidates. Politically subservient district chiefs of administration could be ordered to turn out the vote. Governors typically dominated both regional election commissions and the courts that adjudicated disputes connected with elections. Local economic elites were often pressed into giving illegal cash or in-kind contributions to the governor's campaign and were threatened with reprisals if they supported an opponent.

These efforts greatly shift the odds in favor of the incumbent's re-election. Elections that were held between December 1999 and November 2000 usually resulted in victory for the sitting governor, often by a substantial margin. Only in two instances did governors decide not to run for re-election: but both Nikolai Kondratenko in Krasnodar *krai* and Valery Sudarenkov in Kaluga were able to apply the administrative resources at their disposal to ensure the election of a hand-picked successor. Overall, incumbents or their designated successors won 36 out of 51 elections held over this period.

Along with free and fair elections, a key element underlying the development of democracy is access to information and freedom of the press. The Gorbachev-era achievements in this area, the result of the policy of *glasnost*, were mostly limited to the national media. Since the end of the Soviet Union, national newspapers have had very limited distribution in Russian regions, a result of spiralling costs for delivery and newsprint. Central television, particular the state channel

ORT, is widely seen, but it pays little attention to regional issues. Thus, local television and local newspapers have taken on greater significance. Local television broadcasts are typically limited to a few hours a day, and the staffing and editorial content are tightly controlled by the regional authorities. Broadcast facilities for most regional broadcasts remain under the control of the state, and appointments of station directors, at least until 2000, were subject to approval by regional leaders.

The most influential print media in the provinces are provincial newspapers. Many local newspapers are heavily dependent on financing and privileges obtained from local authorities. Prior to the October 1993 events, many former communist party newspapers were taken over and sponsored by regional soviets. In effect, this sponsorship gave journalists some freedom of manoeuvre, since the soviets were themselves divided or in conflict with the regional executive. With the dissolving of the soviets, these papers were seized by governors or republic presidents. In November 1995 a new law was signed by Yeltsin on federal subsidies to smaller district and city newspapers, but decisions on how the funds would be distributed were left to regional legislatures and governors. Reports on how these funds have been allocated indicate that political factors were often decisive.

As a result of these and other factors, in most regions the press plays the role of official mouthpiece for the local political leadership. Naturally, there is no serious attempt to examine critically the policies and behaviour of the local elite. In those regions where there is an opposition or independent newspaper, its distribution is extremely limited. There have been numerous cases of more blatant attempts to curtail the expression of opposition views, including closing newspapers, withholding necessary newsprint and supplies, conducting repeated 'tax audits', and intimidating – or even killing – journalists. One of the most notorious cases was the 1998 murder in Kalmykia of the editor of the republic's only opposition newspaper, Larissa Yudina. Two of President Ilyumzhinov's former aides were later convicted of the crime. Suppression of the regional press has achieved its desired result: it undermines accountability and prevents the exposure of corruption.

Another factor of potential importance to successful political reform in the regions was the status of local government, particularly in the larger cities. Mayors can serve as a political counterweight to governors, and Yeltsin's team at several times during his presidency attempted to use mayors to put pressure upon them. Mayors tend to be more reform-oriented than governors for several reasons. Urban voters are typically more supportive of reformist politicians than voters in a region as a whole. Economic interests in cities, particularly small and medium-size private enterprises, are also more likely to identify themselves with a reformist programme. Since most cities are net donors to regional budgets, mayors have an interest in fiscal decentralisation and tend to oppose subsidies.

Governors in most regions have continued to resist implementing the law on local government, which would require them to reach some accommodation with mayors on dividing responsibilities. Instead, they have engaged in sustained political warfare with city leaders. In this, governors have had the advantage of control over the budget weapon. Over time, local government has been assigned a greater portion of the burden of supporting healthcare, education, communal services (such as heat and water), and public transportation, but regional governments often selectively disburse funds for maximum political effect. The mayor of the capital city of Khabarovsk, a relatively progressive region, resigned in despair from his post in June 2000, complaining that he was 'tired of being treated like a whipping boy, tired of the endless search for money for coal pur- chases and for funds to keep the city functioning properly' (quoted in *Rossiiskaya gazeta*, 24 June 2000). His city regularly operated under a deficit of from 30–50 per cent of the city budget because the regional government cut funding. In a few regions, governors took more direct action against mayors by manipulating prosecutors to bring criminal charges against mayors in order to remove them from office.

Putin and the Prospects for Reform

The evidence to date makes clear that local elites have taken advantage of the changes in Russia in the 1990s to pursue their own interests in ways that distort and undermine reform. In doing so, they have succeeded in consolidating their hold on power, both economic and political. Part of the blame belongs to misdirected or incomplete policies at the national level, as discussed elsewhere in this volume.

Lax control from the centre – the legacy of Yeltsin's increasing political weakness – was compounded by the advent of elections of governors, which made even more tenuous the centre's control over the political situation in the regions. By the mid-1990s, serious charges of corruption were brought only against former governors, usually after they had been defeated by opposition candidates. The lesson in this for regional leaders is to hold onto their posts by any means possible or to ensure that their successor is loyal – or at least an aide equally tainted by corruption.

One of Vladimir Putin's first priorities as president has been to redress the imbalance that developed between the regions and the centre. Two approaches are possible, with very different implications for democratic development in the regions. One approach would be to use the instruments available to the central government to stimulate the gradual growth of democratic institutions and practices that would limit the powers of regional leaders. These would include reforming the judicial system in the regions, developing truly national political parties, strengthening legislative institutions at the regional level, and supporting democratically elected mayors who may be more interested in pursuing reforms than governors and republic presidents. Measures could also be taken that would provide greater guarantees for independent media in the regions and that would stimulate and protect the growth of civic associations, particularly those whose purpose is to uphold human and civil rights. (One of the best examples of the latter is the Committees of Soldiers' Mothers that investigate unexplained deaths in the military and provide assistance to young men seeking to avoid conscription.) Election reform could provide greater guarantees for the independence of regional election commissions and their ability to prevent the most outrageous violations of fairness.

Putin has apparently rejected this 'organic' approach in favour of an administrative approach that is more in keeping with his own training and background in the KGB. Putin has favoured a series of measures that would impose stricter discipline and a tighter form of hierarchy in order to bring the regions under federal control. This involves changes that would directly affect some of the institutions and relationships discussed in this chapter. In July 2000 the Duma approved Putin's proposed additions to the October 1999 law on regional political institutions to hold provincial authorities accountable for policies that violate the Russian constitution and national legislation. According to the amendments, regional officials must answer for any actions that cause 'massive and crude' violations of civil and human rights that threaten the unity and territorial integrity of the country, national security, or the 'unity of the legal and economic space' of the Russian Federation. Complex and drawn-out procedures were established allowing the president and Russian Duma, after appropriate court decisions, to disperse a regional legislature and call new elections. The new provisions also allow the Russian president, under certain circumstances, to remove a region's chief executive. Again, the procedures require involvement of the court system and Duma. Prior to this, there was no clear mechanism in place to remove corrupt or intransigent regional leaders. It remains to be seen whether the same need for compromise that characterised the Yeltsin years will blunt these efforts and leave considerable discretionary power in the hands of leaders in the regions.

One of the few positive achievements of the Yeltsin years, the rise of democratically oriented mayors of large cities, does not fit in well with the Putin approach. The measures he outlined in mid-2000 included bringing mayors into the administrative 'executive vertical', subordinating them to governors and republic leaders. This would allow governors to remove mayors and chiefs of district administrations who refused to carry out regional laws and directives. Given the current situation in the regions, this means shifting the balance even further in the direction of those who are fundamentally opposed to real changes leading in the direction of greater democracy and freer markets.

PART TWO

Patterns of Public Policy

9

Economic Policy under Yeltsin and Putin

WILLIAM TOMPSON

Beneath the noise and smoke of Russian high politics, a tacit consensus underlay economic policy throughout the Yeltsin era. Despite frequent cabinet shake-ups and changes in official rhetoric, Russian governments throughout the 1990s followed three basic rules: keep inflation under control; do the minimum necessary to keep the IMF engaged; and avoid structural reforms that would threaten the survival of the 'white elephants' of Russian industry (Hanson, 2001). Despite promises of a sharp change in economic policy following the August 1998 financial collapse, the 'post-reform' governments of 1998–9 did more or less exactly what their supposedly 'reformist' predecessors had done. Russian governments throughout the 1990s adopted – but often failed to implement – monetary and fiscal policies designed to please the IMF and contain inflation, while shying away from micro-level structural reforms for fear of their social and political consequences. The main lesson of August 1998 is that this is not a winning formula. Macroeconomic stability cannot last where firms are not subject to real microeconomic discipline – to Kornai's (1986) 'hard budget constraint'. The crisis occurred precisely because the macroeconomic stabilisation of 1995–8 was not underpinned by the micro-level structural changes needed to make it sustainable without massive infusions of external financial support. As economist John Paul Smith observed at the time, 'When the macroeconomic story does not stack up with the microeconomic story, it is always the latter that is proved right' (*Financial Times*, 3 October 1998).

The slow pace of structural reform was not accidental, nor was it the result of Russian reformers' failure to appreciate its importance. Rather, the lack of congruence between macro- and micro-level

developments reflected a fundamental and unavoidable tension between them. Economically, this tension reflected the numerous con-
tradictions between short-term macroeconomic pressures and the
long-term structural needs of the economy. Politically, it reflected
both the interests of those constituencies on which Boris Yeltsin and
his governments relied for support, as well as the limited capacities of
the Russian state itself. The chief aim of this chapter is therefore to
explain how and why this particular mix of policies was implemented
and to assess the prospects for a change of direction under
Vladimir Putin.

Gaidar's Inheritance

It is difficult to exaggerate the structural deformation of the economy
inherited by Russia's radical reformers at the end of 1991. The
structural distortions of the Soviet economy were not dissimilar to
those that afflicted other postcommunist economies, but they were
greater in the Soviet case than elsewhere, largely because so much of
the Soviet Union's basic industrialisation took place under central
planning. Planners did not merely deform an existing industrial base;
to a great extent, they created one from scratch, and they did so on
the basis of a set of priorities that were sharply at odds with the needs
of an internationally integrated Russian market economy. The resulting industrial structure was almost comically inefficient in its use of
resources and heavily oriented towards the defence and heavy industrial priorities of Soviet leaders. Much of the industrial capital
stock was thus virtually worthless in any environment dominated by
the market rather than the Plan. Moreover, while the workforce as a
whole was highly educated by international standards, it was characterised by a high degree of firm or job-specific skills, and its skill
profile did not correspond to the needs of a market economy.

These structural difficulties were compounded by the acute economic crisis facing the country in 1991, a product of both policy
mistakes and political crisis. Real GDP in 1991 dropped by 12–13 per
cent, as localist economic policies and the decay of central institutions
caused ties between enterprises to unravel, and over four million
workdays were lost to strikes. Rising subsidies to back controlled
prices combined with falling production and collapsing tax discipline
to push the state budget deficit to 26 per cent of GDP. Since this
deficit could only be financed by printing money, the money supply
ballooned, wrecking what remained of the system of fixed prices.

Although the Soviet authorities continued to shy away from price liberalisation, wholesale price inflation in 1991 reached 138 per cent and retail price inflation over 90 per cent; food prices jumped 112 per cent. This combination of price controls and monetary incontinence meant that triple-digit inflation coexisted with the shortages produced by Soviet pricing. Fewer than a dozen of the 130 goods designated as basic necessities for everyday life were available through normal retail channels. The external picture was equally dismal. Exports in 1991 fell by 40 per cent in dollar terms and imports by 80 per cent. The Soviet external debt reached $67 billion – roughly 566 per cent of rouble GDP at the market exchange rate. Foreign exchange reserves fell to $60 million, around 10 *hours'* import cover – a product of Western insistence that Russia service its debts until a restructuring could be agreed.

The political challenge facing Russia's reformers was as formidable as the economic task before them. They were revolutionaries who had taken power on behalf of a 'revolutionary class' – the *bourgeoisie* – that did not yet exist. As former prime minister Yegor Gaidar (1995, pp. 28–9) later wrote, 'the social strata essential for the stability of a market economy and a capitalist society were missing. We had no entrepreneurs, no middle class, and no property ownership.' For the revolution to succeed, the reformers had to create a capitalist class, or at least facilitate its speedy emergence – an attempt at social engineering on a scale previously seen only in the creation and consolidation of the Stalinist command economy. In the interim, they had to identify and mobilise potential supporters within the inherited social and economic structure, creating and sustaining coalitions in support of the major strands of reform. Moreover, the reformers were embarking on this revolution from above without a real popular mandate. In so far as Gaidar's unelected cabinet had any democratic legitimacy at all, it was 'borrowed' from the president, whose election victory and opposition to the August putsch had given him unrivalled authority. Yeltsin's mandate, however, was one of opposition to the Soviet state and the communist party rather than support for radical market reforms. Moreover, it was reasonably clear by the end of 1991 that Yeltsin's primary concern was with consolidating his own power; economic reform ranked a distant second (at best) in his priorities. It soon became evident as well that Yeltsin's authority was a non-renewable resource, a resource that was steadily eroded by the unavoidable pain of the transformation, by the errors of Yeltsin and his team, by the corruption of leading officials, and by the president's unnecessarily confrontational and often authoritarian style.

The final problem facing the reformers was the weakness of the state itself. McFaul (1997) has identified three criteria of state strength: the internal cohesiveness, both ideological and institutional, of the state; the relative autonomy of the state from society (that is, the degree to which state structures are or are not captive to particular interests); and the ability of the state to implement policy effectively. On all three counts, he finds the post-Soviet Russian state exceptionally weak. In 1992, it still lacked many of the attributes conventionally associated with statehood: it did not have its own currency or armed forces, it did not control its borders, and it was incapable of performing many basic functions, not least that of tax collection. According to former Gaidar aide Vladimir Mau (1996, p. 66), 'The weak state was an objective reality, which had to be reckoned with when choosing the economic and political strategy to follow. ... This largely predetermined Russia's choice of economic course.' Mau's words certainly ring true with respect to the 'flagship' policies of the first reformist governments: liberalisation and privatisation. On both issues, policy was largely determined by the weakness of the government and the ineffectiveness of the state as a whole.

The Liberalism of Weak States

In a very real sense, Gaidar and his colleagues faced a choice between speed and legitimacy, between seizing the opportunity offered by the 'extraordinary politics' of the immediate post-August 1991 coup period and risking the ultimate success of the project by seeking to build political coalitions which, while providing a political base for reform, might also restrict its pace and scope. They opted for speed, self-consciously adopting the mentality of a 'kamikaze cabinet', which proved at least partly self-fulfilling. In their own minds, their choice was dictated by circumstance. Faced with an economy in free fall, the Gaidar team concluded that they must act decisively and without delay. Notions of gradualism and piecemeal reform no longer seemed relevant; gradualism, in their view, had been tried and had failed. Gaidar later admitted that he had known from the start that many of the necessary preconditions for reform had been lacking when he launched his programme but argued that, given the economic crisis facing the country, 'there was ... no time to sit around and wait while all these preconditions were created' (*Izvestiya*, 19 August 1992). Both the public and the elite might well have been more open to a gradualist approach, whereby the government used the 'traditional' instruments of the old system, like administered price rises and rationing, to stabilise the situation before proceeding with reform. However, given the erosion of central authority and the decay of Soviet economic institutions, the reformers could see no point in expending precious time and political capital shoring up the old system as a prelude to dismantling it – and they doubted whether they could do so if they tried (Gaidar, 1995, p. 25).

'D-Day' was 2 January 1992, when 90 per cent of retail and 80 per cent of producer prices were freed. The main exceptions were energy, some raw materials and some basic foodstuffs. Energy prices, in particular, were freed relatively slowly. This reflected the fear that a rapid convergence between domestic and international energy prices would bankrupt large swathes of industry: accustomed to energy prices held at around 10 per cent of world levels and little concerned with cost-minimisation, Soviet industrial enterprises were fantastically energy-inefficient. Rapid price liberalisation was intended to absorb the massive monetary overhang that had developed during since the 1960s (and particularly after 1987) as well as to establish a sense of relative scarcities. Price signals would provide crucial information about supply and demand, creating new incentives for producers and ending chronic shortages. At the same time, the government moved quickly towards external liberalisation. Quantitative controls on imports were scrapped in January and a flat 5 per cent import tariff was adopted in July. These liberalisation measures were accompanied by steps drastically to curtail federal spending, particularly on such previously sacrosanct items as defence procurement. Fiscal tightening was to be accompanied by tight monetary policies in an effort to ensure that, once the relative price adjustments set in train by liberalisation had taken place and the monetary overhang had been absorbed, prices would stabilise at their new levels.

The other major strand of the government's reforms was the rapid privatisation of state property, initially through a voucher scheme that was to enable virtually the whole of the country's adult population to become asset owners on at least a small scale. This was meant to achieve a number of aims. Above all, rapid privatisation was an exercise in social engineering: it was intended to create a broad class of share owners who, having acquired a stake in the system, would support further reforms. It was also meant to separate economic and political decision-making and thereby to cut failing enterprises off from the state budget. Ultimately, the intention was to foster the emergence of a population of real 'sink-or-swim' firms whose managers would have incentives to use resources efficiently. The reformers recognised that their voucher scheme would produce an economically inefficient ownership structure – a pattern of dispersed ownership in which enterprises were substantially controlled by insiders (mainly managers) with little interest in restructuring. However, they believed that rapid privatisation would make portfolio investment and acquisitions possible. A secondary market in corporate control would quickly emerge and would transform the initial post-privatisation ownership pattern into a more efficient one, in which control passed to effective owners with both the means and the inclination to restructure. Both the reformers and most external observers failed to appreciate how difficult the transition from stage one to stage two of this process would be, not least because Russia lacked the sort of institutions that might resolve, or at least ameliorate, the corporate governance problems posed by the initial pattern of insider control.

For all the radical rhetoric involved, liberalisation and privatisation arguably represented the path of least resistance for the reformers. The system of fixed prices had collapsed by late 1991 and it is doubtful whether even the most determined cabinet could have reimposed wide-ranging price controls and ensured supplies of goods at official prices in sufficient quantities for the system to have any credibility. In the same way, rapid privatisation was seen as a necessity in part because a process of spontaneous privatisation was already well under way (Solnick, 1998). Indeed, one of the government's chief priorities in this sphere was to regain a measure of control over the process. It was also the case that privatisation and liberalisation were policies for which – once the necessary concessions to insiders had been made with respect to the former – there was considerable support among the elite. Just as most managers welcomed privatisation once assured that they would be able to secure control of their enterprises, so most enterprise directors appear to have welcomed the freeing of prices – they had been doing everything possible to circumvent price controls for some time, and most reckoned (often mistakenly) that their output would re-price faster than their inputs.

Political realities also imposed limits on all three major strands of reform. Despite the initial shock of the January 1992 liberalisation package, price liberalisation actually proceeded relatively slowly. National-level controls on hydrocarbons and a few other basic commodities had knock-on effects on other markets, and regional authorities were permitted to introduce local controls, which most did. In addition, numerous tax regulations also interfered with market determination of prices, seriously distorting the operation of product markets. As a result of these and other measures, an estimated 30 per cent of GDP was still covered by price controls in 1995 (OECD, 1995, p. 27). Trade liberalisation was also far from complete. Exports of many commodities (most notably oil) were subject to quotas or very high export duties in an effort to hold down domestic prices, and numerous controls on imports remained, alongside subsidised imports of certain necessities. The distortions introduced by these remaining controls lay at the root of many of the spectacular private fortunes accumulated in the early 1990s. Those in a position to buy industrial goods and commodities at fixed prices could and did re-sell them (whether in Russia or abroad) at much higher prices. Most often, the individuals so positioned were enterprise managers or their close associates, who exploited the arbitrage opportunities provided by price and trade controls to enrich themselves at the expense of their enterprises and the state. Control over the distribution and sale of subsidised or licensed imports – which depended chiefly on official favour – was also lucrative. These processes were self-reinforcing: the rise of a new business elite that had made massive fortunes by extracting rents from the arbitrage between fixed and free prices created a powerful constituency with an interest in further rent-seeking rather than thoroughgoing liberalisation.

The concessions made to bring about rapid privatisation were no less substantial. The key here was to win over Russia's powerful industrial managers. Only when the mass privatisation proposals were amended to offer enterprise insiders the opportunity to secure large stakes in their concerns on concessionary terms was the government able to push its privatisation plans through parliament. The result was a pattern of dispersed ownership and managerial control. In the absence of hard budget constraints, effective competition and functioning capital markets, insider managers were largely able to entrench themselves and to resist both restructuring and liquidation. Operating in an environment of extreme political and economic uncertainty and aware of the limitations of their own newly acquired property rights, large numbers of managers opted for asset-stripping and capital flight over investment and restructuring – arguably a rational, if unattractive, strategy in the circumstances.

Privatisation and liberalisation were all too typical of reform policies more generally. In spheres such as banking and monopolies reform, too, Russia fell into the trap of partial reform identified by Hellman (1998) and others: incomplete early reforms created winners who resisted further reform efforts. In many cases, the incompleteness of the initial measures reflected the need to make concessions to powerful interests that might otherwise block reform altogether. Thus, the bargains struck to overcome *ex ante* constraints on reform measures often made the *ex post* constraints worse. In the case of privatisation, for example, the concessions made to enterprise insiders in order to enable rapid privatisation to take place at all actually impeded the post-privatisation restructuring of former state enterprises (Roland, 1994).

The liberalisation and mass privatisation policies launched by the Gaidar government might have produced better results had they been followed in short order by a range of other structural reforms designed to create the necessary framework for a market economy. That this did not occur was above all due to the fact that the government by late 1992 found itself embroiled in a protracted struggle for macroeconomic stabilisation. The reformers had believed that, after the initial freeing of prices, tight fiscal and monetary policies would bring about macroeconomic stability by late 1992, setting the stage for an output recovery. In the event, it took four years simply to reduce inflation to double digits, and even then the situation was so obviously fragile that the government was engaged in continuous crisis management, lurching from one package of emergency measures to another. Russia's first period of relative stability, in 1996–8, was characterised by constant fiscal crisis and reliance on external support, which could not but undermine confidence in its durability.

The initial attempt to stabilise the economy following the liberalisation shock of January 1992 foundered on the inability of the authorities to resist demands for support from troubled enterprises and on a lack of coordination between the government and the central bank. For much of 1992–3, the Bank of Russia adhered to policies sharply at odds with those of the government, issuing large volumes of soft credits and giving priority to supporting industry rather than reducing inflation. Despite pressure from both the cabinet and the IMF, the bank did not raise its discount rate above the rate of inflation until May 1993. Much of the credit emission undertaken during this period was initiated by the bank acting on its own authority, although the demands of the parliament and the government's spending ministries did aggravate the problem. Bringing the bank into line with the government required a mixture of persuasion and threats, directed at both the bank as an institution and at senior personnel within it. The failure of stabilisation under Gaidar was followed by two more years of failed stabilisation efforts. Typically, the authorities would tighten policy in the early months of the year, only to give way to pressures for easing in the third quarter as the accumulated pressures of the spring combined with the harvest and the approach of winter to break their discipline.

A much more successful approach to stabilisation was adopted from mid-1995, when the so-called 'rouble corridor' was first introduced. Backed by IMF lending and linked to a renewed commitment to prudent macroeconomic management, this exchange-rate based approach to stabilisation brought inflation down rapidly and, to many observers, appeared to have laid the cornerstone for the sort of stable macroeconomic framework that would be needed if investment and growth were to pick up again. Unfortunately, the very success of the strategy in the short term contributed to its undoing. The Bank of Russia's exchange-rate policies could be sustained over the medium term only if the government put its fiscal house in order. The exchange-rate corridor was intended to create conditions (low inflation and exchange-rate stability) that would favour fiscal adjustment. Yet the Bank's success in stabilising the rouble and curbing inflation actually reduced substantially the incentives for the government to press ahead with fiscal tightening. As Granville (1999) observes, from 1992 to mid-1995, there was a very direct link between fiscal deficits and inflation; from mid-1995, the Bank of Russia succeeded in severing this link. At the same time, Granville points out that the very considerable fiscal adjustment that began in 1992 actually stalled in 1995. In short, once the government could run deficits without stoking up inflation, its commitment to fiscal tightening weakened. The financial collapse of August 1998 was in large measure a result of the Bank's attempt to defend the rouble's exchange rate while the government piled up domestic and foreign debt at an unsustainable rate.

Structural Weakness and the August Collapse

The policy of exchange-rate based stabilisation collapsed on 17 August 1998, when the Russian authorities simultaneously devalued the rouble, defaulted on a large volume of domestic government debt and declared a moratorium on the servicing of most private, non-sovereign foreign debt. After almost ten months of mounting pressure, the rouble peg had given way. While Russian officials were anxious to stress the external causes of the collapse – falling oil prices and panicking markets caught in the midst of the Asian financial crisis – the underlying cause was fiscal failure. By 1998, the general government deficit had been fluctuating between 5 and 10 per cent of GDP for the better part of a decade, with no clear evidence of a declining trend. While the stock of rouble-denominated government debt remained fairly low relative to GDP, it was growing at unsustainable rates: the stock of such debt had quadrupled in just over two years, from 4.5 per cent of GDP at the start of 1996 to around 18 per cent of GDP at the end of April 1998.

Fiscal failure was a direct consequence of successive cabinets' failure to make headway on a range of structural reform issues. There was little or no progress on a number of key fronts, including the creation of a functioning bankruptcy mechanism, the establishment of clear property rights and the rule of law, and the imposition of hard budget constraints on firms. The rail, gas and electricity monopolies, which lay at the centre of the economy's web of non-payments and which, as we shall see, performed a quasi-fiscal function as *de facto* subsidy providers, remained largely unreformed. Reform of the expensive and hugely inefficient system of housing and municipal subsidies, which is as regressive as it is inefficient, was taken up relatively late and quickly stalled. Each of these failures served either to reduce budgetary revenues or to prevent further cuts in expenditure.

Ultimately, the failure to impose hard budget constraints mattered most of all: many of the formal legal reforms would have mattered less if the economic environment had imposed its own disciplines on firms. Soft budget constraints were an area of tacit agreement between federal and regional authorities. Both proved reluctant to impose real financial discipline – Kornai's hard budget constraints – on the behemoths of former Soviet industry. This reflected both the power of industrial managers as a lobby and the fear of the social consequences of structural change. This latter concern was particularly acute at regional level, because so many local economies depended more or less entirely on the health of a single enterprise, often an enterprise that could probably never be viable in market conditions. Ensuring their survival therefore required the extension of substantial subsidies. These were initially provided by the state budget and, via the emission of soft credits, the central bank. Although IMF and other pressures forced the government to slash budgetary subsidies and the central bank to stop issuing soft credits to the real sector, only a tiny number of bankruptcies resulted, and most of these affected new private companies in the service sector. While thousands of industrial enterprises persistently failed to pay their debts or turn a profit, almost none were liquidated or forced into restructuring. This provided the best evidence of continued large-scale subsidies: if non-viable enterprises were being kept afloat, someone must be footing the bill for their survival.

What happened after 1992 was not a weaning of Russian industry off its dependence on subsidy but a shift to a less transparent subsidy mechanism. The role of subsidy provider shifted to EES and the other energy and infrastructure monopolies. The instruments used were not soft credits or budgetary funds but payment arrears, barter arrangements and money surrogates (Gaddy and Ickes, 1998; Tompson, 1999). EES and its regional subsidiaries not only could not bankrupt non-payers; they were usually not even permitted to cut them off. They therefore sought whatever payment they could – bills of exchange (*vekselya*), bartered goods, tax offsets and so on. The real value of bartered goods and money surrogates was far less (generally around 50–70 per cent less) than their nominal value. This allowed the utilities to extract something from their debtors while at the same time granting them large real discounts. (The entrenchment of these practices was facilitated by the opportunities they created for tax evasion and corruption.) For a number of years, this arrangement enabled the authorities, with substantial foreign assistance and the aid of some rather unorthodox financial practices, to achieve and maintain a semblance of macroeconomic stability without subjecting enterprises to hard budget constraints. This system broke down in 1998, when the resource-sector exporters and external lenders who had been financing it proved unwilling to carry on. In the end, then, it was the burden of subsidy that broke the budget: not the burden of explicit subsidies as an item of expenditure but the burden of implicit subsidies which meant that the authorities could not or would not collect sufficient revenue for the state to pay its bills.

The record of Russian economic policy since 1991 has not been a happy one (see Table 9.1). Recorded output declined in every year through 1996, before rising slightly in 1997 and falling again in 1998. On the official data, real GDP in 1999 was about 57 per cent of that of a decade earlier. In reality, the output decline was probably rather smaller than it appeared, but there was little doubt that the Russian economy had shrunk substantially over the decade. More importantly, although growth accelerated into 2000, there remained serious doubts about Russia's ability to sustain growth at rates that would bring about convergence with the OECD economies over the medium to long term (Hanson, 2001). The record on inflation control, though better, was still patchy. Annual consumer price inflation was not reduced to double digits until 1996. The Bank of Russia thereafter reduced inflation rapidly, reaching a low of 5.6 per cent for the 12 months to August 1998. Inflation shot up again after the financial collapse, although it did not (contrary to the expectations of most Western observers) spiral into triple digits. The country's foreign debt burden continued to mount, rising from around $67 billion at the time of the Soviet collapse to an estimated $175.6 billion at the end of 1999.

The impact of a decade of market reforms on Russian households is difficult to assess, given problems with the available official data and the difficulty of comparing pre- and post-1992 estimates, given that the latter refer to a system of non-market allocation in which money indicators meant little. It is clear that neither output nor living standards have fallen by anything like as much as the official data suggest, and there is considerable evidence pointing to increasing consumption of goods that were virtually unavailable in the Soviet era. At the same time, crime, corruption and income inequality have increased dramatically. Moreover, indicators of basic human welfare, such as life expectancy, infant mortality and health, paint a grim picture of contemporary Russian life.

Policy Trade-offs and the Micro/Macro Conundrum

In hindsight, it is far from surprising that Russian cabinets settled on the mix of policies they did. The failure to prosecute structural reform was neither accidental nor the result of stupidity on the part of the reformers. In the first place, no government can do everything at once. Some aspects of reform had to take priority over others, and it was not at all clear what a 'proper' sequencing of reforms might look like. Initially, some economists did advance theoretical arguments for the priority of macroeconomic stabilisation – institution-building could wait. Had Russia achieved stabilisation quickly, this might have made sense. However, the struggle for stabilisation was not convincingly won until the end of the decade. In the meantime, the more desperate the government's stabilisation measures became, the more they distorted the development of market institutions and worked against the kind of behavioural changes that reform was mean to bring about.

TABLE 9.1 *Economic and social indicators under Yeltsin*

	1992	1993	1994	1995	1996	1997	1998	1999
Real GDP growth (%)	−14.5	−8.7	−12.6	−4.2	−3.5	0.9	−4.9	3.2
CPI inflation (average)	1353	875	307	197	48	15	28	86
Fiscal balance (% of GDP)*	−10.3	−7.0	−10.7	−6.1	−8.9	−7.0	−5.9	−1.6
Industrial production (1990 = 100)			51	49	46	47	45	
Current account balance ($bn)	4.3	7.5	11.3	8.0	12.5	3.5	1.0	25.0
Exchange rate (average Rb/$)	220	932	2191	4559	5121	5785	9.71**	24.62**
Life expectancy at birth								
Male	62	60	58	58	60	61	61	59
Female	74	72	71	72	72	73	73	72
Gini coefficient***	0.29	0.40	0.41	0.38	0.38	0.38	0.38	n/a
Population (millions, year-end)	148.3	148.0	147.9	147.6	147.1	146.7	146.5	145.9

Source: Goskomstat (1999); IMF, Staff Country Report, 1999; Central Bank of Russia, available from <http://www.cbr.ru>.
Note: * General government balance, including federal, regional and local budgets and off-budget funds.
** Figures for 1998–9 reflect the redenomination of the rouble; 1000 old roubles = 1 new rouble.
*** The Gini coefficient is an index of the concentration of income, with increasing values denoting greater inequality.

Arbitrariness in tax policy, for example, impeded the development of a new set of more or less stable 'rules of the game' that were both predictable and intelligible to economic agents. There has long been wide agreement on the need for fundamental tax reform in Russia. Any tax reform, however, would result in revenue losses, since implementation difficulties generally ensure that almost any significant change to the tax system initially results in a loss of revenue, even if its ultimate effect is to increase the tax take. Yet the permanent fiscal crisis in which the Russian state found itself for most of the 1990s meant that maximising month-to-month revenue collection was a top priority. It could not execute a comprehensive tax reform while maximising current collections. Indeed, the government's desperate revenue hunger had the effect of making the tax system more unstable, unpredictable and arbitrary. It also severely distorted the development of other institutions, particularly financial institutions.

This highlights another aspect of the economic dimension of this micro-macro conundrum. In a developed market economy, macro-economic policy takes institutions as constant, in the short run at least. In a transforming economy such as Russia's, however, macro-economic policies can have significant – and devastating – institutional effects. The reformers were aware of this; indeed, their whole strategy was predicated on the potential of changes in the macro environment to foster institutional and behavioural change. The aim of liberalisation and macroeconomic stabilisation, together with the devolution of property rights, was to prompt agents other than the state to undertake many of the required institutional changes. Thus, the federal government's overriding concern with macroeconomic management largely reflected its own limited capacities and the political incentives it faced. As things turned out, however, the institutional changes wrought by the government's macroeconomic policies were often unintended and seriously dysfunctional. The government's fiscal crisis management, for example, led to severe distortions in the development of the financial system (Tompson, 1997) and to the demonetisation of much of industry (Woodruff, 1999). IMF policy reinforced this emphasis on macroeconomic policy. While the Fund was well aware of the need for structural reform, the release of successive tranches of funds under Russia's various IMF facilities depended more on the meeting of macroeconomic targets than on the implementation of institutional reforms. Given that the latter is necessarily a long-term project, it could hardly have been otherwise. The importance of this incentive is evident if we return to our example of tax reform: the need to secure the release of IMF funds reinforced the incentives to maximise current revenue collection, even at the expense of tax reform.

In any case, political considerations consistently favoured the pursuit of immediate stabilisation goals rather than structural reform. This, too, reflected governmental weakness. The governments of 1992–9 lacked strong social bases of support and presided over a state administration that often opposed their goals and that was in any case extremely ineffective. A government lacking a strong political base will be unable to take on the vested interests opposed, for example, to monopolies reform, and a government lacking effective administrative machine will be unable to implement such reforms as it adopts. By contrast, even a weak government can conduct effective macroeconomic policy, especially if it can rely on outside financial support. Moreover, attempts to tackle such issues as monopolies reform brought the reformers into conflict with key interest groups on which the president and the cabinet relied for support, including regional bosses, manager-owners of major enterprises and key sectoral interests like energy. No government is eager to press ahead with reforms that conflict with the interests of its core constituencies, especially if it rests on an extremely narrow political base. Thus, the politics of liberalisation and stabilisation, difficult as they were, proved easier for successive governments to manage than the politics of structural reform. As Woodruff (1998) has argued, the mid-1990s saw the emergence of a powerful 'strong rouble' coalition to back the government's stabilisation policies. No such coalition emerged in support of, for example, monopolies reform.

This emphasis on political constraints may appear to absolve Russia's leaders and their foreign collaborators of responsibility for their decisions. Up to a point, this is only fair: their actions can only be properly assessed if due attention is given to the opportunities and constraints they faced. However, at critical points avoidable mistakes were made. In particular, the reformers never really made much effort to secure broad social support for reforms. They seemed to view society as a passive object that their chosen policies must transform rather than an active subject whose cooperation in the transformation project must be enlisted. When they did attempt to secure political support for their programme, the radical reformers often won it via compromises and concessions to powerful vested interests that undermined their legitimacy, contradicted their avowed aims and brought the cause of reform into disrepute. Selective liberalisation, insider-friendly voucher schemes and the infamous loans-for-shares auctions of 1995, which preceded President Yeltsin's re-election bid, are all cases in point.

The Role of the West: Financing Non-Reform

Much of the blame for the failings of Russian economic policy has been pinned on the West – particularly the IMF and the World Bank. Critics argue that Western advice to Russia after 1992 took too little account of the peculiar features of the Soviet/Russian economy. The claim that inappropriate Western prescriptions were imposed on Russia is difficult to sustain, if only because the advice given was rather more sophisticated than critics acknowledge and because so little of it was followed. In 1990–2, the major multilateral lenders advocated a range of early steps never adopted by the Russian government, including a currency reform prior to liberalisation, the adoption of an incomes policy for the post-liberalisation period and early moves towards demonopolisation. They stressed the need for a balance between speed and feasibility, and for flexibility of approach. They also acknowledged that the construction of new institutions would take some time, in some cases a decade or more (see Gray and Gelb, 1991, and IMF, 1990 and 1991). These recommendations may or may not have been appropriate – there is good reason to doubt whether they were feasible in Russian conditions – but they bear little resemblance to the policies actually adopted by Russian governments since 1992. Moreover, there remains little reason to question the multilaterals' core recommendations: fiscal discipline, curbs on subsidies, deregulation, market determination of interest rates and an externally oriented economic policy emphasising import liberalisation, a competitive real exchange rate and liberal terms of access for foreign capital.

Yet if Western advice was not followed, Western financial assistance was nevertheless substantial, with Russia becoming the IMF's largest single client by the late 1990s. This is not to suggest that Russian policy-makers simply hoodwinked gullible multilaterals, although at times they certainly tried. Rather, Western advisors and lenders, like the Russian reformers themselves, had to adapt their recommendations to Russian realities, making trade-offs between economic desirability and political feasibility. The problem was that Russian negotiators could exploit an informational advantage when making such assessments. While neither Russian nor Western officials could be certain about what was politically feasible, the former could plausibly claim to know more Russian domestic politics. They could and did exaggerate their political difficulties in order to secure less stringent conditions. Russia played this game with Western governments as well as the IMF. Unlike the IMF's other clients, Russia is a major nuclear power and it is located uncomfortably close to the heart of Europe.

The spectre of an unstable Russia thus proved to be a particularly useful device for unlocking Western assistance. At crucial points, the IMF came under intense pressure from its principal shareholder governments (mainly the United States) to offer softer terms, or accept poorer compliance, than it would have liked. Russia has never borrowed from the Fund under normal IMF conditionality, nor has it ever adhered to all the conditions it accepted. Yet, until late 1998, the funding was never cut off for long, and the Russian elite soon became convinced that it would not be. The result was the worst possible outcome for the IMF: its advice was often ignored, but its deep involvement meant that it shared responsibility for the results of the policies it had helped finance.

Western lenders, then, were too flexible rather than too rigid. Aid was repeatedly disbursed on the basis of promises that were not kept, and it was, ironically, regular injections of Western finance that made it possible to postpone many difficult but necessary reforms. Thus, the West during the 1990s actually financed a great deal of *non*-reform. Western responsibility should not be exaggerated, however. For all the apparent efforts made by Russian governments to please Western lenders – exertions often devoted more to the appearance than to the reality of compliance – the major lines of economic policy after 1992 were determined by Russian governments acting (or failing to act) principally in response to domestic opportunities, incentives and constraints.

An Agenda for Putin

Vladimir Putin's economic inheritance, unlike that of his predecessor, was promising. Contrary to expectations, the devaluation and debt default of 1998 brought relief and recovery. Inflation was contained and real GDP growth reached 3.2 per cent on the official data, following a decline of 4.6 per cent in 1998. The fiscal position in

1999–2000 was the best post-Soviet Russia had ever known. More-over, many of the peculiar pathologies that had afflicted the Russian economy during the 1990s appeared to abate: non-payments, wage arrears and reliance on non-monetary exchange all fell sharply in the wake of the devaluation. Nevertheless, Putin himself acknowledged that devaluation and default had not established the basis for a sustained recovery. The recovery was primarily a reflection of the one-off effects of devaluation on exporting and import-substituting sectors of industry and of an unexpectedly robust recovery in world oil prices in 1999–2000. The oil-price recovery, moreover, highlighted Russia's continuing vulnerability to external conditions: the great surprise of 1999–2000 was to Russia's advantage, but there was no reason to be confident that the next external shock, like the Asian typhoon of 1997, might not be traumatic. Crucially, almost nothing was done during the two years following the August 1998 collapse to address the economy's underlying structural weaknesses.

For those concerned with the longer term, therefore, structural reform remains at the top of the agenda. The critical question is whether and to what extent Putin will break with the economic policies of the last decade and press ahead with long overdue structural reforms. Ironically, the current recovery may well be an impediment to reform, as it reduces the pressure for change. There is some evidence that Putin understands the importance of structural reform. He does seem to recognise that Russia's current problems stem from a lack of reform rather than an excess of it. He also realises that the post-devaluation recovery is largely dependent on favourable external conditions, that the country's inherited industrial capital stock is in desperate need of modernisation or replacement, and that this will require massive investment, much of it foreign. This contrasts with some of his rivals' advocacy of a sort of pseudo-Keynesian 'pump-priming' to generate output growth in industry regardless of quality.

Whether the new President's understanding of Russia's problems is matched by a grasp of the necessary solutions remains to be seen. The team Putin assembled as he took over from Boris Yeltsin was broadly reformist in orientation but included many who favoured adminis-trative solutions to specific problems. And for all its liberal rhetoric, the economic programme prepared for the new government by Economics Minister German Gref and his team contained a fair number of proposals for direct state intervention. A second question is whether Putin will be willing, or able, to fight and win the structural reform battles ahead, particularly since victory in such battles is likely to undermine his public standing, at least in the short term. The government's tax reform drive in mid-2000 was a promising early sign, but many more such battles remain to be waged. The Kasyanov government's reformist rhetoric is encouraging, but the rhetoric of most Russian governments has been liberal; action is another matter.

The final question is how much any president – even one with the sweeping powers Putin enjoys under Russia's 1993 constitution – can actually deliver. He cannot establish either the rule of law or an honest, efficient civil service by presidential decree, let alone impose a less predatory commercial culture. Creating a truly civilised business environment in Russia – the *sine qua non* for the investment-led growth Russia needs – will require action at federal, state and local levels, as well as a fundamental shift in the behaviour and attitudes of Russia's elite. Putin can help engineer this shift, mainly by providing sufficient political and macroeconomic stability for agents to think about the future and by promoting respect for law, at least on the part of the state itself. The predatory character of Russian capitalism is largely a product of the chronic economic and political instability Russia has experienced since 1990. In such an environment, rational actors tend, understandably, to discount heavily the potential future benefits of any long-term undertaking and to focus on short-term gains. Given such high levels of uncertainty, asset-stripping is preferable to investment, rent-seeking to entrepreneurship, and speculation to restructuring. Greater stability is thus a necessary condition for civilising Russian capitalism, albeit not a sufficient one. This would suggest that the most important thing about Vladimir Putin at present is that he is there. For the first time since 1993, the succession question does not head the Russian political agenda and there is widespread confidence that the man now in the Kremlin will be there for some time to come. This expectation gives both the president and the wider elite good reason to think about the longer term. That fact alone constitutes the most compelling ground for at least a cautious optimism about economic policy under Putin.

10

Health and Health Care Policy

JUDITH SHAPIRO

Dramatically rising Russian death rates have returned to the headlines. 'The price of freedom' is the front-page subtitle the *New York Times* gave to its major, well-researched and disturbing series on deteriorating Russian health, published over the course of December 2000. To what extent is that subtitle an accurate diagnosis? This chapter will suggest some reasons why that analysis may miss the central issues.

The United Nations Development Program (1999), surveying a decade of 'the costs of transition', emphasised that 'the biggest single cost has been the loss of lives among young and middle-aged men'. There has been a tragically elevated number of deaths in the transition years, and Russia has been the most dramatic part of this, though not unique among former Soviet republics (Russian women, though evidently more resilient, have not been exempt). However, to attribute millions of deaths to 'the costs of transition' we must consider what we take to be the *counterfactual situation*: that is, what would have happened to health and death in the absence of the end of the USSR? One strong and solid school of thought among Russian demographers argues that most of the excess deaths are a result of longer-term negative health tendencies rather than recent events. The unusual and short-lived period of health improvement at the start of *perestroika*, the high point of Gorbachev's anti-alcohol campaign (White, 1996), is, they claim, the exception. On this view, the deaths in the 1990s are not a cost of transition at all, but a cost of a long-term adverse trend with deep social and economic roots. A powerful datum in support of this is that male life expectancy at age 40 has hardly changed in the century since the 1897 census of the Tsarist Empire.

190

There are, however, many opposing views, finding the causes of a fresh mortality crisis in the transition period, attributed *inter alia* to increased stress, increased consumption of alcohol, other adverse lifestyles, impoverishment, and an already inadequate system of medical care subject to incoherent reform. At present there is no real consensus on this. What is quite clear, for political analysis, is that no serious policies were developed in of the countries that were involved to deal with the rise in deaths. When the situation improved, it did so in the presence of continued policy drift.

Understanding the fresh surge in deaths poses a new challenge. There is an obvious tendency to relate it to the August 1998 collapse of the currency, which also resulted in an abrupt drop in real wages, a surge in poverty, and a loss of hope, the latter strikingly measured by the leading opinion poll organisations. But *how* and *through what mechanisms* did the shock get translated into death?

The basic facts of the up-to-date and grim situation are not in doubt: in the year 1999 Russian male life expectancy at birth again fell below 60 years (see Table 10.3). *Both* male and female life expectancy fell. They had been in a consistent slow recovery since the great mortality rises of 1993 and 1994, which attracted worldwide attention and have been generally considered unprecedented outside of war and famine. As usual, it is the work-age men and women who have been the most affected. In the year 2000 the negative trends in death rates have continued, though at a slower pace. There was a small upturn in infant mortality in 1999, reversed in 2000.

Wide reporting of Russian ill health and death rates are now a part of everyday life. Reporters primed to seek out stories of surprisingly premature death from heart attacks and strokes, and deaths from murders, suicides and accidents, often with a strong alcohol component, can work these accounts into the most unlikely places. Thus, the weather reporter for *Izvestiya* (25 January 2000) begins his forecast for a Moscow audience by discussing a spate of clear suicides by young men in Tomsk, western Siberia, through hypothermia: removing and carefully folding clothing before lying down to freeze to death at night. The cheerful ending is that with the weather in Moscow at that moment (about 0°C), this would be much less likely.

Three Crises Maturing

Unfortunately, though, the new mortality reversal, in an already poor health situation, is not the most urgently demanding health development, even though it may be the most interesting research issue. The 1999–2000 setback in life expectancy is a pale imitation of 1993–4, and simply underlines once more the deeply unsatisfactory chronic condition of Russian adult health. The two leading causes of extra deaths in 1999 and 2000 are familiar ones: increased deaths, and earlier deaths, from cardiovascular diseases, commonly thought of as heart attacks and strokes, and an upturn in violent deaths of all types, with the ordinary or common accident more important than high (male) suicide and murder rates. In comparative perspective, Russian infant mortality rates are comparable or better than countries with the same level of income, and through the decade there has been a gradual unsteady improvement. It is working-age adults whose poor health stands out, in comparison with countries of similar middle-income like those in Latin America. At its worst, in 1994, a Russian 15-year old male could be projected to have only a 50–50 chance of living to collect a pension at 60.

Determining the link between the August 1998 economic crisis and these new developments remains a difficult task. There was no immediate reaction in the overall death rate in 1998. In early 1999 the increase in the death rate bears many signs of being fuelled by an influenza epidemic. Violent deaths still do not rise at this point. It is only in mid-1999 that the number of deaths from directly alcohol-related causes shows a marked jump, along with strong rises in deaths from accidents. That is, there is nearly a one-year time lag between the economic and the health crisis, and it will be complex to consider the causal links.

If 1999–2000 is 'just another mortality jump', there are three major new reasons why we are faced with a more difficult and demanding situation than the 'first Russian mortality crisis' of 1993 and 1994. Each of these maturing crises may be linked to the weakness of the Russian state. Many of these same phenomena are found in other new and weak successor states of the Soviet Union. Policy inattention to all social policy reforms, in conditions of acute shortage of competent administrators and innovators, has been compounded by the great psychological distance of the economic policy elites from the problems of the less successful layers of the population, and by the Moscow equivalent of 'beltway syndrome'. The need for radical design has also had a paralysing effect on political will in the area.

The new crises will be more demanding than the past decade's difficulties. The 'mortality crisis' did not really demand anything of the state, and the tragedies were felt individually. It was for this reason that the Minister of Health, Shevchenko, could outrageously declare the 'low birth rate' the major health priority for 2001. No matter the degree to which this birth rate may be a sign of social distress, it is, after all, a voluntary response, and postponed births are highly remediable, in contrast to premature death.

The deservedly highest profile burst of news has been the description of the way in which evident state weakness has led to an incapacity or lack of will to handle two major and growing threats tuberculosis (TB), particularly as it increasingly takes on a multi-drug resistant form, and the spread of HIV-AIDS. These problems have been maturing for a decade, and in the case of TB in prisons, much longer. The health statistics show us, however, that at this precise point an entirely different level of problem now faces Russia, and further delay will be immeasurably costly.

The third crisis is a crisis of the medical care system itself. The World Health Organisation underscored some of these problems by ranking the Russian health care system 130th in the world in the year 2000, largely because of very low rankings on 'fairness' and 'responsiveness'. The gap between the promises of universal health care and the reality of serious underfunding have now widened, and resemble previous Latin American social insurance systems, effectively covering only a certain proportion of the population who work in urban areas, in steady jobs, and in the formal sector. This view is not so clear from relatively prosperous Moscow. It differs greatly from area to area.

It is not yet clear how much the crisis of medical care organisation has affected and will affect health outcomes. The system does continue to 'muddle' through, but the 'muddle' has accumulated, and created a sense of great distrust. Hospital, medical and out-patient care are no longer free, though they are guaranteed by the constitution. There was always an aspect of this in the old Soviet system, but now it has become a norm. The somewhat arbitrary and uneven nature of the charges, and the fact that they contradict the rules, only adds to the tension of the ill. There are, however, no sharp rises in preventable case-fatality rates in hospitals. Instead, the crisis is manifest as a consumer crisis: it leads to much social distress and it reinforces poverty. Russians have long had a highly medicalised approach to health, and they continue to pay for care and medicine they believe they need, often at the expense of nutrition. The lowest income groups may pay up to one-quarter of their money incomes for medicine, often without a doctor's specific recommendation (Boikov et al., 1998; Ibragimova et al., 2000).

The word 'collapse' has long been misused to describe the Russian medical care situation, and is still not accurate today, But the continued chaos and confusion, strain and deterioration have made it seem that management of the system has simply spun out of control in a number of areas of the country. Much of the population has no idea how much they will need to pay if they fall ill. Through a number of channels, the population appear to pay for about half of their constitutionally free medical care. These caricatures of 'copayments', as they are called in the West, fall heavily on the poor and poorly-connected. Although corruption is widespread in all of Russian economic interactions, survey results reveal that the reported private payment in medical care is not 'pocket-to-pocket' abuse, but paid to official cashiers in the notionally free system. Of course, in a system where doctors still receive a wage below that of bus drivers, and not enough to support a child, the frustrations on that side are also understandable. The below-market wage of doctors supported the Soviet-type extensive system, but it is no longer possible in an age where money matters.

Each of these three maturing crises – TB, AIDS, and the system of medical care delivery – will be examined in turn, before returning to the broader picture. If not addressed by public action, they will dominate the picture for the next few years. If the political will and competence is found, then the general tasks of improving Russian health in a less strained atmosphere can come to the forefront.

In 1999 and 2000 the long-feared snowballing of HIV-positive cases finally arrived. As many as 80 per cent of the cases are the result of transmission through needle-sharing in intravenous drug usage, which has also seen a startling rise in the 1990s. A fairly sober estimate is that St. Petersburg has 70 000 intravenous drug users. UNAIDS, the United Nations lead agency on AIDS, has widely publicised its understanding that nowhere is AIDS growing more rapidly than in Russia.

Confusion and then debate about the true statistics has tended to obscure evaluating the true salience of the problem. The threat has been seen coming for a long time. At one point, it was the medical care system itself that the population feared as the channel for the disease. In light of the debate about figures, one recent 'sentinel indicator' deserves careful attention, but it has been treated as just recent news item: we can calculate that 3 to 4 per cent of potential draftees in Samara tested HIV-positive at the end of 2000. (The comparable figure in Thailand is 10 per cent.) Those bound for higher education are not in the pool of 18-year olds tested, and may perhaps be more vulnerable, but the figure is a high one. It is more disturbing that no one in the Ministry of Health or other agencies has thought of compiling a national picture, using these and other markers. (This is done much more regularly in Ukraine, for example.) The results, instead, seem more disturbing to the Russian Security Council in their implications for army manpower.

Low Russian government credibility on its AIDS figures arose from the low number of HIV positive cases reported in 1987 and 1998: some 11 000. Diagnosed HIV cases are reported *by name* in a national HIV case register, so there is scarcely a conducive atmosphere for encouraging the seeking of medical assistance. However low this figure, in 1999 it jumped dramatically: some 18 thousand new cases were reported, that is a *more than 150 per cent rise*. In 2000 there was a further rise of *nearly 200 per cent*, with 50 000 additional cases. Figures for deaths are as unclear as figures for infection. Even UNAIDS had estimated only 1250 deaths from the first death in the 1980s up to 1999. Of these 850 died in 1999 alone. It is not the numbers, but the trend that matters. The growth seems 'explosive' or 'exponential'.

UNAIDS numbers for Russia are growing very quickly, but they are not as high as a number of the estimates made by individual Russian centres, which may, of course, be prone to exaggeration. As UNAIDS itself notes, constant changes in surveillance procedures are necessary to understand the rapidly changing situation throughout the entire world. The initial failure in Africa serves as a warning.

To get some idea of how the Russian position compares, without tones of moral panic, a good basis for orientation is UNAID's estimated prevalence of HIV in the 15–49 year old population, which in 1999 was nearly two in every thousand, and may be presumed to be rising steadily. For comparison, this is nearly double the rate in the United Kingdom. However, in Ukraine, which may have better reporting than Russia or a worse problem, and most likely both, the figure for 1999 was nearly 1 per cent of the population, or ten per thousand. In 1999, 4000 people were estimated to have died of AIDS in Ukraine, compared to 2000 in France, which has a broadly comparable population. There is no reason to believe the Ukrainian picture will not soon be relevant to Russia, as all the other elements have been the same.

The UNAID's experts worry much less about the actual Russian number than about the apparently exceptional growth rate. They do not think AIDS deaths in Russia are likely to have been much more than twice the reported 850; many countries have substantial undercounts too. (Relatives may prefer 'pneumonia' on a death certificate.) However, the present very high rates of growth could bring the number to the 'half a million' cited often in the press, unless there are counter-measures to increase public awareness and to address the special problems of the new wave of young intravenous drug users.

The image of this group is, however, as a marginal and not particularly valuable layer of society. This exacerbates the major problem, the virtually complete unpreparedness to take any measures, whether it be education on safe sex, harm reduction among intravenous drug users, or any general public awareness programmes. The absence of a national lead is striking. A growing number of regional centres are attempting some increase in activity, but there is no cohesion or direction. Given the general sense of exceptionally stretched funds for medical needs, there has not been public sympathy and concern for the AIDS victims. Indeed, there is very little adult understanding of the extraordinary growth of drug use among young people. In Ukraine AIDS is known to have penetrated the heterosexual, non-drug using world, and the problem of transmission via prostitution is also a major one. Russia will not be far behind. The level of public knowledge on the subject, however, is exceptionally primitive among most layers of the population. Basic ideas about safe sex are missing, and condom use has risen only marginally. The problems will not even be of affording life-prolonging drugs of the newer generation, but of achieving any social consensus to shoulder the burden of decent nursing, hospital, and hospice care for opportunistic infections among young people in the early stages of full-blown AIDS, and to educate about how you can (and cannot) become infected. The costs of insuring that hospitals do not become transmission belts for HIV-infection will be another burden on the over-stretched system. There are more likely to be panics against the victims than purposeful action, without concerted leadership.

A second threat gathering force during a decade also matured in 1999: tuberculosis death rates in Russia jumped by more than 30 per cent, to nearly 30 thousand a year. They had had been on a disturbing and steady 10 per cent annual incline. TB did not come from the outside. Although long considered defeated in the population at large, it had always been endemic to Russia's over-crowded prisons, and Russia continues to have the highest *per capita* prison population in the world. Indeed, TB is a plague that is common to the prisons of the world, and not uniquely to the USSR. However, the combination of economic stringency and decreased help for former prisoners allowed the endemic TB which had long functioned under certain limits simply to get out of control.

One factor that is important in the changed environment has been the emergence of 'multi-drug resistant TB', strains that do not respond to the most common antibiotics. The alternative is an unpleasant cocktail of other drugs, more like chemotherapy than a course of antibiotics. Conditions in which drug supplies are intermittent are a medium for encouraging just such strains. The weakest *m. tuberculosis* bacillus is killed, but then supplies are interrupted, and this allows a period for more resistant microbes to develop.

That the TB epidemic would eventually affect the non-prison community was predictable, and indeed, predicted in the previous edition of this chapter published in 1997: 'It is alarming to read the official report on health statistics for 1995 and to learn that only 25 per cent of people with active, infectious TB who were living in hostels were given separate rooms, and only 18 percent of those living in flats with children. This, however, is an indicator of danger stored up for the future: it does not explain the present mortality crisis.' It is still the case that public concern on the part of what would be the active middle class – if they had an income to match – remains low. TB, like AIDS, is still something that, it is believed, happens to more marginal people and their children. It too, therefore, has not been a priority. The one part of the government which has begun to take it more seriously is actually the prison administration. It should be noted that this problem is not at all confined to Russia, and that even the Baltic states have had to confront this delayed time bomb, though they are apparently attempting it with more attention to the lessons of international experience.

The Crisis of the Virtual Post-Soviet Health Care System

The big idea, the 'conception' of health reform of the last days of the USSR, was that of compulsory medical insurance, which would somehow bring forth resources that had been unobtainable before. This was a poorly understood reform, and it has been carried out in at least 89 different ways, few of which seem to be any sort of example. The problem of 'dual power' between the health authorities and the new funds, OMS or Compulsory Medical Insurance, is often the cause of the greatest inefficiencies and uncertainties.

This big idea was simple: a payroll deduction would pay the insurance for those working, the budget for the others. It was first mooted in the Soviet period, and it has been attractive in every transition country. For Russia, the idea was that the basic funds would be territorial, with a small federal fund. The funds would then, somehow, be able to license competent insurance firms, who would compete to choose and pay for quality and efficient services. It is difficult to separate any inherent failures in this approach from the conditions under which it was implemented. A payroll deduction of 3.6 per cent has been applied to a shrinking base, which itself was inadequate in the first place (Estonia's fund, for example, has a rate closer to 10 per cent). The development of new forms of medical provision is scarcely likely when the entire economy is starved of investment. Instead of a grand scheme for 'purchaser-provider competition' based on adequate resources, we have ended up with new, often untrained, groups of the elite administering an inadequate fund from a payroll tax whose major virtue is that payment compliance has been good. There are at least four major variants of the system at work, but in no case is there real competition, nor did anyone stop to listen to any lessons from the West about the difficulties of such competition.

The roles of the organisations for insurance and for private insurers are poorly understood. It is scarcely surprising that a mature system could not flourish in such a barren environment. Even in the case of British and Swedish health care reforms, reformers underestimated the sheer problem of transactions costs in arranging such contracts. With the exceptional cost and health fluctuations of 1990s Russia, and an absence of real investment opportunities, these concepts are absurdly utopian. Defenders of the insurance principle somehow still hope that these organisations can become purchasers who will force an irrational system to rationalise itself. They point to the fact that, when the budget cuts came, health care did not do as badly as education, because, they claim, of the small amounts coming in from these new funds. Despite the evidence that some territorial funds have been raided for other purposes, they believe that these funds are safer than in the budget. However, after an initial boost to the total public funds available for health care, the budget allocations were subsequently cut. Thus these new funds provide only a fraction of public expenditure, and their procedures for organising payment are very far from transparent. The widespread elite hope for them must be understood as arising from the despair in the old system.

It is symptomatic of the Russian chaos that we do not even have a corridor of consensus on much has been spent on medical care, public, private and shadow. However, a certain standard picture is emerging. The year 1992 appears to have represented a sharp fall over 1991 (Shishkin, 1998), but it remains impossible to judge the data for 1991, a year of intense shortage and suppressed inflation with accompanying black markets without much more intensive examination of what happened in the medical sector.

TABLE 10.1   *State expenditure on health care, Russian Federation, 1992-1997*

Year	Per cent of GDP	Index of real expenditure, 1992 = 100
1992	2.46	100
1993	3.73	135
1994	4.04	124
1995	3. 4	80
1996	3.19	76
1997	3.24	79

Source: Sheiman, 1998.

The pattern of public spending is shown in Table 10.1, but it is not disaggregated by source. Table 10.2 presents a different picture drawn from a representative survey in December 1997. It accords well with, for example, the findings of Ibragimova, Krasilnikova and Ovcharova (2000) on what people spend on medical care, but further research is desirable. The need for 'copayments' reportedly continues to increase. In the 1997 study, three possible estimates were given of private expenditures. Table 10.2 uses the middle estimate. As the funding available has been consistently inadequate, it has been spent, as everywhere in the world, first on the maintenance of salaries and beds, and to the detriment of supplies. This has not prevented wage arrears in the health sector, of course. Although there has been some slow rationalisation of beds and services, it is sadly junior medical personnel, exactly the ones who need to be trained and more highly educated, who have slipped away.

To sum up the present policy outlook, we may observe that the Putin government that was formed in the summer of 2000 contained individuals with a definite conception of what had to be done. The

TABLE 10.2   *Public and private expenditure estimates for Russia, 1997*

Source	Per cent of GDP
1. From the state budget	2.81
2. Contributions of employers to the mandatory medical insurance funds	0.68
3. *Total of the above, 1 + 2*	*3.49*
4. Population expenditure on medical services	1.27
5. Population expenditure on buying medicine in pharmacies	1.46
6. Population expenditure on voluntary health insurance	0.03
4 + 5 + 6	2.76
Grand total	*6.25*

Source: Boikov *et al.*, 1998, p. 113.

basic argument was this: we cannot afford to meet all the medical needs of the population, and offer too many guarantees. So we have effectively arrived at a system of copayments. However, it is not equitable, and the poor pay a greater amount of their income. What we need, therefore, is an official system of copayments, with means-testing for the truly needy. We cannot promise everything, so we must agree on the basic package, which we do guarantee. An enhanced and better-developed insurance system will cope with this best.

A priori, this is a reasonable argument, and it is made on grounds of both equity and efficiency. The consequences of attempting to means test when about one-third of the population is considered officially poor is at best politically fraught. Moreover, it is clear that up until now, it has not been possible to carry through any of the tasks that challenge interest groups. Thus, though the Moscow economists moan about the continued gross over-extension of the health care system, they have not yet been able to put through a simple measure which would change the formula by which the regions receiving federal transfers (most of them) get their health funding based on the number of beds and doctors, not on patients treated, let alone any quality judgements about medical outcomes. The chances for the draft law now in process are not at all clear at this point. The government's 'Gref Programme' of summer 2000 in which they were embodied spoke of a 'window of opportunity' and the closure time could be near.

It should also be clear from Table 10.2 that much expenditure ␣ the Russian population goes on medicines. Many of these are not prescription medicines, and recent international discussion has highlighted the ineffective, useless, or even dangerous nature of some of these. Corvalol, for example, a mixture of alcohol with a barbiturate and another controlled substance not available in Western pharmacies, has been one of the most popular 'cardiac' medications. It is selected for pricing by the State Statistics Committee as one of the most basic and important of ten medications.

A recent Western market survey in Moscow found that people preferred to choose the drugs themselves, even though the average Russian visits a doctor 9 times a year, down from 11 in the Soviet period. For comparison, the British average is 6. In countries like Japan, judicious but considerable use of pharmaceuticals, prescribed by general practitioners, has turned out to be very cost-effective, producing good health with far less use of hospitalisations. The present Russian situation is very different, and even suggests some pent-up demand for medication. Like everything else about the system, it suggests the strong need for patient education, health promotion, and continuing medical education.

If the questions were addressed of what medical care was needed, and how to learn about promoting good health, then the question of whether to have a 'Bismarck' insurance system or a 'Beveridge' (UK or Swedish) state system would be essentially trivial. Unfortunately, the initial forces to begin this task are few. Yet, an orientation in this way would help make the necessary changes in the health system more palatable, and not seem like cost-cutting exercises, but the genuine freeing up of resources for more effective use in the public interest. It is to be hoped that as the government inches forward with its new conceptions, it will also incorporate this approach.

The intense contradiction between inadequate financing and persistent promises for more and better quality care has actually sharpened in the 1990s, in part because of falling expenditure, in part because of rising expectations, as Russians became aware of Western medical practice. This gap has not at all been improved by the chaotic financial situation, the unclear 'dual power' between the new Compulsory Insurance Funds and the local budgets and health departments, and the immense absence of capacity in health economics. The group of policy makers who are planning strategy, though not centralists, are discomfited that the problems have been resolved so differently in each subject of the federation, often in violation of the law on health insurance, so that there is no longer one health system. Policy-makers are no more happy with the large degree of informal payment that has arisen inside the officially free sector, and the favoured solution is to accept this by moving towards a formal system, with means-testing. However, this item has not been high on the reform agenda, and progress in the year 2000 was imperceptible. Even though the 'Gref programme' deliberately put social policy first, and First Deputy Minister of the Economy and Development Mikhail Dmitriev publicly and early expressed his optimism that health reform would be the easiest and first reform, there is no sign whatsoever of real progress. Local reports, instead, are usually and consistently of cuts.

The basic idea for resolving this problem put forward by the reformers who came in with Putin is to develop an affordable basic package for all, with an assumption of private and top-up medical care for others. However, it was bound to bog down in the kind of details that have proved difficult in more prosperous societies. What is 'essential' health care, and who will decide? How can the basic equity of a civilised society be maintained in a two-tier right to life?

Russian Health and Mortality

Medical care is only part of what a health care system, and the entire social system produces health outcomes. The Russian population is not so convinced of this, in part because they have had a highly medicalised and curative culture, and in part because the absence of assured care tends to focus attention on it, rather than on lifestyles. Nonetheless, it is not at all clear what role health care problems played in the crisis in Russian mortality. Some observers have automatically assumed it must explain everything, some the opposite.

The 1999 spike in the death rate reversed a gradual improvement since the worst years, which were 1993 and 1994. In the few short years from 1991 to 1994, Russian men lost six years of life expectancy, Russian women three (Shapiro, 1995). It is popularly assumed that this must have had some connection with the transition, and the successive and different economic difficulties of 1991 and 1992. It is therefore natural to connect this second Russian mortality crisis with the August 1998 economic crisis, which led to a very sharp fall in real wages, as prices rose swiftly but pay did not. Unemployment initially climbed sharply also, though it is now down again. However, as we

TABLE 10.3   *Russian life expectancy at birth, 1897–1999 (selected years)*

	Male	Female
1896–7	29.4	31.7
1926–7	40.2	45.6
1958–9	63.0	71.5
1969–70	63.2	73.4
1978–9	61.7	73.1
1984–5	62.3	73.3
1986–7	64.9	74.5
1988	64.8	74.4
1989	64.2	74.5
1990	63.7	74.3
1991	63.2	74.3
1992	62.0	73.8
1993	58.9	71.9
1994	57.6	71.2
1995	58.3	71.7
1996	59.8	72.5
1997	60.8	72.9
1998	61.3	72.9
1999	59.9	72.4

Source: Goskomstat RF (1998), for years until 1965, and Goskomstat RF (2000).

discuss below, the connections between wage and unemployment rates and death rates would have to be largely on circumstantial evidence at present.

We know the proximate (that is immediate) causes of the rises in Russian mortality. For both periods of sharp rise the two key factors are the same: a rise in deaths from violent causes, which includes common accidents, deaths from lethal quantities of alcohol, as well as murders and suicides, and a rise in deaths attributed to cardiovascular disease (in plain language, heart attacks and strokes), particularly as these show a tendency to strike at younger ages. These are also the two basic reasons why Russian life expectancy is so low.

It is much more complex and demanding, however, to ascertain the root or underlying causes through research. The task could never be easy, as causes are likely to be complementary, rather than competitive. But there has been insufficient research at the level of the individual, and also insufficient comparative study across transition countries, including all the FSU countries, which also have had their own crises with differing patterns. Thus, although there obvious candidates for 'the' cause, and a lot of partial and suggestive information, there is no clear consensus. Which of a number of causes – stress, alcohol, or problems in health care delivery, for example – are crucial? We still do not know. The absence of better evidence remains intensely frustrating for serious policymaking. During the period of improvement of mortality conditions the frustration was, however, more bearable. Now it is expressed more openly (World Bank, 1999).

The Russian mortality crisis is sometimes misleadingly thought of as simply male. (Just as tuberculosis death, like the great majority of infectious disease mortality in Russia, *is* overwhelmingly male.) But in 1999 female life expectancy also fell, expressed in years, about half as much as that for males, as has been the pattern in Russia throughout the postcommunist period. Even here, there was a warning of a possible adverse development. Deaths in the working-age years have been about 80 per cent male, but, as the Russian Ministry of Health reported in 2000, for the first time women's death rates for this group, the non-elderly adults, worsened *more* than they did for men (Minzdrav, 2000). In 1999 there were 10.5 per cent more male deaths, but *16.2 per cent* more female deaths among these middle-aged and younger Russians than there were in 1998. Moreover, the rate of increase in some traditionally 'male' causes of death, such as accidents and poisonings, was also higher for women. There was a particularly marked jump in deaths from circulatory diseases in this non-elderly age group (24.2 per cent as against 9.9 per cent for men), and a 31.6 per cent rise in deaths from respiratory diseases as against 23.2 per cent for men. Although there was a serious influenza epidemic, which caused excess winter deaths in both men and women throughout Europe, the extra jump in fatalities among working-age women is unusual for Russia.

Although both tuberculosis and AIDS are correctly seen as posing major threats if not contained, as explained above, for neither sex in Russia is infectious disease the driving cause of higher mortality. Russia has advanced enough in the 'epidemiological transition' to diseases of civilization so that infectious disease is now a minor factor. However, as noted during the diphtheria epidemic of the early 1990s, these returns from the past are clear signals of social distress and state weakness. This, then, has enlarged and radically transformed a trend with its roots in the old Soviet system, which itself was in great need of reform to meet modern demands. It has grown worse during the 1990s until it now presents a separate crisis of its own. The following section explains the important legacies from the old system, and the development of adverse health trends. It then proceeds to consider the major alternative views of the causes of this crisis, and the extreme politicisation of the debate. We then move to a discussion of the present health care situation, the 'reforms' that have led to the drift to the present chaos, and the policy developments that are proposed in the government's current programme. The final section draws some more general conclusions about the non-making of Russian social policy.

The Soviet Legacy and the Russian Inheritance

In its health problems Russia is the most extreme, but not at all unique, among the successor states of the former Soviet Union, all of which have had some sharp rise in adult mortality. (In Central Asia, this appears to have fallen heavily on women too.) For this reason alone, it would seem necessary to understand how the problems developed. Gorbachev's Minister of Health, Yevgenii Chazov, offered a bitter capsule summary of the Soviet health care legacy at the 19th Conference of the Communist Party in 1988: 'We used to talk with pride about our health system. But we kept quiet about the fact that our infant mortality level was 50th in the world, after Mauritius and Barbados. We used to say with pride that we had more doctors and hospitals than any country in the world, but we kept quiet about the fact that our average life expectancy occupied 32nd place in the world' (Chazov, 1988).

From that time forward, a developing Soviet elite consensus condemned the existing health care system, acknowledging its relatively poor results and stressing its increasingly poor financing. Unfortunately, the discussion concentrated less on the poor health *outcomes*, which Chazov had stressed, and rather more on the straitened and backward material situation of health care *delivery*. With the flowering of *glasnost*, doctors were free to voice their despair at poorly equipped hospitals, sporadic medical supply lines, and abysmal morale in this sector, funded by the famous 'residual principle': they got what was left over. In the spirit of the period, journals published thoughtful insiders' exposures of the medical situation as 'a picture of terrible poverty. And that is no exaggeration' *(Politicheskoe obrazovanie,* no. 1, 1989). Medical experts detailed how the central planning system resulted in all the insulin for the year being produced in one month, at the end of the planning period, but unavailable for most diabetics for long stretches of time. They revealed that a substantial number of the large volume of hospitals and polyclinics had no water supply, or perhaps only a cold-water one, or no sewerage.

Patients then added their notes of discontent at the violation of the ideals of socialist medicine. The Soviet health care system had long advertised that it was universal, free and of high quality. This ideal had remained a highly popular one (Field, 1994), but the reality was sharply different. Low quality was an inevitable accompaniment of the 'extensive' development of the system, with its accent on quantity – that is, on indicators that could be measured by bureaucrats from afar. The health care system caricatured the worst aspects of the whole Soviet economy. More than one-quarter of the population spent some time in hospital during a year, often awaiting diagnosis (more than double the British figure). These hospitals were over-crowded, with beds in corridors. Medical staff, predominantly female, were paid markedly less than the national average wage. Quality nursing, a keystone of modern medical care, was a totally absent tradition. In this atmosphere 'gifts' to staff hardened into normal bribes. Patients had to arrive at hospital with generous supplies of ruble notes to pay for routine services.

There had always been a separate closed health care system for the very top groups, latterly organised under the Fourth Administration of the Ministry of Health, added to which were a whole series of 'departmental' systems for the semi-privileged. These had not been a secret, but public discussion focused resentment. The visible failures of health care delivery thus led to both an elite and a popular backlash, and to what seems today a naive turn to the hope of market mechanisms in health care. This was well before the idea of communism was abandoned in other spheres.

The failures of Soviet medicine are now so well publicised that the student may find it hard to believe the 'socialist principles' of Soviet health care were once very popular internally. Yet we can judge that this was so from in-depth emigre surveys from the 1950s to the 1980s (Millar and Wolchik, 1994). One important reason for earlier support for the Soviet health care system by the population was that they valued the quantities of health care treatment in themselves. Western health care specialists correctly emphasise that it is the outputs – the health status of individuals – that matter for welfare, not quantities of beds, medicines or operations. However, Soviet citizens were not alone in finding it hard to judge the quality of medical care by its results, and finding quantities of care reassuring. This is partly the result of one of the unusual aspects of medical care compared to most other commodities. Even a very sophisticated health care consumer often has to depend on the producer to tell them what they ought to want. Even Soviet emigrants who had lived in the United States for some years in the 1970s and 1980s singled out the principle of Soviet health care as that part of the old system most worth retaining (Millar, 1987).

Before the 1980s a greater proportion of the USSR's resources were devoted to health care. Just when other countries began to spend more proportionately, the stagnating late Brezhnevite USSR began to spend a smaller fraction of its income on delivering medical care. This relative contraction further misfocused the concerns of those most active in determining what needed to be done about health care. There is little doubt that health suffered in part from the low priority given to health care. However, the entire health system needed a new orientation, much more than it needed more resources. In the absence of development of such an orientation, extra resources would be overly hospital-based, overly-technological, and under-manned.

In the late Brezhnev period, published Soviet statistical output had slowed even more dramaically than Soviet productivity. There was therefore considerable shock in Chazov's revelations, and in the wide dissemination of figures which revealed that adult mortality had been rising since 1965 for males (a few years later for females), that infant mortality rose sharply for a period and then did not improve, and that these were multiples of newer, low Western figures. This was naturally then linked with the call for more resources. In the West – until the shift towards understanding of life-style, environmental, socioeconomic and other risk factors in health – the medical model, emphasising delivery of curative care, ruled as well. Russians elite and population had not yet absorbed this shift in health understanding. Given, also, the 'mirror' effect caused by permission to see the new Western health equipment and procedures they lacked, it was probably inevitable that reform would almost entirely focus on getting better equipment (doctors, understandably, were also concerned about higher pay).

Although one of the earliest Gorbachev initiatives, the anti-alcohol camaign was accompanied by a marked improvement in life expectancy in its first two years, underlining the importance of life styles in longevity. It is striking that this was not widely recognised at the time.

Remarkably little attention had been paid to other influences on health, notably smoking. The absence of a democratic component to the anti-alcohol camaign, emphasised by White (1996), also meant that little was done to explain underlying health issues. The idea that people themselves, not the state, might take responsibility for their health was essentially absent.

This is certainly one reason why the backlash against the Soviet legacy began as an elite project. It was, first of all, an attempt on the part of the main actors in the health care sector to enlarge their share of the pie, which was being steadily eroded. These actors were among the very few who were more acutely aware of the failure of the health care system to deliver its real output, measured not in hospital beds occupied but in years of good quality life for the population. The very position of these sector specialists encouraged them to believe that expanding medical care resources (their resources) was central. Thus the truly informed were far too tightly focused on less central issues, and those who might have been better directed were not well-informed. After 1988, when Russian adult mortality trends resumed their upward climb, this misdirection of reform effort assumed ever-greater importance.

As we noted at the outset, it is precisely two causes of death that have been critical in determining changes in death rates for both men and women: steadily growing deaths, at younger and younger ages, from cardio-vascular (heart and circulatory) illnesses, and deaths from 'external' causes, that is accidents, suicides and murders. Therefore it is worth emphasising that up to about 1965 there were some quite positive developments in Soviet Russian health indicators, improvements which help to explain why it was possible to make a successful propaganda pitch for Soviet medicine, inside and outside the USSR. The achievements were not necessarily due to the system; they might well have occurred in spite of the system. But an appeal to broad public sentiment is not usually based on more subtle historical argumentation.

At the start of the century, life expectancy in Russia was very low (30 years for men, 32 years for women, using the data of the 1897 census), which was 15 years below levels in England and Wales, France or the US (Shkolnikov, Meslé and Vallin, 1995). After the First World War and the Russian Civil War – a disastrous period – there were improvements in the 1920s. In the bleak 1930s, however, famine, political persecution and an absence of rising living standards all led to a *widening* of the gap with the West. Thus by 1938 Russia was 20, not 15 years behind the United States. Between 1938/9 and 1958/9, however, Russian life expectancy improved dramatically. Men gained 24 years and women 27 years. More than half of this was due to improvements at very young ages. Russian infant mortality fell by three-quarters in that period, and then halved again in the following decade (Zakharov and Revich, 1992). Thus Russia narrowed the life expectancy gap with the West substantially at this time. It was at its minimum just as Khrushchev was deposed in 1964. Russia, like much of Eastern Europe, seemed to be converging on the West, through the 1950s and to the end of the ebullient Khrushchev period.

Then, across almost all of the Soviet-type economies, life expectancy for males, and sometimes for females too, went into slow reverse. This remarkably uniform process is also, as yet, not completely understood. We know that alcohol consumption increased considerably, as did smoking. The extremely high rate of Russian death due to violent or external causes correlates closely with alcohol consumption, as it has varied over the ears. Animal fat consumption, from meat, milk, and eggs, was not a health concern in the Soviet period: rather it was considered healthy. Until 1990 almost all groups in the population increased this consumption dramatically. These risk factors were combined with an increasingly backward health care service, which failed to take advantage of either the techniques or the knowledge of modern medicine. Almost all developed market economies saw declines in cardiovascular death rates at this time, even in the least advantaged groups in their population. Russian mortality in this category continued to grow, with the notable exception of 1985–7.

In the absence of an understanding of the wider factors that lie behind health, elite and then popular dissatisfaction at the end of the Soviet period focused on the material shortcomings of the medical care system. Attention always returned to the question of how to get *more*: more resources for health care, more medicine, more surgery, more laboratory tests. This was a problem addressed only in the most marginal of ways, as with expensive imports of Western technology and diagnostics for which few were trained. Experiments in health care restructuring that were started in principle were just as often not carried out in practice. With the repressed high inflation of the end of the Gorbachev era, with ever-increasing shortages and ever-decreasing values for accumulated rubles, it would have been difficult to carry out any consistent economically-oriented reform. More importantly, though, there were no interest groups who wished to effect such a reform. It was from this unsatisfactory, gradually worsening, health environment that post-Soviet Russia emerged. Some observers had thought there could be nothing worse than the Soviet health care system. Unfortunately they turned out to be mistaken.

Maturing Crisis

The new Russian Federation inherited a population with increasingly poor health habits, an unsatisfactory environmental situation, non-modernised or deteriorating water and sanitation systems, and a health care system that was short of everything except under-trained personnel and under-equipped hospital beds. This was a recipe for disaster, and perhaps the only surprise was that it was somewhat delayed in revealing itself fully. In 1992 life expectancy dropped sharply; it dropped even more sharply in 1993, and worsened again in 1994 (Table 10.3).

The deteriorating health situation was reflected most sharply in rising adult death rates. There were other indicators, which did not account for much of the increase in death rates, but said a lot about the chaos and inadequacy of the system. Sharply reduced vaccination rates eventually yielded a sharp upturn in diphtheria infection and death rates. The essential cause of the reduction in these rates was the absence of trust in the safety of the vaccines, and the increased willingness of doctors to sign forms for school enrolment nonetheless. There were somewhat more dramatic outbreaks: cholera was allowed a foothold, via Dagestan. These latter indicators received more publicity than the hundreds of thousands of excess deaths, perhaps because they were harder to visualise. The crisis, initially, was virtually ignored. This initial indifference reflected a tradition of passivity in such matters, but also its complexity. Thus the mortality issue took a long time to emerge as politically salient. First of all, there was not a great deal of publicity about the rise in the death rate during 1993 itself. The figures available to the State Statistical Committee were not suppressed, but neither were they explained so that anyone but a narrow circle of people might understand them. Moreover, the 1993 jump was so high that as leading international demographers said later, 'At the time they were simply unbelievable'. Once the more detailed figures were available, it became tragically clear that this was not some statistical artefact.

As an example of the played-down early reporting was the fact that, for the first half of 1993, there was a 20 per cent increase in the death rate, a 6 per cent rise in the murder rate, suicides were up by a third and deaths from alcoholic poisoning by 140 per cent, all of which was laconically mentioned on page 33 of a poorly reproduced and barely circulated monthly report of the State Statistical Committee. The facts of the situation were more generally available by mid-1994, but still did not really attract more than specialist attention until 1995: that is, not until after life expectancy had stopped falling. As soon as it started, though, the debate about the causes of this mortality rise – inside and outside Russia – was rapidly politicised. In the shift to extremes that has long been associated with Russia, it is not perhaps surprising that the debate on causes became highly charged. Indeed, 'genocide' – that is, this surge in deaths – was seriously proposed in the Duma as an item in the proposed impeachment of President Yeltsin.

Even in Western scholarly discussion an element of politicisation must be acknowledged. For some left-leaning analysts, Russian mortality rates were the ultimate condemnation of Gaidarite 'shock therapy'. To others, alcohol was important, but for others still, this was essentially 'blaming the victim'. Moreover, the absence of co-ordination of research effort and the failure to allocate serious resources for epidemiological work has led to a series of partial results, unconvincing to sceptics. A medical model would suggest that the problem lay in the health care delivery system, and its inadequate funding. This has been the approach of the Federal Ministry of Health and its allied institutes, and of the Russian Academy of Medical Sciences.

Two related but distinct hypotheses were proposed soon after-wards: that increased alcohol consumption was critical, and also that a major cause of this might be stress in the medical psychosocial understanding of it, where it is given a precise definition. Rather than just a vague complaint, a good definition in this case might well be this one: 'An unaccustomed set of demands on an individual, the failure to cope with which may be extremely serious.' This emphasis on stress does not mean that rising poverty and inequality do not matter to health, only that their role may well have been an indirect one, coming through the resultant creation of stress and an increase in adverse life-style habits as opposed to poor nutrition.

None of these hypotheses is *a priori* incompatible with a third, demographically sophisticated argument which deserves a serious hearing. It is argued that during the early successful period of the anti-alcohol campaign, many deaths of vulnerable individuals were, essentially, postponed. Without deeper social change, this could not last forever. With the end of the successful period, the vulnerable resumed their dying, and this briefly increased the death rate, since they all 'bunched' so to speak, thus giving the air of a crisis to a 'catching up process'. This is argued most strongly by Anatolii Vishnevsky, who has tried to start a broader discussion. He uses as an important support for this argument the finding of Sergei Zakharov, also of the Centre for Demography and Human Ecology in Moscow, that precisely those cohorts, or birth year groups, which gained the most in life expectancy in the 1985–97 period lost in the early 1990s, and that the gains and losses were surprisingly symmetrical. If those born in 1943 saw a fall in their death rate to a high degree in 1985–7, the reverse would hold for 1993.

This would imply, then, that it is not correct to speak of the new deaths as 'transition costs'. If they would have happened without transition, but only with a return to the usual situation, then they are not. If there had been no *perestroika*, so the argument goes, this more vulnerable group in the population would have died even sooner. Analysis of new data for 1999 and 2000, when it is available, will be a strong test of this approach. There are other elements in the discussion as well. For example, it is widely thought by Russian youth today that environmental causes are responsible for most problems, although the pattern of deaths does not match those we would expect if this was the case. Whilst most who look at economic shocks stress uncertainty, the serious strain on families, up to 40 per cent of whom fell below the official poverty line in 1999, is still regarded seriously by many. Against this, there is the simple fact that the usual victims in cases where poverty is the real whip are more likely to the young and the old.

Despite many words, seminars, colloquia and effort, the investigation of poor Russian adult health remained completely unresolved, just as the new mortality reversal and falling Russian population has attracted worldwide attention. The death rate attracts attention not for humanitarian reasons, but because, together with the falling birth rate, it leads to a projected substantial lowering of Russian population, which, in the Russian political context, is not viewed with equanimity (Putin himself has been particularly alarmist). Reversing the mortality trends, however, would do far more to create the optimistic mood in which the birth rate could recover.

Social Policy: Plus Ça Change?

The chaotic character of Russian health care policy-making must always be seen in the context of broader social policy failure to date. The absence of a social policy programme is not a new charge. 'Some of our opponents assert that social policy, as such, is absent in Russia', complained the 1995–6 Minister of Social Protection, Lyudmila Bezlepkina. (The Ministry of Social Protection was soon thereafter incorporated in the Ministry of Labour.) The charge that 'Russia has no social policy' did indeed gain currency, with attacks coming from both reformers like Yevgenii Gontmakher, head of the government's social policy department, and nationalists like the Liberal Democratic Party's Kalashnikov, who was for some time chairman of the Duma's committee on labour and social questions.

The veteran observer of Russian economic reform, Gertrude Schroeder, always talked of the treadmill of reforms. How much has changed? There is now a written social policy, which was quite deliberately given the opening place within the government pro-gramme that was approved in the summer of 2000. This 'Gref programme' is quite detailed and well-informed. The introduction suggests that the authors accept that the neo-liberal recipes they think would be best for Russia are not on the immediate agenda. The problem is that, once again, the initial waves of enthusiasm of a rejuvenated group of reformers seem insufficient to the task of moving the mountains of inertia represented by entrenched interest groups and bureaucracies. As of early 2001, the hopes that action would be forthcoming soon on any major reform programme have already been dampened.

It thus still remains as true as ever that torn between unpleasant options, administratively weak, deeply divided and ideologically incoherent, the myriad policy centres of the Russian government have moved towards few decisions. Where patently unworkable systems have been decreed, they have often been modified in practice, an old Russian custom. The problem, in this case, is that systems have often proved unworkable because of a sheer absence of funds. The exceptional Russian endowment of national resources has enabled a swift development of the new rich, while state weakness has resulted in another cycle in which massive corruption and increasing informa-lisation made all serious moves to towards a strengthened, if leaner, state impossible.

A window of opportunity has been presented by high world oil prices, a factor which gave the Brezhnevite system an extra lease of life it failed to use. In the new open Russia, there is a positive dynamic of increased exports, increased government revenues, decreased barter and arrears. The problem, of course, is that in such a favourable climate hard decisions are also often postponed until it is too late. It is, however, also a time of some possibilities. The overall economic environment is important, because it is difficult to get social policy to work in conditions of extreme inequality and massive poverty. These conditions, in turn, are a further damper on economic and political development. It is still possible for 2001 to represent the start of a virtuous circle, as the alternative is that Russia will slide back into the continuation of the evidently vicious one that was in progress at the end of the 1990s.

An important step forward would be the involvement of at least part of the population, and a movement away from the intensively passive depoliticisation of people understandably just trying to make ends meet. It has been noted that patient-groups have been among the most active non-governmental organisations within Russia's young and still fragile 'civil society', as an economist would have predicted. The Russian disabled have similarly shown the first signs of the kind of self-awareness that has arisen in the West; and Russian medical workers have shown some signs of self-activity. The economic crisis gave rise to some positive changes, and it is not in the realm of the impossible that the present crisis in health and social policy may do the same. The signals, however, are not at all encouraging. It will take more political will than has so far been apparent to alter this, even though the rather dramatic new crises have been acknowledged officially as urgent, real and of new dimensions.

11
Foreign Policy

ALEX PRAVDA

The most striking features of Russian foreign policy are incoherence and ambivalence. Since the end of the Cold War Moscow has found itself pulled between cooperation with the West and efforts to demonstrate Great Power credentials. Cooperation with the international community has remained the dominant tendency in Russian foreign policy behaviour and even in its more volatile rhetoric. The flexing of economic, military and political muscle has been too disparate to amount to an alternative strategy of Great Power defiance even if frequent enough to cast doubt on Moscow's commitment to cooperation. The reactive and often inconsistent conduct of foreign policy through the 1990s added to the overall image of incoherence. In sum, what we see is an ambivalent foreign policy reflecting the ambiguous nature of Russia as a regional power in terms of capabilities and a Great Power in terms of nostalgia, pride and ambition.

What makes the picture more complicated still is the segmented nature of Russian foreign policy, with objectives and capabilities in the former Soviet area differing from those in the wider world. In the 'near abroad' (the former Soviet Union) Moscow has clearer foreign policy interests and hegemonic ambitions which it typically pursues proactively even where hampered by major resource constraints. Further afield Russia's aims are more ambivalent, its capabilities more limited and its policies more reactive. This chapter reviews the patterns of policy in the 'near' and 'far abroad' and considers the factors shaping them.

Russia and the 'Near Abroad'

Since the end of the USSR, relations with the former Soviet republics have been the most immediately important dimension of Russian foreign policy. Soon after becoming acting president Vladimir Putin echoed his predecessor in highlighting the 'absolute priority' of the 'near abroad' in foreign policy (*Interfax*, 25 January 2000). Putin stressed the importance of this area precisely because Russian policy towards the 'near abroad' has lacked drive and effectiveness. One can trace these policy weaknesses to a combination of complacency, unclear roles and institutional ambiguities. Familiarity with the former republics tended to make Russian officials complacent, especially in the early years, about the need to craft new policies to manage relations with former dependent family members. Designing such policies has been complicated by problems relating to identity and role. Many in Moscow still feel emotionally that Russia is a successor metropolitan power while knowing rationally that they now should treat the ex-republics like normal sovereign states. The new states, for their part, sometimes reinforce this ambivalence by their wariness of Russian imperialist instincts and their understandable sensitivity about newly-won sovereignty. These sensitivities underlie and reinforce the basic ambiguities of the institution supposed to manage the inter-state relations of the former Soviet space – the Commonwealth of Independent States (CIS), which embraces all the former Soviet republics except the Baltic republics. On the one hand, the CIS was created to help the former republics to deal with Russia as independent and equal states (Sakwa and Webber, 1999, pp. 379–80). In Kiev some described the CIS in the early years as a 'framework for civilised divorce'. Moscow has always stressed that the CIS was established not just to promote cooperation and integration. This has fed suspicion of the CIS as a vehicle for Russian hegemony. Meant to foster collaboration, the CIS has been distinguished by lack of cooperation from the smaller member states. Its integrating role has been undermined Moscow's lack of commitment to make multilateralism work and its increasing resort to bilateralism in building within the CIS.

Russian policy has evolved through three stages. Initially, in 1992, Moscow's attitude could be described as one of optimistic *laissez faire*. It concentrated on agreeing the distribution of responsibilities and resources inherited from the USSR and establishing damage-limitation mechanisms. The Yeltsin administration, and notably foreign minister Andrei Kozyrev, seemed to assume that the benign international environment would make it possible for Moscow to build normal relations without much policy effort. There were also vague hopes that the CIS would naturally become a loose confederation and might even grow into something like the EU (Yeltsin, 2000, p. 248).

The second stage, which ran from 1993 to 1996, saw Moscow make more active efforts to ensure that the former Soviet space remained a Russian sphere of influence. Signs of growing assertiveness in the CIS region emerged with military support for Russian separatism in the Dnestr area of Moldova in summer 1992 and, more importantly, moves in autumn 1992 to intervene forcefully and with eventual success in the civil war in Tajikistan. Early 1993 saw Moscow claiming Monroe Doctrine like special rights and responsibilities in the CIS area. Throughout that year Russia used economic and military leverage to press reluctant smaller states to join the Commonwealth; Azerbaijan and Georgia complied in later 1993, Moldova in April 1994. These successes reinforced a more resolute policy on the CIS as a vehicle for Russian influence. Moscow's *Realpolitik* objectives were clearly spelled out in the September 1995 presidential decree, the most authoritative statement to date on overall CIS strategy. The decree gave priority to integration and saw this as a way of consolidating Russia's position as 'the leading force' in the post-Soviet space.

Active steps followed to establish building blocks of integration. In March 1996 quadripartite accords established closer political and economic links between Russia, Belarus, Kazakhstan and Kyrgyzstan (the Community of Integrated States). The following month saw the signature of a treaty pledging Russia and Belarus to move towards a union state. The fanfare accompanying such agreements was widely seen as an effort to compensate for their declaratory nature and lack of substance. In fact the whole elaborate CIS structure, with its summits, councils and committees was increasingly criticised as unproductive. Widespread absenteeism from meetings weakened the authority of agreements – in 1998 barely 15 per cent of the hundreds of documents agreed by the top CIS bodies bore the signatures of all twelve member states (Sakwa and Webber, 1999, p. 396). Such absenteeism was symptomatic of the failings of the CIS from a Russian standpoint. Rather than operating as a vehicle for influence, the Commonwealth had proved difficult to manage, even becoming a forum for criticism of Moscow. This unwelcome development was highlighted by the creation in 1997 of a group of the Commonwealth's strongest dissidents, Georgia, Ukraine, Azerbaijan and Moldova (with the affiliation in 1999 of Uzbekistan GUAM became GUUAM).

The appearance of GUAM pointed up the failings of the CIS. These attracted growing official criticism in 1997–8, with even Yeltsin acknowledging that Moscow had made a mess of CIS policy. Such disenchantment with the CIS marked the beginning of the third and current stage of Russian policy characterised by concentration on bilateral relations. The ritual of CIS multilateralism continues because the institution still has negative as well as positive political uses for Moscow. On the preventive side, CIS forums offer the Russians opportunities to prevent developments that might well become even more objectionable to Moscow were there no Commonwealth. In a more positive vein, the CIS gives Russian leaders a sense of self-importance and provides them with an institutional framework, however flawed, within which to maintain some show of integration potential. It is symptomatic of the situation, though, that the integration model that Moscow highlights remains a bilateral project, the Union with Belarus, whose institutional arrangements while finalised in a December 1999 treaty (*Nezavisimaya gazeta*, 9 December 1999), but remained far from operational in early 2001. Rather than seeking to add others to the Union, the Kremlin has focused on strengthening its network of bilateral ties. Putin has concentrated on trying to improve relations with the more troublesome CIS states, paying visits to Uzbekistan, Turkmenistan, Azerbaijan and Ukraine in the course of his first year in office and negotiating partially successful agreements on specific economic and security questions without linking these to further CIS integration. The pragmatic and tough business-like approach taken by Putin in these negotiations reflects the general tone of current Russian policy in the 'near abroad'.

In assessing the overall nature of Russian policy over the last decade one must be careful to avoid extreme judgements. Moscow has pursued neither simply a policy of aggressive neo-imperialism nor one of liberal cooperation. Rather, it has behaved like a constrained hegemon, relatively cautious in its attempts to build dominant influence in the region. Its hegemonic actions have been curbed by awareness of resource limitations and caution about the costs of power projection. The degree of constraint and caution has varied with issue area, being greatest on Russian minority issues and least in the security sphere where hegemonic tendencies have been most pronounced.

When the USSR disintegrated, leaving 25–6 million Russians beyond the borders of the Russian Federation, many anticipated that Moscow would play the ethnic card to bring pressure to bear on the

Baltic states, Ukraine and Kazakhstan, all of which have large Russian minorities. Yet the Russian diaspora has figured remarkably little in Russian policy in the 'near abroad'. Local military support for Russian separatists in the Dnestr region of Moldova in 1992 proved to be the exception. Moscow has complained regularly about the treatment of the Russian minorities in Estonia (30 per cent) and Latvia (34 per cent) without the issue becoming a major obstacle to reasonable if at times strained relations. Russian troops withdrawals from these states were negotiated relatively smoothly and completed on schedule in 1994. Since then Moscow has continued occasionally to protest about the violation of minority rights but has desisted from taking any action that might risk seriously disrupting ties and causing problems in relations with the West. In fact, Russia has wisely left it to the Western governments and the OSCE to press Tallinn and Riga on minority issues. Within the CIS, Moscow has shown even greater restraint, doing very little to support the large numbers of its compatriots in Kazakhstan and Ukraine. Attempts in the mid-1990s to secure dual citizenship rights were successful only in the case of Turkmenistan and were not vigorously pursued in negotiations with Ukraine where the 11 million-plus Russian minority comprises roughly a fifth of the population. Moscow trod a very cautious policy line throughout the problems Kiev experienced with the independent-minded Russian region of Crimea in the early and mid-1990s. That the Kremlin ignored Russian nationalist calls to help their compatriots testifies to the importance it attributed to avoiding major instability. Similar pragmatism led Moscow to reach compromise in 1997 on the knotty issue of the naval base at Sevastopol and agree to a 20-year lease, so not pressing territorial claims on the city.

The fact that Russia has not played the ethnic card so far does not mean that minority issues will always remain so low on the foreign policy horizon. Putin's efforts to strengthen Russian national identity are paralleled by signs of greater interest in doing more for compatriots in the 'near abroad' (*Izvestiya*, 24 October 2000). While the Kremlin has shown no signs of increasing the use of language and other minority rights issues against other CIS states these sensitive questions continue to offer potential scope for leverage.

Caution is also evident in Moscow's handling of economic relations in the CIS. Here Moscow has had to juggle two concerns: to retain and build ties to further political influence, security and long-term regional economic integrity and yet do so without damaging Russia's national economic interests. The problems of satisfying both sets of concerns have been compounded by the economic environment. The break-up of the USSR adversely affected the economies of all the CIS states and prompted a rapid diversification of trade from the region. The first half of the 1990s saw sharp declines in trade among the CIS states; as a proportion of their overall trade it fell from well over a half in 1992 to just a third in 1997 (Olcott *et al.*, 1999, pp. 59–65). By 1999 only Belarus, Tajikistan and Moldova were still heavily dependent on Russia for their exports; Ukraine, Uzbekistan and Azerbaijan were among the most successful in reorienting their goods to world markets. This diversification has been driven not just by economic rationale but also by a political imperative to reduce dependency on Russia. In exporting more oil to the West, Baku has sought to increase its security as well as its revenues.

For Azerbaijan economic and foreign policy priorities work in tandem, for Russia they typically pull in different directions. Moscow has tended to put economic priorities first. Rather than continuing to paying a premium for its economic hegemony in the region, Russia began drastically to cut its deliveries of subsidised fuel to other CIS states in the early 1990s and succeeded in redirecting more oil and gas to international hard-currency markets where it sold 85 per cent of its exports in 1999. So for national commercial benefit Russia has helped to accelerate rather than attempting to stem the flight from CIS trade. And when presented with opportunities of furthering regional integration at some material cost, Moscow has shown extreme economic prudence. Tough Russian terms for membership of the rouble zone contributed to the failure of that scheme in 1993 (Olcott *et al.*, 1999, pp. 47–8). Concerns about the economic costs of integration with Belarus long delayed agreement on the Union state and continue to complicate its establishment.

Despite its commitment to building a single CIS economic space, Moscow was in the late 1990s among the most protectionist-minded members of the Commonwealth. Russian economic nationalism has greatly added to the considerable problems hampering the effective operation of the elaborate CIS economic mechanism that Moscow initially hoped would increase its own control over the former Soviet economic space. Unable to use bodies such as the inter-state economic committee, Russia has had to negotiate contentious economic questions in multilateral and bilateral settings that give it no inbuilt advantage. In the long tussle over mineral rights in the Caspian Sea Moscow failed to push through the principle of joint control of the seabed by of all the littoral states. Russia found that hegemonic pressure tactics, particularly when employed half-heartedly, were insufficient to overcome the opposition, notably from Azerbaijan supported by several major oil multinationals. Russia compromised by accepting the division of the seabed into national sectors (Becker, 2000, pp. 92–9). The Caspian story illustrates the limitations of Russian muscle, especially in the face of determined resistance from a CIS state enjoying the combined backing of Western and also some Russian commercial interests, including the oil conglomerate Lukoil. Moscow has had to contend with similarly difficult circumstances in the long and unresolved contest over Caspian oil pipelines (ibid., pp. 104–22).

In less complicated bilateral settings, freer from Western involvement, Russia has managed to pursue its objectives with somewhat less difficulty. Relations with Ukraine have long suffered from trade tensions, and Russian complaints about mounting debts for gas deliveries. To counter alleged siphoning of Russian gas transiting Ukraine territory, Moscow plans to build a bypass pipeline through Belarus and Poland. This may be seen as an instance of economic rationale taking precedence over closer political ties with Russia's most important neighbour. However, the bypass threat also helped Putin negotiate an interim settlement on Ukraine gas debt in October 2000 (*Interfax*, 16 October 2000). The agreement reportedly involves a kind of debt for equity deal whereby Russia, through Gazprom, can acquire considerable stakes in the Ukrainian pipeline. The accord seems typical of the Kremlin's wish to marry economic objectives with political ones. Putin is aware that the Russian economy remains too weak either to exercise natural economic hegemony or to afford to pay heavily for political influence. At the same time, he seems to favour greater and more coordinated Russian promotion of its economic presence in the CIS states. With Moscow increasingly sceptical about the Western connection as the key to economic prosperity, efforts to nurture CIS economic ties might pay commercial as well as political and security dividends.

It is in the security field that Russian hegemonic tendencies, and occasionally neo-imperialist instincts, have emerged most clearly and been pursued most forcefully. Moscow has shown a relatively consistent commitment to two policy objectives. The first centres on a strategy of extended border defence which is based on the idea that the best way to protect the Russian Federation is to ensure the security of the former Soviet frontiers. Moscow's reasoning here is

straightforward. The collapse of the USSR left Russia with a frontier
including large sections of undefended, formerly administrative
boundaries and a collection of newly independent states neighbouring
states too weak to secure the old and well fortified Soviet borders.
Moreover, new governments in strategically located states in the
Caucasus and Central Asia were unable to manage local conflicts.
The resulting instability could not only undermine border security but
also spread by contagion to adjoining regions and ethnic republics of
the Russian Federation. What Moscow viewed as legitimate security
concerns appeared to many of the new states as pretexts for Russian
hegemony and neo-imperialism. Such anxieties were reinforced by
Russia's second objective: to keep the 'near abroad' as Russia's
security preserve and sphere of influence in keeping with its Great
Power status. To this end Moscow has sought to build up multilateral
and especially bilateral military ties within the CIS and to counter the
influence of external security organisations throughout the 'near
abroad'.

The strategy of 'outer border' area defence has taken different
forms in different regions of the CIS. In the Caucasus Moscow has
used actively interventionist policies to establish dominance. This is
understandable given the particularly high strategic value of the
region in terms of energy and its close contact with the most unstable
areas of the Russian Federation, notably Chechnya. Azerbaijan and
Georgia have both been targets of especially active Russian pressure,
though with different results. In the late 1990s, after years of using
tough pressure tactics against Baku, Moscow switched to a softer
approach, including a more even-handed stance towards the Azeri-
Armenian conflict in which it had traditionally supported its close ally
Yerevan. This more pragmatic line has yielded better results in the
form of a limited rapprochement on energy issues even though Baku
remains resistant to closer military cooperation. In the case of
Georgia hard pressure tactics have proved more fruitful. Tbilisi's
vulnerability to Abkhaz separatism was the key to its early concessions to Moscow's demand for effective security domination. With
troops already on the ground, Russia managed to turn the conflict
between Georgia and Abkhazia to its advantage. Moscow did so
through a peculiar form of 'peacekeeping' in which it acted as a
'player' rather than a 'referee', exercising pressure on both sides to
maximise leverage (Lynch, 2000, ch. 6). As a result, Georgia became a
part of Moscow's sphere of influence, with its borders patrolled by
Russian troops. However, negotiations continue on the size and stay

of Russian contingents and Tbilisi is actively seeking to diversify its security links within and outside the CIS (Kuzio, 2000, p. 96).

If Russia 'pushed' its way into Caucasian conflicts to increase its leverage on local leaders, in Central Asia Moscow found itself 'pulled' into major security involvement. Russian anxiety in autumn 1992 about radical Islam opposition forces effectively separating Tajikistan from the CIS prompted Moscow to use its forces on the ground to support the government and defend it against internal and external threats (Lynch, 2000, pp. 155–7). Confronted with the formidable problem of stabilising the situation, Moscow managed to bring about negotiated internal accord. It made less progress in trying to establish a collective CIS and Central Asian 'peacekeeping' operation. The neighbouring states have made only nominal contributions and the most powerful of them, Uzbekistan, remains opposed to any institutionalised joint security arrangements for the region. In 1999 Tashkent, along with Baku and Tbilisi, withdrew from the CIS collective security organisation. Increasingly, Russia has had to rely on a network of bilateral agreements, the closest of which are with Kazakhstan, Kyrgyzstan, Armenia, Belarus and Georgia (Olcott *et al.*, 1999, p. 88).

The asymmetry of these accords means that Russia has had to bear the cost of security for the benefits of exercising control. The economic pressures on the defence budget and the large cuts announced for the armed forces have placed in doubt the sustainability of Moscow's security commitments throughout the CIS. Maintaining such a large military presence and security commitment in Central Asia runs the risk of strategic as well as budgetary over-extension. In Yeltsin's last years it looked as if such arguments might bring about partial disengagement (Lynch, 2000, p. 169). The greater stress Putin has placed on defence funding and priorities makes any major retrenchment less likely. The Kremlin has made much play of the growing threat of Islamic fundamentalism in connection with the war in Chechnya and the fighting in Uzbekistan. With talk in spring 2000 of Moscow carrying the struggle with the Taliban into Afghanistan (*Interfax*, 22 May 2000), the Kremlin seems hardly disposed to reduce its commitment to protecting what Primakov has called ' the underbelly of Russia' (*Interfax*, 29 January 1996).

Linking security issues in the CIS directly with those further afield is the problem of keeping the influence of alternative groups and alliances to a minimum within the 'near abroad'. Within the CIS itself Russia's greatest challenge comes from GUUAM whose members share concerns about Moscow's use of border stabilisation and peace-keeping as vehicles to promote Russian security hegemony. To counter such efforts these states have begun to cooperate in both areas. More worrying from a Russian perspective are GUUAM's increasing links with NATO. The group's leading state, Ukraine, signed a Charter in 1997 associating it with NATO and occasionally Kiev talks about the possibility of moving to full membership (Black, 2000, pp. 175–202). Aspirations to join NATO have also been expressed by Georgia and Azerbaijan and Baku is actively considering granting basing rights to the Alliance. Such 'southern' initiatives compound older Russian anxieties about facing NATO expansion to its northern borders through the affiliation of the Baltic states. Moscow has repeatedly stated that would find any such move 'unacceptable' since it would transgress the 'red line' Russia has drawn around the security zone of the whole 'near abroad'. Russian attempts to offer the Balts 'security guarantees' have predictably met with rejection (ibid., pp. 202–21). Moscow's hopes of keeping NATO beyond the 'red line' lie mainly in improving its relations with Washington and possibly encouraging Brussels to assure the Balts with a prospect of EU membership which would be a more acceptable Western affiliation from Russia's standpoint.

Russia and the 'Far Abroad'

In its relations with the wider world Russia has operated under far more severe constraints and behaved more reactively than within the CIS. In the 'far abroad' Russia is obviously a weaker actor, trying to find the elusive balance between the cooperation required to maintain a benign economic and political environment and the assertiveness needed to ensure the kind of security, influence and self-respect expected by a state with superpower memories and Great Power ambitions. Russian policy towards the 'far abroad' has evolved through three main stages: full collaboration in 1992; qualified cooperation from 1993 to 1995; and pragmatic engagement and active multipolarity since 1996.

1. *Full collaboration (1992)*. In its first year as an independent state Russia tried to demonstrate its willingness to collaborate with the West in the hope that this would lead quickly and almost automatically to integration with the international community. On the economic front there were hopes that Russia's new

membership of the IMF (June 1992) would yield large and perhaps even Marshall Plan sums of aid. In the atmosphere of post-Cold War euphoria Moscow conceived of security as an area for integration and aspired to participation in the creation a new security architecture based on the CSCE. Existing security organisations would be transformed and Yeltsin even spoke of Russian membership of NATO as a long-term possibility. Concerned to display its commitment to collaboration, Moscow aligned itself with the West on even the most difficult issues. Russia supported the tough US line towards Libya and Iraq and voted in May 1992 for UN sanctions against Yugoslavia.

This full collaboration stage must be viewed realistically. It is sometimes assumed that it constituted the natural line of Russian foreign policy from which many subsequent developments have represented an unexpected, remarkable and ominous deviation. As a corrective, one might argue that 1992 was the result of the exceptional conditions of post-Soviet euphoria in Western capitals and in Moscow. Full collaboration reflected an enthusiasm for the successful Western model in both domestic and international affairs as well as offer Yeltsin and his foreign minister Andrei Kozyrev a ready substitute for a considered national strategy.

2. *Qualified cooperation (1993–5)*. In late 1992 and through 1993 the policy of full collaboration and Kozyrev himself started to come under critical fire especially from communist and nationalist positions. Even official endorsement of full collaboration became qualified in documents such as the Foreign Policy Concept (April 1993). While placing emphasis on internal rather than external threats to Russian security, the Concept warned against the dangers of excessive economic openness to the West, which might exploit this to reduce Russia to a raw materials exporter (Malcolm *et al.*, pp. 67–9). Scepticism deepened about the benefits of the disappointingly small sums of aid that were forthcoming (Gould-Davies and Woods, 1999, pp. 7–10). Moscow found it difficult to adjust to the realities of conditionality. In policy action too signs emerged of a shift away from complete acquiescence to Western preferences. In 1993 Washington objected to the export of Russian rocket engines to India and threatened sanctions. Instead of complying fully with American wishes, Moscow negotiated a compromise solution (Malcolm *et al.*, 1996, pp. 141–2). This episode marked the beginning of

tougher Russian promotion of its international trade interests, especially where these also advanced national security priorities.

On the security front tensions grew in 1994 as Moscow realised that the Partnership for Peace scheme was not a way of diverting Eastern Europe from pressing to join NATO, as the Russians had initially assumed, but rather a pathway to their eventual membership. The clear intention of Washington to take in new members resulted in Russian delays in signing and implementing its own Partnership Agreement (Antonenko, 1999–2000, pp. 127–8). Objections to NATO expansion as a threat to Russian security grew ever louder against the backdrop of what Moscow saw as typically overbearing Alliance behaviour in the Bosnian conflict (Black, 2000, pp. 12–13). The Bosnian crisis placed Russian willingness to cooperate with the West under increasing strain. Moscow's attempts to mediate between NATO and Belgrade ultimately failed to prevent air strikes (Baranovsky, 1997, p. 396), which the Russians did not actively oppose for fear of precipitating an open rift with the West. Instead, Moscow undertook some low-profile political obstruction and Yeltsin talked in December 1994 about the onset of 'Cold Peace'. The temperature fell further with Western criticism of Moscow's military action in Chechnya and vociferous Russian complaints about NATO. Symptomatic of the declining support for earlier notions of cooperation with the West was the replacement in January 1996 of their beleaguered advocate Kozyrev with the more pragmatic head of the Foreign Intelligence Service, Yevgenii Primakov.

3. *Pragmatic engagement and active multipolarity.* Primakov brought to the Foreign Ministry a more strategic and soberly pragmatic approach to pursuing Russian national state interests formed by his long experience of international affairs, going back to the 1960s, and his recent career in state intelligence. His appointment acted as a catalyst for the transition to a more active *Realpolitik*. Under Kozyrev growing doubts about cooperating with the West had typically produced strong rhetoric, improvised gestures of protest and little or no effective action. Overwhelming concern to use international cooperation to help ease domestic problems had largely crowded out an active foreign policy. In his two-and-a-half years as Foreign Minister Primakov tried, with some success, to shift gear and give Russian foreign policy a more proactive and strategic direction. This effort has

been sustained under Igor Ivanov, who took over his job when Primakov became Prime Minister in August 1998. While Ivanov is a lower-key minister, Moscow has become if anything a more vigorous foreign policy actor. This is due in large part to having in Putin a far more energetic and statist-minded president with a keen interest in taking forward the policy approach Primakov established: pragmatic engagement with the West to manage threats coupled with an active, diverse and 'multipolar' development of Moscow's external relations to give Russia greater presence in international institutions and processes (Gorchakov, 1999, p. 165; *ITAR-TASS*, 29 March 2000).

In this approach both assertiveness and cooperation play a part. On the one hand, Moscow follows what Realists would recognise as a normal pattern of behaviour for a weak state trying to counter and balance threats, adjusting strategy to what its capabilities and international constraints will allow. On the other hand, Russia also seems to conform to some neo-liberal institutionalist expectations. Moscow continues to be influenced by its economic and institutional links with the international community in general and the industrial West in particular. Russia seeks to gain acceptance and appreciates admission to major international clubs, such as the G7 (retitled G8 at the 1997 Denver summit). This desire to be accepted as playing a major role in world affairs through rather than against the international community both encourages and restricts Russian foreign policy assertiveness. Moscow thinks that a degree of assertiveness helps it to earn the respect of the West (Yeltsin, 2000, p. 131). At the same time, Moscow remains anxious to avoid assertiveness leading to conflict and international marginalisation. Russian assertiveness therefore has self-limiting qualities (Mandelbaum, 1998, p. 32). Moscow seeks to adjust its policies to maximise respect while minimising loss of international acceptability and influence. Such self-limiting assertiveness has figured, in varying degree, in Russian attitudes to economic relations with the West, in Moscow's engagement with NATO in Yugoslavia and in its efforts to diversify political reach through a strategy of active multipolarity.

The economic strand connecting Washington and Moscow became particularly strong in the Primakov years, with the IMF making available funds ($6.8 million in 1995 and $10.2 billion in March 1996) that Yeltsin found extremely useful to support both reform policies

and his own re-election in summer 1996. Support continued into
Yeltsin's second term as the financial situation worsened, with the
largest package of $17.1 billion shortly preceding the financial crash
of August 1998 (Gould-Davies and Woods, 1999, pp. 10–17). The
crisis severely undermined the already frail confidence of the Russian
leadership and political class in Western economic advice and aid.
This 'shock therapy' increased awareness of the risks as well as
benefits of greater integration into international financial and economic structures (*Izvestiya*, 8 December 1999). The lessons of August
1998 have encouraged more careful and tougher negotiation, whether
on access to the World Trade Organisation or debt rescheduling
(*Nezavisimaya gazeta*, 28 April 1999; *ITAR-TASS*, 1 November
2000). Putin has tried to strike a balance between the need for
pragmatic self-reliance and cooperation. He has warned against the
emasculating consequences of dependence on foreign loans and
advocated as much reliance as possible on Russian resources (*Russian
TV*, 8 July 2000). It is in this context that Putin has come out as a
strong supporter of efforts to maximise Russia's main hard-currency
exports – energy and arms. In the energy field this has found
reflection in a more determined policy to secure Russian national
interest in the routing of Caspian pipelines. And arms exports
have been given an even higher priority than they received in the
Yeltsin years. At the same time, Putin is aware of the fact that arms
and even oil exports will themselves never resolve the country's
economic problems. He has highlighted the need to attract foreign
investment by ensuring that Russia follows a pragmatic external
policy and abides by the rules of the international commercial game
(*ARD TV*, 9 January 2000). In the debates in Moscow in early 2001
over whether to adhere to the schedule of interest payments on Paris
Club debt, the Kremlin came down in favour of honouring Russia's
commitments.

   As far as the security dimension of the current stage of policy is
concerned, a new approach emerged soon after Primakov took over
the Foreign Ministry. Instead of continuing simply to protest against
the idea of NATO expansion, Moscow accepted its inevitability and
moved to use negotiation and political engagement to try and
alleviate some of the major problems at a time when Brussels was
keen to reach some kind of accord (*ITAR-TASS*, 29 September 1996).
The Founding Act on Mutual Relations, Cooperation and Security
between NATO and the Russian Federation was signed in Paris in
May 1997. Its provisions fell short of Russian expectations on both

military and political fronts. While the act includes assurances on the non-deployment of nuclear weapons beyond NATO's existing borders, provisions regarding conventional forces are more permissive than Moscow would like. Russian anxieties about enlargement bringing military infrastructure closer to their borders were confirmed by the rapidity with which Brussels decided to locate the headquarters for Polish, Danish and German northern forces in Szczecin.

The political provisions of the Act also proved disappointing failed to meet Russian concerns about being marginalised in European security decisions. The Act established an elaborate set of consultative and confidence-building institutions and processes, including a Permanent Joint Council. Moscow assumed that these arrangements would ensure full and timely consultation on all issues, including those relating to the future development of NATO (Antonenko, 1999–2000, p. 130). But Washington made clear that the Russians would play no real part in such discussions. The general weakness of the arrangements was brought home by the inadequate consultation on NATO plans for dealing with the Kosovo crisis. NATO action in Kosovo heightened Russian alarms about military vulnerability as well as security marginalisation. The Kosovo operation underscored the technological gap between NATO and a fast-deteriorating Russian military capability suffering from huge budgetary cuts. Kosovo also showed NATO's ability, in accord with its New Strategic Concept, to conduct operations out-of-area. Many in Moscow saw Western intervention in Yugoslavia as preparing the ground for similar ventures in ethnic conflict areas within the CIS. The supportive attitude to the NATO operation shown by Tbilisi and Baku only increased Russian concern (ibid., pp. 131–3). This may have contributed to Moscow's decision to move in late 1999 to impose control over Chechnya. Western protests against Russian conduct in Chechnya were more rhetorical than real, with action limited to gestures such as the suspension of Russia from the Parliamentary Assembly of the Council of Europe. The Chechnya and Kosovo crises certainly raised tensions between Russia and the West yet did not lead to any lasting rupture in relations. To be sure, NATO strikes prompted a verbal onslaught from Moscow greater than any since the end of the Cold War. Primakov, now prime minister, en route to Washington when the bombing started, pointedly ordered his plane to return to Moscow. Beyond this gesture, there were no serious official threats of counter-measures. On the contrary, the Kremlin was anxious to restrain protest to avoid political isolation (Lynch, 1999, pp. 69–70).

Russian policy towards Kosovo illustrates the way in which Moscow uses limited assertiveness to try and carve out a prominent role in international crisis diplomacy. Russian policy was by no means a coherent and consistent strategy of cooperation with the international community. Policy was often improvised, reacting to opportunities rather than following any strategic plan (Levitin, 2000). Moscow was certainly sympathetic to the Serb cause though equally wary of being used by Milosevic. Moscow saw the only way it could be a real player in the diplomatic game was to help mediate between the two sides and cooperate with the West. Viktor Chernomyrdin's shuttling to Belgrade made an important contribution to the peace plan accepted in June 1999. Such diplomatic mediation and broader cooperation within the Contact Group helped Russia promote its interest in securing a greater role for the UN and OSCE in the Kosovo settlement (Lynch, 1999, pp. 62–5). The Russian position here by no means mainly reflected high-minded internationalism. Support for the involvement of the UN and OSCE in Kosovo as in other areas stems rather from a concern to subordinate NATO, in which Moscow has no influence, to institutions where Russia has a strong voice. Moscow has been distinctly less enthusiastic about allowing extensive UN and OSCE involvement in ethnic disputes within the CIS let alone on its own territory (Hopf, 1999, ch. 3). Still, whatever the *Realpolitik* calculations shaping Russian attitudes, Moscow has shown an interest in promoting cooperation through these and other international bodies.

The fact that Russia managed ultimately to play a constructive role in the Kosovo settlement meant a relatively fast mending of fences with NATO. After tussling over command and deployment arrangements, Russian troops took part in KFOR peace-keeping operations. And in late 1999 Moscow began to resume low-level contacts under the Founding Act arrangements, which it had suspended in protest against the NATO strikes. The consultative arrangements, reactivated fully in 2000, have contributed to a slow improvement in relations just as these have come under new strain from American plans for a National Missile Defence (NMD). Moscow's two main concerns about NMD recall those surrounding Reagan's Strategic Defence Initiative in the 1980s. First, that NMD threatens to undermine the Anti-Ballistic Missile Treaty of 1972 and disrupt strategic stability by triggering a new arms race, with all nuclear powers striving to increase their offensive arsenals. The second concern, less loudly voiced yet more acutely felt, is that the process of creating NMD would lengthen

America's lead in weapons technology and eventually give the US unchallengeable nuclear superiority. The Russian policy response to NMD has combined alarm and assertiveness with a willingness to find some kind of compromise. NMD, coming on top of NATO expansion and Kosovo, has heightened Russian alarm about external threats. In the National Security Concept of 2000 these receive more far more prominence than in the 1997 version, which gave precedence to internal threats. The Concept's greater emphasis on the operational importance of nuclear weapons fits in with the most assertive of the policy responses to NMD which has emerged in Moscow: to counter the American plan by developing Russia's strategic forces, especially the Topol-M missile.

While supporting force modernisation, the Kremlin seems to prefer a political approach to the whole NMD problem. Putin pressed for ratification of the START II treaty (which parliament agreed in April 2000) to strengthen his hand in the START III talks and get deeper cuts in strategic warheads on both sides to reduce US strike capability. The main thrust of his political approach has been to weaken the momentum of NMD with offers to cooperate with Washington combined with attempts to balance against its missile defence plans. Moscow is keen to take forward collaboration on early warning and theatre missile defence to deal with the threat from rogue states by which Washington largely justifies NMD. It may even be willing to contemplate negotiating adjustments to the ABM treaty. As far as efforts to balance against the US are concerned, Russia has encouraged opposition to NMD in Asia as well as Europe. Enlisting support from Beijing on this issue has proved predictably easy. In Western Europe Russian attempts to divert America's allies from supporting NMD have met with little success. There was no positive response to Putin's proposal, launched in summer 2000, for a joint Russian-European non-strategic missile defence system. Nonetheless, Moscow persists in trying to bring Europe into play on this issue while seeking to negotiate with Washington.

Efforts to enlist European and Chinese support in the campaign against NMD form part of a wider approach characteristic of the current stage of Russian policy: active multipolarity. Since the mid-1990s Moscow has been increasingly energetic in rebuilding ties with Soviet-era allies such as Iraq, Libya, Iran and China, who remain relative outsiders in the international community, as well as with accepted club members like India, Japan and the EU. The underlying thrust of this diversified diplomacy is described officially, in the

Foreign Policy Concept of 2000 and in countless speeches, as the promotion of multipolarity, a term which has become a mantra of Russian diplomacy.

As a strategic approach active multipolarity has two components. The first is the building of an extensive network of relations, which Russia needs in order to be able to fulfil its rightful role as 'a leading state', a Great Power in world affairs. Closely related is a second and more competitive component: standing up to American domination. Officially this is couched in progressive terms – Russia seeks to combat the unhealthy unipolar tendencies inherent in US hegemony in order to promote a 'civilised multipolar' world. In fact there is a competitive edge to promoting multipolarity that reflects Moscow's lingering preoccupation with Washington. Measuring up against the US by asserting influence in different parts of the world remains an important measure of Russia's self-respect. Yet gaining self-esteem through assertiveness could prove self-defeating, say Russian critics of the multipolarity approach, since Moscow cannot effectively counter US power and globalisation (*Moskovskie novosti*, 27 February–6 March 2000). The official line continues to nurture a Great Power role. At the same time, the Kremlin remains aware of Russia's need to compensate for economic and military weakness by skilful diplomacy that uses measured assertiveness to gain influence. Reference is often made to the example set by Prince Gorchakov, the foreign minister who managed to build up Russian influence in the aftermath of defeat in the Crimean War (Gorchakov, 1999). Moscow hopes that developing a Great Power diplomacy through active multipolarity will help Russia to punch above its weight and create an international environment favourable to its economic growth.

Moscow has made steady progress in raising its profile in Asia by establishing links with smaller Cold War allies like Vietnam and North Korea, consolidating ties with India and China and improving relations with former adversaries such as Japan. Intensive if fitful moves in the Yeltsin years to normalise relations with Tokyo by making a breakthrough on the long-running Kurile island dispute raised Japanese expectations of finalising a peace treaty by the end of 2000. Putin has taken a more cautious and open-ended approach in the hope that this key problem can eventually be managed through closer economic cooperation. Agreements on trade and energy projects were the most substantial results of summit meetings in 2000 and 2001. Economic diplomacy, albeit of a more assertive kind, has played a prominent part in consolidating Russian relations with India and China. Moscow has led with arms exports, which have not only yielded considerable income (combined these countries account for over half of total sales) but have also helped cement military and political ties. Putin visited both capitals in 2000 and sought to build on the 'strategic partnerships' established under his predecessor. On his November 2000 visit to Beijing Prime Minister Mikhail Kasyanov recalled Primakov's earlier vision of an axis between the three powers. Such notions reflect Moscow's tendency to exaggerate the strategic achievements of its multipolar policy. Too many issues separate Beijing and New Delhi for Moscow to be able to create a tripolar grouping, and the two other countries are markedly less enthusiastic than Moscow about the extent of their 'partnerships'. China certainly shares Russia's interest in opposing NMD and US interventionism. Beijing cooperates with Moscow within the Shanghai Five, a group (including Kazakhstan, Kyrgyzstan and Tajikistan) formed in 1996 to oversee Central Asian border stability. But traditional conflicts of interest continue to worry some in Moscow who warn against supplying too much military equipment to an overpopulated neighbour with a long, if now agreed, border with the Russian Far East which remains rich in minerals but is fast losing its already small population. Preoccupied with strengthening its position relative to the US, Russia may be in danger of losing sight of other and perhaps more vital security interests.

Russian policy in the Middle East and particularly towards Iran brings out the problem of managing assertiveness to maximise the returns of active multipolarity in terms of international influence. Moscow has taken advantage of the rift between Teheran and Washington to enlist Iran as a partner in Central Asia and the Caucasus as well as to capitalise on opportunities in the arms and nuclear technology markets (Freedman, 2000). In 1995 Russia agreed a large nuclear reactor construction contract. American threats of sanctions against Russian firms allegedly involved in exporting dual use nuclear technology elicited a mixture of defiance and compromise. Moscow insisted on the legality of its major contracts, but undertook to prevent export of dual use technology and to curb arms deliveries. Under the terms of an agreement signed by prime minister Viktor Chernomyrdin and US vice-president Al Gore in 1995, Moscow agreed to stop all arms exports to Iran at the end of 1999 in return for the Americans not imposing sanctions. This deal, which involved potential revenue losses for Russia of up to $4 billion, reflected the priority the Kremlin then placed on staying on good terms with

Washington. Under Putin Moscow has taken a more assertive line, disavowing the Iran deal and even announcing plans to ship arms to another 'rogue' state, Libya. On issues of greater strategic importance to Washington in the Middle East, such as Iraq's compliance with UN inspections, it seems doubtful that Putin will go beyond the self-limiting assertiveness of Primakov's 1997 and 1998 mediation attempts, which aimed not so much to support Baghdad as to raise Moscow's profile within the international community as a responsible actor promoting resolution of the conflict (Primakov, 1999, pp. 308–38). Putin seems to be as eager as was Yeltsin to capitalise on Russian diplomatic access to 'outsider' states to earn international respect. At the G8 summit in July 2000 he was quick to make use of his visit to Pyongyang, and the ideas it had produced ideas for incentives to pre-empt a North Korean missile programme, to impress his colleagues as the leader of a major and responsible member of the international community.

The cooling in relations with Washington, associated with the tougher yet less engaged stance on Russia taken by the Bush administration, is likely to have a mixed impact on Moscow's pursuit of active multipolarity. On the one hand, it might strengthen Russian determination to defy US pressure both to boost international standing and to remind Washington of Moscow's wish to be taken into account – preferably as a partner – at a time when America may become increasingly indifferent to Russia's fate. On the other hand, any deterioration in relations with Washington will tend to make Moscow concentrate more on diversification rather than assertiveness, on building relations that strengthen Russia's position without risking adverse reaction from the international community. This constructive development of multipolarity could lead Moscow to focus on further improving ties with the European Union.

Until the mid-1990s a traditional preoccupation with bilateral relations with the major West European states slowed the development of policy towards the EU. It was not until the end of 1997 that Russia ratified its Partnership and Cooperation Agreement (signed in 1994) and not until late 1999 that it published a statement of long-term objectives, which include moving to a 'strategic partnership'. Such a move has to surmount considerable obstacles. In security terms, the fact that the EU is distinguishable from NATO has inclined Moscow to look favourably at efforts to develop a European defence identity and capability. At the same time, Russia remains aware that unless such developments were coupled with a stronger pan-European security structure, they might pose just as many problems as NATO. On the economic front, the path to closer cooperation seems less difficult. Trade and investments links are substantial, with the EU accounting for 40 per cent of Russian foreign trade and around two-thirds of inward investment. While Russia figures only marginally in overall EU trade, it does supply 21 per cent of the Union's natural gas (Gowan, 2000, p. 7). Moscow expects EU enlargement to boost trade just over half of total Russian turnover (*Russian TV*, 29 October 2000).

Enlargement poses considerable political problems as Moscow wants a say in the process, which Brussels refuses to entertain. Russia feels relatively well disposed towards Baltic entry, hoping that this will provide an alternative to NATO membership. At the same time, Moscow remains concerned about being isolated by the new border regimes enlargement will bring. Anxiety is especially acute in relation to the Kaliningrad region, located between Poland and Lithuania, which enlargement will make into an island within the EU. Talks on Kaliningrad suggest that the way forward lies in imaginative visa regimes and development of the region as a free trade zone (Gowan, 2000, pp. 36–7). As with Kaliningrad so in its overall relationship with the EU, Moscow is looking to a combination of political goodwill and economic cooperation to make a 'greater Europe' – combining the benefits of economic and geostrategic advantage with traditional cultural affinity – into the most important pillar of its multipolar policy (*ITAR-TASS*, 26 October 2000; Baranovsky, 2000).

PART THREE

Current Issues

12

Crime and Corruption

LOUISE SHELLEY

The enlightenment thinker Cesare Beccaria wrote that the certainty of punishment was more important than its severity in reducing crime rates. Russia in the first decade of post-Soviet rule has illustrated the validity of Beccaria's pronouncement. While Russia continues to have severe criminal punishments, it has had soaring rates of street crime, organised crime and corruption because of the general impunity of its offenders. The collapse of the social control apparatus, combined with a general lawlessness of society, have contributed to conditions highly conducive to crime commission. In contrast, there is general impunity for all but the lowest offenders on the social and economic spectrum. The globalisation of Russian crime in the 1990s has placed many criminals outside the reach of domestic law enforcement. Foreign law enforcement cannot act against these offenders because the corruption of domestic Russian law enforcement undermines international law enforcement cooperation, a necessity in combating the serious Russian crime that is increasingly transnational.

The Soviet Union had been a very different society in these respects, one with a high degree of certainty and severity of punishment. Throughout the Soviet period, the USSR had one of the world's highest rates of incarceration *per capita*. Despite efforts under Gorbachev to reduce the size of the prison and labour camp population by the hundreds of thousands, the USSR still had one of the highest rates of imprisonment *per capita* in the world. The Soviet criminal justice system was not particularly efficient despite its pronounced success in arresting criminals for reported crimes. This success was explained more by the brutality of the Soviet system and the success of law enforcement in forcing known criminals to confess to crimes that had been committed.

The order of the Soviet period was achieved at the cost of extensive social controls, gross violations of human rights and a penal policy that incarcerated millions in order to deter the possibility of crime prevention. In the late 1980s, crime began to skyrocket due to diminished political control, increased economic hardship, citizens' decreased fear of the state and the diversion of militia resources to manage interethnic conflicts and safeguard public order during rallies and demonstrations. The legacy of the Soviet period is an endemic crime problem that has grown more intractable during the 1990s. The Russian expression, 'The fish rots from the head', has been applied to Russian crime and corruption in the 1990s. With the large-scale corruption of the Yeltsin Family and his associates, there has been a tolerance for high level financial crime and corruption that has pervaded all levels of society.

Crime and Criminals

In the post-Soviet period every form of reported crime has increased. This includes the offences that are a threat to daily life, the serious organised crimes that affect all sectors of the economy and the pervasive corruption. Yet despite this recorded increase many crimes, especially the high level financial crimes of major officials and parliamentarians who possess parliamentary immunity, remain un-recorded and unprosecuted. Such offences include the pyramid schemes that deprived many Russian citizens of their life's savings and the criminalisation of the privatisation process, which prevented many citizens from obtaining any financial stake in the Russian state.

The Soviet Union collapsed, in part, because the system of social and political control ceased to exercise its coercive role. This was most evident in daily life with the weakening of the police through attrition, massive dismissals for corruption and abuse of power and general demoralisation. The decline of militia capacity had an immediate impact on the state's ability to control crime. Despite the reduced capacity of the law enforcement apparatus to act against crime, recorded offences increased markedly in the final years of the Soviet period. In 1985, the year Gorbachev assumed power, there were two million registered crimes and in 1991, the year of the dissolution of the USSR there were 3.2 million. The most serious increases in crime were in the categories of premeditated murder, premeditated assault, armed robbery and theft. The rise in premeditated homicide was closely linked to the rise in organised crime, but other social and economic conditions accounted for the rise in other serious offences. A recent analysis of the overall rise in violence attributes the growth more to aggression within neighbourhoods caused by such factors as a reduction in crimes solved by the police, increase in alcohol consumption and poverty rather than to the impact of organised criminal activity (Ahrend and Andrienko, 2000, p. 37).

The growth in crime continued a trend that began after the death of Stalin. Throughout the Soviet period, there were enormous efforts to hide a rise in crime. The official ideology insisted that crime would wither away along with the state. Therefore, police failed to record crimes whenever possible and incarceration was widely used, which helped reduce the number of potential offenders at liberty. Despite these efforts to suppress the growth of crime, the average annual rate of growth of crime in the USSR in the post-Stalin period (1956–1991) was 5 per cent, whereas the population grew by only 1 per cent. This means that the crime rate grew more rapidly than the population even though there had been a very small increase in the youthful population, the age at which a given population is most likely to commit crimes.

Despite this growth in crime, published crime rates for most serious offences other than violent crimes were significantly below levels in the United States and Western Europe. The explanation for this lay in the extent of social control that characterised authoritarian Soviet society. Citizens were controlled not only by an extensive law enforcement apparatus that regulated every aspect of daily life, but also by the fact that they were dependent on the state for employment. The supremacy of the rights of the state over the individual meant that there was extensive surveillance over the citizenry not only in the political arena but intrusion into their daily life and personal mobility through such regulatory mechanisms as the system of internal passport controls.

The data of the Soviet and post-Soviet periods are not directly comparable because Russia became a separate country and significant population movement occurred as millions of Russians moved to Russia from other parts of the former Soviet Union, particularly the countries of Central Asia. Furthermore, major changes were made in the Criminal Code as the laws linked to the Soviet economy were removed and new laws were introduced that reflected the rather different definitions of criminality that were appropriate to a market economy. Over 60 offences were dropped from the Russian Criminal

Code of 1960 and 70 new ones were inserted in the Russian Criminal Code of 1996. These new offences include crimes linked to computers, fraudulent bankruptcy and trafficking in women, all offences that could not exist in the closed, planned economy of the Soviet Union.

While the crimes of the 1990s are not directly comparable with those of the Soviet period, it is clear that there were notable increases in crime in both the Soviet and post-Soviet periods, and that crime rates increased markedly in Russia during the transition from communism (see Table 12.1, which is based on official statistics). During these years the annual growth of registered crime averaged 7 per cent, whereas the population not only failed to increase but fell by an average of 0.2 per cent a year. In 1999, crime increased by 16 per cent and population fell by 0.3 per cent. Crime grew most notably in economic crime, where the growth rate was over double that for other categories of criminality.

TABLE 12.1   *Russian crime rates, 1992–9*

	1992	1993	1994	1995	1996	1997	1998	1999
All crimes (millions)	2.8	2.8	2.6	2.8	2.6	2.4	2.6	3.0
Of which homicide and attempted homicide (thousands)	23.0	29.2	32.3	31.7	29.4	29.3	29.6	31.1
Convictions (millions)	1.1	1.3	1.4	1.6	1.6	1.4	1.5	1.7

Source: *Rossiya v tsifrakh. Kratkii statisticheskii sbornik* (Moscow: Goskomstat, 2000), p. 112.

Certain characteristics of the crime rates of this period deserve particular analysis. For example, in the transitional period of the 1990s, there was a much higher rate of growth of reported growth in theft of personal property rather than state property. This was at a time in which the theft from enterprises through embezzlement and asset stripping reached its height. At the same time, citizens with property responded to the heightened fear of crime by installing elaborate locks and installing security systems supported by privatised security agencies. The reason for this differentiation in crimes rates was one of enforcement and often complicity between those who engaged in theft of state resources and the law enforcement bodies that were intended to control such crimes.

Youth crime rose dramatically in the first years of the 1990s, and then declined in the second half of the decade. But no such decline was seen with adult offenders. Rates of violence, indeed, grew dramatically both in the domestic and the public sphere. The killings associated with organised crime and banditry were especially notable. Certain large cities with significant criminal groups such as Moscow, St Petersburg and Yekaterinburg saw many killings associated with the division of territory. But violent crime grew in many other areas as well. In the Soviet period, murder weapons were often knives, hunting rifles and other instruments that were available because guns were tightly controlled. In the post-Soviet period, with widespread trafficking in small arms, guns were frequently used for ordinary crimes as well as those linked with organised groups.

The criminal justice system revealed very selective enforcement of the laws during the postcommunist years, and most individuals who were arrested for crimes came from the lowest economic and social level of society. Very few arrests were made of those linked to very high-level economic crimes or to those connected with any of the low-level organised crime groups. Most serious offenders enjoyed immunity from arrest, some of them through their election to national and regional parliaments. For others, their immunity stemmed more from the operational realities of the present-day criminal justice system rather than the institutionalised protection granted to wealthy politicians. Criminals with significant assets or allied with affluent crime groups could bribe themselves out of criminal arrests and investigations. Lawyers could also help find technicalities leading to the release of suspected offenders. The data of the offender population reveal that the criminal courts and labour camps were reserved for the lowest strata of Russian society. Of the 1.7 million offenders charged with crimes in 1999, 56 per cent were persons without a steady income. Some 27 per cent had committed a crime while under the influence of alcohol, narcotics, or other substance; 15 per cent were women and 11 per cent were minors. These are the most defenceless and poorest members of society. The highly significant detention rate of women is further evidence of the impact of the impoverishment of women in the transitional period.

Corruption

There is not one form of corruption in Russia but a multiplicity of forms which function on different levels of society. These include corruption of the bureaucracy, the legal institutions and legal processes, and possibly most important of all, the economy, in this transitional period. All of these have had a very deleterious impact on the possibility of promoting a sustainable transition to democracy in Russia.

The World Bank has conducted assessments of corruption of the countries of the former Soviet Union. The countries of the Commonwealth of Independent States, including Russia, have among the highest levels of corruption of all countries surveyed (World Bank, 2000). Their conclusions on the incidence of corruption in Russia relative to other countries have been confirmed by surveys conducted by Transparency International (New Corruption, 1999). The World Bank has attempted to differentiate between administrative corruption and state capture. State capture, according to their definition, 'refers to the actions of individuals, groups or firms both in the public and private sectors to influence the formation of laws, regulations, decrees and other government policies to their own advantage as a result of the illicit and non-transparent provision of private benefits to public officials', whereas administrative corruption refers to the 'intentional imposition of distortions in the prescribed implementation of existing laws, rules and regulations to provide advantages to either state or non-state actors as a result of the illicit and non-transparent provision of private gains to public officials'. According to the World Bank typology of corruption, Russia rates in the mid-range of former socialist countries in its index of administrative corruption but among the highest on the scale of state capture (World Bank, 2000, pp. xv, xvii–xviii).

The definition of the World Bank is relatively narrow and does not capture the full variety of corruption that currently exists or even the transnational dimensions of the phenomenon. Much of the problem lies in patron-client relationships, the use of *blat* (influence) and networking to promote personal interests that are never manifested in law (Ledeneva, 1998). The corruption of the privatisation process occurred, in part, not because of particular laws or their distortion but in the deliberate absence of laws that allowed individuals to promote their interests at the expense of others and the larger financial benefit of society. The US Department of Justice lawsuit against Harvard University in 1999 for misusing the resources entrusted to it to promote privatisation in Russia reveals the transnational dimension of the problem in a way that is not reflected in World Bank definitions.

The state capture problem in Russia was very evident at the end of the Yeltsin era. When he resigned from office there was institutionalised corruption at all levels of government and possibly irreversible damage to key Russian institutions. Vladimir Putin has expressed his desire to reduce the level of corruption, but his indebtedness to selected oligarchs who facilitated his rapid rise to power may limit his freedom of action at the highest levels. Yet the tone at the top affects attitudes towards corruption at lower levels of society. With impunity for those at the top, those at lower levels feel no incentive to trim their excesses.

The pervasive corruption and the penetration of organised crime into the state and economy cannot be explained only by the failure to create institutions and norms. The explanation lies rather in the legacy of the Soviet system and the flawed process of transition. The transition years were marked by widespread impunity for those in all positions of authority. Russian data for the decade from 1986 to 1996 show a marked decline in the registered number of offences for embezzlement by officials (a 33 per cent decline), bribery (a 17 per cent decline) and misuse of official position (a 33 per cent decline). While reports of crimes declined, the actions taken against offenders declined even more appreciably. Those sentenced for the crime of official embezzlement declined to a tenth of its earlier level. And convictions for bribery went down three times in the same time period.

The Soviet Union collapsed, in part, because of its endemic corruption. The problem did not decrease in the Russian successor state; instead, corruption acquired even more significant proportions with the demise of the Communist Party, the privatisation of state resources and the entry of Russia into the global economy. In the absence of conflict of interest laws, bureaucrats benefited from their positions as regulators of the economy to simultaneously open private business ventures institutions that they themselves would regulate. Consequently, many continued to hold on to their government positions not because of bribes and pay-offs, but because of the business opportunities it offered them.

Privatisation was intended to make communism irreversible and improve state and industrial efficiency. But privatisation, in the event, brought little profit to the state because the mixing of the Soviet system of favours with the new reality resulted in the wholesale transfer of property to a privileged few. The privatisation programme was initiated by a small and well-connected group of insiders who themselves benefited significantly from the programme they were implementing. While many sponsors of the programme claimed the creation of a large share-holding class in Russia, this was a paper transfer that imparted almost no financial value to the citizenry. As a consequence, gross domestic product declined, state revenues decreased and the sale of state assets brought little benefit to the government.

State and industrial efficiency declined because the managers of enterprises engaged in asset stripping, tolling and other mechanisms that moved assets out of the country rather than producing revenues for the state and profits for enterprises. The highly corrupt loans-for-shares deal in 1995 in which powerful individuals in Russia acquired the major holdings in Russian industry for minimal prices established an entrenched oligarchy with no interest in rebuilding the Russian state (Freeland, 2000, pp. 169–89). Facilitating this theft was their cosy relationship with state officials who facilitated this trade in exchange for pay-offs and political support for the Yeltsin government. Foreign loan moneys were siphoned off as well as domestic. Officials charged with overseeing the reconstruction of Soviet infrastructure siphoned off such large quantities from reconstruction loans that completed projects could not function. This affected such key sectors of the Russian economy as the coal, gold and shipping industries.

There was no capacity to address any of these problems because the control system had ceased to function. Law enforcement was neutralised by corruption, inadequate equipment, absence of qualified personnel, and the lack of authority to investigate the crimes of a market economy. The corruption went from the lowest level personnel who were part of a system of institutionalised corruption up to the highest levels of the police and the Procuracy. The problems of criminalisation of the police are very significant. In 1993, for instance, Russian police officials reported that 13 000 internal affairs employees were directly collaborating with organised criminal groups and many more were accepting bribes. A survey conducted in 1998 in one of the two labour camps where former law enforcement and government officials are incarcerated revealed similarly that the majority of inmates had been in the police. But unlike the inmates from the Procuracy, the judiciary or the customs service, they were more likely to be incarcerated for ordinary crimes than those connected with performance of their duties. Less than a third of former internal affairs personnel had committed job-related offences while that was the case for the majority of former procurators and the great majority of customs and judicial personnel. These data suggest the criminalisation of the police is more advanced than in other branches which are suffering primarily from severe corruption. Police personnel who received bribes were part of a system of corruption and passed part of their bribes up the law enforcement hierarchy (Shelley and Repetskaya, 1999).

The inadequate legal system led at the same time to massive abuses in the private investment funds that had been set up in the process of privatisation. This occurred because many so-called economic 'reformers' believed that laws and legal norms would arise spontaneously to protect the property that was created. For almost the entire citizenry, any legal protections came too late. Many citizens lost their life savings because they were defrauded out of what they had. Privatisation, in the event, proved to be the central mechanism for the acquisition of financial power by the former party and Komsomol *nomenklatura* and by organised crime. The political losers of the Soviet era were the financial winners of post-Soviet Russia, a rare case in history in which the discredited elite of the old political system enhanced their financial power after the collapse of the system they had operated. A decree against fraud in the privatisation process was introduced only in late 1993, after a significant share of Russian property had already been privatised.

The mechanism of pyramid schemes, many operated with the tacit consent or outright collusion of regional leaders, was the cause of the Russian citizenry losing their life savings. This was a major mechanism by which property was redistributed from the ordinary citizenry to the new financial elite. There were no laws on the registration or advertising of share funds, which helped to ensure that these funds were often a mechanism to defraud ordinary citizens. As a response to the most noteworthy scandal of them all, MMM, in which 10–12 million citizens had invested, a June 1994 decree was issued 'On the Protection of Interests of Investors'. But there were no mechanisms to ensure it was implemented. Other pyramid schemes were set up throughout the country. But although hundreds of criminal cases were initiated against them, only a few led to convictions. As a result, the equality achieved by 70 years of the Soviet period had disappeared within a few years of the collapse of the Soviet system.

Organised Crime

Russian organised crime is an international phenomenon. While some groups operate solely on a local and regional level, the most important organised crime operates internationally and even globally. While organised crime groups in certain countries engage in a limited range of illicit goods and services and launder their money into the licit economy, Russian organised crime represents one of the world's most diversified forms. Its activities span the full range of illicit goods and services including drugs, gambling, prostitution, trafficking in endangered species, arms sales and then a full range of illicit activities including illegal licensing arrangements, corrupted import–export operations and organised criminalisation of the privatisation process. Its major profits are made from the stripping of businesses that it has forcibly privatised and its control of aluminum and other key elements of a resource-driven economy.

Russian organised crime is not a uniform phenomenon. It differs by regions of the country. Just as legitimate trade is influenced by its trading partners, organised crime in Russia is influenced by the countries with which it participates. Crime in the Russian Far East is closely associated with criminal gangs from Asian countries such as Yakuza in Japan, crime groups in Korea, Vietnam, China and Mongolia. Along the southern borders, there is more contact with the drug trafficking groups of Central Asia; while in the western parts of Russia, the ties are strongest with the crime groups of Eastern and Western Europe. All of the regions of Russia have criminal ties to the United States and to the international financial centres of Europe and their offshore banking institutions.

The structure of Russian organised crime is more flexible and dynamic than the structure of more traditional organised crime groups. It is not a monolithic top-down organisation of the same kind as La Cosa Nostra. Instead it resembles more closely the structure of a company of the new economy, organised along network lines rather than the top-down structure of a traditional company such as a General Motors. Russian law enforcement authorities currently identify the presence of over 8000 crime groups operating within its territory. Many of these groups are a few bandits known to local police departments. But it also points to the different structure of Russian organised crime, which is organised as discrete units that band together for larger operations. These smaller groups may be organised along ethnic lines, may be ex-convicts who served in prison together or have served side by side in the Afghan war. Ethnic groups which may be in violent conflict in the Caucasus may cooperate together in Russia in running extortion rings in local consumer markets or more complex operations such as trafficking in stolen automobiles.

Russians have attempted to blame the organised crime problem on ethnic groups present within Russia, particularly individuals from the Caucasus and to a lesser extent Central Asia. These groups are clearly identifiable within organised crime in Russia, just as ethnic minorities have contributed significantly to organised crime in the United States, Japan and other countries. Individuals of ethnic minorities have assumed a disproportionate representation in the traditional organised crime groups known as 'thieves-in-law'. Among the approximately 600 identified thieves-in-law from the former USSR, individuals who have been adopted into the established criminal underworld after elaborate initiation rituals, only a third currently reside in Russia. But this is not the most pernicious form of Russian organised crime; it has been given disproportionate attention because of their use of violence, isolation from the institutions of society and elaborate rituals. These groups, in fact, are not as powerful or as wealthy as some of the identified crime groups such as the Soltnsevo group in Moscow, which is dominated by ethnic Russians.

Moreover, many of the organised crime emanating from Russia that is investigated and prosecuted in the West involves individuals tied to Komsomol and party structures. The origins of this crime lie deep in the Soviet period. It is these individuals who had access to the resources of the Russian state rather than the ethnic criminals who were at the margins of the society engaging in smaller businesses who are a very significant part of Russian organised crime today. Links can be seen between *nomenklatura* organised crime and that of ethnic groups making it difficult to differentiate between these phenomena. All of these groups have used high levels of corruption to facilitate their objectives.

Russian organised crime, in contrast to many criminal organisations, is able to draw on many highly trained specialists who were left adrift by the collapse of the former Soviet Union. These include military specialists, mathematicians and other scientists and former members of the KGB. All of these have made their distinct contributions to organised crime. For example, former members of the KGB have worked as money launderers for Russian, Colombian and other crime groups, Russian scientists have worked with the Italian organised crime to commit elaborate tax evasion schemes and military members have trafficked in small and large arms to Asian and Colombian organised groups. The presence of such specialists and the ability to hire such services gives a competitive advantage not only to Russian organised crimes groups but also to the groups with whom they work together in cooperative relationships.

A distinctive feature of Russian organised crime is the rapid accumulation of very significant assets. Unknown on an international scale before the collapse of the USSR, Russian criminal gangs have accumulated billions in assets in the 1990s. The true extent of their capital resources will never be known because much of it is parked in anonymous bank accounts and carefully masked trusts that are housed in offshore locations. There are literally over 10 000 Russian banks in the Caribbean alone, and this is just one area of the world that is used to house their money. Cyprus, Switzerland, Austria are highly used by Russian organised crime but even such far-flung locations as the Marshall Islands and Nauru in the South Pacific are locales of significant Russian money laundering.

The capital that Russian organised crime has acquired has allowed them to invest significantly in real estate overseas and to enter financial markets in ways that are less easy to detect than through the purchase of commercial and residential real estate. Russian organised crime infiltration into their domestic banking sector has facilitated their transfer of money into legitimate financial institutions internationally. Indicative of this was the criminal investigation of the Bank of New York in 1999, and Swiss investigations into Yeltsin entourage accounts in leading banks in their country.

Unlike many organised crime groups internationally, Russian organised crime repatriates little of its profits. They rest in safe havens overseas and do not return to build hotels, buy farmland or consumer industries as is the case with other international crime groups. The Colombians have brought home a significant share of their profits, buying real estate in Bogota and cattle ranches in rural areas. Italian organised crime has entered into the food production sector as well as building hotels and resorts and numerous apartment houses in the south. Economic development occurs in Southern China with the proceeds of trafficking in human beings. Apart from the money invested in Moscow real estate, there is little evidence of organised crime money returning to the regions where it originated. Prior to the financial collapse of August 1998, some money was returning to Yekaterinburg to open small stores catering for consumers, but the pace of this process diminished dramatically after this convulsion. Even small-scale investment in the provinces of Russia has disappeared as criminals find it more advantageous to invest their capital outside of their country. Many are already residing outside the country and therefore lack an incentive to invest in their communities as is the case with Colombian, Italian and some other crime groups. In Russia it is more common for criminal groups to use charitable organisations to launder their money rather than to make actual investments.

Russian organised criminal groups enjoy some competitive advantages over other groups of this kind. They are able to draw on certain categories of specialists that are hard for other criminal groups to recruit such as military personnel, and technicians with high levels of technology and intelligence gathering skills. Russian criminals, many with backgrounds in the former KGB, have great expertise in covertly moving money and have become excellent money launderers. They provide these skills not only to their own associates but to other groups. Their technological skills have allowed them to penetrate banking systems, to set up pyramid schemes operating globally through the internet and to market Russian-produced child pornography internationally. They thrive in their overseas activities not only through corruption but through their understanding of the ways in which foreign lawyers and banks can be used to function in a global environment. They have excelled in establishing front companies and offshore accounts to not only hide assets but to siphon off and dilute the equity stakes of other shareholders who are not part of their group. Furthermore, they have proved expert at using expensive litigation abroad to ward off investigative journalists who seek to expose their criminal activity. At home, they use violence to strike not only at their competitors but also to kill or discourage reporters who threaten their economic monopolies and their power base.

Much organised crime operates with a short-term mentality focusing primarily on today's profits with little thought to the future. This is particularly true of Russian organised crime, which has a 'raider' mentality towards its own economy and its own people. Russian organised crime is not interested in investing back in its economy, and even more damagingly, it does not seek to maximise profits from the sale of its commodities. Whereas Chinese traffickers seek to control their human cargo from recruitment to delivery to maximise their returns, Russians sell off trafficked women to intermediaries and fail to obtain the price they could secure if they controlled their delivery of services. Drug cartels in other countries seek similarly to control all aspects of the trade from cultivation to refinement and delivery. A share of the profits is then reinvested to improve production and transports. Russian organised crime does not do the same with its primary commodities. Oil and aluminum are sold below world market prices and little if any of the return is reinvested to improve production and delivery. The 'flashy' lifestyles of Russian criminals allows many to draw attention to themselves. Many escape prosecution both at home and abroad because of the corruption of law enforcement. They are able to neutralise any efforts to control their actions at home through massive pay-offs to the police, procuracy and judiciary. Many of the most powerful get themselves elected to local and national office, which gives them immunity. The same forces work internationally. As long as they are not engaged in active criminal activity abroad, there is little law enforcement agencies in other countries can do to prosecute them in the absence of cooperation with the law enforcement authorities within Russia itself.

Conclusion

Crime and corruption issues, prior to the collapse of the Soviet Union, were seen as peripheral issues, not central to the evolution of the Soviet state. The decade since the collapse of the USSR has revealed the centrality of these issues to the demise of the Soviet state and their importance in determining the future development of Russia. The failure to recognise their importance has had costly consequences for Russians and for the international investors and multilateral institutions which lent to Russia.

The crime and corruption issue is certainly a matter of daily concern to Russian citizens. It diminishes their quality of life and increases their cost of living. The corruption of the Russian state and of its state and private financial institutions has had disastrous consequences for the citizenry. The mass of the population have lost their life savings in phony pyramid schemes and repeated collapses of unmonitored banks penetrated by organised crime. Crony capitalist privatisations have given Russian citizens no equity stake in the future. Despite the distribution of most of the state's assets in the 1990s to its citizenry, the majority of Russian citizens ended the decade poorer than they started. This fact is explained more by the criminalisation of state functions and economic redistribution policies than by the decline of the Russian domestic product.

The rise of an oligarchy, made possible by high-level corruption and its ties to organised crime, has wiped out any possibility for a real market economy and a functioning democracy in the near future. A middle class, the backbone of democracy in other countries, has failed to emerge because of the unequal distribution of wealth that has restored the economic inequalities that the Soviet revolution was supposed to erase. Vladimir Putin understands that he needs to reduce the level of corruption to improve economic performance. But his past and his ties to the oligarchs limit his freedom of movement. Yet all does not depend on the top. Civil society and the media can also play an important role in combating the problems of organised crime and corruption. Putin's moves against the independent media, however, and the still limited role of civil society, make the chances of controlling these problems by these means highly questionable. Russia, it seems, still lacks the political will to address the problems that sap its ability to grow economically and to develop viable legal and government institutions.

13
Politics and the Media

SARAH OATES

The media were a central instrument of political control in the USSR, and they remain a battleground for power in postcommunist Russia. The Russian media struggle with two very powerful forces in an attempt to build a modern broadcast and print industry: the Soviet legacy of heavy-handed propaganda, and the chaotic politics of a new democracy. With fairly liberal laws protecting the freedom of speech on the one hand and relatively overt control by the government on the other, the media are neither a watchdog nor a lapdog for the government. Although the presidential administration has been tightening its control over the media in recent years, enough diversity remains to present a range of opinions to Russian citizens. Rather ominously, however, there are signs that control of the media and the limiting of access by citizens to information has been accelerating. In this chapter we look in turn at three main themes: Soviet censorship and control of the media, the current Russian media system, and the challenges faced by the Russian media in the post-Soviet era. A wealth of evidence suggests that the concept of media objectivity and freedom is still poorly developed in Russia; perhaps more surprisingly, it is not always well understood, even by journalists themselves.

Media in the Soviet Era

Soviet leaders were quick to identify the importance of the media to educate the public about their new socialist values and to encourage support of the regime itself. In addition to control through censorship and direction from party officials, the Soviet authorities fostered a journalistic culture that demanded total support of the ideology and

254

policies espoused by the leaders of the Communist Party of the Soviet Union. The development of the 'internal censor' on the part of journalists was very effective at controlling the media. In order to get and keep their jobs, journalists had to prove their ability to produce stories and broadcasts that were completely supportive of the party line. If journalists chose to work in the extremely visible sphere of broadcast journalism, it was necessary for them to toe the party line completely.

Both print and broadcast media (first radio, later television) were considered critical propaganda tools by the party authorities. As a result, the Soviet Union had newspapers with some of the largest circulations in the world. For example, in 1980 the Communist Party flagship paper *Pravda* (Truth) had a daily circulation of nearly 11 million while another important central newspaper, *Izvestiya* (News) had a circulation of 7 million in the same year. Certainly, much of what was printed was ignored or merely put to use in other ways by consumers, most notably as toilet paper when that commodity was scarce. Nonetheless, recent research indicates that people who lived through Soviet times retain two important characteristics from the plethora of print media: they enjoy reading a large range of print media, and they are quite good at extracting useful information from even relatively banal statements of the official position. In addition, many were pleased that the media, both print and broadcast, supported a positive image of the great Soviet state, something in which they took great pride even while they were aware of its shortcomings.

There was an enormous amount of printed material available to Soviet citizens. Aside from the huge circulations of the biggest newspapers, more than 8400 newspapers, magazines and periodicals were being published in 1990. Despite the lack of objectivity and unadulterated news, sociological studies showed that many adults were eager consumers of newspapers. For example, a survey in Leningrad (now St Petersburg) in the early 1970s found that 75 per cent of those surveyed read a newspaper every day and a further 19 per cent did so three or four times a week, suggesting that virtually every adult in the city was a regular newspaper reader (Firsov and Muzdybaev, 1975). In addition, people energetically wrote and sent millions of letters to the editors of major newspapers, particularly as this was one of the few effective ways to complain about minor issues and problems in the Soviet state. The total postbag of the national press was estimated at 60–70 million in the early 1980s, and letters departments were often the papers' largest (White, 1983).

The Growth of Television

Television also supported the positive image of the Soviet state, but was understandably more monolithic than the print media. Initially far behind the West, the Soviets aggressively developed the availability of television. While only about 5 per cent of the Soviet population could watch television in 1960, at least one channel was available to about 99 per cent of the country by the 1990s. This was a remarkable technological achievement in a country as vast as Russia, in which 13 per cent of homes still lacked running water and 60 per cent had no telephone lines by the 1990s. The availability of television, both through a satellite system of broadcasting and the massive output of television sets, shows that the Soviet administration very much valued the ability of television to inculcate the masses with a positive view of the policies it was promoting. According to official data, at least three-quarters of all households across its vast territory had television sets by the later years of Soviet rule, and the typical audience for the main nightly news programme reached 80 per cent of the adult population, including the entire armed forces (Mickiewicz, 1988, p. 8).

By the early 1980s, there were two national television networks: Ostankino on Channel 1 and Russian State Television on Channel 2. In addition, much of the country could see either the Moscow channel on Channel 3 or St Petersburg television on Channel 4. Local programming would sometimes be transmitted on the main channels in much the same way that was practised in national services in other countries. Although this allowed for a better geographical focus for the viewers, they were unlikely to find anything scandalous or unusual by flipping the dial – until the advent of *glasnost* (often understood as 'openness' but better translated as 'transparency') under Mikhail Gorbachev in the late 1980s.

Soviet television was not, of course, all news reports about record-breaking harvests and the achievements of the Soviet space industry (the fullest available account is Mickiewicz, 1988). It also featured nature programmes, concerts and opera, and reports from overseas (albeit with an ideological slant). Sports programmes, and feature films, were particularly popular. And there were even games shows. A particularly banal example were the popular shows called 'Let's Go, Gals!' and 'Let's Go, Lads!' that featured Soviet young people showing off their skills in silly games, such as competing to see who could build a wall with the fewest bricks while being driven around on a city bus. The love of this type of light-hearted programme, complete with an irreverent host, would re-emerge in the post-Soviet years when Russian television channels began to compete for viewers. Participants in focus groups, conducted under the author's guidance in Moscow and the regions in the early months of 2000, recalled with particular fondness Soviet-era programmes on travel and animals; the wife of the former president, Naina Yeltsin, herself expressed a particular liking for the television films of the Soviet period, with their simple and optimistic story lines.

Media content varied over the course of the Soviet regime, but it always mirrored the policy of the state. Thus, the media were most conservative under Stalin, but there was a brief period of relative openness during the leadership of Nikita Khrushchev in the late 1950s and early 1960s. This period saw the publication of some dissident writers, including Alexander Solzhenitsyn's fictionalised account of prison camp life, *A Day in the Life of Ivan Denisovitch*. Tighter censorship returned once Khrushchev had been ousted from power and Leonid Brezhnev had taken over as party leader. There was a wide variety of titles for different readerships, from chess players to female farmers and football fans, but all of them supported the regime and its policies, and all of them came ultimately under the control of party officials.

What Soviet leaders failed to appreciate was that television was indeed a powerful weapon, but one that could work against the regime as well as for it. Secure in the knowledge that they controlled the journalists and the broadcast signals, they seemed unaware that the attentive audience spread across the Soviet Union would be very responsive to even the most subtle suggestions for change. They had created both an impressive media network and a well-primed audience, highly educated and with a lively interest in the wider world. During the mid-1980s, both of those elements in society began to work against the interests of the Communist Party as it sought to cling to power in a changing society.

Glasnost and the Russian Media

The introduction of *glasnost* by Mikhail Gorbachev after 1985 prompted change at an exponential rate in the Soviet media. Not surprisingly, many Western observers were suspicious of the introduction of any sort of openness into the Soviet media system, perceiving it as an attempt by the Communist Party to increase its hold on power or as a cynical exercise in public relations. However, while the initial changes in the mid-1980s were quite modest and restrained, they had far-reaching effects in a society that previously had been tightly controlled. *Glasnost* started what became an unstoppable process that moved from slight openness to full freedom of speech within the course of a few years.

While Soviet citizens had been writing letters to editors of newspapers for decades, *glasnost* allowed more generalised complaints to be covered in regular articles and editorials. The earliest ventures into more 'transparent' press coverage, in retrospect, seem very tame. For example, *Pravda* created a sensation in February 1986 by referring to special shops and other facilities for Communist Party members. Far greater revelations were to follow. By the late 1980s, print, radio and television were running stories revealing Second World War atrocities by Soviet troops, challenging Soviet rule in the Baltic states, questioning the war in Afghanistan, and even criticising the ideals of Leninism. While some newspapers clung to a more conservative party line, others emerged with an openly pro-Western ideology. A former tourist throwaway newspaper, *Moscow News*, emerged as one of the most aggressive supporters of the new scope that the printed media had begun to enjoy at this time. Another paper that had formerly been the mouthpiece of an official public education society, *Argumenty i fakty* (Arguments and Facts), was similarly outspoken.

In its eagerness to make up for decades of bland, feel-good coverage, Soviet television began to produce almost unremitting images of the failures of the communist regime. The sorts of stories they began to carry included an anguished Russian mother talking about losing her son in the military, an exposé of mental hospitals, and coverage of the push for independence by Lithuania, Latvia and Estonia. New shows and presenters started to gain immense popularity, typically trading in the staid, measured tones of traditional announcers for a fast-paced, controversial style that featured more jeans and T-shirts than suits and ties, and gave a greater emphasis to young people and their particular concerns.

When Gorbachev tried to continue to use television as a propaganda tool, he found he had lost control of its immense power. For example, he pushed for the live broadcast of the first session of the new Soviet parliament in 1989. Gorbachev thought the broadcast would strengthen his image as a liberal Communist leader. Instead, viewers saw members of the new Congress – many of whom had been elected in the first relatively free elections in Soviet history – stand up to challenge Gorbachev, the party and even the tenets of Communism itself on live national television. One of those who challenged Gorbachev was the former dissident, scientist Andrei Sakharov. Short of a return to a much stricter authoritarian regime, it would have been hard for Gorbachev and his supporters to re-establish control after broadcasts of this kind. But in itself it meant no more than an 'unprecedented freedom to complain about an almost unprecedented drop in living standards and a particularly tyrannical history' (Wedgwood Benn, 1992, p. 49), with no real power to change the system.

One way of tracking the enormous changes in the Russian media is to compare the coverage of two disasters, one early in Gorbachev's period of rule and one three years later. When the Chernobyl nuclear reactor blew up in the Ukraine in April 1986, the Soviet media refused to concede the nature or scope of the accident for days. As a result, millions of Soviet citizens as well as people in East European countries were unaware of their exposure to highly dangerous radiation and could do nothing to minimise the risks. It is particularly distressing that there was little information on how to protect children, who are especially vulnerable to radiation poisoning. By contrast, riots in April 1989 in the Georgian city of Tbilisi, then part of the Soviet Union, were covered by the Soviet media, including reports that gave support to Georgians who were demonstrating against Soviet power in their native land. Whereas the Soviet media had lacked the initiative or power to even report on a huge nuclear disaster with enormous public health consequences, just a few years later they could directly challenge the government line and question the party's actions in a nationalist demonstration.

The media's new freedom was clearly apparent in August 1991, after the attempt by the National Emergency Committee to seize power. The coup plotters, who held Gorbachev under house arrest in his Black Sea vacation home, managed to order the military into Moscow and seize control of the central media. However, journalists quickly arranged to publish a one-off issue under their joint auspices called *Obshchaya gazeta* (Common Newspaper). At the central television facility in Moscow, armed soldiers arrived to enforce the coup. Even the presence of the military could not stop journalists from opposing the return to repressive methods. They fought back, at first in small ways by failing to cooperate fully and finally through direct defiance in reporting on the resistance at the barricades in Moscow. Even as the coup plotters were holding press conferences to claim that the country would return to authoritarian rule, Channel 1 was broadcasting images of street protests in major cities and putting out calls for resistance. In the end, Soviet-created television had the scope and power to contribute significantly to the downfall of the regime itself.

The Russian Media in an Emerging Nation

The end of Soviet rule brought enormous change for all of Russia, including the media. The state no longer had a monopoly on the mass media, which meant that private groups could start their own publications, radio stations or even television networks. Practically, however, this was enormously difficult because of the economic problems of the young Russian state. In addition, Soviet rules and norms of doing business remained in place, stifling both Russian entrepreneurs and foreign investors in the media sphere. Soviet mass media equipment had become badly outdated as the regime ran out of money. The circulation of the print media plunged, due to both a lack of funding to produce the publications and the inability of consumers to afford them. Even newspapers such as the once-mighty *Pravda* floundered in the new market economy, escaping closure only by investment from a left-wing Greek tycoon.

Today, Russia has both state and private media, many of them merging public and private funds to stay afloat. As many Russians can no longer afford newspapers, television has become even more dominant as an information source (see Table 13.1). While Russia has a mixture of state-run and private television, many Russian citizens are in practice limited to one of the national state-controlled channels. The state-controlled first channel (*Obshchestvennoe Rossiiskoe Televidenie* or ORT) and the second channel (*Rossiiskoe Televidenie i Radio* or RTR) reach virtually all of the country. The Russian government owns all of RTR but only 51 per cent of ORT. While it clearly has full control of RTR, the situation at ORT is more complex. In particular, the financier Boris Berezovsky owns a substantial minority shareholding, which gives him disproportionate influence on the only television channel that reaches virtually the entire country. This is in addition to his control of another channel, TV-6, and the influence he can exert through the newspapers he controls, including the influential dailies *Kommersant*, *Nezavisimaya gazeta* and *Novye izvestiya*. TV-Centre, broadcast on the third channel, is funded mostly by the Moscow city administration and

TABLE 13.1 *Patterns of media consumption, 2000 (percentages)*

	Television	National press	Local press
Practically every day	70	11	8
Two or three times a week	16	18	10
Once a week	5	26	17
Less than once a week	3	14	18
Never	6	30	46

Source: *Monitoring obshchestvennogo mneniya: ekonomicheskie i sotsial'nye peremeny*, no. 4, 2000, p. 18 (n = 1800).

generally reflects the views of its energetic mayor, Yuri Luzhkov. The Russian government also launched the Culture Channel on Channel 5 to show ballets, concerts and other cultural fare (it does not run advertisements). The present structure of television ownership is shown in Table 13.2.

The major private television networks are NTV, which is broadcast on Channel 4, and TV-6, which is broadcast on Channel 6. The broadcast coverage of the private channels is mostly in European Russia, although they have partners that carry all or part of their programming throughout the country and abroad. In 1999, NTV officials estimated that they had about 40 million viewers across the country, while TV-6 claimed a potential audience of more than 100 million across Russia and the other CIS countries. According to the survey evidence, 87 per cent of regular TV viewers in Russia watched ORT daily, 83 per cent watched RTR, 72 per cent watched NTV, 51 per cent watched TV-6 and 35 per cent watched TV-Centre. The importance that government attached to this form of influence became starkly apparent on Easter weekend 2001 when NTV's editorial staff was summarily replaced by a pro-Kremlin group backed by the Gazprom conglomerate. Although the media company was in debt and Gusinsky himself had been charged with money laundering and briefly imprisoned, the move was widely seen as an attempt to wrest editorial control from the most powerful critical voice against the Putin regime. Gusinsky's newspaper *Segodnya* (Today) and his weekly news magazine *Itogi* (Events) also disappeared, at least temporarily. The two main radio stations, Radio Rossiya and Radio Mayak, are wholly state-owned and reach more than 90 per cent of the population.

Studies of the Russian media during elections have found that newspapers and television both overtly and covertly support their

TABLE 13.2   *Major television channels in Russia*

Channel	Name	Ownership
1	Russian Public Television (ORT)	51 per cent owned by the state, the rest by a mix of public and private corporations (including banks and natural resource companies)
2	Russian Television and Radio (RTR)	State-owned
3	TV-Centre	Funded primarily by the City of Moscow
4	NTV	Private; now controlled by state interests
5	Culture	State-owned; cultural channel created by presidential decree in 1997. Only channel that does not carry advertising
6	TV-6	Private

favourite candidates. In the case of newspapers, it is common practice for politicians and parties to buy 'secret advertising' – favourable articles about themselves that are not clearly designated as advertising. On television, news programmes often skew their stories in favour of their political patrons. Media analysts claim it is common for politicians and parties to bribe journalists for anything ranging from a favourable mention on the news to a better slot for a political advertisement. Understandably, few journalists admit even to being offered bribes.

While the state monopoly on mass media was abolished at the start of the 1990s, economic problems have provided little opportunity for media outlets to grow. In a brief 'honeymoon' period after the unsuccessful coup of 1991, most of the media were unanimous in their praise of the new Yeltsin government and the destruction of the Soviet system. But as the problems of a new democracy began to accumulate, most notably the rampant inflation that came with the collapse of the communist economy, the Russian media quickly reverted to the trend of the *perestroika* era, unafraid to report on the myriad problems in the new society. Many of the problems – the spectacular rise in crime, the new poverty of the working class, the financial scandals of the elite – made for exciting and dynamic reporting. In addition, it made for a great deal of anger on the part of the new government, whose leaders felt that they had to endure a relentless barrage of negative media coverage that did not make allowance for the difficult situation they had inherited from the Soviet administration.

Despite these early tensions, the new Russian state provided important laws to protect media freedom and independence. Formally, censorship itself was abolished by the Soviet media law of 1990, and by the corresponding Russian law of December 1991. Freedom of speech is guaranteed more generally under Article 29 of the 1993 Russian constitution. However, there are limits – the same article of the constitution forbids the dissemination of propaganda that spreads social, religious or national hatred. In addition, government secrets cannot be published. The final part of Article 29 guarantees 'freedom of mass information' and once again outlaws censorship. However, significant problems still remain in the legal protection of a free and fair media in Russia, including the lack of a law on broadcasting because of wrangling over its possible content.

Yet it is more the lack of a tradition of a free media than any dearth of written laws that creates problems for media development in Russia. The country has neither the British tradition of a state-funded media that still maintains significant editorial independence, nor the type of competitive private media outlets found in the United States. After the collapse of the Soviet regime, many groups of journalists wanted to take over and run their own newspapers, magazines or even television stations. However, the primary television channels with the largest reach – Channels 1 and 2 – remained under government control. Although many publications made an attempt to run themselves as independent businesses, it soon became clear that a shaky market economy could not support the plethora of publications that had thrived in the Soviet era. Those that do survive have to deal with twin pressures from funding sources in the government and the demands of their advertisers. Even if advertisers have no direct interest in editorial content, they do demand popular content, a desire that can run counter to the government's need to inform or even propagandise the viewers and readers. In this sense, the Russian media have the worst of both worlds – not only government influence, but also pressure from their advertisers.

Bias in the Russian Media

Even with these constraints, there is variation and choice among the Russian media. NTV, founded in 1994, built its reputation on its daring coverage of the first war in Chechnya. While the state-controlled television stations such as ORT were claiming Russian victories, NTV revealed the darker side of the war as untrained recruits died needlessly. After NTV dispatches continually contradicted the more optimistic reports on ORT, the state-controlled station was forced into more honest coverage of the conflict. Nonetheless, NTV bowed to pressure to ignore some serious problems of former president Boris Yeltsin – notably that he was in very poor health – when reporting the 1996 presidential campaign (its head even joined Yeltsin's staff for the period of the campaign). Despite pursuing its own political interests from time to time, NTV remained arguably the most objective major television outlet in Russia up to its takeover by pro-Kremlin interests in 2001.

There are in fact few restraints on those who fund the media from influencing editorial content on television, particularly news programming. Thus, there is a clear bias toward the Putin administration and the government it appoints on the two major state channels (ORT and RTR). The influence of media moguls, notably Boris Berezovsky, is clear on channels in which he controls most of the shares (such as TV-6). There is little respect for objectivity across any of the media, although the European Institute for the Media have suggested that radio remains freer of this sort of influence than either television or the print media. A wide range of interests is represented across all media outlets – including the various branches of the government as well as the media moguls – but virtually all news sources are biased, particularly state-run television.

Some of the most interesting studies of bias on television news have focused on election coverage. Optimally, national television, whether state-funded as in Britain or dependent on advertising revenue as in the United States, should provide voters with unbiased and clear information on their electoral choices. Studies show that most media in Russia conspicuously failed to do this in the 1999 and 2000 elections. The state-controlled television channels, notably ORT and RTR, openly promoted pro-government parties in the December 1999 Duma election, and Putin himself in the 2000 presidential campaign. Meanwhile, the mayor of Moscow used 'his' channel – TV-Centre, which is mostly funded by the city administration – to promote his favoured party and his personal political ambitions. NTV also championed its favourite parties and politicians in the 1999 and 2000 elections (particularly the liberal politician Grigorii Yavlinsky, a personal friend of Gusinsky).

According to the detailed monitoring of coverage that was undertaken for the European Institute of the Media, in the 1999 parliamentary elections ORT (Channel 1) gave 28 per cent of its election news coverage to the Kremlin-backed Unity party, while NTV gave the same party just 5 per cent of its election news coverage. Instead, NTV gave a third of its news coverage to Fatherland-All Russia, which was widely seen as the most serious challenger to the Kremlin and its allies. During the presidential elections, Channels 1 and 2 virtually became 'infomercials' for Putin, presenting him as a strong, decisive leader of the country. Putin, in fact, made no use of his free-time allocation on television, and engaged in none of the arranged debates among the leading candidates. He still secured about a third of all television coverage (as much as his three leading challengers put together), and about half of all the news and current affairs reporting on all television channels (EIM, 2000a).

The 1999 Duma election marked the rise of a new and worrying development, the use of *kompromat* (compromising material) or 'black propaganda' on Russian television. Some news shows that claimed to be 'analytical' programmes began to present negative material on political rivals, with little substantiation or reply from the victim of the attacks. For example, programmes on Channel 1 during the parliamentary campaign showed photos of the Moscow mayor's opulent country home and then flashed documents on the screen to suggest money laundering. In another show, ORT presenter Sergei Dorenko also showed gruesome shots of hip replacement surgery complete with buzzing sound effects for the bone saw. This was to suggest that Kremlin rival Yevgenii Primakov – who had just turned 70 – was too old and infirm to run for office because he had undergone the same operation. This sort of coverage became enormously popular with the viewers, not only destroying the reputation of some politicians on the bias of little or no evidence, but also crowding out more balanced presentations of political candidates and their actual qualifications for office.

In addition to the problems of news bias, a lack of money at state-controlled networks prevents the production of interesting entertainment programmes or even their purchase from abroad. As a result, Russian broadcasters typically offer a hodgepodge of inexpensive imports, including a wildly popular Mexican soap opera called *The Rich Also Cry*. Other offerings in recent years have included the American evening soap opera, *Santa Barbara*, and *Dr. Quinn: Medicine Woman*. While intellectuals complain of the lack of a native film industry to produce high-quality Russian drama, many of the Western imports are extremely popular. While the shows may have little social relevance for Russian viewers (such as shows about an American doctor in the Wild West), they do keep them tuned into television in general.

There are other media outlets, notably newspapers, the radio and the internet, to provide alternative information, although they have far less reach and influence than television. For example, a correspondent from Radio Liberty, which provides radio broadcasts as well as an influential internet newsletter on the former Soviet Union, disappeared in the winter of 1999 while filing reports about the war in Chechnya. The correspondent, Andrei Babitsky, had been providing reports that often contradicted the official Russian line about the military campaign in which they had become engaged. At first Russian officials claimed he must have been killed or kidnapped by the Chechens, but it eventually emerged he had been held by Russian forces to stop his reporting. After intense international pressure, mostly from US-based Radio Liberty, Babitsky was released. But his detention by the Russian military is a chilling message to other reporters who might try to defy the government information monopoly on events in Chechnya or on other news stories.

What do Russians themselves think about the media in their country? Focus groups conducted in Moscow, Voronezh and Ulyanovsk in the first half of 2000 suggest that Russians adjust to the lack of objectivity in news sources by using a variety of ways to filter the information that is made available to them. In particular, older people enjoy reading a range of newspapers – often shared with friends or family to cut the costs – as well as flipping across the television channels to get a greater diversity of coverage. However, they are often less bothered by biased news coverage than they are by the reporting of unpleasant social realities, and by a plethora of violence.

Ordinary Russians, in fact, seem relatively comfortable with the idea of the media as a political player, rather than an unbiased watchdog or commentator on political life. Much as in Soviet times, they expect television to instil a sense of pride about the country and find news coverage of Chechnya, corruption, crime and other problems depressing and unpatriotic. For this reason, they often preferred the coverage on state-funded television such as ORT, even though they were aware that it was less objective than the news broadcasts on NTV. Unsurprisingly, younger viewers who did not have to cope with the information shortages that existed in the Soviet period are less careful and analytical consumers of all forms of media.

Conclusions

The Russian media have become less free since the heady days of *glasnost* and the collapse of the Soviet coup in 1991. Perhaps most significantly, the consolidation of power in the executive branch and the lack of a real rule of law have left the media very vulnerable to government political and economic control. This is exacerbated by the lack of a tradition of journalistic freedom and objectivity. This lack of commitment to the journalistic ethic as it is understood in the West is particularly apparent during election campaigns. Trust in television has declined steadily since the end of the Soviet era, when the media were seen as voicing the discontent of the masses. Even NTV, the most powerful private television station in Russia, has failed to keep its distance from political power games in Russia. It can be debated as to how much this was really feasible for NTV, particularly in a country in which the executive branch can manipulate its power to award or discontinue a licence to broadcast.

However, it is distressing that broadcasters themselves seem not to understand the need for objectivity to build a responsible, independent media. As a result, voters may be able to receive different 'slants' on political news on a range of channels, but cannot obtain unbiased information from any single source. This is particularly worrying as about half of the voters have no access to television channels beyond those controlled by the presidential administration and its close associates (ORT and RTR). At the same time there has been a growth of quite questionable news practices, which bring the worst excesses of smear tactics into prime-time news programming. This type of 'black propaganda' has been noted in many parts of the media, but was particularly flagrant on ORT during the 1999 and 2000 elections.

Meanwhile, a lack of financing and support, even at the largest television stations, leaves journalists vulnerable to bribery and coercion from a variety of groups. Even if there were a culture of journalistic objectivity and public service, it would be virtually impossible to maintain in a system in which government support is inadequate to cover the running costs of the media. In addition, even major television stations have had to weather times at which their salaries and other costs were simply not paid by the government because of its periodic financial crises. Advertising revenues are a further source of funds, particularly for the independent media, but they are generally not sufficient to support most media outlets. Without some sort of powerful government or business sponsor,

most media outlets could not exist. By the same token, it is understood in Russian journalism that the sponsor will influence editorial
content. While there is no longer the full control over information
flows that existed in the Soviet era – as the Russian government was
reminded when they were slow to release information about the
Kursk submarine disaster in the summer of 2000 – there are effective
ways to limit critical reporting.

Underlining the problems relating to objectivity and independence
are the problems that menace Russian society at large, namely crime,
lawlessness and violence. Unsurprisingly, journalists are often targets
of this violence because of their high profile. Russia was shocked
when popular television host and ORT executive Vladimir Listyev
was murdered in the spring of 1995. Many other journalists have been
killed, beaten, threatened or kidnapped, particularly in attempting to
cover the Chechen conflict or expose the Russian mafia, or even the
activities of their local administration. Although Russian journalists
have shown amazing bravery in harrowing situations, the dangers of
the profession must serve as a deterrent to those who would like to
report objectively on their society.

It does not help that there is increasing government pressure, in the
form of arrests and illegal detainments of prominent figures in
journalism, to toe the government line. This is a particularly effective
technique, as journalists throughout Russian media organisations are
aware that if high-profile figures – such as Radio Liberty correspondent Babitsky or NTV financial backer Gusinsky – can be detained
on vague pretexts there can be little security for journalists anywhere.
As there is also little respect for the rule of law, even the elaborate
guarantees of media freedom in the Russian constitution are of little
help. Rather, officials can claim that journalists were breaching
military security (in the case of Babitsky) or engaged in financial
fraud (in the case of Gusinsky). Whether the charges stick is less
important than the factor of intimidation in itself. Journalists,
certainly, have various means of fighting intimidation through their
own media outlets and through international coverage of their plight.
But at the start of a new century, it seemed that Russia's new
president might be prepared to weather the international opprobrium
he would incur by violating the civil rights of journalists if this was the
price he had to pay for silencing the critics of the federal government.

14

Values and the Construction of a National Identity

VERA TOLZ

Scholars regard clearly defined state borders and the membership of a nation as a precondition for successful democratisation. The Russian Federation faces considerable problems in this area. After the demise of the USSR, Russians were confronted with the failure of their previous attempts at nation- and state-building. Indeed, as the liberal politician Galina Starovoitova noted in late 1991, if the USSR disintegrated Russia would 'have virtually the same ports as it had when Peter I came to power'. Accordingly, in the 1990s, the answer to the question 'who are we, the Russian people?' suddenly became more uncertain than it had been since first posed in the eighteenth century. Since that time, two main issues have influenced the construction of Russian national identity – the existence of the land-based empire, in which Russians actively intermingled with other ethnic groups, and the comparison between Russia and the West. In this empire the geographical and political boundaries between the metropolis and the colonies were blurred. So were, in many instances, ethnic boundaries between its different peoples. From the Russian point of view, particularly unclear were the boundaries between themselves and other East Slavs (Ukrainians and Belarusians). With the disintegration of the USSR, Russians were faced with the need to rethink some of the stereotypes that they had held concerning their relationship with non-Russians.

In most instances, Russian intellectuals and politicians of the pre-revolutionary and Soviet periods constructed various images of Russia by emphasising either its differences or similarities with Western Europe and North America. The main question that elites confronted was whether Russia should modernise by copying the examples of Western countries or whether it should try to identify its own path of development. In 1992 the then acting prime minister, Yegor Gaidar, expressed hope that Russia would become a civic nation and would be able to shake off the burden of the past and start anew the process of reinventing itself as a European democratic state with a market economy. The reality proved to be far more complex. Gaidar's, it emerged, was not the only vision of the new Russia, and historical legacies turned out to be more persistent than he and his supporters had anticipated. This chapter looks at the debate on what is Russia and who are the Russians among intellectual and political elites after the collapse of the USSR and the impact of this debate on public opinion. This debate is not a purely intellectual exercise. The way in which Russian elites and the broader public imagine the proper borders of the Russian national homeland and define membership of the Russian nation has a direct impact on the government's internal and foreign policies and in determining the future of Russia and of the other countries of the former Soviet Union.

Theoretical and Historical Background

Scholars regard nations as a modern phenomenon, the consequence of the social organisation of industrial society. Such a society cannot function without its members being bound by a common culture, which political and intellectual elites create and which is transmitted through a universal system of education. In Western Europe, where in the course of the nineteenth century modern nations were created, strong states had been in existence and their boundaries determined the membership of national communities, and nations were perceived as civic communities whose members were all citizens of the state bound by loyalty to its political institutions. In Eastern and Central Europe, whose peoples lived in pre-modern empires, nations were imagined by the elites as ethnic communities, bound by common language, culture and history.

In Russia, both civic and ethnic elements of nationhood were weakened by the peculiar form of Russian state-building. In the pre-revolutionary period, the attitude of the Russians towards their state and their views of themselves were shaped by the existence of their land-based empire. Living side by side with representatives of other ethnic groups for centuries, Russians failed to acquire a fully developed ethnic national identity. In turn, due to the lateness of Russian industrialisation (it began only at the turn of the twentieth century), the absence of necessary political freedoms and of a civil society, civic identity, based on inclusive citizenship, also could not be forged among the different peoples of the empire. This peculiarity of the Russian situation was well understood by pre-revolutionary and émigré Russian thinkers, who argued that Russians managed to create a new type of community, different from nations as they existed in Europe. According to this position, the Russian empire could not be compared to either land-based or overseas European empires. In this new community, the argument went, peoples of different ethnic origins, cultural and religious backgrounds peacefully coexisted, both retaining their essential ethnic characteristics and contributing to the creation of a supranational pan-Russian culture. Such a view was, however, largely confined to the multi-ethnic, yet fully Russified, imperial elite. Members of society at large continued to hold pre-national religious and regional identities. Moreover, at the turn of the twentieth century, among some non-Russian nationalities, local intellectuals began to construct their own visions of ethnic nations, based on non-Russian languages and cultures.

After the October revolution, the Soviet government pursued highly contradictory policies. Many of these policies were conducive to the creation of modern nations – rapid industrialisation, urbanisation, destruction of village-based traditional cultures, and the introduction of a universal system of education. Among the non-Russians of the USSR, ethnic nationalism was encouraged. Indeed, by creating ethnically based administrative units, educating local elites, encouraging the development of non-Russian languages and cultures and introducing an ascribed category of ethnic nationality in internal passports the government stimulated the development of and, in many instances, even created from scratch, ethnic nations among various peoples of the empire. At the same time, however, Soviet ideologists propagated the idea that all citizens of the USSR constituted a new community of 'a single Soviet people' united by loyalty to the communist state. Without renouncing their local ethnic heritage, all Soviet citizens, with time, were expected to be able to partake in Russian culture, albeit in a Sovietised version. Whereas non-Russians enjoyed privileged access to jobs and education in their own ethnic administrative units, Russians enjoyed such privileges throughout the entire country. As a result, the majority of Russians were unaware that they lived in a multi-ethnic empire – they saw it as a Russian state – and they viewed the USSR rather than their own union republic, the RSFSR, as their homeland. Thus, in contrast to non-Russians, the Russian ethnic identity continued to be blurred. Civic identity continued to be undermined by the existence of the authoritarian state, which submerged society.

Only in the 1960s did some Russians for the first time begin to question whether the maintenance of this multi-ethnic community was in their interest. Alexander Solzhenitsyn, among others, argued that the preservation of the USSR led Russians to make unnecessary economic sacrifices and distorted their cultural tradition. Thus, he urged Russians to shake off 'the burden of Central Asia and the Caucasus', to allow the independence of the Baltic republics, and thus pave the way for the creation of a Russian nation-state. But who would be the members of the Russian nation and where would be the borders of the new Russian state? For Solzhenitsyn and those who shared his views, ideally, the Russian nation was to consist of the three east Slavic peoples, including Ukrainians and Belarusians. Linguistic and cultural similarities between eastern Slavs and their alleged common history were regarded by these Russian nationalists as the markers of common national identity.

By the end of Gorbachev's *perestroika* the idea that the preservation of the empire was not in the interest of the Russians was embraced by Boris Yeltsin's government. The Russian leader argued that the federation should become a new nation-state of all the people who resided there. However, the few years in which the Russian leadership contrasted the new federation and its Soviet predecessor were not long enough to make Russians fully identify with the Russian Federation as a legitimate form of Russian national statehood. Therefore, after the disintegration of the Soviet Union, the idea that Russians were ultimately an imperial people and could survive as a distinct community only within some form of a union remained strong. At the same time, politicians and intellectuals who argued that the time had come for Russians to put the 'imperial temptation' behind them and build a modern nation-state could not agree on the geography of the state and on membership of the nation.

Defining the Boundaries of the Russian Nation

In the 1990s, five main definitions of the Russian nation were put forward by intellectuals and politicians:

- Russians defined as an imperial people or through their mission to create a supranational state

- Russians as a nation of all eastern Slavs, united by common origin and culture
- Russians as a community of Russian speakers, regardless of their ethnic origin
- Russians defined racially, with blood ties constituting the basis of common identity
- Russians as members of a civic nation of all citizens of the federation regardless of their ethnic and cultural background

Imperial People

The most outspoken advocates of the definition of Russians in terms of their imperial mission are Communists and those Russian nationalists who, in the 1990 republican parliamentary elections, created a joint Bloc of Public and Patriotic Movements with the goal of preserving the USSR. Since December 1991, the communist and nationalist press has been dominated by the belief that eventually the union will be recreated, otherwise the Russians will completely disappear as a distinct community. As philosopher Yuri Borodai (1992, p. 130) put it: 'I can say frankly and openly that I am an imperialist ... I believe in the resurrection of the Russian state after Golgotha'. The communist-nationalist opposition in parliament views the recreation of the union as its programme- maximum. The Communist Party leader, Gennadii Zyuganov, argues that the Russian empire and the USSR constituted a unique Russian civilisation, all of whose members had a common identity. So does the leader of the extreme nationalists, Vladimir Zhirinovsky. Inspired by such convictions, Communists and nationalists persuaded the Duma to adopt a resolution in March 1996 which proclaimed the Belovezh Accord of December 1991 that had dissolved the USSR null and void.

The view that Russians should preserve their union identity is expressed not just by extreme right-wingers and communists, but also by some liberals. The author of one of the first scholarly articles explaining to Russians the Western notion of a civic nation, Vadim Mezhuev (1996, p. 103), argues similarly that the creation of a nation-state should not be the goal of the Russian people today. As the citizens of the federation are not ready to form a civic nation, he argues, attempts to create a nation-state would either lead to the forced Russification of non-Russians and/or to the disintegration of Russia. Instead, Russians should continue to fulfil their mission of maintaining a unique supranational state. In turn, during the 1996 presidential election campaign, Yeltsin and some liberal members of his entourage paid tribute to the position that Russian identity was difficult to disentangle from the union one. Then, some liberals in the government began to refer cautiously to the possibility of reviving some form of a union. In May 1996 *Nezavisimaya gazeta* published a working paper of the Council for Foreign and Defence Policy that went so far as to claim that the revival of the union was feasible. Although the Council was a non-governmental body, some of its participants were also members of Yeltsin's Presidential Council. The authors of the paper believed that the formation of a Russian national statehood was impossible unless a fully-fledged economic, political and military union was revived on the territory of the defunct USSR. In this same period Yeltsin began advocating CIS citizenship, which would strengthen the union identity of all former Soviet citizens. Yeltsin and the organisers of his election campaign evidently believed that such policies would appeal to the Russian electorate. It seems, however, that this perception was erroneous. Although opinion polls indicate a strong nostalgia for the Soviet Union among Russians, only a small minority (around 7–8 per cent) support Russia's re-unification with the Transcaucasus, Central Asia and the Baltics (Kuskovets and Klyamkin, 1997).

Community of Eastern Slavs

The attitude towards Ukraine and Belarus on the part of the Russians is rather different. Opinion polls conducted in 1997 indicated that up to 64 per cent of respondents supported the idea of merging Ukraine and Russia into one state and 75 per cent endorsed a union with Belarus (Tolz, 1998b, p. 292). The polls showed that the majority of respondents saw Ukrainians and Belarusians as part of the Russian nation.

The reason for this view is the cultural and linguistic affinities between eastern Slavs and above all the way in which Russians view their national history. Until 1905, the tsarist government denied that Ukrainians and Belarusians were nationalities in their own right and classified them as part of the pan-Russian people. Although the Soviet government recognised Ukrainians and Belarusians as separate nations, since the 1930s Soviet historiography promoted the view that in the medieval period all east Slavs were part of one Russian nationality and that Kiev Rus was the first Russian state.

In the post-communist period, the majority of Russian nationalists began to argue that, if the fully-fledged union could not be recreated, at least a community of all eastern Slavs should be preserved. Moreover, many nationalists and communists revived the pre-revolutionary view of denying Ukrainians and Belarusians separate identities altogether. In his writings Communist leader Zyuganov unequivocally included Ukrainians and Belarusians in the Russian nation, citing nineteenth-century Russian authors as his authority. Even the liberal press tends to see Ukrainian independence as an anomaly, a ploy of Ukrainian elites with little popular resonance. In turn, the working paper of the Council for Foreign and Defence Policy singled out Ukraine and Belarus as the countries of greatest importance for Russia. Yeltsin's government shared this view, as its successive agreements on the formation of a union with Belarus have indicated. Their December 1999 treaty on the creation of a union accepted that both countries would retain their sovereignty, but it was likely that Belarusian national identity would be weakened in such circumstances. This, in turn, will have serious implications for setting the boundaries of the Russian nation. On numerous occasions, members of the Russian government have indicated their desire to have a similar arrangement with Ukraine and expressed dissatisfaction with the rejection of such an option by the majority of the Ukrainian political elite.

A Community of Russian Speakers

Another definition of the Russian nation is through language as the main marker of national identity. In the pre-revolutionary period, many Russian intellectuals and the government attributed great importance to the Russian language as a force unifying different ethnic and social groups in the empire. In the Soviet period, Russification made many non-Russians, especially other eastern Slavs, view themselves as Russians and, accordingly, they identified themselves as Russians in internal passports and censuses. In the course of industrialisation, millions of Russians settled outside the borders of the Russian republic. Therefore, when the USSR disintegrated and approximately 25 million Russians and another 5 million Russian speakers found themselves outside the borders of the Federation, they were proclaimed by some intellectuals and politicians as part of the divided Russian nation. The advocates of such a definition of the nation are aware of the weak nature of the ties between Russian-speaking communities in the newly independent states and the low level of their identification with the Federation. This is not regarded as a reason to look for other definitions of the Russian nation.

Instead, they believe that the Russian government should try to regain areas where Russians and Russian speakers live in compact settlements in the 'near abroad'. They also argue that the national consciousness of Russians/Russian speakers outside the Federation should be strengthened by nationalist propaganda, which will emphasise the role of Orthodox Christianity and common history. Scholars began to publish studies, tracing the history of settlements of the Russians throughout the former empire, in order to advise politicians on where the 'proper' borders of the new Russian state should be.

In 1993–4, under the influence of opposition forces in the parliament and of some members within the government, Yeltsin began to promote the view of the Russian nation as a community of Russian speakers throughout the former USSR. The defence of the rights of the Russian speaking 'diaspora' accordingly became the main focus of Russian foreign policy. The Russian diaspora was an artificially constructed category and its precise membership had never been clearly defined by politicians. Appeals of Russian politicians to Russian speakers in the 'near abroad' had little response from these politically-disengaged people, most of whom did not identify with the Federation. In addition, the refusal of all the newly independent states, with the exception of Turkmenistan and Tajikistan, to agree to the Russian proposal of dual citizenship, meant in 1995 a virtual collapse of the Russian policy towards the 'near abroad'.

Among ordinary Russians, support for the idea that Russian speakers in the non-Russian newly independent states are part of the Russian nation has been sizeable. According to a poll conducted in 1995 by the Moscow-based Public Opinion Foundation, a significant minority (33 per cent) thought Russia should incorporate territories of other newly independent states where Russian speakers lived in a compact majority (Klyamkin and Lapkin, 1995, pp. 94 and 96). Yet only 8 per cent thought the government should use any radical measures to achieve the incorporation of Russian-populated areas of the 'near abroad' into the Federation.

Racial Definitions

To some extent, the multi-ethnic nature of the land-based Russian empire and the high degree of ethnic assimilation in the USSR acted as a safeguard against racial prejudice. In the pre-revolutionary period, overt racism was manifested in the theories of the extreme right-wing anti-Semitic movement, the Black Hundreds. These ideas were revived in the late 1960s and the 1970s, when for the first time the view of Russia as the most exploited among the union republics was formulated by nationalists. At this time, geographer Lev Gumilev began to argue that nations were biological rather than social phenomena. Initially, such views were confined to a very limited number of fairly obscure journals, but in the period of *glasnost* they began to be widely publicised.

In the postcommunist period purely racist groups have proliferated, as their leaders began to appeal to popular resentment against the growing influx of refugees and to exploit popular frustrations over economic hardships. Those advocating a racial definition of Russianness argue that in order to survive Russians should safeguard themselves from the harmful influences of other 'ethnoses'. As the leader of the Russian Party, Nikolai Bondarik, put it in his party's newspaper in 1993: 'In Russia, there must be only a Russian government, a Russian parliament consisting of ethnic Russians belonging to the Great Nation by blood and spirit'. The advocates of a racial definition of a nation do not explain *how* the purity of Russian blood is to be established. Indeed, the purists' search for a true Russian in racial terms would immediately encounter difficulties with the un-challenged symbol of Russianness – Pushkin, whose grandfather was an Abyssinian. If the ideologists of the Black Hundreds saw Jews as the main 'enemy' of the Russian people, contemporary extremists add to this list the peoples of Central Asia and the Caucasus. Nikolai Lysenko of the National Republican Party of Russia and Alexander Barkashov of Russian National Unity call for the introduction of laws forbidding mixed marriages and for the imposition of restrictions on people from the Caucasus and Central Asia who live in the federation.

Popular support for such groups is limited. Yet the anti-Chechen propaganda of the government and of the media since the mid-1990s has contributed to the rise of anti-Muslim, racist feelings. Opinion polls in early 2000 indicated that up to 80 per cent of those polled regarded Islam as a 'bad thing' (by contrast, in 1992, only 17 per cent subscribed to such views) (Goble, 2000). Particularly since the resumption of regular military operations in 1999, the Chechens have been portrayed in the media and by politicians as 'treacherous' and 'savage' enemies of Russia, who threaten its cultural and religious traditions. In the words of Vladimir Putin, Chechens 'would not be content with remaining inside' the borders of their republic and, if

Chechen 'extremists' were not stopped, 'we will have the Islamisation of Russia' (*The Times*, 21 March 2000).

Civic Identity

Views of this kind on what it means to be a Russian and where the borders of the Russian state should be are rooted in either the pre-revolutionary or Soviet past, and their advocates apply and adapt concepts that have been elaborated under entirely different circumstances.

There is, however, a novel idea concerning Russian identity, which entered intellectual and political discourse in the late 1980s and gathered strength in the post-communist period. This is the idea of a civic Russian (*rossiiskaya*) nation whose members are all citizens of the Russian Federation (*rossiyane*) regardless of their ethnic origin and culture, united by loyalty to their new political institutions and to the constitution. The main advocate of the civic Russian nation is the prominent ethnographer and former head of the State Committee on Nationalities, Valerii Tishkov. Tishkov calls on the Russian government to introduce state symbols and encourage the development of common values that would have a meaning for all citizens of Russia, not only ethnic Russians. Supporters of the concept of a civic nation of *rossiyane* remind the government that, given that 18 per cent of federation citizens are non-Russians, the forging of a compound civic identity is the only way to preserve the integrity of the state.

Attempts to forge a civic identity among all peoples of the federation informed government policies in 1991–2. No specific Russian ethnic characteristics are reflected in the 1991 Russian citizenship law, which does not even require a basic knowledge of the Russian language as a condition for obtaining citizenship. Although in 1993–5 the government defined the Russian nation as a community of Russian speakers throughout the former USSR, the 1993 Russian constitution mentions the civic Russian (*rossiiskaya*) nation as a community of Federation citizens. Similarly, the 1996 'Concept of State Nationalities Policy' defines as a main goal of the Russian leadership the maintenance and further development of 'the traditions of interaction between the Slavic, Turkic, Caucasian, Finno-Ugric, Mongol and other peoples' of the Federation.

After Yeltsin's re-election as president in 1996, he resumed attempts at constructing a nation of *rossiyane* within the borders of the federation. Yeltsin's call to society to search for a new 'Russian idea,' in his first post-election address to the nation in July 1996, should be seen in this light. The expression 'Russian idea' was invented by the famous philosopher Vladimir Solovev at the turn of the twentieth century to mean 'the purpose for Russia's existence in world history'. Informed by Romantic definitions of a nation, intellectuals searched for a particular lesson that Russia could teach the world. This messianism, to some extent, continued to inform the policies of the Soviet government, whose members believed in the universal value of communist ideology.

Against this background, many liberals attacked Yeltsin's proposal. The mentioning of a 'Russian idea' revived memories of a messianic vision of Russia, spreading either Orthodox Christianity or communism beyond its borders. Liberals also feared that the government yet again was trying to invent a new political ideology for Russia. In fact, it seems that Yeltsin's goal was far more modest – it was a desperate attempt to unite a polarised society by promoting a vision of a civic nation based on values its members could share.

The notion of a civic nation of all citizens of the federation enjoys fairly broad support among Russians, whose ethnic identity has traditionally been weak. According to a study conducted in July 1996 by the All-Russian Centre for the Study of Public Opinion (VTsIOM), 53 per cent defined Russians as all those who lived in the Russian Federation and regarded themselves as Russian (irrespective of ethnicity). In turn, according to a 1997 survey by the Moscow Institute of Sociological Analysis, only 16 per cent of those polled perceived Russia as a 'state of ethnic Russians' (see Tables 14.1 and 14.2). However, Yeltsin's attempt at identifying a set of common values that would unite rich and poor, Muscovites and the periphery, supporters of his own policies and those who regularly voted for the opposition, proved to be a failure. The most common idea, put forward by those who responded to the president's call was the encouragement of state patriotism. This approach is not new. From the time of Peter and Catherine the Great, Russian rulers have felt that it was up to them to unite society by promoting state patriotism – namely, people's unity around the tsar (or the party leadership) due to their pride of belonging to and serving a strong state. However, in 1917 and 1991, state patriotism could not prevent the disintegration of the country when it was in deep crisis. Thus, Yeltsin's critics immediately pointed out that with the state being so weak, attempts to unite society by instilling state patriotism were doomed. In spite of this disappointing experience, Vladimir Putin appears to believe that the revival of a strong state and the unification of society through a pride of belonging to it represent the only way forward.

TABLE 14.1   *Popular perceptions of Russia (percentages)*

A state whose status in the world is determined by the wellbeing of its citizens	52
A state with a market economy and democratic freedoms	41
A multiethnic state of equal citizens regardless of ethnicity	35
A mighty military power	21
A state of ethnic Russians	16
A Christian Orthodox state	13
As it was under communist rule	12
An empire within the borders of the USSR	7

Source: based on a survey conducted by the Moscow Institute of Socio-logical Analysis, May 1997; 1519 respondents from 12 regions of the Russian Federation were asked to choose not more than three of the above definitions of Russia.

The main critics of the idea of the civic nation are the intellectual and political elites of the ethnic republics. Like ethnic minorities elsewhere, they view the concept of a civic nation as an attempt by central government to disguise its assimilation policies. Ethnically based units of government offer their elites a wide range of political and economic privileges, which they are most unwilling to lose. Tishkov and other supporters of civic nationalism have called on the Russian government to gradually move away from an ethnically-based federation – an administrative structure that in the case of the USSR, Yugoslavia and Czechoslovakia proved to be unviable. Optimists in the Russian government deny the similarity between the USSR, other unsuccessful ethnically-based federations, and the Russian Federation. They point out that in the RF a minority (33 per cent) of non-Russians actually live in their 'own' administrative units. According to opinion polls, among non-Russians who live outside their ethnic areas a civic (*rossiiskaya*) identity prevails. Indeed, non-Russians in Russia today are far more Russified and versed in Russian culture than was the case with the majority of non-Russians who were allotted union republics in the USSR.

Russian Identity between West and East

While trying to define the membership of the Russian nation and create images of the postcommunist Russian homeland, intellectuals and politicians constantly raise the question of Russia's relationship

TABLE 14.2 *Popular perceptions of the national homeland and Russian identity (percentages)*

1. When you are talking about the homeland, what do you usually mean?

Russia	34.5
City/village of birth and childhood	30.9
City/village of residence for most of one's life	16.3
Soviet Union	10.3
Republic of residence	3.6
Difficult to answer	2.5
None/other	1.8

2. Do you agree that Russians are all those who live in Russia and regard themselves as Russian, or is this definition not sufficient?

Yes, Russians are all who live in Russia and regard themselves as Russian	54.6
This definition is not sufficient	36.0
Difficult to answer	9.4

3. Which of the following criteria are particularly important for a person to be considered Russian?

To cherish the traditions of the Russian people	54.3
To have Russian as a native language	53.4
To live according to the moral ideals of Russia	39.7
To have Russian ancestors	36.8
To be an Orthodox Christian	18.9
To be Russian according to one's passport entry	11.8
Difficult to answer/something else	9.5

Source: based on a survey conducted by the All-Russian Centre for the Study of Public Opinion (VTsIOM), July 1996 (n = 2404).

with the 'West'. This is hardly surprising. Since the time Russia's 'modernisation' began in the early eighteenth century, Western Europe and, since the nineteenth century, also the United States, have been Russia's 'other', against which Russian identity has been constructed. Sometimes Russian nation-builders have imagined the West as a unified, undifferentiated category; at other times, individual countries within Europe, or the United States, have served as models or anti-models for Russia to emulate or reject. The famous Slavophile–Westerniser debate of the nineteenth century was precisely about Russia's difference or similarity with Europe. The Slavophiles dwelt on what they perceived as Russia's unique qualities – the spirit of collectivity, support for autocracy, the search for inner 'truth'.

Westernisers, by contrast, hoped that Russia would eventually be able to follow the Western path of development and establish a constitutional government. However, later in the century, even the Westernisers became doubtful about their foreign models. In response to their direct experience of living in Western Europe as political refugees, they began to condemn the evils of capitalism and express the hope that Russia would find its own way of development. Many Westernisers thus turned to socialism either in a specific Russian variant, which reflected the hope that peasant communes could constitute a basis for a new society, or in a Marxist version.

The growing disillusionment with the West led Russian nation-builders to raise the question of Russia's relationship to the East. After all, geographically the Russian empire was located partly in Asia, and many of the empire's subjects were non-European. In the late nineteenth century a view emerged that Russia constituted a world of its own, a unique continental multiethnic civilisation. In the 1920s, the émigré movement, the Eurasians, brought these ideas to a logical conclusion by completing the dissociation of Russia from Europe by declaring its affinity with Asia.

In the Soviet period, Lenin's vision of the capitalist West as the main adversary, an anti-model in a political sense as well as a positive example of technological development, by the mid-1930 was superseded by an overwhelmingly hostile attitude towards Western Europe and North America. This sharp division of the world was reconsidered in Mikhail Gorbachev's period and replaced by the idea of USSR/Russia as an unquestionable part of Europe, isolation from which was harmful for Russia. In the early 1990s this approach was enthusiastically taken up by Yeltsin and members of his government, particularly foreign minister Andrei Kozyrev and economics minister Yegor Gaidar, who regarded as their main goal the achievement of Russia's integration into Western political, security and economic structures. For Kozyrev, the developed countries of the West were Russia's 'natural allies', and the West was described as a 'world of civilisation'. According to Gaidar, in order to enter this world, Russia had to abandon its traditional, 'pathological' forms of state and society.

Such a position had many opponents. Gorbachev's and later Yeltsin's pro-Western policies were attacked by nationalists and communists, who have been united not only by their support for the preservation of the USSR/recreation of a union but also by their anti-Westernism. Using various anti-Western pronouncements by prerevolutionary and émigré Russian thinkers and Soviet ideologists, the opposition constructed an image of Russia whose unique identity the West had been determined to destroy. In an article in a leading opposition newspaper in June 1992, the journalist Sergei Morozov argued that 'The Moscow principality, which later became Russia, was designed by its leaders to be a counterbalance to the Catholic West', with a foreign policy that was 'a rejection of the West.' Another conservative nationalist, Shamil Sultanov, was sure that 'the decadent, hypocritical and atheistic civilization [of the West] ... cannot last long' (Sultanov, 1992, p. 143). In the view of Gennadii Zyuganov, one of Russia's main missions in history has been to prevent the spread of the evil influence of the West to other parts of the world. Gorbachev, Yeltsin and other 'Westernisers' were agents of Western powers, carrying out a plot to destroy Russia. The 'West' for these authors is the 'Atlanticist, maritime powers' – above all the United States and Great Britain. The attitude towards continental European powers, such as Germany and France, is more favourable, and some nationalists have maintained close contacts with right-wing politicians in these countries.

Rejecting the Westernisers' image of the new Russia, their opponents have turned to the heritage of the 1920s Eurasians to construct an alternative. The Russia of the opposition is a continental, Eurasian power, a bridge between different cultures and civilisations of East and West. Sultanov argued that 'The double-headed eagle of the Russian empire manifestly expressed the main geopolitical and geo-historical essence of the country: its inner Eurasian character'. The Russia of the opposition is more of the East than of the West, and 'the future belongs' to the former.

The 1990 elections to the Russian parliament indicated that there was more public support for the Westernisers' vision of Russia than for that of the nationalist-communist opposition. However, both public opinion and the positions of initial Westernisers began to change in 1992. Members of the reformist parliamentary faction, Democratic Russia, as well as members of Yeltsin's administration began to reject the Kozyrev–Gaidar vision. In the spring of 1992, the presidential advisor on foreign policy matters, Sergei Stankevich, offered a moderate version of Eurasianism as a middle ground between radical Westernisers and the opposition. For Stankevich, because of Russia's history and its not exclusively European geography, it constituted a unique, continental civilization, with special interests in the CIS and Baltic countries that the West must recognise.

By mid-1993 many elements of Kozyrev's approach were abandoned by Yeltsin's government and a position much closer to that of Stankevich was adopted. Meanwhile, polls began to indicate a change in public opinion, with a growing feeling that Russia should promote its own (never, in fact, clearly defined) 'indigenous' values.

Why did such a shift occur? First, given Russia's history, attempts to construct an identity that would be based on the idea of congruence between Russia and an 'imagined' West were unrealistic from the outset. However, the political discourse created through those efforts instilled in the population hopes that in a foreseeable future their lives would be radically transformed for the better. Instead, economic reforms, closely associated with Western and particularly US advice, had a negative impact on the lives of many ordinary people. In introducing reforms, Yeltsin's government failed to formulate any notion of national goals other than material ones that could help the population cope with the sacrifices and suffering which the economic reforms had inflicted. Disillusionment with reforms was accompanied by criticism of the West. Among pro-Western liberal intellectuals support for Russia's total 'Westernisation' began to decline as the view became more popular that Russia had again been 'rejected' by Europe as its integration into Western alliance systems had proved slow and painful. By the mid-1990, liberals began to share with conservatives the view that, as Russia had lost its superpower status, the United States was trying unilaterally to set the terms of world politics, even in those areas which Russia had traditionally viewed as central to its national interests.

Some scholars see this shift from overembracing Westernism to a much more suspicious attitude towards the West's intentions as an indication that anti-Westernism is becoming the main component of a compound new Russian identity which is being forged after the demise of the USSR (for instance McDaniel, 1996; Urban, 1998). This view may be too gloomy. First, intellectuals and politicians who deny the European nature of Russian culture and believe in a threat posed to the existence of Russia by the West do not dominate the government. The most influential politicians acknowledge that Russia is much closer to Europe than to any country in Asia, and express a persistent desire to see Russia admitted into the political and economic institutions of the West. Thus, in his opening statement at the EU–Russia summit in May 2000, Putin reiterated that Russia 'was, is and will be a European country by its location, its culture, and its attitude toward economic integration'. Even Communist Party leaders agree that various Western political and economic practices have to be introduced in Russia; they do not reject regular parliamentary elections and some elements of a market economy.

Secondly, as for the Russian population, however strong is its dissatisfaction with the current state of affairs, most people do support political liberties and do not want the return to a planned command-administrative economy of the Communist era (Rose, 1998, Table 1). And finally, anti-Western feelings as expressed by the majority of Russians and especially the criticism of the West on the part of liberals and moderates are largely aimed at the United States rather than Western Europe. Unpopular economic reforms are mostly associated with American advice; and the NATO bombing of Serbia in 1999, which was sharply opposed by the majority of Russians, was blamed almost solely on the United States. Some journalists even argued that the bombing amounted to a war waged by the United States against Europe, of which Russia was a part; and there was widespread support, even among liberals, when Yeltsin warned the US president in December 1999 'not for a minute, or even a half-minute' to forget that Russia had a full arsenal of nuclear weapons.

Conclusion

The demise of the USSR delivered a considerable blow to the perceptions of many Russians about their identity. The common view that Russians were, above all, the creators and preservers of a unique multi-ethnic community seemed all but discredited in 1991. Under the circumstances it is not surprising that the search for a new 'Russian idea' was put on the agenda of intellectual and political elites. The question of a new Russian identity has been vigorously debated in the media and, in consequence, has attracted the attention of the broader public. As this chapter has shown, the ways in which the elites and the public define the Russian nation have a direct impact on policies, particularly in relation to ethnic minorities in the federation itself, to Ukraine and Belarus, to Russian speakers in the 'near abroad' and to CIS integration.

The outcome of the debate about the membership and the boundaries of the Russian nation is not yet clear. It seems that the most conducive path of nation-building on the territory of the former USSR is the formation of a civic nation of *rossiyane* out of all citizens of the federation regardless of their ethnicity. This is the way in which the Russian constitution defines the nation. However, the nation of *rossiyane* does not yet exist and the obstacles to its formation are still formidable. Among them, particularly significant are the rift between rich and poor and between capital and periphery; disputed state borders, particularly in North Caucasus; and the rise of xenophobia towards non-Russians, especially Muslims, among the Russian population.

PART FOUR

Conclusion

15

Russian Democratisation in Comparative Perspective

ZVI GITELMAN

In the past decade there has been considerable debate over whether the Russian Federation has evolved into a democratic state. When the communist regimes of the Soviet Union and Eastern Europe collapsed in 1989–91, many in the West made the facile assumption that democratic systems would replace them, as if there were no alternatives to communism other than democracy. In hindsight, we realise that no single type of system has replaced communism and that the formerly communist states in Eastern Europe and the territories of the Former Soviet Union range from those that seem fully democratic to the distinctly undemocratic. How can one understand this variance? What, after all, is democracy? How and why among a group of states, all of which started from the same communist base, do some appear to be democracies today and others do not?

What is Democracy?

Democracy is a system of government that meets four essential conditions: (1) meaningful, extensive and non-violent competition for power at predictable intervals; (2) the opportunity for all to participate in politics; and (3) civil and political liberties 'sufficient to ensure the integrity of political competition and participation' (Diamond, Linz and Lipset, 1988, p. 4) What differentiates democratic governments or organisations from others is that anyone can aspire to leadership, and can dissent from leaders' opinions and preferences. Moreover, leadership is responsive to the rank-and-file.

A more elaborate set of criteria for democracy is posited by Robert Dahl. These are: freedom to form and join organisations; freedom of expression; the right to vote; eligibility for public office; the right to compete for support/votes; alternative sources of information; free and fair elections; and institutions for making government policies depend on votes and other expressions of preference (Dahl, 1971). Both definitions encompass the sources of authority for government, the purposes served by government, and the procedures for constituting it. These are the critical issues for democracies. Samuel Huntington, like many before him, believes that what distinguishes democracy from other forms of government is the emphasis on procedure – contestation and participation. These must imply freedom of expression and assembly, for without such freedoms, genuine contestation and participation cannot occur (Huntington, 1991).

Lisa Anderson postulates that the adoption and consolidation of democratic regimes depend on 'the capacity of the state to extract adequate resources and implement public policy, and the ability of social groups to resist arbitrary and capricious government and to demand acknowledgment and enforcement of the rule of law' (Anderson, 1999).

Contrary to what most American and British citizens might assume, democracy has not been and is not now the 'normative' or modal form of government in the world. Democracy made its first appearance in the modern world only a little over 200 years ago when the American and then the French revolutions inaugurated it. If one looks at a map of the world today, it can be seen that democracy has been the dominant form of government in the second half of this century only in North America and Western Europe, Oceania, India, Israel and a very few countries in Asia, Africa and Latin America. According to Huntington, in 1990 about two-thirds of the countries of the world did not have democratic regimes. Beginning in the mid-1970s, as Huntington sees it, a 'third wave' of democratisation has swept over southern and Eastern Europe as well as Latin America. (The first two 'waves' were in 1828–1926 in Europe and the United States and in 1943–62 in Europe, East Asia and parts of Latin America.) But across both time and space democracy has been the exceptional form of government rather than the rule.

Democracy, like other forms of government, should not be seen as an absolute, but as a spectrum. Political systems are not easily classified as either democratic or non-democratic. There are more and less democratic political systems and organisations, and the same system may vary over time in the extent to which it is democratic. This is crucial for our discussion of Russia. Especially after only a decade of postcommunist political life, preceded by seven decades of communism and centuries of tsarist autocracy, the proper question is not so much whether Russia *is* democratic or not, but whether it is *becoming* more or less democratic.

Transition, Democratisation and Consolidation

Analysts have described three stages of post-1991 politics in Russia and other formerly communist states: transition, democratisation and consolidation. There is no consensus on the importance or utility of any of the three terms. Some argue that while a transition from communism has been made, it is not clear to what the transition has been. Others point to the return to power in Hungary, Poland and Lithuania of former communists, the vigorous competition given to Boris Yeltsin by a coalition of Communists in the 1996 Russian presidential election and their continuing dominance of the Duma as evidence that the transition from communism is by no means assured. While some claim that the transitions from communism are paralleled by transitions from authoritarian governments in southern Europe (Greece, Portugal, Spain) and Latin America (Argentina, Brazil) and that there are critical features common to these transitions, others argue that the transitions are different in important ways. For example, in southern Europe the only issue was democratisation, whereas in eastern Europe and the former Soviet Union it is the creation of a new economy, class system, sets of international relations and even states themselves (Bunce, 1995; Schmitter and Karl, 1994).

There are similar disagreements over the most effective way of 'democratising' a political system. Should economic and political reform be introduced simultaneously, and, if not, which should come first? What is the most effective and long-lasting way of democratising – by agreement among elites, by pressures 'from below' (among ordinary people), or by some combination of these? What should be the role of external actors – states, international organisations, private groups – in spurring the growth of democracy in a country? Can democratisation be accomplished in a relatively short period, or can does it require slow, organic growth over many years if it is to be firmly implanted? (Linz and Stepan, 1996).

Analysts realise that democratisation may be temporary and superficial. Therefore, they have considered how and when a democracy can be 'consolidated'. Some reject the very notion that there is some point at which a democracy can be assumed to be permanent or 'consolidated'. After all, the argument goes, if democracy is a process and not a result, 'if the democratic project can never be completed, then how can we understand the term 'consolidation' with its implication of democracy as an end state?' (Bunce, 1995, p. 125). What are the measuring rods of consolidation – the absence of large-scale protest against the system or the presence of relatively durable coalitions and widespread support for the institutions and procedures of democracy?

Huntington asserts that consolidation is a meaningful concept. A democracy is consolidated when citizens learn that 'democracy rests on the premise that governments will fail and that hence institutionalised ways have to exist for changing them. ... Democracies become consolidated when people learn that democracy is a solution to the problem of tyranny, but not necessarily to anything else' (Huntington, 1991, p. 263). In other words, when people persist in supporting a democratic system even though the particular government is not meeting their expectations, democracy is consolidated. More concretely, Huntington proposes a 'two-turnover test' for measuring democratic consolidation. If the party or group that takes power in the initial election at the time of transition loses a subsequent election but turns over power peacefully, and if the new winners, in turn, hand over power to the winners of the next election, the democratic system can then be considered consolidated. Moreover, he notes, 'A striking feature of the first fifteen years of the third wave was the virtual absence of major antidemocratic movements in the new democracies' (ibid.) However, this has not been true in Russia where unreconstructed Communists, nationalist authoritarians (including even some monarchists) and other anti-democratic groupings have obtained significant proportions of the vote in parliamentary and presidential elections. Perhaps in no other European former Soviet republic, except Belarus, have authoritarian alternatives been as visible and popular as in Russia.

The Prospects for Democracy in Russia

As we see, there is broad consensus on what democracy is, though not on how a system becomes democratic. What are the prospects of Russia becoming democratic? This, too, is a matter of considerable debate. The debate centres on the importance of economics and of political culture, that is, a group or nation's subjective orientation toward and understanding of politics. Over 40 years ago, Seymour

Martin Lipset argued that democracies emerge only in societies that are relatively prosperous (Lipset, 1959, 1994). He continues to believe that 'economic well being comes close to being a necessary condition for democracy. The poorer a polity, the less amenable its leaders ... will be to giving up power, their only source of status and wealth' (Lipset, 1999). Potentially always one of the world's richest countries, Russia remains poor by European standards and her economic status should not be conducive to democracy. Nevertheless, as a Russian political scientist points out, India, a poor country, is a democracy, while Singapore, a rich one, is not (Melville, 1999). Lipset also believes that relatively high levels of education and low income disparities are other requisites for the emergence of democracy. In addition, he sees democracy requiring 'a supportive culture, the acceptance by the citizenry and political elites of the principles underlying freedom of speech, media and assembly; rights of political parties, rule of law, human rights, and the like. Such norms do not evolve overnight'.

Some believe that culture is quite stable and puts its stamp on the institutions of a state, creating an inertia difficult to reverse. They would argue that in light of Russia's autocratic past, there is a 'natural tendency' toward non-democratic forms of government. Others see political culture as more malleable. As William Zimmerman points out, there are two variants of this approach, one holding that 'the core attitudes that constitute a political culture are driven by societal and technological change and evolve as society changes'. The other stresses the role of institutions and incentive structures. 'If the institutions are right, political culture follows, rather than drives, successful institutionalization [*sic*]. ... Change the institutions, change the political culture' (Zimmerman, 1995). Institutional change was seen as the way to democratise Germany after World War One, but it proved insufficient to overcome that country's authoritarian heritage. Following the next world war, the allies attempted to change not only Germany's institutions but also its political culture, including family patterns, attitudes toward authority and towards peoples of different religions, races and cultures. This attempt to alter the political culture directly, rather than relying on institutions, seems to have been more effective.

The German experience may provide some lessons for those interested in changing Russian political culture in a more democratic direction. Constitutional lawyers, political scientists, educators and human rights activists, from within Russia and without, have been attempting to alter both Russia's institutions and, to a lesser extent, because it is much more difficult and a longer-term undertaking, Russia's political culture. But, unlike Germany and Japan in 1945, Russia has not had democratic rule imposed on it by occupying powers who invested a great deal in the political resocialisation of the population. Militating against rapid democratisation are Russia's history and traditions of authoritarian rule; disunity among democratic politicians who have not been able to unite in a single electoral list, let alone a political party, over the course of several parliamentary and presidential elections; prolonged economic crisis; and the training and experience of most of the leaders of the formerly Soviet states. As one observer points out, despite the collapse of the Soviet state and its economy, there has been 'remarkable elite stability' (Solnick, 1999). Unlike Poland, the Czech Republic and the Baltic states – but like the Central Asian States, Romania, Serbia, Croatia and other states that have not moved very far toward democracy – the postcommunist leadership in Russia has come largely from former elites and not from the democratic opposition. Moldova's president, at the start of the new century, was the former first secretary of its communist party and a member of the leadership of the CPSU; Alexander Lukashenka, the dictatorial president of Belarus, was a regional party official in that republic; the presidents of Kazakhstan, Turkmenistan, Uzbekistan, Georgia, and Azerbaijan were first secretaries of their republics' communist parties before the fall of the Soviet Union (Nazarbaev, Niyazov, Karimov, Shevardnadze, and Aliev, respectively). Boris Yeltsin himself had been a member of the Politburo of the CPSU, and party leader in Moscow.

Moreover, unlike Hungarian, Polish and even Czech communists, Russian communists did not have several years of experience in negotiating with an opposition and at least partly accommodating it. Thus, their authoritarian reflexes were largely undisturbed. One of the criticisms of Boris Yeltsin's rule was that under a democratic veneer it was quite authoritarian. But, some argued, presidential power and dominance of the other branches of government was needed in a period of transition to democracy because only a strong presidency could push Russia along the road away from its authoritarian past. Yet, when Yeltsin resigned in favour of Vladimir Putin, the latter took advantage of the ongoing conflict in Chechnya to rationalise the need for an extension and even expansion of presidential power. Since late 1999, little has been heard of limiting that power. Instead, as we have seen in earlier chapters of this book, Putin has gone after the few media that are critical of him and his government by arresting Vladimir Gusinsky, head of Media-Most, the largest independent media conglomerate, and by curbing the power of the regional governors. To be sure, many of the latter rule their regions like feudal fiefs, but Putin's drive to reduce the number of Russia's regions from 89 to seven 'federal districts', and to curb the powers of the governors, is designed to enhance central power, not to democratise the regions. Putin's high ratings in opinion polls, even in the wake of the Kursk submarine disaster in summer 2000, indicate that most people favour a strong or even dictatorial leadership. Moreover, disunity among democratic politicians has not only weakened their influence in the institutions of governance, but has diminished their appeal as people worthy of support and of office-holding.

The authoritarian traditions of Russia and most of the other Soviet successor states mean that people are not used to democratic behaviour and values, such as welcoming pluralism in thinking and behaving, tolerance of dissidence, support for the seemingly less efficient methods of democratic decisionmaking. They do not easily see the advantages of debate, discussion, and non-conformity, and not deferring to a class of 'superiors'. Recent surveys show that Russians have far less favourable attitudes toward democracy than people in scores of other countries. Studies in the early 1990s conducted by scholars with little familiarity with Soviet culture and traditions optimistically concluded that there was broad support for democracy among the population of the Russian Federation (see for instance Gibson and Duch, 1994). The World Values Survey, however, which compares over 60 countries, found in 1999–2000 that whereas over all the countries 89 per cent of respondents gave a positive account of democracy, in Russia only 56 per cent did so (Inglehart, 2000). Russians are very dissatisfied with their government's performance; they are less trusting and tolerant, less healthy and less happy, than people in many other countries. Inglehart finds that such attitudes are correlated with scepticism about democracy. 'Culture seems to shape democracy far more than democracy shapes culture. This is bad news for anyone seeking a quick and easy solution to the problems of democratization.' Since, he argues, 'cultural factors are ultimately more decisive than economic ones' in bringing democracy about, an improvement in the Russian economy would not by itself substantially increase the prospects for democracy (ibid.).

But there are forces that could impel the Russian Federation toward democracy. They include revulsion by many against the communist political and economic systems; Western pressure for democratisation and the desire by many to be accepted as part of

'Europe'; growing exposure to the cultures and political systems of the West; and the democratic strains in the Russian political tradition upon which even Russian nationalists can draw. Indeed, most surveys taken in Russia in the last decade show that democratic attitudes and support for a market economy are strongest among the young, those who have had the least experience of communism and the most of the West. Roughly speaking, younger cohorts are more inclined toward pluralism of opinions, are sceptical about the existence of a 'single truth', optimistic about the future of democracy in Russia and reluctant to return to communist practices in economics, culture and politics. The university-educated are also more likely to support democratic values than those with less education. They tend to be more favourable toward the market economy and more willing to gamble that political and economic change will be ultimately for the better, and less inclined to retain an oppressive but familiar political system and a stagnant but minimally providing economic system. On the other hand, middle aged men, farm workers, the unemployed and underemployed, those dependent for their livelihood on one of the enormous industrial 'dinosaurs' that can no longer be justified in economic terms are understandably desperate. It is among such people that the 'solutions' proffered by non-democratic politicians such as Vladimir Zhirinovsky, leader of the misnamed Liberal Democratic Party, or Gennadii Zyuganov, the Communist leader, find their greatest appeal. But some have concluded that since it is among the younger people that support for democracy is strongest, all other things being equal, time is working in favour of broader mass support for democracy in Russia.

Huntington lists several factors that influence whether or not a country will go in a democratic direction. These include prior democratic experience; a high level of economic development; a consensual and non-violent transition; and absence of severe social and economic problems. Russia has had only fleeting prior democratic experience. On economic development Russia would rank much higher than the Central Asian successor states, and ahead of Moldova, Belarus and Ukraine and the republics of the Caucasus, but behind the three Baltic republics. Indeed, those people who are worse off economically within Russia are generally the least favourable toward reform and democracy. The transition in Russia was largely consensual, though both in 1991 and 1993 some violence accompanied major changes. Unfortunately, the problems facing the country are very severe and inclined to lead some to seek quick, non-democratic 'solutions'. Among these problems, as we have seen in Chapter 12, are skyrocketing crime rates, including tens of thousands of murders, and hundreds of 'contract murders' that are rarely resolved. Other newly visible problems are capitalist-style poverty, homelessness, dramatic increases in the gap between the rich and poor, high rates of divorce and alcoholism – the latter contributing to a shocking decline in longevity, especially among men – unemployment, and corruption. To the extent that these are associated with 'democracy', as opposed to communism, these social and economic problems weaken popular support for political democracy.

Moreover, the prolonged, demoralising and terribly costly war in Chechnya is a multifaceted problem: the Chechens have already humiliated the armed forces and political leadership, divided Russia's politicians, thrust the vexed problem of the nature of the federation and centre-periphery relations into the forefront of Russians' consciousness, and, worst of all, cost thousands of lives. The humiliation of Russia has another dimension, the loss of empire and of control over a huge multi-republic state. Not only has Russia lost her status as the dominant region of a world superpower, she has also lost control of Eastern Europe and of the roughly 140 million non-Russians in the old Soviet Union. Russia finds herself the weakened defender of 25 million Russians now living outside Russia, some of whom have fled wars in Tajikistan and the Caucasus and discrimination in the Baltic and Central Asia for their ancestral homeland. That homeland is hard put to provide the refugees with even the bare necessities of refugee existence.

Democratisation in Russia in Comparative Perspective

Analysts agree that Russia is not a consolidated democracy, but there is no consensus on how to label its political system in a more positive way. Many point to the 'hybrid' nature of a regime that exhibits both democratic and non-democratic characteristics (Bunce, 2000). One scholar describes Russia not as a democracy but as a system with a 'durable division of power among a fairly stable group of elite actors' (Solnick, 1999), though this was written before Putin began his campaign against the oligarchs, regional governors and other 'elite actors'. Other writers have called the Russian system 'soft Bonapartism', a 'personalist, populist, plebiscitary regime, that rests on the administrative and coercive apparatuses of the state and that by seemingly elevating itself above society, acts as an arbitrator and preserver of the new bourgeoisie's interests as a whole' (Gill and

Markwick, 2000). Should Putin continue successfully to erode the power of the 'new bourgeoisie' and other elites, analysts may begin to perceive the system in different terms.

Obviously, it is very difficult to predict how the Russian system will evolve even in the near future. Can one extrapolate from the experiences of other democratising societies in order to make an educated guess about the direction in which Russia will go? Some have suggested that the way in which the transition from authoritarianism was made is critical to the prospects for democracy. Transitions may be led by existing elites or by the opposition. They may result from the overthrow of the regime or from its collapse from within. They may be consensual ('pacted') or they may be produced by conflict. Elite-led transitions are less likely to lead to democratisation since the elites were the leaders of an authoritarian system, and this is certainly the case in Russia and many of the other successor states, as noted earlier. The transition in Russia was not exclusively the result of an internal collapse, though that was the long-term cause, but violence was rather limited and the process of transition did not leave the deep scars it might have. This is, of course, propitious for democracy. The transition also had elements of both conflict and consensus. Therefore, the transition process itself does not point clearly toward or away from the consolidation of democracy in Russia.

According to Linz and Stepan, in order to become consolidated democracies need five interacting areas: a lively civil society, a relatively autonomous 'political society' (institutions and procedural rules), the rule of law, a functioning state bureaucracy, and an 'economic society' (norms, institutions and regulations that mediate between the state and the market) (Linz and Stepan, 1996, pp. xiv, 11). A democracy is 'consolidated' when no major group tries to overthrow the democratic system, a strong majority of the public believes that democratic procedures and institutions are the most appropriate way to govern collective life, and conflicts are resolved within the democratic process.

Once again, the evidence from Russia is mixed. Some observers see a civil society emerging, one in which autonomous groups mediate between the state and the citizenry, though the most powerful groups seem closely tied not just to the state but to a particular government and even a particular person, whether Yeltsin or Putin or a local ruler. One element of civil society is stable, visible political parties that serve to aggregate and articulate the political interests of the citizenry. It has often been remarked that the only genuine party in Russia today is the Communist Party, since all others seem to be *ad hoc* coalitions of electoral candidates, lacking permanent structures, clear programmes and stable constituencies (see Chapter 5). Indeed, political institutions themselves are still being moulded. The shape of the executive and legislature, relations between the 89 subjects of the federation and the centre, and other basic institutional arrangements, are not yet stabilised. The rule of law seems to be taking hold, though, as we noted in Chapter 6, it is much too early to conclude that it is firmly established. The state bureaucracy is problematic for several reasons: Soviet-era habits still prevail and corruption is widespread, though apparently less than in Ukraine and other new states. Relations between the state and the market seem to be volatile, especially as the market is not yet fully developed. Local and foreign businessmen complain of what they see as capricious economic regulation and exploitative taxation, favouritism, and irrational and unpredictable state economic policies.

Part of the problem of both political and economic institutionalisation may lie in the choice made between parliamentary and presidential forms of democracy. Linz and Stepan argue that the choice of parliamentary or semipresidential constitutions in Greece, Spain and Portugal gave those new democracies 'greater degrees of freedom' than if they had chosen American-style presidentialism as their constitutional framework. Parliamentarism is generally more favourable to democratic consolidation than presidentialism because it gives the political system greater efficacy, the capacity to construct majorities and the 'ability to terminate a crisis of government without it becoming a crisis of the regime' (ibid., p. 141). Hungary, the Czech Republic and Slovenia have adopted the parliamentary system and 'it is perhaps no accident' that they are closer to consolidation than any postcommunist country with a directly elected president who has significant powers. The three major Slavic republics of the former Soviet Union – Russia, Ukraine and Belarus – all have presidential forms, as do the Central Asian states.

In addition to the choice of presidentialism, there are other choices made which have militated against rapid democratisation. Several policies of the late Soviet period weakened the state but did not create new democratically legitimated central state structures. Gorbachev's programme of *perestroika* and *glasnost* was one of these. The previously hollow institutions of Soviet federalism provided the framework for the political mobilisation of ethnicity. That was more effective than ideological mobilisation in a state in which political alternatives had not been discussable for the better part of a century.

Appealing to one's 'primordial' ethnic identity was a far more effective short-term strategy than trying to win one over to a new, complicated political programme, even had clear programmes existed. Moreover, many of the nationalisms that emerged from under the facade of Soviet 'proletarian internationalism' were exclusivist, militant and intolerant, not very compatible with democratic thinking and acting. Local and regional elections shifted the focus from civic to ethnic issues, spurring the disintegration of the state. Most of the successor states have put independence ahead of democratisation and have therefore emphasised collective rights over individual rights, and have put economic restructuring ahead of political restructuring. According to Linz and Stepan, had political reform and consolidation preceded economic reform, the state would have been stronger and better able to implement the economic reforms.

This raises the question of whether the sequencing of political and economic reform influences the success of democratisation. Linz and Stepan argue that in Spain the primacy of political reform, followed by socioeconomic reform and only then economic reform, was probably the optimal sequence for the consolidation of democracy. However, most analysts of the postcommunist states argue for the simultaneity of economic and political reform as the optimal strategy. Linz and Stepan also suggest that political reform should precede economic reform because democracy legitimates the market, not the reverse. Democratic regulatory state power is needed to make the market work. 'Effective privatization [*sic*] ... is best done by relatively strong states that are able to implement a coherent policy. ... Effective privatization entails less state scope but greater state capacity. ... A state with rapidly eroding capacity simply cannot manage a process of effective privatization' (Linz and Stepan, 1996, p. 436). Furthermore, if there is a strong popular commitment to the new democratic forms of government, this can be a cushion against the blows of economic restructuring. The postcommunist Polish system seems to have enjoyed this advantage. Painful economic restructuring was tolerated by a public firmly committed, perhaps not so much to democracy as to not returning to communist dictatorship. By now, it is clear that the Polish economy has succeeded in making the transition to the market, and economic success serves as a legitimation of the political system with which it is associated. Support for specific achievements of a system can grow into 'diffuse support', that is, a generalised support of the system that gives it the slack to survive temporary setbacks.

Comparable survey data show that the postcommunist polities of

Hungary, Poland and the Czech Republic obtain much more support than do those of Russia, Belarus and Ukraine.

> Respondents in the six former Warsaw Pact countries of East Central Europe gave a mean positive rating of 62 to the post-Communist political system (a rise of 16 points over the positive rating they gave to the Communist political system). In sharp contrast, in the three former Soviet Union countries (Russia, Ukraine, and Belarus), a mean of only 29 gave the post-Communist political system a positive rating (a decrease of 26 points from those who gave the Communist system a positive rating) (ibid., p. 446).

In addition, there is a much lower willingness to defer material gratification in the former Soviet Union than in East Central Europe, possibly because of greater pessimism regarding the economy, state disintegration and armed conflicts, shame and humiliation over the loss of empire and the disintegration of the Soviet state.

Thus, it seems reasonable to conclude that democracy is better established in the northern tier of East Central Europe (Poland, Czech Republic, Hungary), in the three Baltic states and in Slovenia than it is in Russia, but in this respect Russia is ahead of Belarus, the Central Asian states, and perhaps other former Soviet republics. Even where reform Communists have returned to power, they have accepted the rules of the game both in the elections themselves and in the way they have been exercising power. They have been accepted by the parties they defeated and by the public and thereby strengthened confidence in the fairness of democratic procedures. On the other hand, in his election campaign in 1996 Gennadii Zyuganov was careful not to be specific about what he and his party would do should they come to power in Russia, and one could not assume they would adhere to the rules of the democratic game. More than the East European parties, a Russian Communist party or coalition is likely to revert to practices of earlier times – or even Stalinism.

There is no reason to assume either that democracy can never be firmly established in Russia or that it must inevitably be. It is reasonable to expect that postcommunist states will reach different degrees of democratisation or not democratise at all. We come back to the idea that democracy is a spectrum, and the states emerging from the Soviet Union, though they all seemed to start at the same point, are likely to range themselves across this spectrum. Scholars will continue to debate the determinants of democracy and why one country reaches one point on the spectrum and another a different point. Political culture, level of economic and cultural development, external influences, and social problems are all factors in the equation. But perhaps the most important is elite choices. Precisely in periods of transition, elites make fateful choices among alternative directions in which they can lead their countries. As Linz and Stepan note, 'Democratic institutions have to be not only created but crafted, nurtured and developed' (ibid., p. 457). Russia seems to have been halted, at least temporarily, at the creation stage. This is due in large part to the contradictory nature of Yeltsin's impulses, which alternated between those of a populist democrat and those of the provincial party boss he once was. A range of freedoms never enjoyed by Russia's citizens was not only introduced but has been maintained, but neither Yeltsin nor Putin has even tried to form an institutionalised constituency for democracy (a party, for example). Yeltsin's seemingly arbitrary hiring and firing of assistants, advisers and ministers was more reminiscent of a royal court than of a modern democracy.

If one were to draw up a balance sheet of democratisation in Russia to date, on the positive side one might list broad freedom of expression; the right to organise; a broad franchise (unlike in Estonia and Latvia); no ethnic discrimination emanating from the government; freedom of travel and of emigration; and the lifting of most restrictions on private economic activity. On the other side of the balance sheet would be presidential control of some of the media, especially television; the imbalance of power within the federal government which gives the president overwhelming power *vis-à-vis* the legislature; the '*nomenklatura* privatisation' that gave individuals privileged access to vast resources; and the close ties between many interest groups and the government. The preoccupation with Chechnya, the genuine strength of the communist constituency and the failure of reformers to unite and articulate a clear and appealing programme are other roadblocks on what might otherwise have been a smoother path to democracy.

Over 150 years ago, the first Russian novel, written by Nikolai Gogol whom Ukrainians claim as one of their own, concluded with this observation: 'And you Russia – aren't you racing headlong like the fastest troika imaginable. ... And where do you fly to, Russia? Answer me! ... She doesn't answer. The carriage bells break into an enchanted tinkling, the air is torn to shreds and turns into wind; everything on earth flashes past, and, casting worried, sidelong glances, other nations and countries step out of her way.' At the start of the twenty-first century it is still not clear where Russia is racing. While outsiders continue to cast 'worried, sidelong glances' they cannot permit themselves merely to 'step out of her way'.

Guide to Further Reading

The listing that follows suggests a number of items that students and others may find useful to consult on the themes that are covered by each chapter of this book. Current developments in Russian politics and related themes are regularly considered in academic journals such as *Europe-Asia Studies* (formerly *Soviet Studies*, eight issues annually); the *Journal of Communist Studies and Transition Politics* (quarterly); *Post-Soviet Affairs* (quarterly); *Communist and Post-Communist Studies* (quarterly); and *Problems of Post-Communism* (six issues annually). Legal and constitutional issues across the postcommunist countries generally are given particular attention in the *Review of Socialist Law* (quarterly) and the *East European Constitutional Review* (quarterly). The *Current Digest of the Post-Soviet Press* (weekly) is a digest of translations from newspapers and journals; the *BBC Summary of World Broadcasts* (from 2001 superseded by Global Newsline) and the *Foreign Broadcast Information Service* (daily) include radio and television broadcasts as well as periodical material. Pockney (1991) and Ryan (1993) provide useful collections of statistics on social and economic developments over the Soviet and early post-Soviet periods.

Internet resources may be most conveniently consulted through one of the gateways that provide a specialist service. See for instance the websites maintained at the University of Pittsburgh < http://www.ucis.pitt/edu/rees-web > and at the School of Slavonic and East European Studies in London < http://www.ssees.ac.uk/ruttia.htm > . The daily news service maintained by Radio Free Europe and Radio Liberty may be consulted at < http:// www.rferl.org/newsline > .

Chapter 1   From Communism to Democracy

The Soviet experience may helpfully be considered within the larger debate about the nature of communist rule and the reasons for its demise (at least in Europe). See for instance Malia (1994), Courtois (1999) and Furet (1999), and for more academic treatments Westoby (1989) and Lane (1996). There are several good accounts of the experience of communist rule in the USSR itself, including Hosking (1992), Keep (1996) and Service (1997). On its ruling group in particular see Lane and Ross (1999) and Mawdsley and White (2000). The Gorbachev period is well covered in Sakwa (1990), Miller (1993), White (1994) and Brown (1996); Gorbachev published his own memoirs (1996) and a best-selling account of *perestroika* (1987) as well as some later reflections (1999). Different interpretations of the decline of Soviet rule are presented in Strayer (1998) and Kramer (2000).

On the postcommunist period, see for instance Löwenhardt (1995), Sakwa (1996), Murrell (1997), Urban *et al.* (1997), Shevtsova (1999), Gill and Markwick (2000) and White (2000). The prospects under Putin are assessed in Breslauer and Bonnell (2000). For an illuminating essay on 'postcommunism' as a phenomenon, see Sakwa (1999).

Chapter 2   The Presidency: From Yeltsin to Putin

Given the dynamic nature of Russian political institution building, elite transformation, and policy making, many of the best information sources for the Russian presidency and government are to be found on the internet and in scholarly journals. There is a growing number of good English-language web sites from both Russian governmental and academic institutions, with leading politicians such as Anatolii Chubais and Boris Nemtsov also maintaining their own sites. For information on the development of the post-Soviet presidency and executive branch, see Colton (1995a), Easter (1997), Nichols (1999) and especially Huskey (1999). Broader issues of postcommunist institutional design are addressed in Frye (1997), Taras (1997), and Elster *et al.* (1998). Good discussions of presidentialism in a broader cross-national comparative light are provided in Linz and Valenzuela (1994) and Carey and Shugart (1998). For information on the life and career of Boris Yeltsin, see his three autobiographical volumes (1990, 1994 and 2000) and a definitive biography by Aron (2000). Putin's autobiography (2000) provides information on his background and thinking as he came into the presidency. Useful discussions of postcommunist elite politics are found in Lane and Ross (1999) and Rivera (2000). For a discussion of the informal politics of the oligarchs see Freeland (2000) and Schroder (1999).

Chapter 3   Parliamentary Politics in Russia

The Russian Constitution of December 1993 is available in several convenient editions, including Belyakov and Raymond (1994), which includes commentaries, in Smith (1996), and in Finer *et al.* (1995), which contains the texts of other constitutions. The text may also be consulted on the internet < http://www.fipc.ru/fipc/constit > . On representative institutions since the late Soviet period see Remington (2001), and on the contemporary Duma Remington (2000) and Smith and Remington (2001). Ostrow (2000) offers a comparative perspective.

Chapter 4   Elections and Votes

For a comprehensive account and analysis of Russian elections up to 1996, see White, Rose and McAllister (1997). The most sophisticated analysis of the Russian electorate up to the present is Colton (2000). On the most recent elections see White (2000), Colton and McFaul (2000), and Sakwa (2000). A comprehensive inventory of results is available in Munro and Rose (2001).

Movements in public opinion may be followed through the *New Russia Barometer* (sponsored by the Centre for the Study of Public Policy, University of Strathclyde, since 1992; see < http://www.cspp.strath.ac.uk >), as well as through the bulletin of the All-Russian Centre for the Study of Public Opinion, *Monitoring obshchestvennogo mneniya* (six issues annually since 1993, with an English translation of the questions asked; an electronic archive may be accessed at < http://www.rissoavptes.org >). Some of the issues of analysis that relate to survey research in postcommunist Russia, and to the results that have been obtained, are considered in Wyman (1997) and Alexander (1997, 2000). Attitudes towards the electoral system itself are examined in Pammett (1999). A wider study, relating developments in postcommunist Russia to those in Hungary, the Czech Republic, Slovakia and Ukraine, is available in Miller, White and Heywood (1997).

Chapter 5   Parties and Organised Interests

Good studies of the former Communist Party of the Soviet Union include Schapiro (1970) and Hill and Frank (1986), with the concept of democratic centralism examined by Waller (1981) and the end of the party-state discussed by Gill (1994) and White (1991). The travails of the emergent party and representative system are discussed by Dallin (1993), Fish (1995), Hosking *et al.* (1992), Sedaitis and Butterfield (1991), Tolz (1990), Urban *et al.* (1997) and Urban and Gel'man (1997). One of the most comprehensive discussions of the features of the contemporary Russian party system is provided by Lowenhardt (1998), and a good brief overview is in Golosov (1998). Lentini (1995) provides useful material for the earlier period. Regional party development is examined by Brown (1998), Gel'man and Golosov (1998) and Golosov (1995, 1997, 1999). The development of the CPRF is analysed by Flikke (1999), Sakwa (1998) and Urban and Solovei (1997); its leader's views may be consulted in Zyuganov (1997). To place the development of the Russian representative system in comparative context see Lewis (1996) and Kitschelt *et al.* (1999). Attitudes towards political parties themselves are considered in Pammett (2000).

Chapter 6   Russia and the Rule of Law

For background on the pre-revolutionary and Soviet legal systems, see Berman (1966), Smith (1996) and Solomon (1997). Constitutional developments are analysed in Sharlet (1993, 1996 and 1999) and Ahdieh (1997); for the constitution itself see the citations in the further reading to Chapter 3. The Procuracy and the courts in post-Soviet Russia are analysed in Smith (1997) and Huskey (1997). Useful discussions of the process of drafting new legislation and the influence of Western advisers appear in Maggs (1999) and Sharlet (1997 and 1998). Jury trials are discussed in Thaman (1995). The published proceedings of a symposium at Syracuse University (2000) provides information on plea bargaining, immunity, wiretapping, search and seizure procedures, as well as the current functioning of jury trials. For discussions of organised crime and the problems of law enforcement see Smith (1999) and Shelley (2000). Annual reports on human rights in Russia are available from the Glasnost Defense Fund, Human Rights Watch, and Amnesty International websites.

Chapter 7   From Federalisation to Recentralisation

For a full discussion of the national and federal dimensions of postcommunist Russian politics, see Bremmer and Taras (1997), Smith (1999), Stavrakis *et al.* (1997) and Ross (2001). Intergovernmental transfers are considered in Wallich (1994) and Lavrov and Makushkin (2000).

Chapter 8   Politics in the Regions

Background on Soviet and the early post-Soviet regional developments is contained in Hough (1969) and Friedgut and Hahn (1994). Recent case studies of politics in specific regions include Novgorod (Petro, 1999), Omsk (Le Huerou, 1999), Primor'e krai (Chernyakova, 2000), Pskov (Slider, 1999), and Sverdlovsk (Startsev, 1999). Elite behaviour in Bryansk and Smolensk is examined in Lallemand (1999). Specific aspects of regional politics and economics are treated in Johnson (2000) – the banking system, Glasnost Defense Foundation (1999) – mass media, Whitmore (1998) and Lussier (2000) – elections, Woodruff (1999) – barter and regional finances, and Tavernise (2000) – bankruptcy and ownership issues. Region-by-region reports of human rights violations can be found at < http://fsumonitor.-com > ; press freedom rankings are at < http://www.freepress.ru > ; investment climate rankings are at < http://www.ekspert.ru/ratings/regions > . A more optimistic view of regional devolution and reform is expressed in Kupchan (2000).

Chapter 9   Economic policy under Yeltsin and Putin

Book-length treatments of a subject as rapidly changing as post-Soviet Russian political economy are always in danger of being out of date before they appear. However, Gros and Steinherr (1995), despite its age, remains an outstanding introduction to the problems of economic transition. More recent accounts of Russian economic policy in the 1990s (and the politics thereof) are to be found in Shleifer and Treisman (2000), which handles both economic problems and political constraints extremely well, Gustafson (1999) and Hough (2001), while Woodruff (1999) provides a fascinating account of the most important – and anomalous – of the post-Soviet transition pathologies to afflict the Russian economy, the problem of de-monetisation. On the manysided relationship between politics and business see Rutland (2000). Several websites may be consulted, including those of the Central Bank of the Russian Federation (< http://www.cbu.ru > , in English and Russian); the Finance Ministry's Economic Expert Group (< http://www.iet.ru > , also in

English and Russian); and *Russian Economic Trends*, including their monthly updates (< http://www.hhs.se/sie/ret/ret.htm >), in addition to the sites maintained by Goskomstat and outside agencies, especially the IMF and World Bank.

Chapter 10   Health and Health Care Policy

The single best English-language overview of Russian health care policy for the student of Russian politics at present is the collection edited by Field and Twigg (2000). This is less strong on the hotly-debated topic of the health situation itself, as opposed to health-care reform. Other easily available items balance this. For the medical-care finance debate, the key items are on the web in English, including Shishkin (1998) and (1999), and the earlier article by Rozenfeld, which is in the seminal Rand conference papers (1996) available without charge at < http://www.rand.org/publications/CF/CF124/index.html > . The short form of the 'Gref Programme' is available in English at < http://www.csr.ru/english/action.html > , the website of his Centre for Strategic Research. On other social policy, Eatwell, Ellman, Karlsson, Nuti and Shapiro (2000) offers a view of what has happened in the key social policy areas and alternative scenarios, plus a chapter on health alone. Cook, Orenstein and Rueschemeyer (1999) focus on social policy as a political process. To look directly at the health crisis issues, you might start with websites: for TB see < http://www.russia.phri.org > and for AIDS, < http://www.unaids.org > . There are links to follow from there. For somewhat more complex but accessible coverage, the basics are laid out by Russian demographers in Rand (1996); Davis (2000) is an important view of the medical care process from an economist's perspective, in Cornia and Pannicia (2000).

Chapter 11   Foreign Policy

General accounts of Russian foreign policy may be found in Petro and Rubinstein (1996), Donaldson and Nogee (1998) and Bowker and Ross (2000). For more detailed analyses see Kanet and Kozhemiakin (1997), Mandelbaum (1998), and Hopf (1999). Security aspects, especially relations with NATO, are covered in Baranovsky (1997) and Black (2000). On the 'near abroad' dimension see Olcott *et al.* (1999); and on relations with Asia, see Chufrin (1999). The interplay between domestic and international factors is examined in Malcolm *et al.* (1996) and Wallander (1996). For the military see Barylski (1998). Purisanian (2000) places Russian foreign policy within the context of international relations theory.

Chapter 12   Crime and Corruption

Useful reading for understanding more about the problem of Russian organized crime include the following: Center for Strategic and International Studies Task Force Report (2000); Klebnikov (2000); Handelman (1995); and

Williams (1997). To understand more about corruption the following are recommended: World Bank (2000); Freeland (2000); Ledeneva (1998); and Wedel (1998). To gain more recent information it is useful to check the websites of Transparency International, the World Bank and the Center for Transnational Crime and Corruption.

Chapter 13　Politics and the Media

There are several full accounts of glasnost and media politics in the late Soviet period, including Benn (1989 and 1992), Laqueur (1989), Mickiewicz (1988), Remington (1988), Nove (1989) and an early classic, Inkeles (1950). The postcommunist period is covered authoritatively, for television, in Mickiewicz (1999), and for Russia and the other CIS countries, in McCormack (1999). On the role of the media in elections and campaigns, see particularly the reports that were produced by the European Institute for the Media immediately after the 1995 Duma, 1996 presidential, and 1999 Duma and 2000 presidential elections (Lange, 1996a, 1996b, EIM 2000a, 2000b), and also Helvey (1999) and Kaid (1999). Several websites are useful, including < http://www.eim.org > (European Institute for the Media) and < http://www.ctr.columbia.edu/vii/monroe > (The Post-Soviet Media Law and Policy Newsletter).

Chapter 14　Values and the Construction of a National Identity

There is a large literature on theories of nationalism and nation-building. See, in particular, Gellner (1983) and Balakrishnan (1996). Russian nation-building in the pre-revolutionary period is analysed by McDaniel (1996) and Hosking (1997). Illuminating discussion of Soviet nationalities policies can be found in Suny (1993) and Martin (2000). Debates about Russian identity in the period of *perestroika* are analysed by Szporluk (1989). There are several other works that discuss the construction of the postcommunist Russian national identity and the impact of the elite debate about identity on internal and foreign policies. See, or instance, Szporluk (1994), Bonnell (1996), Tishkov (1997), Tolz (1978a and b), Urban (1998), and Prizel (1999).

Chapter 15　Russian Democratisation in Comparative Perspective

Among the better known works on the nature of democracy are Dahl (1971), Lipset (1959, 1994) and Diamond, Linz and Lipset (1988). On democratisation generally, see Rustow (1970), O'Donnell, Schmitter and Whitehead (1986), Przeworski (1991) and Huntington (1991). An attempt to synthesise the experiences of Latin America, the former Soviet Union and southern and eastern Europe is Linz and Stepan (1996). On transitions from authoritarianism, see Schmitter and Karl (1994), Bunce (1995), Terry (1993) and Zimmerman (1995).

Bibliography

Afanas'ev, Mikhail (1997) *Klientelizm i rossiiskaya gosudarstvennost'*. Moscow: Moskovskii obshchestvennyi nauchnyi fond.

Ahdieh, Robert B. (1997) *Russia's Constitutional Revolution: legal consciousness and the transition to democracy, 1985–1996*. University Park: Pennsylvania State University Press.

Ahrend, Rudiger and Andrienko Yury (2000) 'Crime in Russia: understanding its development during transition: a regional approach', *Transition*, August–October.

Alexander, James A. (1997) 'Surveying Attitudes in Russia: a representation of formlessness', *Communist and Post-Communist Studies*, vol. 30, no. 2 (June), pp. 107–27.

Alexander, James A. (2000) *Political Culture in Post-Communist Russia*. London: Macmillan.

Amnesty International Annual Reports, available from < http://www.amnesty-usa.org >.

Anderson, Lisa (ed.) *Transitions to Democracy*. New York: Columbia University Press.

Antonenko, Oksana (1999–2000) 'Russia, NATO and European Security after Kosovo', *Survival*, vol. 41, no. 4, pp. 124–44.

Aron, Leon (2000) *Yeltsin: a revolutionary life*. London: HarperCollins.

Avdeev, Alexandre *et al.* (1998) 'The Reactions of a Heterogeneous Population to Perturbation: an interpretative model of mortality trends in Russia', *Population: an English selection*, vol. 10, no. 2, pp. 267–302

Bahry, Donna (1987) *Outside Moscow: power, politics, and budgetary policy in the soviet republics*. New York: Columbia University Press.

Balakrishnan, Gopal (1996) *Mapping the Nation*. London: Verso.

Baranovsky, Vladimir (ed.) (1997) *Russian and Europe: the emerging security agenda*. Oxford: Oxford University Press/SIPRI.

Baranovsky, Vladimir (2000) 'Russia: a Part of Europe or Apart from Europe?', *International Affairs*, vol. 76, no. 3 (July), pp. 443–58.

Barylski, Robert V. (1998) *The Solder in Russian Policies: duty, dictatorship and democracy under Gorbachev and Yeltsin*. New Brunswick and London: Transaction.

Becker, Abraham S. (2000) 'Russia and Caspian Oil: Moscow loses control', *Post-Soviet Affairs@*, vol. 16, no. 2 (April–June), p.. 91–132.

Bell, Daniel (1960) *The End of Ideology: on the exhaustion of political ideas in the fifties*. Glencoe: Free Press.

Belyakov, Vladimir V. and Raymond, Walter J. (eds) (1994) *Constitution of the Russian Federation*. Laurenceville VA: Brunswick.

Berman, Harold (1966) *Justice in the USSR*. Cambridge MA: Harvard University Press.

Bialer, Seweryn (1980) *Stalin's Successors: leadership, stability, and change in the Soviet Union*. Cambridge and New York: Cambridge University Press.

Biryukov, Nikolai and Sergeev, Viktor (1993) *Russia's Road to Democracy: parliament, communism and traditional culture.* Aldershot: Edward Elgar.

Black, J. L. (2000) *Russia Faces NATO Expansion: bearing gifts or bearing arms?* Lanham MD: Rowman and Littlefield.

Boikov, V. *et al.* (1998) 'Raskhody naseleniya na meditsinskuyu pomoshch' i lekarstvennye sredstva', *Voprosy ekonomiki,* no. 10 (October), pp. 101–17.

Bonnell, Victoria E. (ed.) (1996) *Identities in Transition: Eastern Europe and Russia after the collapse of communism.* Berkeley: University of California International and Area Studies

Bonnell, Victoria E. and Breslauer, George W. (eds) (2000) *Russia in the New Century: stability or disorder?* Boulder CO: Westview.

Borisova, Yevgenia (2000) 'And the Winner Is?', *Moscow Times,* 9 September.

Borodai, Yu (1992) 'Totalitarizm: khronika i likhoradochnyi krizis', *Nash sovremennik,* no. 7, pp. 121–30.

Bowker, Michael and Ross, Cameron (eds) (2000) *Russia After the Cold War.* London: Longman.

Bremmer, Ian and Taras, Ray (eds) (1996) *New States, New Politics: building the post-Soviet nations,* 2nd edn Cambridge and New York: Cambridge University Press.

Brown, Archie (1996) *The Gorbachev Factor.* Oxford: Oxford University Press.

Brown, Archie (ed.) (2001) *Contemporary Russian Politics: a reader.* Oxford: Oxford University Press.

Brown, Ruth (1998) 'Party Development in the Regions: when parties start to play a role in politics', *Journal of Communist Studies and Transition Politics,* vol. 14, nos 1 and 2 (March–June), pp. 9–30.

Brubaker, Rogers (1996) *Nationalism Reframed: nationhood and the national question in the new Europe.* Cambridge and New York: Cambridge University Press.

Bunce, Valerie (1995) 'Should Transitologists be Grounded?', *Slavic Review,* vol. 54, no. 1 (Spring), pp. 111–27.

Bunce, Valerie (1999) *Subversive Institutions: the design and destruction of socialism and the state.* Cambridge and New York: Cambridge University Press.

Bunce, Valerie (2000) 'Comparative Democratization: big and bounded generalizations', *Comparative Political Studies,* vol. 33, nos 6 and 7, (August–September), pp. 703–34.

Butler, William E. (1988) *Soviet Law,* 2nd edn London: Butterworth.

Carey, John M., and Shugart, Matthew S. (1998) *Executive Decree Authority: calling out the tanks, or filling out the forms.* Cambridge and New York: Cambridge University Press.

Center for Strategic and International Studies Task Force Report (2000) *Russian Organized Crime and Corruption: Putin's challenge.* Washington DC: Center for Strategic and International Studies.

Chazov, Yevgenii I. (1988) in *XIX Vsesoyuznaya konferentsiya Kommunisticheskoi partii Sovetskogo Soyuza, 28 iyunya – 1 iyulya 1988 g. Stenograficheskii otchet,* 2 vols. Moscow: Politizdat.

Chernyakova, Nonna (2000) 'The Wild World of Russia's Far East', *Transitions Online,* 15 May. Available from < http://www.tol.cz >.

Chinarikhina, Galina (1996) 'Dogovor kak sposob razgranicheniya polno-mochii i predmetov vedeniya mezhdu sub'ektami federativnykh otnoshenii v Rossii', *Vlast'*, no. 9, pp. 20–5.

Chufrin, Gennady (ed.) (1999) *Russia and Asia: the emerging security agenda*. Oxford: Oxford University Press/SIPRI.

Clem, Ralph S. and Craumer, Peter R. (1995a) 'The Politics of Russia's Regions: a geographical analysis of the Russian election and constitutional plebiscite of December 1993', *Post-Soviet Geography*, vol. 36, no. 2 (February), pp. 67–86.

Clem, Ralph S. and Craumer, Peter R. (1995b) 'The Geography of the Russian 1995 Parliamentary Election: continuity, change and correlates', *Post-Soviet Geography*, vol. 36, no. 10 (December), pp. 587–616.

Colton, Timothy J. (1995a) 'Superpresidentialism and Russia's Backward State', *Post-Soviet Affairs*, vol. 11, no. 2 (April–June), pp. 144–8.

Colton, Timothy J. (1995b) 'Boris Yeltsin, Russia's All-Thumbs Democrat', in Timothy Colton and Robert Tucker (eds), *Patterns in Post-Soviet Leadership*. Boulder CO: Westview.

Colton, Timothy J. (2000) *Transitional Citizens: voters and what influences them in the new Russia*. Cambridge MA: Harvard University Press

Colton, Timothy J. and Michael McFaul (2000) 'Reinventing Russia's Party of Power: "Unity" and the 1999 Duma Election', *Post-Soviet Affairs*, vol. 16, no. 3 (July–September), pp. 201–24.

Cook, Linda (1997) *Labor and Liberalization: trade unions in the new Russia*. New York: Twentieth Century Press.

Cook, Linda, Orenstein, Mitchell and Rueschemeyer, Marilyn (eds) (1999) *Left Parties and Social Policy in Postcommunist Europe*. Boulder CO: Westview.

Cornia, Giovanni Andrea and Panniccia, Renato (2000) *The Mortality Crisis in Transitional Economies*. Oxford: Oxford University Press.

Courtois, Stephane *et al.* (1999) *The Black Book of Communism: crimes, terror, repression*. Cambridge MA and London: Harvard University Press.

Dahl, Robert (1971) *Polyarchy: participation and opposition*. London and New Haven CT: Yale University Press.

Dallin, Alexander (ed.) (1993) *Political Parties in Russia*. Berkeley: University of California.

Davis, Christopher (2000) in Cornia and Panniccia (2000).

Derrida, Jacques (1994) *Spectres of Marx*. London: Routledge.

Diamond, Larry, Linz, Juan and Lipset, Seymour Martin (eds) (1988) *Politics in Developing Countries: comparing experiences with democracy*. Boulder, CO: Lynne Rienner.

Donaldson, Robert H. and Nogee, Joseph L. (1998) *The Foreign Policy of Russia: changing systems, enduring interests*. Armonk NY: Sharpe.

Dunlop, John B. (1998) *Russia Confronts Chechnya: roots of a separatist conflict*. Cambridge and New York: Cambridge University Press.

Duverger, Maurice (1954) *Political Parties: their organization and activity in the modern state*. London: Methuen.

Easter, Gerald M. (1997) 'Preference for Presidentialism: postcommunist regime change in Russia and the NIS', *World Politics*, vol. 49, no. 2 (January), pp. 184–211.

Eatwell, John, Ellman, Michael Karlsson, Mats and Shapiro, Judith (2000) *Hard Budgets, Soft States: economics of social policy choices in central and eastern Europe.* London: IPPR.

Elazar, Daniel J. (1997) 'Contrasting Unitary and Federal Systems', *International Political Science Review*, vol. 18, no. 3, pp. 237–52.

Elster, Jon, Offe, Claus and Preuss, Ulrich K. (1998) *Institutional Design in Post-Communist Societies: rebuilding the ship of state.* Cambridge and New York: Cambridge University Press.

European Institute for the Media (2000a) *Monitoring the Media Coverage of the December 1999 Parliamentary Elections in Russia: final report.* Dusseldorf: European Institute for the Media.

European Institute for the Media (2000b) *Monitoring the Media Coverage of the March 2000 Presidential Elections in Russia: final report.* Dusseldorf : European Institute for the Media.

Federal'noe Sobranie – parlament Rossiiskoi Federatsii (2000) Gosudarstvennaya Duma. Analiticheskoe upravlenie, Analiticheskii vestnik, No. 3: *Statisticheskie kharakeristiki zakonodatel'noi deiatel'nosti Gosudarstvennoi Dumy vtorogo sozyva (1996–1999).* Moscow.

Federativnyi Dogovor: dokumenty, kommentarii (1992) Moscow: Respublika.

Field, Mark (1994) 'Postcommunist medicine: morbidity, mortality, and the deteriorating health situation', in Millar and Wolchik (1994), pp. 178–95.

Field, Mark, and Twigg, Judyth (eds) (2000) *Russia's Torn Safety Nets: health and social welfare during the transition.* New York: St. Martin's.

Finer, S. E., Bogdanor, Vernon and Rudden, Bernard (eds) (1995) *Comparing Constitutions.* Oxford: Clarendon Press.

Firsov, B. M. and Muzdybaev, K. (1975) 'K stroeniyu sistemy pokazatelei ispol'zovaniya srestv massovoi kommunikatsii', *Sotsiologicheskie issledovaniya*, no. 1, pp. 113–20.

Fish, Steven (1991) 'The Emergence of Independent Associations and the Transformation of Russian Political Society', *The Journal of Communist Studies*, vol. 7, no. 3 (September), pp. 299–334.

Fish, M. Stephen (1995a) *Democracy from Scratch: opposition and regime in the new Russian revolution.* Princeton NJ: Princeton University Press.

Fish, M. Stephen (1995b) 'The Advent of Multipartism in Russia, 1993–95', *Post-Soviet Affairs*, vol. 11, no. 4 (October–December), pp. 340–83.

Flikke, Geir (1999) 'Patriotic Left-Centrism: the zigzags of the Communist Party of the Russian Federation', *Europe-Asia Studies*, vol. 51, no. 2 (March), pp. 275–98.

Fond 'Tsentr Strategicheskikh Razrabotok' (2000) 'Osnovnye napravleniya sotsial'no-ekonomicheskoi politiki Pravitel'stva Rossiiskoi Federatsii na dolgosrochnuyu perspektivu: strategiya razvitiya Rossiiskoi Federatsii do 2010 goda'. Moscow. Available from < http://www.csr.ru/about-publications/plan2010.html >.

Freedman, Robert O. (2000) 'Russian–Iranian Relations under Yeltsin', *The Soviet and Post-Soviet Review*, vol. 25, no. 3, pp. 265–84.

Freeland, Chrystia (2000) *Sale of the Century: Russia's wild ride from communism to capitalism.* London: Little, Brown and New York: Times Books.

Friedgut, Theodore and Hahn, Jeffrey (eds) (1994) *Local Power and Post-Soviet Politics.* Armonk NY: Sharpe.

Friedman, Robert I. (2000) *Red Mafiya: how the Russian mob has invaded America*. Boston: Little, Brown.

Frye, Timothy (1997) 'A Politics of Institutional Choice: Post-Communist Presidencies', *Comparative Political Studies*, vol. 30, no. 5 (October), pp. 523–52.

Fukuyama, Francis (1989) 'The End of History', *The National Interest*, vol. 16 (Summer), pp. 3–16.

Fukuyama, Francis (1992) *The End of History and the Last Man*. New York: Free Press.

Furet, Francois (1999) *The Passing of an Illusion: the idea of communism in the twentieth century*. Chicago: University of Chicago Press.

Gaddy, Clifford and Ickes, Barry W. (1998) 'Russia's Virtual Economy', *Foreign Affairs*, vol. 77, no. 5 (September–October), pp. 53–67.

Gaidar, Yegor (1995) 'Russian Reform', in Yegor Gaidar and Karl-Otto Pöhl (eds) *Russian Reform/International Money*. Cambridge MA: MIT Press.

Gellner, Ernest (1983) *Nation and Nationalism*. Oxford: Basil Blackwell

Gel'man, V. Ya (2000) 'Institutsional'nyi dizain: sozdavaya "pravila igry" ', in Gel'man, G. Golosov and E. Meleshkina (eds), *Pervyi elektoral'nyi tsikl v Rossii, 1993–1996 gg*. Moscow: Ves' mir.

Gel'man, Vladimir and Golosov, Grigorii (1998) 'Regional Party System Formation in Russia: the deviant case of Sverdlovsk Oblast', *Journal of Communist Studies and Transition Politics*, vol. 14, no. 1–2 (March–June), pp. 31–53.

Getty, J. Arch and Roberta T. Manning, (eds) (1993) *Stalinist Terror: new perspectives*. Cambridge and New York: Cambridge University Press.

Gibson, James and Duch, Raymond (1994) 'Postmaterialism and the Emerging Soviet Democracy', *Political Research Quarterly*, vol. 47, no. 1 (March), pp. 5–39.

Gill, Graeme (1994) *The Collapse of the Single-Party System: the disintegration of the Communist Party of the Soviet Union*. Cambridge and New York: Cambridge University Press.

Gill, Graeme and Markwick, Roger (2000) *Russia's Stillborn Democracy? From Gorbachev to Yeltsin*. Oxford and New York: Oxford University Press.

Glasnost Defense Foundation (1999) *The Silent Regions*. Moscow: Sashcko.

Glasnost Defense Fund, available from < http://www.gdf.ru > .

Goble, Paul (2000) 'Idel-Ural and the Future of Russia', *RFE/RL NewsLine*, 17 May.

Golosov, Grigorii V. (1995) 'New Russian Political Parties and the Transition to Democracy: the case of western Siberia', *Government and Opposition*, vol. 30, no. 1 (Winter), pp. 110–19.

Golosov, Grigorii V. (1997) 'Russian Political Parties and the "Bosses": evidence from the 1994 provincial elections in western Siberia', *Party Politics*, vol. 3, no. 1 (January), pp. 5–21.

Golosov, Grigorii V. (1998) 'Who Survives? Party origins, organizational development and electoral performance in post-communist Russia', *Political Studies*, vol. 46 (Special Issue), pp. 511–43.

Golosov, Grigorii V. (1999) 'From Adygeya to Yaroslavl: Factors of Party Development in the Regions of Russia, 1995–1998', *Europe-Asia Studies*, vol. 51, no. 8 (December), pp. 1333–66.

Golosov, Grigorii V. (2000) 'Proiskhozhdenie sovremennykh rossiiskikh politicheskikh partii, 1987–1993', in V. Gel'man, G. V. Golosov and E. Meleshkina (eds), *Pervyi elektoral'nyi tsikl v Rossii, 1993–1996 gg.*, Moscow, Ves'mir.

Golovin, V. G. (1994) 'Ekonomicheskie vzglyady politicheskikh partii i blokov Rossii', in *Partii i partiinye sistemy sovremennoi Evropy*, Moscow: INION.

Gorbachev, Mikhail S. (1987) *Perestroika: new thinking for our country and the world*. London: Collins and New York: Harper and Row.

Gorbachev, Mikhail S. (1996) *Memoirs*. New York and London: Doubleday.

Gorbachev, Mikhail S. (1999) *On My Country and the World*. New York: Columbia University Press.

Gorbacheva, Raisa (1991) *Na nadeyus'*. Moscow: Novosti.

'Gorchakov: an Epoch in Russian Diplomacy' (1999) in *International Affairs* (Moscow), vol. 45, no. 1, pp. 154–66.

Gordon, L. and Klopov, E. (eds) (1993) *Novye sotsial'nye dvizheniya v Rossii.* Moscow: Progress–Kompleks.

Goskomstat (1998) *Naselenie Rossii za 100 let (1897–1997).* Moscow: Goskomstat.

Goskomstat (1999) *Russia in Figures.* Moscow: Goskomstat.

Goskomstat (2000) *Demograficheskii Ezhegodnik 2000.* Moscow: Goskomstat.

Gosudarstvennaya Duma (1999) *Stenogramma zasedanii: Byulleten'*, no. 306 (448), (24 dekabrya), pp. 1–4.

Gould-Davies, Nigel and Woods, Ngaire (1999) 'Russia and the IMF', *International Affairs*, vol. 75, no. 1 (January), pp. 1–22.

Government of the Russian Federation (2000) 'Action Plan of the Government of the Russian Federation in the Area of Social Policy and Economic Modernization for the Years 2000–2001 (directive 1072-r)'. An English version is available Moscow: < http://www.csr.ru/english/action.html >. Alternatively, a Russian version can be found at < http://www.gov.ru/ main/ministry/isp-vlast47.html >

Gowan, David (2000) *How the EU Can Help Russia*. London: Centre for European Reform.

Granville, Brigitte (1999) *The Problem of Monetary Stabilisation'*. London, Mimeo.

Gray, Cheryl and Gelb, Alan (1991) *The Transformation of Economies in Central and Eastern Europe: issues, progress and prospects.* Washington: World Bank.

'Gref Programme': see Fond (2000) 'Tsentr strategicheskikh razrabotok' and also Government of the Russian Federation (2000).

Greskovits, Bela (1998) *The Political Economy of Protest and Patience: east European and Latin American transformations compared.* Budapest: Central European University Press.

Gros, Daniel and Steinherr, Alfred (1995) *Winds of Change: economic transition in central and eastern Europe.* London: Longman.

Guboglo, M. N. (ed.) (1997) *Federalizm vlasti i vlast' federalizma*, Moscow: IntelTekh.

Gustafson, Thane (1999) *Capitalism Russian-Style*. Cambridge and New York: Cambridge University Press.

Hahn, Jeffrey W. (ed.) (1996) *Democratization in Russia: the development of legislative institutions*. Armonk NY: Sharpe.

Hanauer, Laurence (1996) 'Tatarstan and the Prospects for Federalism in Russia: a commentary', *Security Dialogue*, vol. 27, no. 1, pp. 81–6

Handelman, Stephen (1995) *Comrade Criminal: Russia's new mafiya*. London and New Haven CT: Yale University Press.

Hanson, Philip (2001) 'Barriers to Long-term Economic Growth in Russia', *Economy and Society* (forthcoming).

Hellman, Joel S. (1998) 'Winners Take All: the politics of partial reform in postcommunist countries', *World Politics*, vol. 50, no. 2 (January), pp. 203–34.

Helvey, Laura Roselle (1999) 'Television and the Campaign', in Timothy Colton and Jerry Hough (eds), *Growing Pains: Russian democracy and the election of 1993*. Washington, DC: Brookings Institution.

Hill, Ronald J. and Frank, Peter (1986) *The Soviet Communist Party*, 3rd edn. London: George Allen & Unwin.

Hofstadter, Richard (1970) *The Idea of a Party System: the rise of legitimate opposition in the United States, 1780–1840*. Berkeley: University of California Press.

Hopf, Ted (ed.) (1999) *Understandings of Russian Foreign Policy*. University Park: Pennsylvania University Press.

Hosking, Geoffrey (1992) *A History of the Soviet Union, 1917–1991*. London: Fontana.

Hosking, Geoffrey (1997) *Russia: People and Empire, 1552–1917*. London: HarperCollins.

Hosking, Geoffrey A., Aves, Jonathan and Duncan, Peter J. S. (1992) *The Road to Post-Communism: independent political movements in the Soviet Union*. London: Pinter.

Hough, Jerry F. (1969) *The Soviet Prefects*. Cambridge MA: Harvard University Press.

Hough, Jerry F. (1997) *Democratization and Revolution in the USSR, 1985–1991*. Washington DC: Brookings Institution.

Hough, Jerry F. (2001) *The Logic of Economic Reform in Russia*. Washington DC: Brookings Institution.

Hough, Jerry F., and Fainsod, Merle (1979) *How the Soviet Union Is Governed*. Cambridge MA: Harvard University Press.

Human Rights Watch World Report, available from < http://www.hrw.org >.

Hughes, James (1994) 'Regionalism in Russia: The Rise and Fall of Siberian Agreement', *Europe-Asia Studies*, vol. 46, no. 7, pp. 1133–62.

Huntington, Samuel (1991) *The Third Wave: democratization in the late twentieth century*. Norman and London: University of Oklahoma Press.

Huskey, Eugene (1997) 'Russian Judicial Reform after Communism', in Solomon (1997).

Huskey, Eugene (ed.) (1992) *Executive Power and Soviet Politics*. Armonk, NY: Sharpe.

Huskey, Eugene (1999) *Presidential Power In Russia*. Armonk, NY: M.E. Sharpe.

Ibragimova, Dilyara, Marina Krasilnikova and Lilia Ovcharova, (2000) 'Uchastie naseleniya v oplate meditsinskikh i obrazovatel'nykh uslug', *Monitoring obshchestvennogo mneniya: ekonomecheskie i sotsial'nye peremeny, no. 2* (March–April), pp. 7–16.

IMF (1990) *The Economy of the USSR*. Washington: World Bank.

IMF (1991) *A Study of the Soviet Economy* (3 vols) Paris: OECD.

Imidzh ideal'nogo prezidenta (po resultam gruppovykh diskussii) (2000) Moscow: Romir. Available from < http://www.romir.ru/election/03 2000 > .

Inglehart, Ronald (1984) 'The Changing Structure of Political Cleavages in Western Societies', in Russell J. Dalton *et al.*, (eds), *Electoral Change in Advanced Industrial Democracies: realignment or dealignment?* Princeton NJ: Princeton University Press.

Inglehart, Ronald (2000) 'Political Culture and Democratic Institutions: Russia in Global Perspective', paper presented at the annual meeting of the American Political Science Association.

Inkeles, Alex (1950) *Public Opinion in Soviet Russia: a study in mass persuasion*. Cambridge MA: Harvard University Press.

International Foundation for Electoral Systems (2000) *The 1999 Election to the Russian State Duma: findings and recommendations*. Available from < http://www.ifes.ru > .

Johnson, Juliet (2000) *A Fistful of Rubles: the rise and fall of the Russian banking system*. Ithaca NY: Cornell University Press.

Kaid, Lynda Lee (1999) *Television and Politics in Evolving European Democracies*. Commack NJ: Nova.

Kanet, Roger and Kozhemiakin, Alexander V. (eds) (1997) *The Foreign Policy of the Russian Federation*. Basingstoke: Macmillan.

Katz, Richard S. and Mair, Peter (1994) *How Parties Organise: change and adaptation in party organizations in western democracies*. London, Sage.

Keep, John L. H. (1996) *Last of the Empires: a history of the Soviet Union, 1945–1991*. Oxford: Oxford University Press.

Khakimov, Raphael S. (1996) 'Prospects of Federalism in Russia: A View from Tatarstan', *Security Dialogue*, vol. 27, no. 1, pp. 71–6.

Kitschelt, Herbert, Mansfeldova, Zdenka Markowski Radoslav and Toka, Gabor (1999) *Post-Communist Party Systems*. Cambridge and New York: Cambridge University Press.

Klebnikov, Paul (2000) *Godfather of the Kremlin: Boris Berezovsky and the looting of Russia*. New York: Harcourt.

Klyamkin, I. M. and Lapkin, V. V. (1995) 'Russkii vopros v Rossii', *Polis*, no. 5, pp. 78–96

Konstitutsii respublik v sostave Rossiiskoi Federatsii (2 vols) (1996) Moscow: Izvestiya.

Kornai, János (1986) 'The Soft Budget Constraint', *Kyklos*, vol. 39, no. 1, pp. 3–30.

Kramer, Mark (ed.) (2000) *The Collapse of the Soviet Union*. Boulder CO: Westview.

Kryshtanovskaya, Olga and White, Stephen (1996) 'From Soviet Nomenklatura to Russian Elite', *Europe-Asia Studies*, vol. 48, no. 5 (July), pp. 711–33.

Kto est' chto: politicheskaya Moskva, 1993. (1993) Moscow: Catallaxy.

Kupchan, Clifford (2000) 'Devolution Drives Russian Reform', *The Washingon Quarterly*, vol. 23, no. 2 (Spring), pp. 67–77.

Kuskovets, T. and Klyamkin, I. (1997) 'Postsovetskii chelovek,' *Informatsionno-analiticheskii byulleten'*, nos 1–2.

Kuzio, Taras (2000) 'Geopolitical Pluralism in the CIS: the emergence of GUUAM', *European Security*, vol. 9, no. 2, pp. 81–114.

Lallemand, Jean-Charles (1999) "Politics for the Few: elites in Bryansk and Smolensk', *Post-Soviet Affairs*, vol. 15, no. 4 (October–December), pp. 312–35.

Lane, David (1996) *The Rise and Fall of State Socialism*. Cambridge: Polity.

Lane, David and Ross, Cameron (1999) *The Transition from Communism to Capitalism: ruling elites from Gorbachev to Yeltsin*. New York: St. Martin's.

Lange, Bernd-Peter (ed.) (1996a) *Monitoring the Media Coverage of the 1995 Russian Parliamentary Elections: final report*. Düsseldorf: European Institute for the Media.

Lange, Bernd-Peter (ed.) (1996b) *Monitoring the Media Coverage of the 1996 Russian Presidential Elections: final report*. Düsseldorf: European Institute for the Media.

Laqueur, Walter Z. (1989) *The Long Road to Freedom: Russia and Glasnost*. London: Unwin Hyman.

Lavrov, A. M. and Matushkin, Alexei G. (2000) *The Fiscal Structure of the Russian Federation: financial flows between the center and the regions*. Armonk NY: Sharpe.

Le Huerou, Anne (1999) 'Elites in Omsk', *Post-Soviet Affairs*, vol. 15, no. 4 (October–December), pp. 362–86.

Ledeneva, Alena V. (1998) *Russia's Economy of Favours: blat, networking and informal exchange*. Cambridge: Cambridge University Press.

Lentini, Peter (ed.) (1995) *Elections and Political Order in Russia*. Budapest: Central European University Press.

Leon, David A. *et al.* (1997) 'Huge variation in Russian mortality rates 1984–94: artefact, alcohol, or what?', *The Lancet*, vol. 350, no. 9075 (9 August), pp. 383–8.

Levada, Yuri (2000) 'Problema emotsional'nogo balansa obshchestva', *Monitoring obshchestvennogo mneniya: ekonomicheskie i sotsial'nye peremey, no.* 2 (March–April), pp. 35–44.

Levitin, Oleg (2000) 'Inside Moscow's Kosovo Muddle', *Survival*, vol. 42, no. 1, pp. 130–40.

Lewis, Paul (1993) 'Civil Society and the Development of Political Parties in East-Central Europe', *The Journal of Communist Studies*, vol. 9, no. 4 (December), pp. 5–20.

Lewis, Paul G. (ed.) (1996) *Party Structure and Organization in East-Central Europe*. Cheltenham: Edward Elgar.

Lieven, Anatol (1998) *Chechnya: tombstone of Russian power*, London and New Haven CT: Yale University Press.

Linz, Juan and Stepan, Alfred (1996) *Problems of Democratic Transition and Consolidation*. Baltimore: The Johns Hopkins University Press.

Linz, Juan J. and Valenzuela, Arturo (eds) (1994) *The Failure of Presidential Democracy*. Baltimore and London: Johns Hopkins University Press.

Lipset, Seymour Martin (1959) 'Some Social Requisites of Democracy', *American Political Science Review*, vol. 53, no. 1 (March), pp. 69–105.

Lipset, Seymour Martin (1994) 'The Social Requisites of Democracy Revisited', *American Sociological Review*, vol. 59, no. 1 (February), pp. 1–22.

Lipset, Seymour Martin (1999) 'On the General Conditions for Democracy', in Lisa Anderson (ed.), *Transitions to Democracy*. New York: Columbia University Press.

Löwenhardt, John (1995) *The Reincarnation of Russia: struggling with the legacy of communism, 1990–4*. Durham NC: Duke University Press.

Löwenhardt, John (ed.) (1998) *Party Politics in Post-Communist Russia*. London and Portland OR: Frank Cass.

Luneev, V.V. (1997) *Prestupnost' XX veka*. Moscow: Norma.

Lussier, Danielle (2000) 'Country Files: Russia: Special Report 1999: a year of dirty tricks', *Transitions Online*.

Lynch, Dov (1999) ' "Walking the Tightrope": the Kosovo conflict and Russia in European security 1998–August 1999', *European Security*, vol. 8, no. 4, pp. 57–83.

Lynch, Dov (2000) *Russian Peacekeeping Strategies in the CIS. The Cases of Moldova, Georgia and Tajikistan*. Basingstoke: Macmillan.

Maggs, Peter B. (1999) 'The Process of Codification in Russia: lessons learned from the uniform commercial code', *McGill Law Journal*, vol. 44, no. 2 (August), pp. 281–300.

Malcolm, Neil, Pravda, Alex, Alison, Roy and Light, Margot (1996) *Internal Factors in Russian Foreign Policy*. Oxford: Oxford University Press.

Malia, Martin (1994) *The Soviet Tragedy: a history of socialism in Russia*. New York: Free Press.

Mandelbaum, Michael (ed.) (1998) *The New Russian Foreign Policy*. New York: Council on Foreign Relations.

Martin, Terry (2000) 'Modernization or Neo-Traditionalism? ascribed nationality and soviet primordialism' in Sheila Fitzpatrick (ed.), *Stalinism: new directions*. London: Routledge.

Mau, Vladimir (1996) *The Political History of Economic Reform in Russia*. London: CRCE.

Mawdsley, Evan and White, Stephen (2000) *The Soviet Political Elite from Lenin to Gorbachev*. Oxford and New York: Oxford University Press.

McAuley, Mary (1997) *Russia's Politics of Uncertainty*. Cambridge and New York: Cambridge University Press.

McCormack, Gillian (ed.) (1999) *Media in the CIS*. Düsseldorf: European Institute for the Media.

McDaniel, Tim (1996) *The Agony of the Russian Idea*. Princeton NJ: Princeton University Press.

McFaul, Michael (1997) 'When Capitalism and Democracy Collide in Transition: Russia's "weak" state as an impediment to democratic consolidation', Working Paper no. 1, Program in New Approaches to Russian Security, Cambridge MA: Davis Center, Harvard University.

McFaul, Michael (2001) *Russia's Troubled Transition from Communism to Democracy: institutional change during revolutionary transformations*. Ithaca NY: Cornell University Press.

Medvekov, Yuri, Medvekova, Olga and Hudson, George (1996) 'The December 1993 Russian Election: geographical patterns and contextual factors', *Russian Review*, vol. 55, no. 1 (January), pp. 80–98.

Melville, Andrei (1999) 'Post-Communist Russia: Democratic Transitions

Bibliography 319

and Transition Theories', in Lisa Anderson (ed.), *Transitions to Democracy*. New York: Columbia University Press.

Mendras, Marie (1999) 'How Regional Elites Preserve Their Power', *Post-Soviet Affairs*, vol. 15, no. 4 (October–December), pp. 295–311.

Mezhuev, V. (1996) *Mezhdu proshlym i budushchim*. Moscow: Institut filosofii RAN.

Michels, Robert (1962) *Political Parties: a sociological study of the oligarchical tendencies of modern democracy*. New York: Free Press.

Mickiewicz, Ellen (1988) *Split Signals: television and politics in the Soviet Union*. New York: Oxford University Press.

Mickiewicz, Ellen (1999) *Changing Channels: television and the struggle for power in Russia*, revised and expanded edn. Durham NC: Duke University Press.

Millar, James R. (1987) *Politics, Work, and Daily Life in the USSR: a survey of former Soviet citizens*. New York: Cambridge University Press.

Millar, James R. and Wolchik, Sharon L. (eds) (1994) *The Social Legacy of Communism*. New York: Cambridge University Press.

Miller, John (1993) *Mikhail Gorbachev and the End of Soviet Power*. London: Macmillan.

Miller, William L., White, Stephen and Heywood, Paul (1997) *Values and Political Change in Postcommunist Europe*. London: Macmillan and New York: St Martin's.

Mishler, William and Willerton, John P. (2000) *The Dynamics of Presidential Popularity in Post-Communist Russia: how exceptional is Russian politics?* Glasgow: Centre for the Study of Public Policy, University of Strathclyde.

Mishler, William, Willerton, John P. and Smith, Gordon (2000) 'Presidential Decrees and the "Hegemonic" Russian Presidency', paper presented at the VI ICCEES Congress, Tampere, Finland, 29 July–3 September.

Moscow Helsinki Group (2000) *The Human Rights Situation in the Russian Federation, 1999: annual report*. Moscow. An English version is available from < http://www.fsumonitor.com >.

Moser, Robert G. (1998) 'The Electoral Effects of Presidentialism in Post-Soviet Russia', *Journal of Communist Studies and Transition Politics*, vol. 14, nos 1 and 2 (March–June), pp. 54–65.

Munro, Neil and Rose, Richard (2001) *Elections in the Russian Federation*. Glasgow: Centre for the Study of Public Policy, University of Strathclyde.

Murrell, G. D. G. (1997) *Russia's Transition to Democracy: an internal political history, 1989–1996*. Brighton: Sussex Academic Press.

'New Corruption Indexes of Transparency International: Wide Range of Scores' (1999) *Transition*, vol. 10, no. 5, pp. 1–3.

Nichols, Thomas M. (1999) *The Russian Presidency: society and politics in the second Russian Republic*. London: Macmillan.

Nove, Alec (1989) *Glasnost in Action: cultural renaissance in Russia*. Boston: Unwin Hyman.

O'Donnell, Guillermo, Schmitter, Philippe C. and Whitehead, Laurence (eds) (1986) *Transitions from Authoritarian Rule: prospects for democracy*. Baltimore MD: Johns Hopkins University Press.

OECD (1995) *Economic Surveys: The Russian Federation 1995* Paris: OECD.

Olcott, Martha, Aslund, Anders and Garnett, Sherman W. (1999) *Getting it Wrong: regional cooperation and the commonwealth of independent states.* Washington DC: Carnegie Endowment for International Peace.

Organisation for Co-operation and Security in Europe. (Office for Democratic Institutions and Human Rights) (2000) *Russian Federation Presidential Election, 26 March 2000: final report.*

Orttung, Robert W. (ed.) (2000) *The Republics and Regions of the Russian Federation: a guide to politics, policies and leaders.* Armonk NY: Sharpe.

Ostrow, Joel M. (2000) *Comparing Post-Soviet Legislatures: a theory of institutional design and political conflict.* Columbus OH: Ohio State University Press.

Pammett, Jon H. (1999) 'Elections and Democracy in Russia', *Communist and Post-Communist Studies*, vol. 32, no. 1 (March), pp. 45–60.

Pammett, Jon H. and DeBandeleben, Joan (2000) 'Citizen Orientations to Political Parties in Russia', *Party Politics*, vol. 6, no. 3 (July), pp. 373–84.

Panebianco, A. (1988) *Political Parties: organisation and power.* Cambridge and New York: Cambridge University Press.

Petro, Nicolai and Rubinstein, Alvin Z. (1996) *Russian Foreign Policy: from empire to nation-state.* New York: Longman.

Petro, Nicolai (1999) 'The Novgorod Region: a Russian success story', *Post-Soviet Affairs*, vol. 15, no. 3 (July–September), pp. 235–61.

Petrov, Nikolai (2000) *Vybory-2000: politicheskii vkus i poslevkusie.* Moscow: Carnegie Centre Election Bulletin No. 3.

Pilkington, Hilary (ed.) (1996) *Gender, Generation and Identity in Contemporary Russia.* London: Routledge.

Pirani, Simon and Farrell, Ellis (1999) 'Western financial institutions and Russian capitalism', paper presented the conference on the World Crisis of Capitalism and the Post-Soviet States, Moscow, 30 October–1 November (1999)

Pockney, B. P. (1991) *Soviet Statistics since 1950.* New York: St Martin's.

Pospelov, P. N. *et al.* (eds) (1970) *Istoriya Kommunisticheskoi partii Sovetskogo Soyuza*, vol. 5, book 1. Moscow: Izdatel'stvo politicheskoi literatury.

Primakov, Evgenii (1999) *Gody v bolshoi politike.* Moscow: Sovershenno sekretno.

Prizel, Ilya (1999) *National Identity and Foreign Policy: nationalism and leadership in Poland, Russia and Ukraine.* Cambridge and New York: Cambridge University Press

Przeworski, Adam (1991) *Democracy and the Market: political and economic reforms in eastern Europe and Latin America.* Cambridge and New York: Cambridge University Press.

Public Health Research Institute (2000) 'TB in Russia'. Available from < http://www.russia.phri.org/tbinrussia.htm >.

Pursiainen, Christer (2000) *Russian Foreign Policy and International Relations Theory.* Aldershot and Burlington VT: Ashgate.

Putin, Vladimir (2000) *First Person.* London: Hutchinson and New York: HarperCollins.

Radzikhovsky, Leonid (2000) 'Unlimited power', *Prism: the Jamestown Foundation*, vol. 6, no. 5 (May), part 1.

Remington, Thomas F. (1988) *The Truth of Authority: ideology and communication in the Soviet Union.* Pittsburgh: University of Pittsburgh Press.

Remington, Thomas F. (2000) 'The Evolution of Executive-Legislative Relations in Russia since 1993', *Slavic Review*, vol. 59, no. 3 (Fall), pp. 499–520.

Remington, Thomas F. (2001) *The Russian Parliament: institutional evolution in a transitional regime, 1989–1999*. London and New Haven CT: Yale University Press.

Remington, Thomas F., Smith, Steven S. and Haspel, Moshe (1998) 'Decrees, Laws, and Inter-Branch Relations in the Russian Federation', *Post-Soviet Affairs*, vol. 14, no. 4 (October–December), pp. 287–322.

Rivera, Sharon Werning (2000) 'The Elite in Post-communist Russia: a changing of the guard?', *Europe-Asia Studies*, vol. 52, no. 3 (May), pp. 413–32.

Rokkan, Stein (1997) 'Cleavage Structures and Party Systems', in Rokkan, *State Formation, Nation-Building, and Mass Politics in Europe*, Oxford: Oxford University Press.

Roland, Gérard (1994) 'On the Speed and Sequencing of Privatisation and Restructuring', *Economic Journal*, vol. 104, no. 5 (September), pp. 1158–68.

Rose, Richard (1998) *Getting Things Done with Social Capital: New Russia Barometer VII*. Glasgow: Centre for the Study of Public Policy, University of Strathclyde.

Rose, Richard (2000) *Russia Between Elections: New Russia barometer VIII*. Glasgow: Centre for the Study of Public Policy, University of Strathclyde.

Rose, Richard, White, Stephen and Munro, Neil (2001) 'A Floating Party System', *Europe-Asia Studies*, vol. 53, no. 3 (May), pp. 419–43.

Ross, Cameron (ed.) (2001) *Regional Politics in Russia*. Manchester: Manchester University Press.

Rossiya (2000) *Rossiya v tsifrakh*. Moscow: Goskomstat.

Rustow, Dankwart (1970) 'Transitions to Democracy: toward a dynamic model', *Comparative Politics*, vol. 2, no. 3 (April), pp. 337–63.

Rutland, Peter (ed.) (2000) *Business and the State in Contemporary Russia*. Boulder CO: Westview.

Ryan, Michael, (comp) (1993) *Social Trends in Contemporary Russia: a statistical source-book*. London: Macmillan.

Sakwa, Richard (1990) *Gorbachev and his Reforms, 1985–1990*. Hemel Hempstead: Philip Allan.

Sakwa, Richard (1996) *Russian Politics and Society*, 2nd edn. London: Routledge.

Sakwa, Richard (1997) 'The Regime System in Russia', *Contemporary Politics*, vol. 3, no. 1 (March), pp. 7–25.

Sakwa, Richard (1998) 'Left or Right: the CPRF and problems of democratic consolidation in Russia', in Löwenhardt (1998).

Sakwa, Richard (1999) *Postcommunism*. Buckingham: Open University Press.

Sakwa, Richard (2000) 'Russia's "Permanent" (Uninterrupted) Elections of 1999–2000', *Journal of Communist Studies and Transition Politics*, vol. 16, no. 3 (September), pp. 85–112.

Sakwa, Richard and Webber, Mark (1999) 'The Commonwealth of Independent States, 1991–1998: stagnation and survival', *Europe-Asia Studies*, vol. 51, no. 3 (May), pp. 379–415.

Sartori, Giovanni (1976) *Parties and Party Systems: a framework for analysis*. Cambridge and New York: Cambridge University Press.

Sartori, Giovanni (1987) *The Theory of Democracy Revisited.* Chatham NJ: Chatham House Publishers.

Schapiro, Leonard (1970) *The Communist Party of the Soviet Union,* 2nd edn. London: Methuen.

Schmitter, Philippe C. (1992) 'Interest Systems and the Consolidation of Democracies', in Gary Marks and Larry Diamond (eds), *Reexamining Democracy.* Newbury Park CA and London: Sage.

Schmitter, Phillipe and Karl, Terry Lyn (1994) 'The Conceptual Travels of Transitologists and Consolidologists: how far should they attempt to go?', *Slavic Review,* vol. 53, no. 1 (Spring), pp. 173–85.

Schroder, Hans-Henning (1999) 'El'tsin and the Oligarchs: the role of financial groups in Russian politics between 1993 and July 1998', *Europe-Asia Studies,* vol. 51, no. 6 (September), pp. 957–88.

Sedaitis, Judith B. and Butterfield, Jim (eds) (1991) *Perestroika From Below: social movements in the Soviet Union.* London: Westview.

Sergeyev, Victor M. (1998) *The Wild East: crime and lawlessness in post-communist Russia.* Armonk NY: Sharpe.

Service, Robert (1997) *A History of Twentieth-Century Russia.* London: Allen Lane.

Shapiro, Judith (1995) 'The Russian mortality crisis and its causes', in Anders Aslund (ed.), *Russian Economic Reform at Risk.* London: Pinter.

Sharlet, Robert (1993) 'Russian Constitutional Crisis: law and politics under Yel'tsin', *Post-Soviet Affairs,* vol. 9, no. 4 (October–December), pp. 314–36.

Sharlet, Robert (1994) 'The Prospects for Federalism in Russian Constitutional Politics', *Publius: the journal of federalism,* vol. 24 (Spring), pp. 115–27

Sharlet, Robert (1996) 'Transitional Constitutionalism: politics and law in the second Russian Republic', *Wisconsin International Law Journal,* vol. 14, no. 3, pp. 1–27.

Sharlet, Robert (1997) 'Bringing the Rule of Law to Russia and the Newly Independent States', in Karen Dawisha (ed.), *The International Dimension of Post-Communist Transitions in Russia and the New States of Eurasia.* Armonk NY: Sharpe.

Sharlet, Robert (1998) 'Legal Transplants and Political Mutations: the reception of constitutional law in Russia and the newly independent states', *East European Constitutional Review,* vol. 7, no. 4 (Fall), pp. 59–68.

Sharlet, Robert (1999) 'Constitutional Implementation and State-Building: progress and problems of law reform in Russia', in Smith (ed.) (1999).

Shelley, Louise I. (1996) *Policing Soviet Society: the evolution of state control.* London and New York: Routledge, 1996.

Shelley, Louise (2000) 'Is the Russian State Coping with Organized Crime and Corruption?', in Sperling (2000).

Shelley, Louise and Repetskaya, Anna (1999) 'Analysis: corruption research among convicted government and law enforcement officials', *Organized Crime Watch,* vol. 1, no. 3, pp. 1–2.

Shevtsova, Lilia (1999) *Yeltsin's Russia: myths and reality.* Washington DC: Carnegie Endowment.

Shishkin, Sergey (1998) 'Priorities of the Russian Health Care Reform', *Croatian Medical Journal,* vol. 39, no. 3. Available from < http://www.ie-t.ru/personal/shishkin/dubr-t32.htm > .

Shishkin, Sergei (1999a) 'The Challenges for the Russian Health Care Reform' *Eurohealth*, vol. 4, no. 6, (special issue, winter), pp. 59–60.

Shishkin, Sergei (1999b) 'Problems of Transition from Tax-Based System of Health Care Finance to Mandatory Health Insurance Model in Russia', *Croatian Medical Journal*, vol. 40, no. 2 (March). Available from < http:// www.vms.hr/cmj/1999/4002/400211.htm > .

Shkolnikov, Vladimir and Nemtsov, Alexander (1997) 'The anti-alcohol campaign and variations in Russian mortality', in J.-L. Bobadilla *et al.* (eds), *Premature Death in the New Independent States*. Washington DC: National Academy Press.

Shkolnikov, Vladimir, Andreev, Evgenii and Maleva, Tatyana (eds) (2000) *Neravenstvo i smertnost' v Rossii*. Moscow: Signal for Moscow Carnegie Center.

Shkolnikov, Vladimir, Meslé, France and Vallin, Jacques (1995) 'La crise sanitaire en Russie, 1970–1993', *Population*, vol. 50, no. 4–5 (July–October), pp. 907–82

Shleifer, Andrei and Triesman, Daniel (2000) *Without a Map: political tactics and economic reform in Russia*. Cambridge MA: MIT Press.

Shmelev, Nikolai (1988) 'Ekonomika i zdravyi smysl', *Znamya*, no. 7 (July), pp. 179–84.

Slider, Darrell (1999) 'Pskov Under the LDPR: dysfunctional federalism in one oblast', *Europe-Asia Studies*, vol. 51, no. 5 (July), pp. 755–67.

Slider, Darrell, Gimpelson, Vladimir and Chugrov, Sergei (1994) 'Political Tendencies in Russia's Regions: evidence from the 1993 parliamentary elections', *Slavic Review*, vol. 53, no. 3 (Fall), pp. 711–32.

Smith, Gordon B. (1996) *Reforming the Russian Legal System*. Cambridge: Cambridge University Press.

Smith, Gordon B. (1997) 'The Struggle over the Procuracy', in Solomon (1997).

Smith, Gordon B. (1999) 'The Disjuncture between Legal Reform and Law Enforcement: the challenge facing the post-Yeltsin leadership', in Smith (ed.) (1999).

Smith, Gordon B. (ed.) (1999) *State-Building in Russia: the Yeltsin legacy and the challenge of the future*. Armonk NY: Sharpe.

Smith, Graham (1998) *The Post-Soviet States: mapping the politics of transition*. London: Arnold.

Smith, Steven S. and Remington, Thomas F. (2001) *The Politics of Institutional Choice: formation of the Russian State Duma*. Princeton NJ: Princeton University Press.

Solnick, Steven (1998) 'Will Russia Survive? center and periphery in the Russian Federation', in Barnett Rubin and Jack Snyder (eds), *Post-Soviet Political Order: conflict and state-building*. London: Routledge.

Solnick, Steven (1999) 'Russia's "Transition": is democracy delayed democracy denied?', *Social Research*, vol. 6, no. 3 (Fall), pp. 789–824.

Solomon, Peter H. (ed.) (1997) *Reforming Justice in Russia, 1864–1996*. Armonk NY: Sharpe.

Sperling, Valerie (ed.) (2000) *Building the Russian State: institutional crisis and the quest for democratic governance*. Boulder: Westview.

Stavrakis, Peter J., DeBardeleben, Joan and Black, Larry (eds) (1997) *Beyond the Monolith: the emergence of regionalism in post-Soviet Russia*. Washington DC: Woodrow Wilson Press.

Startsev, Yaroslav (1999) 'Gubernatorial Politics in Sverdlovsk Oblast', *Post-Soviet Affairs*, vol. 15, no. 3 (October–December) pp. 336–61.

Stepan, Alfred (1999) 'Federalism and Democracy: beyond the US model', *Journal of Democracy*, vol. 10, no. 4 (October), pp. 19–34

Strayer, Robert (1998) *Why did the Soviet Union Collapse? understanding historical change*. Armonk NY: Sharpe.

Sultanov, Sh. (1992) 'Dukh yevraziitsa', *Nash sovremennik*, no. 7, pp. 143–8.

Suny, Ronald G. (1993) *The Revenge of the Past: nationalism, revolution, and the collapse of the Soviet Union*. Stanford: Stanford University Press.

Suverennyi Tatarstan (1997) Moscow: INSAN.

Syracuse Journal of International Law and Commerce (2000) Symposium on 'Prosecuting Transnational Crimes: Cross-Cultural Insights for the Former Soviet Union', vol. 27, no. 1 (Winter), pp. 1–75.

Szporluk, Roman (1989) 'Dilemmas of Russian Nationalism', *Problems of Communism*, vol. 39, no. 4 (July–August), pp. 15–35

Szporluk, Roman (ed.) (1994) *National Identity and Ethnicity in Russia and the New States of Eurasia*. Armonk: Sharpe

Taras, Ray (ed.) (1997) *Postcommunist Presidents*. Cambridge and New York: Cambridge University Press.

Tavernise, Sabrina (2000) 'Using Bankruptcy as a Takeover Tool', *New York Times*, 7 October.

Terry, Sarah Meiklejohn (1993) 'Thinking About Post-Communist Transitions: how different are they?', *Slavic Review*, vol. 52, no. 2 (Summer), pp. 333–7.

Thaman, Stephen C. (1995) 'The Resurrection of Trial by Jury in Russia', *Stanford Journal of International Law*, vol. 31, no. 2 (Winter), pp. 61–273.

Tishkov, Valery (1997) *Ethnicity, Nationalism and Conflict in and after the Soviet Union*. London: Sage

Tolz, Vera (1998a) ' "Conflicting Homeland Myths" and Nation-State Building in Postcommunist Russia', *Slavic Review*, vol. 57, no. 2 (Summer), pp. 267–94.

Tolz, Vera (1998b) 'Forging the Nation: national identity and nation building in post-communist Russia', *Europe-Asia Studies*, vol. 50, no. 6 (September), pp. 993–1022.

Tolz, Vera (2001) *Russia: inventing the nation*. London: Arnold.

Tompson, William (1997) 'Old Habits Die Hard: fiscal imperatives, state regulation and the role of Russia's banks', *Europe-Asia Studies*, vol. 49, no. 7 (November), pp. 1159–85.

Tompson, William (1999) 'The Price of Everything and the Value of Nothing? unravelling the workings of Russia's "virtual economy" ', *Economy and Society* vol. 28, no. 2 (May), pp. 256–80.

Tsentr (1985) Tsentr po khraneniyu dokumentov noveishei istorii, Moscow, *fond* 89, *perechen'* 36, document 16.

Turovskii, Rostislav (2000) 'Osnovnye itogi vyborov v odnomandatnykh okrugakh' in *Rossiya v izbiratel'nom tsikle 1999–2000 godov*. Moscow: Carnegie Center.

UNAIDS, 'Report on the global HIV/AIDS epidemic – December 2000'. Available from < http://www.unaids.org/epidemic_update/report_dec00/index_dec.html#ful 1 > .

Urban, Joan Barth and Solovei, Valerii D. (1997) *Russia's Communists at the Crossroads*. Boulder CO: Westview.

Urban, Michael (1998) 'Remythologising the Russian State', *Europe-Asia Studies*, vol. 50, no. 6 (September), pp. 969–92.

Urban, Michael and Gel'man, Vladimir (1997) 'The Development of Political Parties in Russia', in Karen Dawisha and Bruce Parrott, (eds), *Democratic Change and Authoritarian Reactions in Russia, Ukraine, Belarus and Moldova*. Cambridge and New York: Cambridge University Press.

Urban, Michael, with Igrunov, Vyacheslav and Mitrokhin, Sergei (1997) *The Rebirth of Politics in Russia*. Cambridge and New York: Cambridge University Press.

Wallander, Celeste A. (ed.) (1996) *The Sources of Russian Foreign Policy after the Cold War*. Boulder CO: Westview.

Waller, Michael (1981) *Democratic Centralism: an historical commentary*. New York: St Martins Press.

Waller, Michael (1993) 'Political Actors and Political Roles in East-Central Europe', *Journal of Communist Studies*, vol. 9, no. 4 (December), pp. 21–36.

Wallich, Christine (1997) 'Reforming Intergovernmental Relations, Russia and The Challenge of Fiscal Federalism' in B. Kaminski (ed.), *Economic Transition in Russia and the New States of Eurasia*. Armonk NY: Sharpe.

Ware, Alan (1996) *Political Parties and Party Systems*. Oxford: Oxford University Press.

Wedel, Janine (1998) *Collision and Collusion: the strange case of western aid to eastern Europe 1989–98*. New York: St. Martin's Press.

Wedgwood Benn, David (1989) *Persuasion and Soviet Politics*. Oxford: Blackwell.

Wedgwood Benn, David (1992) *From Glasnost to Freedom of Speech: Russian openness and international relations*. London: Royal Institute of International Affairs.

Welch, Stephen (1993) *The Concept of Political Culture*. Basingstoke: Macmillan.

Westoby, Adam (1989) *The Evolution of Communism*. Cambridge: Polity.

White, Anne (1999) *Democratization in Russia under Gorbachev 1985–91: the birth of a voluntary sector*, Basingstoke, Macmillan.

White, Stephen (1983) 'Political Communications in the USSR: letters to party, state and press', *Political Studies*, vol. 31, no. 1 (January), pp. 43–60

White, Stephen (1991) 'Rethinking the CPSU', *Soviet Studies*, vol. 43, no. 3, pp. 405–28.

White, Stephen (1994) *After Gorbachev*, revised 4th edn. Cambridge and New York: Cambridge University Press.

White, Stephen (1996) *Russia Goes Dry*. Cambridge and New York: Cambridge University Press.

White, Stephen (2000a) 'Russia, Elections, Democracy', *Government and Opposition, vol.* 35, no. 3 (July), pp. 302–24

White, Stephen (2000b) *Russia's New Politics: the management of a post-revolutionary society*. Cambridge and New York: Cambridge University Press.

White, Stephen and Nelson, Daniel (eds) (2001) *The Politics of the Post-communist World* (2 vols). Aldershot: Ashgate.

White, Stephen, Rose, Richard and McAllister, Ian (1997) *How Russia Votes*. Chatham NJ: Chatham House.

White, Stephen, Wyman, Matthew and Oates, Sarah (1997) 'Parties and Voters in the 1995 Russian Duma Election', *Europe-Asia Studies*, vol. 49, no. 5 (July), pp. 767–98.

Whitmore, Brian (1998) 'Power Plays in the Provinces', *Transitions*, vol. 5, no. 9 (September), pp. 71–7.

Willerton, John P. (1992) *Patronage and Politics in the USSR*. Cambridge and New York: Cambridge University Press.

Williams, Phil (ed.) (1997) *Russian Organized Crime: the new threat?*. London and Portland OR: Frank Cass.

Woodruff, David (1998) 'Why Market Liberalism and the Ruble's Value are Sinking Together', *East European Constitutional Review*, vol. 7, no. 4 (Fall), pp. 73–6.

Woodruff, David (1999) *Money Unmade: barter and the fate of Russian capitalism*. Ithaca NY: Cornell University Press.

World Bank (1999) *A Health Sector Strategy for the Europe and Central Asia Region*, Washington DC: World Bank.

World Bank (2000) Anticorruption in Transition: a contribution to the policy debate. Washington DC: World Bank.

Wyman, Matthew (1996) 'Developments in Russian Voting Behaviour: 1993 and 1995 compared', *Journal of Communist Studies and Transition Politics*, vol. 12, no. 3 (September), pp. 277–92.

Wyman, Matthew (1997) *Public Opinion in Postcommunist Russia*. London: Macmillan.

Wyman, Matthew, White, Stephen and Oates, Sarah (eds) (1998) *Elections and Voters in Post-communist Russia*. Cheltenham and Northampton MA: Edward Elgar.

Wyman, Matthew, White, Stephen McAllister, Ian and Oates, Sarah (2001) 'Regional Voting Patterns in Postcommunist Russia', in Ross (2001).

Yakobson, Lev (1998), 'Ekonomika zdravookhraneniya', Bureau of Economic Analysis, *Obzor ekonomicheskoi politiki v Rossii za 1998 god*. Moscow: Bureau of Economic Analysis. Available from <http://www.beafnd.org/russian/activity/library/fundamental/98_ch14_r.doc>.

Yeltsin, Boris (1990) *Against the Grain: An Autobiography*. London: Cape and New York: Summit Books.

Yeltsin, Boris (1994) *The Struggle for Russia*. New York: Random House. (Also published as *The View from the Kremlin*. London: HarperCollins.)

Yeltsin, Boris (2000) *Midnight Diaries*. London: Weidenfeld and Nicolson.

Zakharov, Sergei (1999) 'Cohort Analysis of the Russia's Population Mortality: long- and short-term effects of generations' inequality in the face of death', *Studies on Russian Economic Development*, vol. 10, no. 2, pp. 199–211.

Zakharov, Sergei and Boris Revich (1992) *Mladencheskaya smertnost' v Rossii. Istoricheskii i regional'nyi aspekt*. Moscow: Centre for Demography and Human Ecology Working Papers, no. 7 (August).

Zimmerman, William (1995) 'Synoptic Thinking and Political Culture in Post-Soviet Russia', *Slavic Review*, vol. 54, no. 3 (Fall), pp. 630–41.

Zyuganov, Gennadii (1997) *My Russia: the political autobiography of Gennady Zyuganov*. Armonk NY: Sharpe.

Index